Praise for *You Daughters of Freedom*

'Clare Wright's *You Daughters of Freedom* is the uplifting story of a time Australia led the world in including women in our democratic project. It is a reminder of our proud legacy and a clarion call for who we can be.'

PENNY WONG

'A thrilling tale, superbly told, of Australia's women voters leading the world.'

JUDITH BRETT

'Here, one of the country's most accomplished historians and storytellers relates Australian women's fight for the vote in all of its passion, intensity and drama. *You Daughters of Freedom* delivers a neglected chapter in the story of democracy with a sparkle rivalling that of the many remarkable women who populate its pages.'

FRANK BONGIORNO

'A rare achievement. Grand, bold and brilliantly written, *You Daughters of Freedom* is a book that promises to shift our entire understanding of the nation's founding. At a time when democracy is under threat, Clare Wright reminds us of the largely forgotten history of democratic idealism that propelled Australian women to the forefront of the international fight for the franchise and full citizenship rights.'

MARK McKENNA

'The essential story of our greatest reformers, and one of our proudest achievements as a nation.'

GEORGE MEGALOGENIS

'Finally, the enthralling story of the Australian women who won the vote, then took the battle to the world.'

ANNE SUMMERS

'Clare Wright shines a light on the corners of history into which even the loudest, most defiant of women change-makers have been pushed and forgotten. How lucky we are to have her.'

CLEMENTINE FORD

ALSO BY CLARE WRIGHT

Beyond the Ladies Lounge: Australia's female publicans

The Forgotten Rebels of Eureka

We Are the Rebels: the women and men who made Eureka

You Daughters of Freedom

*The Australians who won the vote
and inspired the world*

CLARE WRIGHT

TEXT PUBLISHING
MELBOURNE AUSTRALIA

textpublishing.com.au
textpublishing.co.uk

The Text Publishing Company
Swann House, 22 William Street, Melbourne, Victoria 3000, Australia

The Text Publishing Company (UK) Ltd
130 Wood Street, London EC2V 6DL, United Kingdom

First published in 2018 by The Text Publishing Company

Book design by W. H. Chong
Cover photograph by Fred Kroh
Typeset in Adobe Caslon 12/16.25 by J & M Typesetting
Index by Karen Gillen

Printed and bound in Australia by Griffin Press, an accredited ISO/NZS 14001:2004 Environmental Management System printer

The paper used in this book is manufactured only from wood grown in sustainable regrowth forests.

ISBN: 9781925603934 (hardback)
ISBN: 9781925626896 (ebook)

A catalogue record for this book is available from the National Library of Australia

To my grandmothers
Alice, Sally and Sara

Power concedes nothing without a demand.
It never did and it never will.

FREDERICK DOUGLASS, 1857

Contents

AUTHOR'S NOTE

This is an evidence-based non-fiction account of how Australia became the first nation in the world to give white women full political equality, and what certain women chose to do with those basic rights and historic privileges.

While I have engaged with the scholarship on gender, race, citizenship, colonialism, imperialism, internationalism and transnationalism to frame my questions going into the archive, and to make sense of what I have found there, what follows is a narrative account predominantly based on primary sources. Three points of clarification are necessary.

First: the issue of precedence. From the passage of the Commonwealth Franchise Act in 1902, white women in Australia enjoyed full and universal adult suffrage: that is, there was nothing in legislation to distinguish them from male voters. No property qualification; the same age and residency requirements. Australian women were eligible to sit in parliament as well as vote. No other women in the world were so entitled until Finland followed suit in 1906. New Zealand women won the vote in 1893, but could not sit in parliament until 1919. Nor was New Zealand a nation, as Australia became in 1901—it remained a colony or dominion of Britain until 1947. Women in Wyoming could vote from 1869 and in Utah from 1870 but their enfranchisement was viewed as politically marginal and attracted little global attention.

Second: only *white* women in Australia were accorded the

privilege of the vote. The racial qualifier takes a good deal of the gloss off patriotic gloating. The story told in this book should not be read as a celebratory nationalist narrative, nor be seen to imply a tacit assumption of white women's moral or spiritual superiority.

Finally, the terms *suffragist* and *suffragette* are not inter-changeable. Suffragists are people who advocate for votes for women. Men can be suffragists, and they were. The term is a generic descrip-tion of a political position, akin to the terms *socialist*, *capitalist* or *environmentalist*. Suffragettes, by contrast, were a specific group of (mostly) women defined by their membership of certain suffrage organisations at a certain time in British history.

Abbreviations

ABA	Australian Bicentennial Authority
ANZWVC	Australian and New Zealand Women Voters' Committee
ASL	Artists' Suffrage League
AWNL	Australian Women's National League
ILP	Independent Labour Party (UK)
IWSA	International Woman Suffrage Alliance
NUWSS	National Union of Women's Suffrage Societies
NWCC	National Women's Consultative Committee
ULPSA	United Labor Party of South Australia
WCTU	Woman's Christian Temperance Union
WFL	Women's Federal League (Aus.)
	Women's Freedom League (UK)
WFPA	Women's Federal Political Association
WPA	Women's Political Association (Vic.)
	Women's Progressive Association (NSW)
WPSC	Women's Political and Social Crusade
WSL	Womanhood Suffrage League (NSW)
	Woman's Suffrage League (Vic.)
	Women's Suffrage League (SA)
WSPU	Women's Social and Political Union

You Daughters of Freedom

The Big Picture

Canberra, 2018

> A banner is a thing to float in the wind, to flicker in the breeze,
> to flirt its colours for your pleasure, to half-show and half-conceal,
> a device you long to unravel; you do not want to read it,
> you want to worship it.

MARY LOWNDES
On Banners and Banner-making, 1909

If you're ever in Canberra, Australia's national capital, whether for the first time or the one millionth, it's worth a visit to Parliament House. The walls have stories to tell.

As you walk from Queen's Terrace towards the House of Representatives, you pass the Great Hall to your right. The Great Hall, as its name suggests, is vast, its native timber panelling both warm and sleek—the ambitious veneer of home-grown, post-colonial representation. The Great Hall must be impressive when filled to the gunnels with pollies and punters on feast days like the annual Parliamentary Midwinter Ball, but whenever I've been to Parliament House it's been empty save for huddled groups of Chinese and Indian tourists pointing iPhones in every direction. But I like to pop my head in nonetheless, if only because the Great Hall houses a stunningly beautiful tapestry, conceived by artist Arthur Boyd. According to the parliamentary website, the artwork was executed by the Victorian Tapestry Workshop and designed to bring 'the essence of the Australian landscape' into the heart of Australia's political life.[1] The tapestry took fourteen full-time weavers over two years to complete.

On another wall in the Great Hall hangs a sixteen-metre-long embroidery, designed by artist Kay Lawrence and wrought by '500 highly skilled women' from all of the Australian state and territory embroidery guilds…'a logistical challenge that would foster team-work between women across the country'. The embroidery tells the story of human settlement in Australia, from pre-European times to 1900.[2] Both artworks were commissioned for the opening of the new Parliament House in May 1988. The Great Hall is a fitting place to start any female-centric tour of Australian democracy. Crafting the story of the nation has always been women's work—on the ground, if rarely in history's written page.

Walk further into the Members' Hall—the centre of Parliament House, directly under the flag mast—and you'll be greeted by a welcoming committee of framed portraits of Australia's past prime ministers. Move along the row and watch the sombre frockcoats and bushy moustaches give way to sombre suits and ties and clean-shaven chins.[3] There are also portraits of governors-general in the Members' Hall gallery and one of the G-G's boss, Australia's head of state, Queen Elizabeth II, painted in London in 1954 by William Dargie. The portraits constitute part of the Historic Memorials Collection, founded in 1911 by Prime Minister Andrew Fisher.

Only two of the faces in the Members' Hall belong to women: Australia's first female governor-general, Quentin Bryce (2008–14) and Australia's reigning sovereign, Queen Elizabeth II (1952–). Australia's first and, to date, only female prime minister, Julia Gillard (2010–13), has yet to be immortalised in oils.

Plonked in the middle of the Members' Hall, directly across from the portrait of the Queen, resplendent in her bright yellow 'wattle dress', is a display cabinet. Here, safely housed under glass, are the 1963 Yirrkala bark petitions. According to the website foundingdocs.com.au, these small but precious items—part traditional Indigenous artwork, part Westminster-style petition—are the 'first documents bridging Commonwealth law as it then stood, and the Indigenous laws of the land'.[4] Queen Elizabeth watches over the material legacy of the colonial project her royal ancestors commenced in 1788.

Proceed now through a narrow corridor, beyond the House of Representatives and the Senate, and you'll reach the Main Committee Room. Here the wall is adorned with Tom Roberts' 'Big Picture', officially known as *The Opening of the First Parliament of the Commonwealth of Australia by His Royal Highness the Duke of Cornwall and York, 9 May 1901*. Hence the shorthand: the Big Picture. The Big Picture, like the Great Hall, is immense. Unlike the hall, the painting is permanently peopled. A multitude of Edwardian VIPs stand frozen in the moment of parliamentary initiation. The famous painting, which depicts the first sitting of the new Federal Parliament (in the Exhibition Building in Melbourne, because in 1901 Canberra was a sheep run, not a city) is on permanent loan from the Royal Collection. It's not easy to own your own history.[5]

As you rounded the corner into the narrow corridor, veering left at the Wattle Queen (or right at Dame Quentin), you might have noticed another glass display case. The item in it is 2.5 metres high and 1.4 metres wide. Apart from its impressive dimensions, the object is also strikingly beautiful. All greens, flowing white and flashes of red. But the tucked-away positioning, not visible from the main hall, suggests that you needn't dally en route to the Big Picture.

If you do stop here, however, you'll find a national treasure: an object that art historian Myra Scott has called 'a triumphant celebration of Australia's leadership in political reform'; an object representing 'the first time in England that art had been co-opted for a mass people's movement, with cultural and ideological issues, for political ends'.[6]

Like the bark petitions, which used art to bridge a gulf between two systems of law—one sovereign, one imperial—this object, according to Scott, 'redefined the issue from one of internal politics…to one of statesmanship and discussion between two countries…a symbolic appeal from one government to another at a level of international diplomacy'.

The issue? Women's suffrage. The countries? England and Australia. The statesmen? Australian women.

⚵

This object you are standing before was made by Australian artist Dora Meeson Coates while she was living in London in the summer of 1908. It is a banner, a huge banner, a women's suffrage banner, one she designed and painted *for the Commonwealth*, as she later explained, and carried in the internationally renowned Women's Coronation Procession of 1911. Organised by Britain's suffragettes—militant campaigners for votes for women—and held on the eve of King George V's coronation in the sweltering summer of 1911, this monster march was hailed as *the greatest procession ever known in the world's history*.[7] Of the one thousand banners that were carried that day down London's streets by forty thousand defiant women, Meeson Coates' was exceptional.

Banners made for the great pre-war suffragette rallies were generally embroidered. But this one was painted, oil on hessian. It was also uncommonly large, requiring four people to keep it upright in the five-hour parade. But it was the banner's message, and its controversial meaning, that attracted the world's attention. The imagery was drawn from the classical style that was the fashion of the day. Mother Britannia, draped in a white gown, holding her sceptre, hip and head cocked, staring into the middle distance. Daughter Minerva, bearing the heraldry of Australia's recently federated states on her shield, leaning forward, reaching out, palm upturned, beseeching but also offering advice. Her counsel? *Trust the Women Mother As I Have Done*. Not a footnote but a banner headline, etched in upright capital letters above the women's heads. Take my hand, Mother, follow me.

Paraded before an international audience, it was a banner replete with allegorical effrontery, signifying what all the world knew: Australia was the nation that had *pioneered [women] into citizenship*, as contemporary American journalist Jessie Ackermann readily acknowledged.[8] *The purest type of democracy the human race has ever known*, wrote another reporter in 1903, *flourishes to-day beneath Australian skies*. It was in recognition of this remarkable fact—that the daughters of empire had outpaced the mother country in winning their political sovereignty—that Dora Meeson Coates had fashioned her suffrage banner, behind which a proud Australian contingent would march in support of her unenfranchised sisters.

Unlike Tom Roberts' Big Picture—the implied centrepiece of Australia's democratic history at Parliament House—Meeson Coates' banner is owned by the Australian people. After languishing in obscurity, unceremoniously folded and gathering dust atop a cupboard in a storeroom in London for most of the twentieth century, it was purchased by the Australian government as a bicentennial gift to 'the women of Australia'. *Women's Banner is Coming Home*, declared a Canberra newspaper, though no boomerang effect was in play. Dora Meeson Coates had created the banner in her Chelsea studio, and on British soil it had to that date remained.[9] Due to the ardent campaigning of a few female MPs, Senator Margaret Reynolds in particular, the banner was 'handed over' by Prime Minister Bob Hawke at an upbeat ceremony on International Women's Day, 1988. Damaged by decades of neglect, the banner was then sent off for conservation work and again forsaken. A fat folder of bureaucratic paperwork in the National Archives of Australia reveals the sorry tale of how Meeson Coates' banner travelled from her Chelsea studio to a roundabout corridor in Canberra.

Owned by the Australian people. Purchased for the Australian people. Representing the world-leading achievements of the Australian people. Yet almost completely unknown to the vast majority of Australian people.

When, in mid-2017, I asked the custodians of Parliament House's art collection for information on the object's provenance, they knew little beyond the bare facts of its purchase and return.[10] In the thirty years since it 'came home', the banner had become untethered from its remarkable story.

Half-shown and half-concealed. A device you long to unravel.

⚕

I first became aware of Dora Meeson Coates' banner in August 2014. I was in Canberra for the preview screening of a documentary series I had worked on, held at the cinema in Parliament House. Later, tipsy on free champagne and applause, I took a wander around the building. When I stumbled upon the banner I was transfixed, both by its beauty as an artwork and by the remarkable fact that I'd never known of its existence—despite the fact that my first foray into television was a documentary called *Utopia Girls*, broadcast on the ABC in 2012, about how Australian women won the vote.

Did I *really* not know about this incredible object taking up valuable real estate in the big house of Australian democracy? Or had I just misplaced the memory?

Either way, I was ashamed of myself. Bad feminist.

A year later, I found myself in another cinema. The occasion was the Melbourne premiere of the Hollywood feature film *Suffragette*. The film portrayed the political awakening of a working-class woman whose life changes forever when she joins Emmeline Pankhurst's Women's Social and Political Union (WSPU) and becomes a militant campaigner for votes for women. Emmeline, played by Meryl Streep, is the goodie; Prime Minister Asquith is the baddie. The working woman at the centre of the story is loosely based on suffragette Annie Kenney, but is really an Everywoman, whose hero's journey takes her from somnolent drudge to politically awakened, window-smashing, speech-giving freedom fighter. I was invited to speak on a post-screening panel, and asked by the organisers to answer any historical questions the audience might have about the British suffrage campaign.

If you ask most Australians what they know of the British suffragette movement, the charismatic Pankhurst women might figure. Bombs in letterboxes, force-feeding and a lady who threw herself in front of a racehorse. The film would join the dots in fictionalised form, and I could temper the artistic licence with some facts.

But I had mistakenly assumed that Australian women (the audience was almost exclusively women) already knew their own history. I soon found myself giving a mini-lecture on the winning of women's suffrage in Australia, on Australia's pre-eminence in the world movement and the significance of Australian women as role models to, and leaders within, the British suffrage campaign depicted in the film.

Australia's participation in the British campaign was not only unrepresented in the movie, but also practically unknown in Australia—the parameters of mainstream knowledge about Australia's role in big world events confined to war and sport. What about politics? And in particular, what about the activism and statesmanship of women?

It's not so surprising that *Suffragette*—a Hollywood movie about a moment in British history—did not have much to say about Australian women's role. (The film was widely criticised for its failure to depict women of colour, but not its omission of the antipodean angle.) What was more alarming to me was how little Australian audiences knew of their foremothers' part in making that history.

But they wanted to know. I discovered that night an appetite for our own history—a hunger even—that this book sets out both to whet and to satisfy.

Academics might know the names of the Australians who walked onto the world stage as leading ladies, not bit parts, but these women are not part of a broader, mainstream historical consciousness. They are not depicted on our own television and movie screens, not popularised as icons in advertising and tourism campaigns, not subsidised by government-sponsored tourist trails.[11]

Imagine a pilgrimage to London, to Westminster, to view the spot where Muriel Matters, known globally as *that daring Australian girl*, became the first woman to speak in the British Parliament. Her words, before being dragged off to prison: *Votes for Women!*

Or to Hyde Park, to re-enact the day in 1908 when half a million people gathered to listen to suffragette leaders preach the gospel of women's enfranchisement. On one of the stages stood an Australian woman, Nellie Martel, proudly proclaiming that she was the only speaker there who had the right to vote, the right that all others coveted.

Or a trip to Hammersmith, to the spot where Dora Montefiore—the woman who established the first suffrage society in New South Wales in 1891—was later holed up in a siege after refusing to pay her British taxes until she won the same right to the franchise that she held in Sydney.

Or to an overflowing Albert Hall, where Vida Goldstein *electrified the house* with her tales of what Australian women had done with their citizenship rights and why British women needed to maintain their rage in the fight for their own rights and freedoms.

Entitlements that were cheekily trumpeted by a huge banner painted by an Australian woman and carried by Australian women in a procession that would be reported around the world.

The story of British women's struggle for suffrage cannot be written too many times. In 2018, the centenary year of (some)

British women getting the (partial) vote, a slew of new books will be published, exhibitions held and honorary marches staged. It is a monumental story containing all the elements of a blockbuster: heroes and villains, oppressors and the oppressed, charismatic leaders, violent conflict, blood sacrifice and, eventually, a victory for truth, justice and the liberal way. But Australia's part in that epic drama needs to be told for the first time.

That *a baby nation* (as Vida called Australia) played more than a crawl-on role in this story of mass democratic protest makes its telling all the more exhilarating.

At the turn of the twentieth century, women's suffrage was described as *the great world movement...the most insistent political problem of the day*.[12] How to understand what could motivate women to take to the streets—against social norms of propriety, facing vilification from the press, imprisonment and physical violence from police and bystanders alike—to claim their piece of the democratic pie? How to understand why Australian women would feel compelled to travel the great distance to continue the fight in Great Britain, when their own long battle was finally won at home? Were they masochists or altruists? Attention-seekers or do-gooders? It's hard to grasp now— when the very concept of democracy is under attack—why they cared so much about democratic citizenship rights.

A Lowy Institute survey in 2017 found that only sixty per cent of Australians believed that democracy was the best system of government. Thirty-three per cent of eighteen- to twenty-nine-year-olds responded that in some circumstances, a non-democratic form of government can be preferable.[13] Research in other western nations reveals a similar level of disenchantment, particularly among young people.[14] Voter dissatisfaction appears to be highest in the United States—the spiritual home of modern democracy—where nine out of ten Americans no longer have faith in their political system.[15] And that was before President Donald Trump was elected.

Given the present state of disillusionment with democracy, it is important to remember that people once cared so very much about defending it, sharing in it and exercising their right to it.

ψ

They say the past is a foreign country. One aspect of first wave feminism that seems particularly strange to modern sensibilities is the tacit notion that women's enfranchisement would lead to the political and social purification of the world, due to women's innate moral and spiritual superiority. In her 1896 essay 'Why Women Need Woman Suffrage; and Why We Need It Now', Dora Montefiore argued that women have *a power for self sacrifice, a power of perceiving with the eye of intuition and of faith…that hidden spiritual power in her sex*. Because a woman's soul had been *sufficiently purified*, women were needed to *instil fresh life into the dead body of politics*.[16] The idea that women were better than men because they were innately 'pure', less inclined to bad habits, was hardwired into generations of women raised in the Victorian era.[17]

Today's generation of democrats, whether rusted on or tenuously attached, are less likely to hold that women having citizenship rights will inexorably lead to social or political purity, let alone global peace. To a twenty-first-century mindset, the first wave feminists' focus on vice, on 'evils' such as drinking, gambling and sexual licentiousness, can seem like killjoy prudery.

But in the early-twentieth-century context, measures such as raising the age of consent and ending the sexual double standard represented a radical attempt to redefine women's bodies as sites of power every bit as contested as the ballot box. Self-government in the public sphere (the vote) was intended to be mirrored in the so-called private sphere (the body). Campaigns for sexual sovereignty were just as threatening to the established order as today's movement for Indigenous sovereignty (a treaty) is to conservative Australian governments.

Feminists pursued a new national and global social order based on mutual care and protection, equality of rights and responsibilities and freedom from sexual, economic and political oppression. They may have looked like wowsers in their bonnets and button-up gowns, but they were actually warriors.

We need to understand what mattered to women in the past—not what we think now should have mattered to them, or not mattered to them quite so much—and how women sought and achieved the legal, civil and social reforms *they* thought were necessary at the time.

In the two decades preceding World War I, women's suffrage was perceived to usher in a new dawn in the history of humanity. Its dominance as the cause célèbre of the era was acknowledged by leading thinkers of the age. Like a pop star, it only needed one name. It was the Cause.

The suffrage crusade, wrote British journalist Alfred Gardiner in 1913, *is the most significant revolution that has come over society in the first years of the 20th century...not political but elemental...the formal embodiment of a spiritual renascence.*[18] The cause stood for rebellion, emancipation, spiritual renewal and a fundamental change in the sexual, political and industrial structure of society. *Its insurgence is worldwide*, wrote Gardiner, *for this reason I think the woman suffrage crusade will, in the eyes of the historian, overshadow all the other events of these tumultuous times.*[19] The cause focused its tactical energies on one solution to the problem of gendered inequality and oppression: the vote.

Because Australia was the first—and for many years the only—country to have national parliamentary suffrage, Australia became the focus of the world's attention. *Students of social questions, professors and pupils came to Australia*, wrote Jessie Ackermann in 1913, *until in time Australia became the Mecca for observation concerning up-to-date legislation in the interest of all the people—the whole of the people.*[20] New Zealand was in the spotlight too, but New Zealand was not a nation-state; she had not placed adult suffrage as a cornerstone of her constitution. Australia was the poison taster of the world: in the *noonday glare*, as Ackermann put it.

As a nation, Australia played a leading part in the cause as inspiration, model and innovator. As individual Australians, many women played leading parts as activists, agitators, intellectuals and educators. Ackermann observed that *the freest girls in the world* were to be found in Australia; *girls who could make a mark upon the age in which they lived*. The task ahead was to abolish demoralising old-time, old-world usages and establish new ones more in keeping with the spirit of freedom and progress. This was the promise of the twentieth century. Ackermann was convinced that *the world's greatest reforms must be brought about by girls, and Australia is the natural starting point...where they enjoy the advantages of citizenship.*[21]

This history of idealism and experimentation has largely been lost to popular memory, overshadowed by the cataclysm of World War I. A new dawn of political, industrial and social awakening was replaced, all too quickly, by the darkness of death and grief.

There has not only been a loss to world history of Australia's role in the great story of the age. There has also been a loss to Australian history of our national self-consciousness as a country of leaders, thinkers and innovators. We have become accustomed to seeing ourselves as country cousins in the world's political affairs: signatories, allies and partners, but not movers and shakers; not agenda-setters. What's worse, except on the sporting field, we expect little of ourselves. *Australia bids for Global Village Idiot status once more*, reads a 2017 headline in CRIKEY.[22] The content of the article is about cyber-security, but the headline plays off an assumption of Australia's inadequacy, regardless of the issue. When I was a kid, at least we were proud we'd invented the black box recorder and the goon bag. Now we're not so sure what we've got to contribute.

Australians at the birth of a new nation and the dawn of a new century did not expect it to be so. In 1902, while debating the Commonwealth Franchise Act that would forever shatter the legislative framework of national governments towards their citizens by making women the political equals of men, Queensland senator Thomas Glassey made this bold prediction:

> I believe that when the history of the first Parliament of the Commonwealth comes to be written, the conferring of this immense boon upon so many people, not as a privilege, but on the grounds of justice and equity, will receive the commendation of the historian.[23]

Instead, the unique achievement became an academic annotation rather than the clarion call of a young and proud nation.

Today, we've largely forgotten that at the turn of the twentieth century, Australia was famed for its reformist drive and progressive agenda. Our inventions and start-ups were in democratic legislation, welfare reforms, industrial arbitration and other experiments (including immigration restriction based on racial exclusion) brewed up in the social laboratory. And women were often both the entrepreneurs *and* the door-to-door salesmen, roaming from country to country spruiking Australia's wares. Australian women were not only nationalising, but also globalising, actors—with the energy, skill, courage and ambition to change the world.

This history, too, is part of the Big Picture.

This is the story of how the world's newest nation became a global exemplar, exporting to the world a model of democracy that was, at once, ahead of its time and perfectly of the moment.

This is the story that Dora Meeson Coates' impudent banner promises to reveal, if only its matted threads can be unravelled.

PART 1

PURITY

Ideas have wings.

BESSIE RISCHBIETH
1964

1

The Rising Sun

Sydney, 1901

Lily Tardent was an intrepid girl. At eleven years of age, she convinced her father to let her accompany him on his last hike of the year. Mr H. A. Tardent and his friend Mr J. E. Vance—both members of the Biggenden Alpine Club—were planning a climb to the top of Biggenden Bluff, 3000 feet above sea level and overlooking the rich plains of Queensland's North Burnett. The climb was a five-hour round trip up a steep, winding goat track: arduous for adults and certainly gruelling for a child. But Lily had her mind set. The party reached the top by evening and, as the QUEENSLANDER reported, *there they saw the setting sun of the 19th century.*

But Lily, her father and Mr Vance had not made this trek to watch the orange and crimson bruise of the sunset. After dark—they were to spend the night on top of the mountain—they lit huge bonfires and *hoisted on the top of an improvised cairn the Australian Federal flag.* Next to it, Mr Tardent raised the flag of the Swiss Republic, his mother country by birth. According to Lily's dad, these were *the two freest and happiest flags in the world.*

The party woke as *the sun, like a huge ball of melting gold, emerged from the billows of the Pacific Ocean, and shed the first rays of its glory on the friendly flags of the oldest and the youngest confederation in the world.*

This was no ordinary day and no ordinary sunrise. This was a sunrise for poets. A sunrise for patriots. Today was Tuesday 1 January 1901—and *Little Lily Tardent* was later credited with *the honour of being the Australian who has first seen the rising sun of the Australian Commonwealth and of the 20th century.*[1]

⚕

It fell to New South Wales, the 'Mother Colony', to host the official celebrations for the *eventful trinity* of *the birth of a year, a century and also a nation.*[2] From New Year's Day, there would be a whole week of rejoicing, with processions, pageants, illuminations, milestone events and a great deal of bunting. There would also be the swearing-in ceremony of the first governor-general, Lord Hopetoun. *The crowning and final act of half a century of political evolution and of national aspiration,*[3] played out before tens of thousands of people in the sweltering January heat.

Elsewhere across the new nation—everywhere across it, in fact—Australia's five million citizens came together to witness what one enthusiast called *one of the most momentous events in human history.* In his letter to the editor of the SYDNEY MORNING HERALD, New South Wales member of parliament E. W. O'Sullivan explained that the Commonwealth of Australia was *destined to be the greatest power in the Southern world, the leader of liberty and progress, and the creator of a state of civilisation that all the world will be glad to follow.*[4]

The BATHURST ADVOCATE was more sober, but no less confident in reflecting on how far the young nation had come: at the beginning *practically an unknown land…mostly criminals…a few tribes of blacks*, it had achieved *a progress which is one of the chief marvels of the age.*[5]

Australia's federal unity was considered exceptional by world standards for one key reason: it had come about without slaughter. In other, older, countries *the wavering corn has sailed over sunlit fields once red with blood*, but with Australia *it was not so.*[6] In Australia, to unite the colonies, to draft a constitution, to elect a provisional government—all this had occurred, it was said, without conflict, division or enmity. *One may truly say*, boasted the ADELAIDE OBSERVER, *that never a drop of white man's blood has been spilt in a white man's war on the Australian Continent.*[7] (According to the OBSERVER, the Eureka Stockade, when the British military turned its rifles and bayonets on a community of white men and women refusing to pay their mining licence fees until such taxation afforded representation, was but *a trifling exception* to the rule that settler Australians were *too busy with the hard practical duties of colonization…to think of flying at each other's throats*. The OBSERVER didn't bother to reflect at all on the most basic process of colonisation: the murder, through dispossession and 'dispersal', of tens of thousands of Indigenous Australians.

All around the new nation in the optimistic summer of 1901, newspapers harped on the same story. Australia was *the fairest of Britain's daughters fair.*[8] On 1 January 1901 *Dawn's white Fingers now disclose the Day! Night has departed on her starry way.*[9] The miners of Broken Hill were treated to a lecture by the Reverend Angwin, who reassured them that Australia's *clean national life* would provide *an example to the entire world of that righteousness alone which can exalt a nation.*[10] The forces of right were white, and, like the dawn of day, they eradicated the darkness that lurked in the shadows.

The Adelaide CHRONICLE published a poem by Will X. Redman, alias Will Scarlet, titled 'The New-Born Nation'. While fashionably turgid, it neatly captured the spirit of the age.

> On a snow-white wild war-horse Australia sits on high…
> In her strong right hand she holdeth, with a grip like the
>   grip of Thor…
> The flag of Federation, whose shaft is of glinting steel;
> Ah! See, now the sun uprises with a glow like firelit gold,
> With glory flooding a country where never a slave was
>   sold.
> With her new-born flag saluting, Australia greets the
>   sun—
> The bright sun of Federation, whose day hath at last
>   begun.[11]

The virtue of a free birth, untainted by a history of bondage. A wild, untrammelled freedom. A white-hot glistening future, waved in the faces of a world shackled to the past. A new dawn.

The metaphors for purity and danger, for a bright future emerging from a dark past, came thick and fast, communicating something that generally went unspoken, but which the Ovens and Murray Advertiser articulated in its coverage of the 'Dawn of Australian Unity': *very few of the aboriginals are left to witness this our crowning day, to witness the triumph of the white race.*[12]

It was, of course, demonstrably untrue that Australia's First People had all but 'died out'. But why let the facts get in the way of a good origin story?

The cover image of the New South Wales government's official program for the inauguration events in Sydney draws on all these strands of artfully curated symbolism. The beautiful young Minerva, crouched on the shores of a wide brown continent, peeking out from behind the federation flag and the British flag. At her feet, the bounty of the Australian soil, native flora cradling the shields of the former colonies, now states. Minerva peers into the distance, where the rays of the dawning sun illuminate the shimmering Pacific Ocean. She is heralding the rise of Truth, Justice, Peace and Charity: the idealised woman embodying the idealised nation.

Australia was the Daughter Land represented by Minerva the virgin goddess, speaking to the civic virtue of nationhood and the morality of good government.[13] As a self-consciously modern nation, Australia paradoxically drew on the tropes of antiquity to tell her story, knowing her citizens readily understood the visual code.[14]

But lest today's readers confuse the imagery of patriotism with the ideology of republicanism, a further verse of Will Redman's poem complicates the narrative.

> I swear to be loyal to England, the mother that gave to
> me birth;

All the while she is Mistress of Ocean, until she is
    Queen of the Earth.

This is why Minerva shelters behind the dual flags of Britain
and Australia as she watches the dawn of a new era. Australia's
freedom rested on her place in the British Empire, her security
assured by 'sharing the twin benefits of parliamentary democracy
and imperial military protection'.[15] The family of empire was a tight
one. The new nation was now part of a British imperial cluster that
included the colonies of South Africa, Canada and New Zealand
as well as other territories under direct Crown rule, such as India.
Minerva could do all the banner-waving she wished: she could not
loosen the apron strings with the mother country. *These daughters
of the imperial mother*, observed one contemporary, *will share in the
greater conclave of the nation and make manifest in counsel the blood-tie
and common racial instinct.*[16]

So there was no ambivalence about whether Australia was
still part of the family circle—but had nationhood changed her kin
status? What becomes of the daughter when she is no longer politically nubile?

Rudyard Kipling expressed the status anxiety in his wildly
popular poem 'The Young Queen', first published in THE TIMES
in October 1900 and syndicated in publications around the world,
including the NEW-YORK TRIBUNE. Kipling's Old Queen—England,
but also literally Queen Victoria, who in 1901 was eighty-two and
had been on the throne for sixty-four years—receives her daughter
mounted on a 'red-splashed charger'. (The blood is a legacy of the
Boer War, not Australia's frontier wars.) She asks:

How can I crown thee further, O Queen of the
    Sovereign South?...
Daughter no more but Sister, and doubly daughter
    so—

But lest it appear that Daughter/Sister Australia, in reaching
her constitutional majority, may now enjoy an equality with Mother

England, Kipling makes it clear where she stands in the hierarchy of
empire:

> And the Young Queen out of the Southland kneeled
>   down at the Old Queen's knee
> And asked for a mother's blessing on the excellent
>   years to be.[17]

Australia was not a sovereign state. She could not make war or
peace with foreign powers. To enter into treaties or even communi-
cate with the leader of a foreign country, she required the consent of
the Colonial Office. According to the wonderfully titled 'doctrine of
colonial repugnancy', no Commonwealth laws could be at odds with
British legislation. Australia might be classified as a self-governing
dominion, but Kipling was quite accurate to depict her kneeling for
her mother's blessing—notwithstanding the fact that the old girl
wasn't quite what she used to be.

By the turn of the twentieth century, the British Empire was
past her prime. Despite having 398 million subjects, she had been
overtaken militarily by European rivals, and outdone industrially by
the United States and Germany.[18] With the empire in geopolitical
decline, it was more important than ever to keep up appearances.
On big family occasions, each member knew exactly where to sit and
how to behave at the imperial table. And there was no bigger festiv-
ity than the Commonwealth of Australia Inauguration Day. Future
prime minister Alfred Deakin dubbed 1 January 1901 *the birthday of
a whole people.*[19]

⚕

It was a moment for anticipation and expectation. In her autobiography, *Thirty Years in Australia*, the novelist Ada Cambridge
remembered the occasion of Federation as a turning point:

> On the last day of 1900 I sat at my writing window
>   to watch the drop of the time-ball that regulates all

the government clocks...I cannot describe the state of
tension we were in, the sense of fateful happenings that
possessed that day...Australia believed herself on the
threshold of the Golden Age.[20]

Indeed, the turn of the twentieth century was a watershed
moment for the women's movement the world over. English suffragist Alice Zimmern described *a universal awakening of women and a
universal appeal to the world to recognise that women as well as men are
people.*[21] The theme of women waking up to the wonders of their
own potential, and the horrors of their debasement, would inform
suffrage art and literature around the world. Political ignorance and
self-effacement were to be relegated to the dark, cocooned days of
the past. In 1899, the popular American writer Kate Chopin titled
her new novel THE AWAKENING. It is the story of a woman's journey
of self-discovery as she struggles to reconcile the constraints of
motherhood with her desire for freedom and sexual independence—
symbolised by learning to swim—and ends with her suicide in the
ocean. That may all sound trite to modern ears, but at the time of its
release, THE AWAKENING was explosive, panned by (male) critics and
adored by young fans.

If women were waking to their own power, they were doing
so in the illuminating rays of a new era of hope and optimism. The
arts and crafts of the period—jewellery, ceramics, stained glass
and graphic art—all draw on a common visual language: a bugler
heralding the dawn; a sun rising on the horizon, the words Votes
for Women encircling it. Sunrise over the sea became a significant
feature in feminist iconography reflecting the aspirations of international womanhood.[22]

The cover of the literary journal SHAFTS featured on its cover a
girl goddess before a rising sun. *Light comes to those who dare to think*,
was the journal's motto, and a poem appeared on the cover:

Oh swiftly speed, ye Shafts of Light,
All round the shadows fly;

Fair breaks the dawn; fast rolls the night
From Woman's darkened sky.

Speed, light, forward motion: such were the characteristics of the Coming Woman.

Not that you would know it from the popular characterisations that appeared in the press. Louisa Lawson, mother of the famous bard Henry, wrote an article called 'The New Woman' for her newspaper THE DAWN in May 1899, summarising the vilification to which this archetype was subjected. *Of the limited number of stock-butts for the funny man's witticisms*, Lawson wrote, *perhaps the New Woman is the most profitable.*

> It should be easy to recognise her, with her hard face, big feet, spectacles, and the 'gigham' [umbrella], which she flourishes as she talks and bangs over the heads of men when they do not agree with her. Although unsexed she has a husband and numerous family, which she system-atically neglects, particularly the baby.[23]

Australian publications such as the BULLETIN (to which Henry Lawson contributed his verse), painted modern women as hysterical, malicious liars with diseased imaginations and an innate desire to harm men.[24] They were the *winter-faced women* and the *flat-chested sisterhood*.[25] Puritanical. Irrational. High on rhetoric; low on logic. At once childlike and animalistic. More akin to 'the servile races' than upstanding Anglo-Saxon men.

Real new women, as opposed to the cartoon or allegorical version, were encouraged though publications like SHAFTS and THE DAWN towards affectionate parenting, companionable marriage, higher education, outdoor exercise and 'rational dress'—the abandonment of whalebone stays and crinolines in favour of gowns tailored for a natural figure and, in some cases, the bifurcated skirts and tunics known as bloomers.

Women were also emboldened to take their newfound social confidence into the domestic sphere, and particularly the bedroom, in order to protect themselves from men's perceived and legal sexual entitlements. At the turn of the twentieth century men could and did take their wives to court to enforce their conjugal rights, obtaining judicial orders to 'return' non-complying wives to the waiting arms of their husbands.[26] Sexual freedom, however, was not a widespread feminist goal at this time. The feminist line on the body was rather: self-government for women and self-control for men. At the time of Federation, sovereignty in Australia was both a national and a women's issue. The political has always been personal.

But if the New Woman was ridiculed, the suffragists had a few satirical tricks up their own sleeves. Feminist artists depicted the anti-suffragists as the folk character Dame Partington, trying 'in vain to sweep back the tide of New Dawn pro-suffrage women blessed by the rays of the rising sun'.[27] In England, a humorous postcard by suffragist Ernestine Mills appropriates Mrs Partington and her mop, the folkloric symbol of futility: like Sisyphus, only female. Here *The New Mrs Partington* is repelling waves whose crests are labelled *professional women, mothers, working women, medical women, liberal women, conservative women, taxpayers, factory workers, writers, civil servants*.[28] A tidal wave of change threatening to wash away the worn-out footprints of custom.

In Norway, suffrage activist Gudrun Drewson predicted that *On the whole, we begin to see the glory of the rising sun, which will give us, within a little while, the bright, clear day.* It was in Australia, noted American journalist Jessie Ackermann, where the twin tides of feminism and federalism surged together, that women could most feel *the dawn of conscious power which has come upon them.*[29]

The national birthday cake being served in Sydney on 1 January 1901 wasn't an appeasement. As we shall see, for Australia's white women, it was sweet reward for timely effort.

2

A Condition Akin to Stupor

Melbourne, 1900

Australia's first birthday party was long and lavish, with parties and parades in every capital city and country town. But for Margaret Heffernan, incarcerated within the cold bluestone of Pentridge Prison for the murder of her baby, there was nothing to celebrate.

The story of Maggie's arrest, trial and sentencing had made the papers throughout Australia, but her situation was common enough: uneducated girl meets boy; boy seduces girl with promises of marriage, then bolts when she falls pregnant. In nineteenth-century parlance she is now a 'fallen woman': a disgrace to her family and a social pariah.

Concealing her condition, and with hopes of locating her lover, Maggie fled from her *highly respected* family in rural Yackandandah[1] to Melbourne. She worked as a servant at the Junction Hotel in Preston until her shameful secret could no longer be hidden, and gave birth to a baby boy in a room at the pub. When her employer, a Mrs Ralph, discovered Maggie she sent her to the Women's Hospital in Carlton where she remained until 9 January 1900. Then she was discharged to the streets with two shillings in her pocket.

This is when things got really grim for Maggie. Indeed, *fate seemed to be against the girl*, as one newspaper later surmised.[2] Homeless, she knocked on the doors of two church charities, who turned her away. On 14 January, she wrote to her parents *and acquainted them with her position*. On the day of the letter's arrival, her parents missed their daily trip to town to collect the mail. The following day, the post office burned to the ground. *As she got no answer to her letter*, Maggie considered herself *cast off by the family.*

There was no such thing as a single mother's pension, and no prospect of employment for a girl nursing the evidence of her sin. What Maggie did next would catapult her from a mere statistic to a media sensation. After a week of sleeping rough, and suffering from what the doctors termed puerperal insanity—what we would today would call postnatal psychosis—Maggie wandered down to Prince's Bridge. There, concealed beneath the bridge, she held her starving, screaming baby under the murky water of the Yarra River until he screamed no more. When the little corpse washed up on the banks a few days later, the hospital identified him by sight as Maggie's child. She was arrested in the home of her new employer, a rich woman on the right side of the river who had advertised for a wet nurse and wasn't inclined to ask too many questions.

The case was sad, but clear cut. *Before Mr Justice Hodges, at the Criminal Court today*, reported the SYDNEY MORNING HERALD on 22 February 1900, Margaret Heffernan

> *was charged with murdering her child by throwing it into the Yarra. Accused, who appeared to feel her position acutely, entered the dock on the arm of an attendant and through-out the hearing of the case remained in a condition akin to stupor.*[3]

The judge determined that *finding herself on the banks of the Yarra the temptation was too strong for her, and undressing the infant she slipped it into the water. She did this with averted head and did not look back.*[4] When the jury returned with a verdict of guilty, *coupled with a strong recommendation for mercy*, Maggie collapsed. Asked if she had anything to say, she whispered in the ear of a female warder, *I intended to take the child to Sydney.* The sentence of death was then passed, *and the woman, who had fainted, was carried from court and driven to gaol in a cab.* If Maggie had been in the mood for gallows humour, she might have found it amusing to reflect that some pregnant women committed minor crimes so that they could deliver their babies in prison, where they at least had a roof over their heads and three lousy meals a day.

The casebooks at the Royal Women's Hospital reveal that Maggie was but a small drop in a vast ocean of female affliction. In the 1880s and '90s, two-thirds of the women admitted there were under thirty years old, and three-quarters of them were pregnant. Of the married women, at least a third were 'shotgun' weddings. Ten per cent of admissions had tuberculosis and thirty per cent had gonorrhea—according to the hospital's Dr O'Sullivan, one of the *greatest evils of modern civilization.*[5]

By the time of Maggie's confinement, doctors knew that it was the gonococcus bacterium that caused chronic infection, sterility, extra-uterine pregnancy, genital malformation and blindness in the newborn, rather than university studies or bicycle riding, which had been the theory. But still, argues medical historian Janet McCalman, it was rarely acknowledged that in the realm of venereal infection, 'the guilty were not women but the selfish and profligate men who gave it to them'.[6] Bacterial theory was still underdeveloped. Post-abortion sepsis was becoming more common, and exnuptial conceptions accounted for a large proportion of its victims—although married women did use abortion as a (terrifying) form of birth control. As for childbirth itself, that was a game of Russian roulette in which putrid infections and hit-or-miss medicine were the live bullets. To be young, poor and female in the late nineteenth century was a recipe for suffering.

And, as Maggie Heffernan's case showed, the justice system wasn't much kinder.

When Maggie was born, women weren't eligible to serve on a jury; there was certainly no such thing as a female barrister. The only respectable jobs available to women were teaching, nursing and domestic service. Married women couldn't own property, or get a divorce or even a bank loan if their husbands abandoned or abused them. Post-primary education for girls was a preserve of the wealthy. There was no maternity allowance, no state welfare and no childcare services. (Unless you count baby-farming, which was the career path of Frances Knorr, the previous Australian woman to become a press sensation. Pregnant and broke, her husband in gaol, she took the children of other desperate women into her care. Some she looked after, some she sold to childless couples, some she strangled and buried in her back garden. After two such infants' bodies were dug up, Frances Knorr was hanged at the Old Melbourne Gaol in 1894, aged twenty-six.)

Changing any of this—the conditions of daily life, the lack of access to justice, the inability to rise from the mire of poverty and misery—seemed impossible. And the basic reason for that, it seemed obvious to many, was that women couldn't vote. They had no civic role in making the laws that governed them. Socially and economically, women were shackled by their dependence on men. Morally, they were bound by the sexual double standard. And politically, they were hamstrung by their disenfranchisement. The veteran American suffrage campaigner Susan B. Anthony adroitly summed up the situation in an 1870 speech: *women are in chains.*

Or behind bars. Which was where Vida Goldstein found Margaret Heffernan in the Australian summer of 1900. Languishing in a damp, airless cell of H. M. Prison Pentridge under sentence of death.

3

The Shrieking Sisterhood

Victoria, 1854–1900

Susan B. Anthony's words were not aimed only at the patriarchal systems of power and privilege that made men the masters and women their slaves; they were also intended as a rebuke to women themselves. The full quote is this:

> The fact is, women are in chains, and their servitude is
> all the more debasing because they do not realize it.[1]

Women, according to feminists like Anthony and her fellow Americans Elizabeth Cady Stanton and Carrie Chapman Catt, needed to wake up to their own subjugation and to rise from the stupor of centuries of political and sexual oppression.

Vida Goldstein was one woman who was utterly alive to the great challenge of the times.

Vida—the name is the Latin feminine for David—was born on 13 April 1869, in Portland, in the far west of Victoria.[2] Her father, Jacob Robert Yannasch Goldstein, was the son of a Polish Jewish father and Dutch Irish mother.[3] After migrating to Australia in 1859, Jacob became fully integrated into Anglo society and never practised as a Jew himself. When he met Vida's mother, Isabella, he was working as a businessman in Portland. Isabella, née Hawkins, was Australian-born, the daughter of wealthy Scots Presbyterian squatters in the rich farming land of the Western District. The odd couple was married in 1868. Vida was their first child; Elsie, Lina, Selwyn and Aileen followed.

In 1877, when Vida was eight, the Goldsteins relocated

permanently to Melbourne. She was educated at home by governesses and then at the Presbyterian Ladies College, which had built a reputation for educating the daughters of the colonial elite to the same standard as their sons. PLC's founding principal, Charles Henry Pearson, thought it absurd that women should not be trained in medicine and law but permitted *that they should amass large fortunes by singing and acting on the public stage*.[4] Tall, graceful and attractive, Vida had the external attributes for a career as an entertainer, but her intelligence coupled with a first-rate education set her on another path. Vida's teachers found her extraordinarily hardworking—to the extent that she suffered a nervous breakdown in her final year—but also vivacious, spirited and possessing a firm conscience.

The Goldstein family attended the Scots Church in Collins Street where former PLC girl Nellie Mitchell, later Dame Nellie Melba, sang in the choir. The charismatic minister was Charles Strong, a progressive liberal and social reformer whose controversial views on science and religion eventually saw him split from the orthodox Presbyterian Church and establish his own independent ministry at the Australian Church. The Goldstein family followed him there, as did many of Melbourne's intellectual elite, including Alfred Deakin.

This was where Vida developed her passionate commitment to the underprivileged and her zeal for social reform. When Reverend Strong took his anti-slum campaign into the dismal back streets of Collingwood, Isabella Goldstein and her daughter were with him. Vida witnessed first-hand the misery and turmoil in the slum houses where women tended to large families, suffering violence and abuse at the hands of drunken husbands, while babies starved and children resorted to petty crime. She would later explain her support for socialism by speaking of her *personal observation of how the poor and working classes live*. She had seen too much *to be satisfied with a system which makes their lives one unceasing round of toil, deprivation and anxiety*.[5]

Vida's mother also led her eldest daughter into the work that would ultimately consume her life: the struggle for women's rights.

⚱

The earliest call for women's rights by a woman in Australia is generally credited to Henrietta Dugdale. In 1869 the Melbourne ARGUS published her letter decrying the inadequacy of a married women's property bill then before parliament. It was personal: Dugdale had herself lost her property to a profligate husband whom she could neither live with nor divorce.[6] Her letter criticised the bill as *but a poor and partial remedy for a great and crying evil*, particularly for deserted wives. *This is a piece of the grossest injustice,* she went on,

> and being unjust the consequences can only be evil. In the case of a young woman so deserted it is three to one but she either falls a victim to some vile seducer, and ultimately ends her shortened career in Bourke-street or the River Yarra.[7]

But the question of the female franchise went back further. In 1857, Victorian MP George Higinbotham (the sympathetic but insufficiently gutsy politician at whom Dugdale's wrath was now directed) had raised it when debating a bill to extend manhood suffrage in Victoria. *Giving the right of voting to females,* he argued twelve years prior to the publication of John Stuart Mill's famous essay 'The Subjection of Women', *will be one step towards that general and complete political equality which it appears to be the chief purpose of this age to effect.* Earlier still, women in Ballarat—women who had fought for the same voting rights that unpropertied men had won after the mass democratic protest movements at Eureka—pressed for their own inclusion in the newly democratised political machinery of the colony.[8]

Opponents viewed the call for the female franchise as *one of all the crazy ideas going around*,[9] not just wrong but risible. *Although I entertain great respect and regard for the female sex*, chortled conservative premier James Francis, *I consider the qualifications of the ladies are already sufficiently charming without adding to their influence in society by conferring on them the right to vote for members of the Legislature.* Former premier James McPherson expressed a similar view, adding that *nature has drawn distinctions between the sexes which can not be ignored.* MacPherson was a member of the Legislative Assembly, the so-called 'people's house'. The responses from the elite Legislative Council were worse.

But despite the ridicule and vilification to which members of *the shrieking sisterhood* were routinely subjected, the movement for women's rights intensified in the post-goldrush years. By 1884, Australia had its first organised women's suffrage association, established in a private parlour in Melbourne by Henrietta Dugdale and Annie Lowe. As Vida would later note, women's suffrage had now *reached the region of practical politics.*[10] George Higinbotham was not present but sent a sizable donation. In 1889 Dr William Maloney, a dapper thirty-four-year-old medical practitioner and ardent socialist, introduced into the Legislative Assembly the first bill *to remove all sex disabilities in regard to voting.* Maloney's bill failed but his commitment to women's suffrage would make him one of the prime movers for change in the next two decades.

By the end of the 1880s, two-thirds of women in Victoria earned their own living and paid taxes. But not one of them got representation for their taxation. And to add insult to injury, women's rights advocates—including male supporters like Higinbotham and Maloney—had to put up with the longstanding accusation that most women couldn't really care less about getting the vote; that suffrage was just a new-fangled fad espoused by a few noisy, carping, dried-up old bluestockings.

In 1891, Premier James Munro promised to introduce a female suffrage bill into parliament if Victoria's women could demonstrate that their sex really did want the vote. Rising to the challenge,

Henrietta Dugdale mobilised a legion of female foot soldiers to spend six exhausting weeks collecting signatures for a massive petition. The core supporters would be easy: respectable middle-class reformers from the burgeoning suffrage and temperance societies. But for the first time women now came together across class lines. Volunteers trudged through the working-class slums of Fitzroy and Carlton as well as the genteel neighbourhoods of Hawthorn and South Yarra. Regional districts organised their own petitions, with volunteers knocking on doors and talking over fences. Isabella Goldstein was one of those women. And where mother went, so did daughter. When other girls of her class were busy attending balls and starting families, Vida trudged the streets helping her mother collect signatures.

The volunteer army collected an astonishing thirty thousand signatures in six weeks. All of the individual paper petitions were stuck onto bolts of cotton, and proud delegates lugged the 260-metre roll into the parliament building, where it took four attendants to place the petition before the House. This was the largest petition ever presented to a colonial parliament. Win or lose, women's suffrage could no longer be dismissed as the shrill bleating of a few radicals.

The 1891 franchise bill did fail, but the petition converted Premier Munro, who now became a staunch advocate of women's suffrage, berating the recalcitrant members of parliament for over an hour:

> The whole thing is a scandalous disgrace. If you believe that women are differently constituted to men, remove taxation from them; but if you are a democrat, and believe in government of the people by the people and for the people, then give the people fair play, and when you tax women, give them the vote as well.

That was how Vida got her first taste for the blood sport of politics. Campaigning in the slums, collecting signatures—witnessing the power of collective action—set the course for her lifelong undertaking to improve the lives of women and children.

That year, Vida was twenty-one. Smart, witty and beautiful, she collected marriage proposals like others collected the daily mail. (A dashing young member of her father's militia unit, John Monash, was one of her unsuccessful suitors. She found him frivolous; he dismissed her as haughty—after she'd rejected his affections.) But Vida vowed she would never marry. She wanted to devote her life to bettering the conditions of all women and children, and she believed, justifiably, that her own marriage and childbearing would make this impossible.

Beyond that, her private life is a mystery. Although she was friendly, warm and vivacious, with devoted male and female friends, almost everything we know about her comes from her reported speeches, her journalism and other published sources. Even her travel diaries read like reportage. Vida was a public woman. She lived and breathed politics.

In 1893 Vida and her sisters opened a school—co-educational, since they believed it was 'unnatural' to separate the sexes in education—run out of the family home in St Kilda. (The financial crash of that year hit independently wealthy families like the Goldsteins hard, and meant the girls needed a source of income.) Vida continued her slum work. She helped organise a committee to raise funds to found the Queen Victoria Hospital, staffed entirely by women.

In 1899, when her friend Annette Bear Crawford died, Vida assumed from her the leadership of the movement for women's emancipation in Victoria. She closed the school to devote herself full time to the women's cause. It was her belief that conditions for women would never change until they had the vote: women's lives would not be improved; women themselves would not be taken seriously as credible, worthwhile human beings without political power.[11]

Vida made her first public speech at a woman suffrage meeting at the Prahran Town Hall in July 1899. A month later she addressed a packed audience at the Melbourne Town Hall, where she shared the stage with Alfred Deakin, Reverend Strong and the Mayor of Melbourne. She spoke in what would become her characteristic style: calm, rational, measured; able to reach every corner of the hall (in those days before amplification) without raising her voice in a 'manly' fashion. TABLE TALK noted after the speech that *she is a living demonstration of the time-honoured fallacy that an 'advanced' woman cannot be womanly.*[12] The AGE was similarly impressed. *Miss Vida Goldstein showed by the grace and aptness of her remarks*, it reported, *that there is no reason why a woman's presence should not be as acceptable on a public platform as in the drawing room.*[13] The papers didn't report what Vida actually said at these meetings. Her presence on the stage was newsworthy enough.

In September 1900 Vida began publishing a monthly journal, the WOMAN'S SPHERE, *as registered proprietor, with full editorial control.*[14] As she revealed in its first issue, Vida had received an offer from an unnamed benefactor to start a journal to represent *all interested in the local movement for advancing the highest interests of women*, the only stipulation being that she assume complete charge of the operation. Though it *entailed embarrassing responsibility*, she jumped at the opportunity. *It is no use to make any other promise than that I will do my best*, Vida announced in her first editorial. *I shall try not to blame anyone but myself, if you, ladies and gentlemen, do not find my paper worthy of your penny, and a little esteem and possibly affection.*

The journal's title was, of course, tongue-in-cheek, a play on the notion that a woman's place was in the home. There were no social notes—no descriptions of who'd worn what gown to what soirée. Nor were there recipes or etiquette tips like those found in the women's pages of other journals. ('What a Girl Should Learn': *to sew; to cook; to mend; to be gentle; to value time; to dress neatly; to keep a secret...to make good break; to be sweet-tempered...to be a womanly woman under all circumstances.*[15])

Rather, Vida's WOMAN'S SPHERE contained what she called

serious reading: colonial politics, parliamentary reports, a regular column called 'The World Turns' containing updates from the women's movement in other countries, notices of meetings and demonstrations, and arguments one could use against anti-suffragists. For example, to the charge: *It will be the cause of dissension in families*, the ready answer could be: *It will not cause dissension except where dissension already exists.*

The journal named its supporters in parliament—and also called out its adversaries. Advertising was accepted from typewriter and bicycle companies, coffee shops and organisations such as the *School of Physical Culture and Medical Gymnastics* and the Working Men's College, which promised *classes open to women*. There were no ads for corsets.

Above all, Vida's ambition was that her paper would obtain the *friendship of even a small percentage of my country-women who love their land and know it can never prosper until half of humanity has its rights—and performs its duties.* At thirty and proudly native-born, never having travelled abroad, Vida was an avowed democrat and Australian patriot. And she was now at the helm of an *organ of communication* that would find a wide audience for her activism.

So when Vida Goldstein walked into Maggie Heffernan's prison cell, it was always going to be a turning point. Remembering the popularity of the monster petition nine years earlier, Vida decided to use the tactic again. She would make Maggie's case a cause célèbre.

⚓

The following is the text of the petition on behalf of Maggie Heffernan, announced the Melbourne AGE on Saturday 3 March 1900.

The paper proceeded to print the contents of the petition of the Women's Political and Social Crusade *in toto*. The petition called for the death sentence to be commuted on the grounds that Maggie's conviction rested on incorrect medical testimony. The judge had directed that she was not criminally insane because she remembered her actions and knew she had done wrong. But puerperal insanity, argued the petition, was not the same *form of disorder* as insanity; the *legal definitions of disease* were biased against postnatal women, thus producing a *legal fiction*.

The injustice done by the court, however, was not merely a technicality. There was a moral dimension:

> Your petitioners believe that the unfortunate girl is deserving not so much of legal punishment as the deepest sympathy...Seduced, betrayed, deserted, homeless, friendless, left to starve in the streets, in a physically exhausted condition, with nothing but water to give to a newly born babe. The hanging of such an unfortunate creature...would be an outrage on our common humanity.[16]

Public opinion had always tended towards mercy for Maggie, but now Vida's campaign provided a tangible goal. Vida orchestrated a letter-writing campaign, wrote articles for the WOMAN'S SPHERE and led deputations. The Trades Hall Council, a powerful labour lobby group, unanimously endorsed the views of one such WPSC deputation. Public meetings were held, and support rolled in from across colonial borders.

A letter to the editor of the Sydney TRUTH, signed by Justice, denounced the behaviour of charities who had closed their doors to Maggie: *Christian (so-called) institutions and Christian (?) women who turned aside and withheld the hand of sympathy from the poor fallen one. Shame! Shame on all such!*[17] Justice's censure went beyond religious humbug to call out social hypocrisy:

> May the day be not far distant when the betrayer must take his place by the side of his victim and bear with her the penalty. Will the day never come when it will be no longer the woman only who pays?

Vida noted in the WOMAN'S SPHERE that Judge Hodges had adjudicated in a case a few weeks before Maggie's in which a man had returned home drunk and cut his wife's throat with a razor *almost severing her head from her body*.[18] The man was found guilty of manslaughter and sentenced to two years imprisonment, *Judge Hodges remarking that drink had led him to commit the crime.*

Maggie's petition received seventeen thousand signatures. *Faced with just such a largely-signed petition*, the lieutenant-governor commuted the death sentence to four years' imprisonment.

Vida had proved that she was not only a dedicated follower, but also an influential leader. And she did more than just chalk up Maggie's reprieve as a feather in her political cap. There is evidence that she maintained an acquaintanceship, possibly even a friendship, with Maggie.

Maggie didn't see out her four-year term. She was released from Pentridge on 21 December 1901, eleven days shy of the first anniversary of Federation.

Not, sadly, as a reward for good conduct: the Melbourne TOCSIN reported a few months earlier that *a lady who has all along taken a great interest in the case heard that Maggie Heffernan had developed consumption*.[19] Nine months after her incarceration, Maggie showed pronounced symptoms of phthisis—fevers, night sweats, fatigue and weight loss—and yet,

> when not ill enough to rest in hospital, she was kept hard at work in the laundry, where the steam is so dense that at times it is impossible to breathe, and at night she was compelled to sleep on the floor, with a piece of coir matting as mattress.

TOCSIN surmised that if the mysterious *friend outside, who was watching her interests*, had not intervened to *set the wheels in motion to secure her release*, Maggie would still be coughing her lungs up in her bluestone bunker. A Royal Commission into the penal system was needed, the paper argued, and no one would have agreed more fervently than Vida. She published an article on penal reform in the Woman's Sphere arguing that the current system was no more than *a State manufactory of criminals.*[20]

How could Australia claim the righteousness that supposedly exalted the new nation, freed from its penal past, when injustice still yoked the vulnerable and the poor? For a democrat and a patriot like Vida, such hypocrisy simply wouldn't do.

4

They Did What They Could

Sydney, 1891

Liberal-leaning Victoria was the first place in Australia where women's rights were actively debated. But, like the rising tide of Federation itself, such paradigm-shifting deliberations did not occur in geopolitical isolation. Outrage was infectious. On 29 March 1891, seven years after the first Australian women's suffrage organisation was convened in a Melbourne drawing room, the inaugural meeting of the Womanhood Suffrage League (WSL) of New South Wales was held in a modest home at 77 Darlinghurst Road, Paddington. The house belonged to Mrs Dora Montefiore.

At that time Dora had been widowed for two years and had two small children. She was luckier, however, than most women in that situation: her late husband's family, the Montefiores, were Establishment. They had been among the earliest free Jewish settlers in New South Wales; the Montefiore name connoted leadership, respectability and entrepreneurial flair in every field of endeavour, including grazing, mining, shipping and land speculation. Dora's marital home had been the Octagon, the oldest (and highest) building in Darling Point.[1] Originally built with convict labour as a government watchtower, it was perched on a hill with a commanding view over Sydney's magnificent harbour. And Dora's own family background was similarly privileged.

Born Dorothy Fuller in Surrey, England, five days before Christmas in 1851, Dora grew up (as she wrote in her 1927 autobiography) in *the Victorian nursery*, sheltered, *nest-like*, from the outside world by servants and governesses.[2] Francis Fuller educated his daughters along with his sons: when Dora was old enough, she attended Mrs Creswell's school at Brighton. The eighth of thirteen children, Dora was quick-witted and clever, with a natural gift for languages. Not pretty, though: short and squat, with her curly dark hair, long nose and wide mouth, she was never going to be the belle of the ball.

In 1874, the script of Dora's insulated life changed when her eldest brother, who had been living in Tasmania, called for one of his sisters to 'come out' to him. His *delicate* wife needed help with the children and the housekeeping, and lord knew good help was hard to find in the colonies. *It was decided that I should be the one to undertake this duty*, Dora recalled: sailing to Australia was not her choice. But the forced realignment in Dora's worldview would be the making of her, particularly after she left her brother's household (for reasons unknown) and took herself off to Sydney where, in 1881, she married George, the scion of the celebrated Montefiores. They married according to Church of England rites, with the bride's father present. Class proved thicker than holy water.

In 1889, when George died of a strangulated hernia, thirty-year-old Dora found herself in reduced but not desperate circumstances.[3] She could feed, clothe and house her two children, six-year-old Florence and two-year-old Gilbert, although she was forced to leave the Octagon and move to Paddington, a drop in both altitude and social status. But Dora was truly floored when informed by her solicitor that *in law, the child of the married woman has only one parent, and that is the father.*[4]

The fact that she could not legally assert custody of her children, even if nobody was at this moment threatening to take them away from her, shaped the course of the rest of Dora's long life. As she would write in her autobiography:

> I was forced by a sense of duty towards other women
> who were not so free as [I] was to act publicly in the

cause that was dear to [me], in order to help bring about before the public the question of the gross disabilities under which women were suffering.

This motivation, to help women who did not have the social and economic advantages she enjoyed, drove Dora to seek the political remedies that no woman possessed. Finally emerging from the cocoon of privilege, she *found herself constantly up against wrong and unsympathetic laws, and without political power to alter or abolish such laws.*[5] In that first grief-stricken year of her widowhood, Dora began to meet other women who were in the same position, all *suffering under the same sex disabilities.*

What did they do with their newfound solidarity? *We discussed, and rebelled, and longed to make things better for our children.* Discussion, rebellion, longing. An economical recipe for change.

⚑

Dora's decision to form a suffrage society was influenced by a chance meeting with Sir George Grey, a true Renaissance man whose colonial careers included army officer, explorer, linguist, land speculator and 'suppressor' of native rebellions. He had been governor of two British colonies: New Zealand and the Cape Colony in South Africa. He was also a liberal and a democrat who championed the principles of social equality and 'pure democracy': the anti-aristocratic concept of one man, one vote.

By 1891 Grey was living in Sydney. He was eighty years old and three-quarters senile, and he was attending the Australasian Constitutional Convention on 2 March. The delegates had been appointed by the parliaments of each Australian colony, plus New Zealand, to explore the possibility of federation and to *consider and report upon an adequate scheme for an Australian Constitution.*[6]

In Grey, Dora found a political mentor. She began to accompany him to meetings, where she was generally the only woman in the room. *He spoke to me of the enfranchisement of women in the colonies,* Dora recalled, *where things moved more rapidly than in older countries, and said that such legislation would lead the way for similar reforms in Great Britain and elsewhere.*[7]

Grey also persuaded Dora that the present historical moment was a unique opportunity.

> He added that now that the question of Federated Australia was becoming a fait accompli, each state in the Federation was making its own special laws, and in consequence, the women in each state must agitate and organise for political enfranchisement.

Whereas Victoria had had its own suffrage society since Henrietta Dugdale and Annie Lowe rallied the troops in 1884, New South Wales only had individual advocates. Women like the formidable Louisa Lawson, and the independently wealthy Miss Rose Scott, who had been a Sydney celebrity for a decade, famed for her intellectual 'at homes' where politicians, writers and artists would gather to discuss the fashionable topics of the day. But there was no suffrage organisation. *That should be your work,* George Grey told Dora Montefiore.

After the inaugural Womanhood Suffrage League meeting at Darlinghurst Road, Dora found new premises for meetings: the tea rooms of Quong Tart in George Street. *Mr Quong Tart,* reported an American newspaper on the issue of the Chinese in Australia, *speaks good English, sings Scotch songs, has an English wife, and takes a prominent part in religious, moral, and philanthropic movements.*[8] Tart had made his fortune selling tea, and his rooms were renowned for their noisy and topical meetings. In the month of April 1891 alone, he opened them up to the Single Tax Conference, the Opium League (against the importation of opium to Australia), the Cyclists Union and the Sydney Horticultural Society. He was an accommodating host, fond of concluding these meeting with the words, *this evening is devoted to harmony.*[9]

As honorary secretary of the newly minted WSL, Dora was less inclined to accord. She was, from the start, dead set against *accepting any form of fancy franchise.*[10] Just as George Grey believed in 'pure democracy', so Dora Montefiore rejected the watered-down version of women's suffrage based on ownership of property. In New South Wales, men could vote regardless of whether they owned property. In the ideological and strategic battle between the so-called *whole-loafers* and the *half-loafers*, Dora set her democratic course towards full adult suffrage.

The latest female-led political lobby group was newsworthy. Papers around the nation reported the event, though often with a fair swag of derision. *A Womanhood Suffrage League has been formed in Sydney*, wrote the AUSTRALIAN STAR, *to advance the cause of the fair agitators.*[11] An Adelaide paper included the news in a column of titbits from around the world:

> German Emperor stirring up the French...
> The Governor will attend the Birthday races...
> Johnston, the Ballarat murderer, has been pronounced
>   sane...
> A Womanhood Suffrage League has been formed in
>   New South Wales...
> Portugal in a bad state—revolution and bankruptcy
>   both threatening...
> A Melbourne bookmaker charged with bigamy. The
>   odds are 2 to 1 against him.[12]

Dora was not dissuaded from her purpose, despite the fact that the press was *so ignorant, prejudiced and malicious that the general population thought we were a band of ill-behaved viragos with raucous voices and abominable manners.*[13]

She continued to hold meetings with a core group of invited members, including Rose Scott and Louisa Lawson. Then, in early June, over 150 people gathered to debate the rules of the league and elect a committee. The first order of business: to send a circular to all parliamentary candidates in the upcoming elections *asking whether they were in favour of woman suffrage.*[14] The era of practical politics had dawned.

At that first public meeting on 4 June 1891, 'the cause' was stated plainly: *Women had been looked upon somewhat as chattels, men being so to speak their owners. Women had, however, proved their right to think and act for themselves.*[15] This was the idea that motivated such respectable middle-class women to march out of their comfortable drawing rooms and throw their bonnets into the political arena: women had long been enslaved; now they had earnt their right to liberty.

But it was more than that. Justice demanded their enfranchisement, whether 'proved' or not, and the opportunity for justice was at hand. If the Federation was to go ahead it would have to abide by its own stated principles, as outlined by the likes of George Grey.

> The Commonwealth of Australia, to be 'broad based upon the people's will', must listen to the real voice of the people, at least half of whom were women.

This became the first motion passed.

Many of the other sentiments voiced were staples of the suffrage movements in England and America. Women, contended a Mrs Pottie, *deserved better than to be classed with convicted criminals, lunatics, idiots and infants.* Louisa Lawson put forward a second motion: *that the right to the ballot was needed by women because without it they had no power to protect and keep pure their chosen sphere of home.* Women were hamstrung (argued Lawson, the mother of a famous drunkard) in their role as moral guardians. *Against intemperance, gambling and impurity [men] hold us responsible and yet take away the only weapon with which to fight.* Only the vote could arm women to purify politics and scrub society clean of its ills.

Mrs Wolstenholme, a deserted wife who had opened a school to pay her way, proposed a third motion, one that pertained directly to the reason Dora Montefiore had woken the sleeping giant of female umbrage in the first place: *The special hardship to women of their legal helplessness in the matter of custody of their own children.*

The inaugural public meeting concluded with a vote of thanks to the Hon. W. H. Suttor for *chivalrously giving his assistance to their cause* in acting as chair. The themes that would set the parameters of the women's suffrage debate in the context of Federation were set: women in the new Commonwealth would not be treated like criminals or lunatics, but rather would be entitled to the same democratic rights as adult men, in order that they could properly carry out their maternal role as purifiers and protectors of the race. The vote was the means by which women's citizenship duties could be discharged in the new nation. There could be no Commonwealth without the common cause of a universal federal franchise.

⟱

Dora Montefiore had no desire to antagonise men. She wanted to educate them, to bring them along on the journey she had herself unexpectedly found herself on. *I am cordially in favour of...anything that brings men and women to work together and to understand and sympathise with each other,* she explained. She believed this was the spirit of the age: *pens take the place of swords, the platform and the parliament the battlefield. The reign of physical combat has given way to mental combat.*

Women, aided by noble men, would reform Australia's political life. *I would have a federation in all things,* Dora fantasised. *Then, and only then, will you bring about a socialism of love and unselfishness.* Dora had used the two years of her widowhood productively. She'd assessed her own position, and found it structural, not situational. She studied the causes and the potential remedies of her disadvantage. *I have carefully stored up and written down every argument I have heard against woman's suffrage,* she now told her new allies at the league. *I have spoken to, and listened to some of the leading men of this country on this subject.* And she took the temperature of the times, assessing the hotspots, the potential allies and the fiery opponents: *I recognise in this subject as Mr Barton does of Federation 'that there are strong prejudices to overcome, old fallacies to be exposed, distrust dispelled, doubt scattered'.* (Edmund Barton, Attorney-General of New South Wales, a staunch federalist and a delegate to the 1891 constitutional convention, was an outspoken enemy of women's suffrage.)

Dora knew that the ideas—and perhaps the tactics—that were beginning to take shape in her were big, dangerous and open to ridicule. *Will you call this the dream of the idealist?…Remember, the ideal of one age becomes the reality of the next.*

But there was no question in Dora's mind that one life had been left behind, a skin shed:

> If every woman could live in a sheltered home, and be fondly loved and nobly protected, the world might never have heard of woman suffrage, though the right would have remained. But if our young girls must go out into the world and fight side by side with men where the struggle is thickest, for daily bread…if our widows and deserted wives must stand at the head of the family and keep off from the little ones the buffets of a world that is not always kindly…then it is more than right, it is expedient, nay, absolutely necessary that woman and the interests of women should be represented in our Legislative Chamber. The good of our children, the good of our country, the good of our sex demand it.

As years slipped by and one decade folded inexorably into the next, Mrs George Montefiore—no longer a girl but a forty-year-old widow, a mother, a newly minted feminist and increasingly a socialist— saw clearly that she dwelled on the threshold of history. She told the league members gathered around her that they were pioneers.

> By-and-by, our daughters and our grand-daughters, who stand in the dawn of the twentieth-century—the

women's century—will say: '…they only tottered on the narrow path which has merged into the broad road on which we walk so freely'. But we hope they will say, if they remember the little band of women who stand here to-night, 'They did what they could'.

And for the time being, Dora felt she had done all that she could in Sydney. In 1892, she packed up her Paddington home and sailed for France on *a study tour*, with nine-year-old Florence and five-year-old Gilbert in tow. Dora's autobiography gives no indication of why she decided to leave Australia so soon after establishing the Womanhood Suffrage League.

Was she confident that, with Rose Scott now at its helm, the league would successfully reap what she had sowed in the fertile fields of Federation? Did she feel her newfound talents as an organiser and a speaker had outgrown the shores of her adopted home, as she hints? *Our woman movement (not undertaken, let me remind my readers, to prove our equality with men, but to gain equality of opportunity with men) is an international one.*[16]

Perhaps she remembered Sir George Grey's conviction that reforms in the antipodes would *lead the way*. Whatever the impetus, Dora Montefiore would seek in the Old World the opportunities to capitalise on all she had gained, lost and learnt in the New.

She sailed with one lesson front of mind: *And I would say to men—'Trust the women of your country; they will not fail you.'*[17]

5

Setting the Torrens on Fire

South Australia, 1894

It's Sydney, as the saying goes, or the bush. But it was in Adelaide—sandstone City of Churches—that the face of democracy would be irrevocably remodelled. And all because of a tiny freedom fighter in widow's weeds.

When a plump Protestant Irishwoman stepped off an immigrant ship at the Port of Adelaide in December 1879, there was nothing to suggest that she would rewrite the rules of the political world. Mary Lee, fifty-eight years old, recently widowed and a mother of seven, had sailed to Australia on domestic business: to care for her critically ill son, John. But he died soon after she arrived and Mary, unable to afford the passage home, was stuck in the colonial outpost on the Torrens River.

Within ten years she had become a star gladiator in the largest arena she could find: votes for women. The issue was, as Sir John Cockburn, South Australia's premier from 1889–90, put it, *the great question of the century, perhaps we may say it is the great question of all time.*[1]

South Australia was founded, like Mary herself, as a model citizen. The only colony to refuse transportation from England, settled in a controlled, ordered fashion, it thought itself a paragon of virtue—an experiment in 'systematic colonisation'—with a comparatively progressive character to rival Victoria's. (Universal manhood suffrage was established in South Australia as early as 1856.)

There were, however, more women earning money from prostitution per capita than in any other Australian city, and thousands more providing cheap labour for Adelaide's rapid industrialisation. Coincidence? South Australia's feminists thought not: Mary Lee was in no doubt that only women's suffrage would improve the social and economic position of women. Taking a different tack from Dora Montefiore, who urged education, Mary came down in favour of direct action, and began writing incendiary letters to the paper:

> Could women have ever descended to such depths of misery and degradation if women had a voice in making the laws for women? Let us be up and doing. Let every woman who can influence an elector see that he seizes his vote as a sledgehammer...[2]

Over the next decade, Mary's firecracker exuberance and relentless activity won her a reputation as a shrew. *Poor Mary Lee!*, wrote one gentleman to the ADELAIDE OBSERVER, *how she does froth and foam and stew and scold.*[3] But more importantly, she was gaining a network of influential contacts within the Adelaide establishment, including the darling of South Australian letters herself, Catherine Helen Spence.

Spence called herself *a professional journalist and reviewer... authoress, poetess, philanthropist, reformer;*[4] Vida Goldstein referred to her as *the prominent social and political economist.*[5] She was a long-time agitator for social reform in education and prisons, and she is thought to have written the first book about women by an Australian woman: CLARA MORRISON, a goldrush tale published in 1854, the year of the Eureka Stockade. (The book was published anonymously in London.)

By the 1860s she had landed on the issue that would become her life's work: electoral reform. In 1861, she printed a thousand copies of a pamphlet titled A PLEA FOR PURE DEMOCRACY, outlining her system for proportional representation. She admitted herself that the publication *did not set the Torrens on fire.*[6] But her ideas about how to erode *the preserve of the wealthy* in parliament had powerful supporters. She corresponded with John Stuart Mill, who told her *it gave him great pleasure to see that a new idea both of the theory and practice of politics had been taken up and expanded by a woman and one from that Australian colony.*[7] Mill and his colleague, Thomas Hare, thought Spence's pamphlet *the best argument from the popular side that had appeared.*

Spence, for her part, found Mill—who favoured retaining some forms of property qualification—too cautious in his approach. *I took this reform more boldly*, Spence boasted: *I was prepared to trust the people.* She was certain that *in our new colonies* her innovations would be met with more favour than in *the old countries bound by precedent and prejudiced by vested interests.*

In this pioneering thinker and activist, Mary Lee had found a powerful ally.

Mary was a tireless letter writer and pulpit-thumping public speaker. Her blistering attacks on men and their follies were frequently published in the Adelaide newspapers.

> Will not South Australian women join forces and storm this last miserable subterfuge? Will they not unite and insist with an emphasis which cannot be misunderstood or evaded that it is their right as citizens of a young state, which claims to be free, that its women shall be free?[8]

But she knew that writing to the press would not be enough. Nor would friends in high places (and she had many, including Julia Holder, wife of Liberal MP Frederick Holder, and Elizabeth Webb Nicholls, president of the South Australian Woman's Christian Temperance Union). As the prosperity of the 1880s waned and workers everywhere began to fall on hard times, Mary cannily predicted that winning the vote for women would require the support of the labour movement.

And in South Australia, alone among the colonies, the female franchise was a live possibility. As South Australians liked to remind people, their political landscape was different from those of the other colonies. In South Australia, the conservative minority was not in the same position to delay electoral reform as it was elsewhere.[9] In Victoria, for example, suffrage bill after suffrage bill had passed the lower house but been stymied by the landed elite in the upper house. South Australia had the most broad-based representation in its upper house, its constitution ensuring that squatters didn't completely dominate. In fact, South Australia prided itself on this quiet little innovation.

So, Mary Lee deduced, she had a chance to actually get a suffrage bill passed—if she could get labour on side.

There had been a suffrage bill, introduced in 1886 by Dr Edward Stirling, that would have granted the vote to women with property. But South Australia had never had a property franchise, and the Trades and Labour Council smelled a rat. The bill was talked down by conservatives as well as by members with labour sympathies, like the liberal Charles Cameron Kingston, who mocked the suffragists and their supporters, asking whether their demands would one day extend to the absurd spectre of women sitting in parliament.[10]

Mary Lee's strategy, then, was to emphasise the link betweeen women's suffrage and the improvement of conditions for working women. In 1891, the same year that Dora Montefiore inaugurated the Womanhood Suffrage League of New South Wales and Vida Goldstein trawled the slums of Melbourne getting signatures for the monster petition, Mary established a new organisation. *We find that the Working Women's Trades Union of South Australia*, she wrote in a letter to the editor, *with a courage born of desperation, resolved to lead the way.*[11]

Mary's method was a simple, if arduous, pincer movement. Bustling about in her voluminous black frocks, she visited count-less sweatshops and factories, directly urging the exploited female workforce to join her union. At the same time, she was lobbying the male union leadership, arguing that having female voters would improve the electoral chances of the newly formed United Labor Party of South Australia.[12] Mary Lee was like a ferocious little terrier, yapping at everybody's heels. You just couldn't shake her off. And by the end of 1891 she had done enough hectoring, door-knocking, cajoling, pamphleting, letter-writing and speech-making to achieve the seemingly impossible, gaining the ULPSA's official endorsement of universal adult suffrage.

The decisive moment came after the general election of early 1894. The United Labor Party swept a record number of seats in an informal alliance with the liberal government that gave it the numbers to withstand the conservative opposition. Suddenly, South Australia had become the only colony in Australia with a non-conservative majority in its upper house.

The new premier, Charles Cameron Kingston, had undergone *a personal volte face* a year earlier, introducing a female franchise bill based on adult suffrage. *It was characteristic of the wise to alter opinions*, he said of his dramatic backflip.[13] Wisdom? Or did Mary Lee's associate, Julia Holder, change Kingston's mind?[14] Her husband Frederick had the ear of the premier, who—at a hulking six feet tall and, in Alfred Deakin's opinion, a man of *great ability, indomitable will and fearless courage…[that] verged upon unscrupulousness*[15]—was a better man to have in your corner than not.

In July 1894, with the newly liberalised upper house in place, Kingston reintroduced his Adult Suffrage Bill, the legislation designed to enfranchise the women of South Australia. *Either the proposal is right or it is wrong*, noted the OBSERVER. *If it is right Parliament, being representative of the people, ought to adopt it and bear the consequences; if it is wrong, they should reject it.*[16] The Women's Suffrage League (of which Mary Lee had been a founder member six years earlier) presented a petition to parliament with 11,600 names declaring the proposal was right.

⚓

On 17 December 1894, a blistering summer day, the Adult Suffrage Bill was introduced for the third time by Sir John Cockburn, a member of Kingston's ministry. The Ladies Gallery was jam-packed with women, including seventy-three-year-old Mary Lee. Catherine Helen Spence had arrived home from a speaking tour of America five days earlier to find *the women's suffrage movement wavering in the balance.*[17] Now she too was in the anxious crowd. Women filled the aisles, sat on the cushioned benches next to the speaker, sat on the stairs and even lifted their skirts to climb up behind the parliamentary clock. The House had never been so full, as the papers were quick to notice:

> If so many scores of women can absent themselves from their family circles by day and night in the mere hope of seeing parliament grant to them their rights of citizenship, what stories of deserted hearths shall we not hear when women are transformed into active politicians?[18]

The debate went on long into the night. Kingston's government needed a two-thirds majority to get the bill up, and it was fairly certain it had the numbers. But the conservatives were stonewalling. *Delicate women should be considered as well as the screaming sisterhood,* averred Mr Grainger. *Women do not yet know how to vote and there will be more informal votes than ever before.* Mr Griffiths preferred to play party politics, referring to the suffrage bill as *payment to the ladies for the support they have given to the government, who have been bought cheap by the Labor Party.*[19] On and on it went, one hackneyed argument after another: most women didn't want the vote; women would become 'manly'; they would stop having children; they were too emotional, too uneducated; they would only vote as their husbands directed; they would only vote for the most handsome candidate; what would women want next?

Eventually the House was adjourned. Many of the women went straight to the Café de Paris, where a welcome-home soirée for Miss Spence was still in swing.

The next morning the House was again buzzing. The suffragists were not the only ones who had been up all night. Staring down the barrel of defeat, the conservatives now decided upon a breathtakingly risky course of action. They abandoned their opposition to the bill, adding instead a last-minute amendment to strike out clause 4, which read: *until otherwise provided by the Act no woman shall be capable of being elected to Parliament as a member of either House thereof.*

Clause 4 stipulated that women would be ineligible to run for parliamentary office: without it, the bill offered the broadest franchise anywhere in the world. No man in his right mind would vote for that—even a Labor man. Not even the women were asking to be allowed to run for election! Indeed, Mary Lee, in a deputation to Frederick Holder, had made it patently clear that women did not aspire to being *lady candidates*. The conservatives were sure this outlandish amendment would sink the bill.

The debate took up where it had left off in the wee hours of the morning. Mr Brooker *strongly appealed* to give the *women their just right. For thousands of years women had been treated little better than serfs*, he pleaded.[20] *Cultivated women don't want the franchise*, Mr Johnston countered. You are *a striking instance of the necessity for woman's suffrage*, jibed Vaiben Louis Solomon. *Oh, divide, divide!*

Divide they finally did. At 11.35 a.m., the vote was taken. The count was thirty-one in favour and fourteen against. The bill was passed.

The Ayes were sonorous and cheery, reported the OBSERVER, *the noes like muffled bells.* The gallery erupted in *loud cheering. There's the hen convention,* Mr Grainger moaned, loud enough for the press reporter to hear him.[21]

Sniping was all he had left, for the conservatives' spoiling tactic had backfired in spectacular fashion. This extraordinary act of political miscalculation meant that South Australian women, including Indigenous women, now had full political equality, making them the most highly enfranchised women in the world.

⚚

The most highly enfranchised—but not, of course, the first.

That distinction belongs to the women of New Zealand, who had fought long and hard for their democratic rights. (Mrs Mary Muller, credited by contemporaries as the *pioneer worker...in the epoch-making 50s* [22] was in this respect the New Zealand counterpart of Henrietta Dugdale.)

Kate Sheppard of the Woman's Christian Temperance Union worked with *untiring energy* and a *clear and logical brain* in her role as franchise superintendent for the colony to bring about electoral reform. The strong association between women's suffrage and temperance did not go unnoticed by the New Zealand liquor trades, who said *many unkind and unpleasant things [about] the Franchise Superintendent.* [23]

In 1891, an electoral bill was introduced to parliament, including a clause that *women should be eligible as members of the House of Representatives.* This may be where the South Australian conservatives got their bright idea: in this instance it proved *an exceedingly adroit move*, as W. Sidney Smith wrote in 1902, giving the Antis (as opponents of suffrage were known) *more ammunition.* Kate Sheppard unsuccessfully wrote to oppose the amendment. The bill was defeated, just as its architects had intended.

In 1892, a coalition called the Franchise Leagues of New Zealand circulated a monster petition, as the Victorian women had done so dramatically a year earlier. Women trudged the length and breadth of the islands collecting signatures. Lady Anna Stout—young and petite despite her Dickensian name—headed the Dunedin

Women's Franchise League. Lady Stout later praised *the efforts of the minority who were brave enough to face the ridicule, opprobrium and martyrdom of pioneers.*[24]

One of the signatories to the petition was a young Australian-born artist named Dora Meeson, who was honing the skills that would one day see her paint an illustrious suffrage banner.

Like Vida Goldstein, Dora was born in Victoria in 1869. She was one of three daughters of John Meeson, a peripatetic school-master, and his wife Amelia. In 1876, the Meeson family sailed for England, but by 1880 had relocated again, this time to Dunedin. A serious girl with a long face and sad eyes, Dora Meeson spent her adolescence in New Zealand developing her love and talent for art. In 1890, she went to London to study at the Slade School, which had recently begun enrolling female students.

By 1893, she was back in New Zealand, studying at the Christchurch School of Art. It was here in Christchurch that Dora and her sister, Amy, signed the suffrage petition attesting to the proposition that *large numbers of Women in the Colony have for several years petitioned Parliament to extend the franchise to them.*[25] The Meeson girls' names were among over thirty thousand signatures that were added to the latest petition, almost a quarter of all those eligible: that is, adult white women. It was, as one MP noted, *the most numerously signed petition ever presented to any Parliament in Australasia.*[26]

A new electoral bill was extended to women, this time without the eligibility clause—and also without a property qualification—but with the support of the government. The bill passed by two votes and the Antis conceded they had been *beaten in a fair fight.*

No country need fear this privilege being given to the adult popula-tion, premier Richard 'King Dick' Seddon assured the rest of the world in 1893, as New Zealand ventured further down the road of progressive legislative reform than any other self-governing democ-racy had yet dared.[27] Kate Sheppard correctly predicted that New

Zealand's first election with female voters would *attract the attention of the civilized world.*[28]

It was New Zealand statesman William Pember Reeves who later proposed the 'one fine morning theory' of New Zealand suffrage: that women themselves didn't want the vote, nor did any *New Zealand female orator or leader of women* stand in the forefront and agitate for reform; rather *one fine morning of September 1893*, a hundred thousand women *woke to find themselves enfranchised.*[29] He would also claim, in his influential book STATE EXPERIMENTS IN AUSTRALIA AND NEW ZEALAND, that the part played by women in gaining the South Australian franchise was *useful but strictly subordinate.*[30]

Women on both sides of the ditch vigorously contested the claim that suffrage was a 'gift' bestowed by progressive men on indifferent women. Elizabeth Nicholls was among those who testified to women's efforts to win their rights:

> How they lobbied the members, how they interviewed some and argued with others and stimulated a third; how they deluged the press with letters; how they attended the House in throngs at all hours of the night to see fair play; how they used every means in their power to secure their end.[31]

It was with pride and satisfaction *that at last they triumphed.*

6

A Series of Miracles

Adelaide, 1897

The autumn of 1897 was to be a busy season for nineteen-year-old Miss Muriel Matters. The aspiring actress already had several bookings. There was a concert at the Fullerton Literary and Musical Society in May, where she would recite 'The Ride of Jennie McNeil', followed by, *in humorous vein*, 'Shadows'. In June, she would perform at the Norwood Town Hall in the three-hander Ruth's Romance, a comedy in one act, with Muriel in the role of Ruth.

So far this autumn, the notices had been good. With her halo of blonde hair and pretty features, Muriel knew she stood out from a crowd. The Bunyip had reported on this Wednesday's performance of Ruth's Romance for the Gawler Benevolent Association, singling out Miss Matters as *especially good*.[1] It was not quite A Doll's House, which was Muriel's favourite play from which to recite (particularly the passages when Nora is told that a woman is expected to stay home to raise children and Ibsen has her say: 'No, my first duty is to myself.'[2]) But Ruth's Romance, a smash on Broadway when it opened five years before, was not too shabby. And she did like the line *I don't wonder when a woman passes twenty, single life begins to pall on her. She wants a change.*

Muriel Lilah Matters was born on 12 November 1877 in Bowden, South Australia, the third of ten children. Her father, John, was a wayward spirit holding out against the stockbroking career that had absorbed his older brothers and which would eventually tether him to respectability too. Muriel's Welsh-born mother, Emma, worked hard to keep her large brood in school and out of doors, and Muriel helped her mother with the younger siblings. When she wasn't playing little mother, she tried on more satisfying roles: singing, piano and poetry recitals at church gatherings and temperance meetings. *Art*, she realised, could be her *magic weapon*.[3]

This week, the attention of Muriel's family must have been divided, despite the success of her Gawler performance, because the Federal Constitutional Convention was meeting in Adelaide. The convention had attracted the disapproval of the Gawler Wesleyan Society Sunday School teachers, who met to express their regret at *the general desecration of the Sabbath by the members of the Federal Convention* in choosing to sit on a Sunday.

Nonetheless, the Matters family Wesleyans were in favour of Federation. More importantly, they were in favour of the womanhood suffrage clauses that would be debated over this heady month of April 1897: Muriel's brother Charles was a personal friend of Mrs Mary Lee and an active member of her Women's Suffrage League.

Muriel could not remember a time when she was not interested in the woman question. So, while she worked hard to recall her lines and hit her marks on the small stages of Gawler, Fullerton and Norwood, she would have one eye on the action playing out on the big stage at Adelaide's Parliament House.

⚕

The birth of the Commonwealth of Australia may appear in hindsight as an inevitability. At the time, it was anything but. The terms were fiercely contested over many years and negotiated through a series of constitutional conventions held in Melbourne, Sydney and Adelaide from 1891 to 1897. Alfred Deakin would say later that Federation was *secured by a series of miracles...any one of a thousand minor incidents might have deferred it for years or generations*.[4]

Each colony had their own parliaments with their own constitutions: creating a nation would require diminishing some powers of the colonies, or expanding some of their laws to benefit all across the new Commonwealth. Federation wasn't simply instrumental.[5] It was an active, dynamic process. The thrashing out of powers, jurisdictions and processes—what the government could do, what the courts could do, what the people could do, who could be 'the people'—was fraught.

Everything was up for grabs. And the suffragists were front and centre in the scrum, determined bridesmaids leaping for the political bouquet.

By 1897, there were organised and effective suffrage societies operating in all colonies bar Tasmania: the women's suffrage movement reached critical mass right at the moment when a huge public platform was emerging, along with a mechanism for change. The convergence of feminism and Federation produced the perfect storm for democratic reform.

Annie Golding, secretary of the Newtown Branch of the New South Wales Womanhood Suffrage League, realised the potency of this unique moment in world history. *Are women of the people?* she asked. *Are they not half the people, and are their claims not to be considered?*[6]

Women who publicly voiced their ambitions were still pilloried in press and parliament, but it was no longer a novelty to see letters to the editor published under women's own names instead of pseudonyms like Justicia, or their brothers' names. Catherine Helen Spence noted that when she first took up the reform cudgels, *women as platform speakers were unheard of.*[7] Now women made eloquent speeches to packed houses. It was commonplace for women to send deputations to MPs, and to see women (Vida Goldstein was famous for it) sitting in the galleries of the legislatures, taking notes on how each member voted on each bill.

And in South Australia, at least, women would be able to vote in the Federal referendum—the one that would be held once the constitutional conventions nutted out the form of a draft constitution. Suffragists now began lobbying convention delegates to make sure, as Golding put it, *their claims were considered.*

The 1897 Convention differed from the 1891 version in one fundamental respect: delegates were elected, not appointed. This was to be the People's Convention. While the 1891 delegates had all been politicians, any citizen could (theoretically) stand for election for a berth at the 1897 convention. Even women—thanks to the advances in South Australia.

Catherine Helen Spence reluctantly put up her hand. It was her brother's idea, and at first she found it *startling.* No other woman in Australia—indeed in the whole empire—had ever stood for public office. In the end she agreed to go where no woman had gone before in order to advocate not for her sex, but for her pet cause: *it was as the advocate of effective voting that I took my stand.* Here was Spence's 'pure democracy'—one man, one vote, the principle that majorities must rule, *but that minorities shall be adequately represented.*

Having held back her nomination form until five minutes before the noon deadline so that no one could query her validity, she gained 7500 votes: twenty-second out of thirty-three candidates. One wag in the press lamented that *Miss Spence was a good man lost.*[8] (She always maintained that she would have done better if Charles Kingston had not played some grubby politics to sow the seeds of doubt about her entitlement to stand.)

But the sex of a single delegate was not really the point. Vida Goldstein, analysing the situation from Victoria, articulated the crux of the matter: if Federation went ahead, South Australian women could help *frame Commonwealth legislation* while all other Australian women, herself included, watched helplessly from the sidelines of citizenship. *This position was intolerable,* she concluded, *and the women made the most of it.*

Around Australia, women mobilised. They petitioned candidates in the popular ballots—and after the ballots they petitioned the elected delegates—to ensure that when a constitution was eventually drafted for an Australian Federation, women's suffrage would be included. Not content to be grasping bridesmaids, Australia's female political activists demanded to be equal partners in the union.

7

National Housekeeping

Adelaide, 1897

The very first petition presented to the delegates in Adelaide, on 23 March 1897, belonged to the Womanhood Suffrage League of New South Wales. After Dora Montefiore left Australia, the WSL was effectively run by Rose Scott and Maybanke Wolstensholme; but by 1895, a new kid had arrived on the block—and Nellie Martel was a kid with a twinkle in her eye to scare the devil.

Nellie was born Ellen Alma Charleston in Cornwall on 30 September 1855, the seventh of thirteen children brought up on a blacksmith's wages; spirited, ambitious and astute, despite a limited education. Her *out-and-out Radical* father, John Charleston, worked closely with the tin miners and industrial class of Cornwall. Some of her brothers were apprenticed to the local ironworks. Unlike Dora Montefiore, Nellie had never been sheltered, *nest-like*, from the outside world.

At twenty-four she had the gumption to follow two of her siblings out to Australia. After a stop in Adelaide to see her brother,[1] Nellie arrived in Sydney in January 1880, *sans* either a chaperone or a calling, but with striking blonde locks, high cheekbones and a vivacious personality. When she married Charles Martel in 1885 she described herself as an elocutionist, though she did not advertise her services in the newspapers. Charles was a photographer by trade and a real estate speculator by temperament. He would go bankrupt several times, while Nellie worked her way onto the social circuit, giving *dramatic and humorous recitals* at literary soirées and other fashionable gatherings.[2] With Nellie's vivacity, charm and hospitality, the Martels were a popular couple in 1890s Sydney.

In 1889, Nellie and Charles returned to England for a visit—Nellie's first time in London—and the experience changed her life. There she witnessed the great East End tailors' strike, where unions protested against the sweated conditions of the Russian Jewish immigrants who worked up to eighteen hours a day for piece rates, not wages.

In September 1900, with ten thousand workers on strike, a wide-eyed Nellie Martel witnessed one of the street demonstrations organised, as she put it, *to show Londoners how one end of London lived*. She was shocked to see the *emaciated* and *stooped* frames of the marchers, *a halting, miserable body of men*. And she asked herself: *what about the women?…if the men had the look of starvation in their faces*, how much worse must it be for the women of the slums?

In Sydney, Nellie had worked hard to leave her past behind her. But now, in London, she recalled the conditions of her Cornish childhood. *I had known enough of the sacrifices of women*, she later wrote, *to know that their condition must have been manifold worse than that of their husbands, or fathers, or brothers who walked in that fearful and awful procession*.[3] She remembered, too, her father's belief that it was essential for women to have the vote—*for any party that has a power, or a section of society that has a power over the other must in time oppress the unrepresented*. The *uplifting of men* could only occur by the uplifting of women.

Though the poverty of London was worse than anything Nellie had seen in Australia, *I determined that from that moment that my future life should be spent in working for the welfare of the country in which I had made my home*.

Nellie was convinced that women in Australia had a singular advantage over their sisters in England. *In young countries*, she wrote, *women are in greater demand, their opinions are sought after because the country begins within the homes*. And she predicted that, with a federalist movement brewing, the time would be ripe to seize that advantage: *The natural housekeeper can become the national housekeeper, as nation-keeping is only house-keeping on a larger scale.* Like all good Victorian daughters, Nellie knew how to keep house. Unlike most women, she would soon have the opportunity to test her management skills on the most public of stages.

⽔

Charles and Nellie returned to Sydney in 1891, just as Dora Montefiore was gathering like-minded souls in her Paddington home. Nellie soon shimmied her way into the WSL hierarchy—chairing meetings and serving on deputations to politicians—to be elected eventually to the WSL Council, along with sisters Belle and Annie Golding.

By 1897 she held the position of recording secretary, responsible for managing all petitions, including this most pressing one to the Adelaide constitutional convention, which she now signed and handed to New South Wales colonial secretary Sir William Brunker—*a benevolent looking old gentlemen*[4]—just before proceedings commenced.

The first of the petition's five points was the most crucial.

> That in framing a Federal Constitution for Australasia, the determination of the persons to whom the Federal franchise shall be granted is a question of great importance and your honourable Convention will probably consider whether or not such franchise shall be uniform throughout all the colonies...[5]

The petition pointed out that the women of most of the colonies were still suffering *under a disability from which the women of South Australia have been relieved.* Women would be taxpayers under a federal government, as well as *patriotic and lawabiding citizens.* They were *justified* in demanding a voice in choosing representatives to the Federal Parliament, *so that united Australia may become a true democracy, resting upon the will of the whole people, and not half the people.*

The text of the petition was soon published around the country, including in full in Louisa Lawson's THE DAWN. With New South Wales sticking its foot in the Federation door, Victorian women wedged it open further. By 3 April the United Council for Women's Suffrage in Victoria had proposed its own similar resolution. As Vida Goldstein noted, the Commonwealth Constitution *must base the electoral laws on the freest in existence at the time of Federation.* A uniform franchise should mean that all Australian women would enjoy the same rights as South Australian women: *political rights in their completest form.*[6]

Predictably, not all the press was favourable to the idea. *I don't suppose the franchise will be embodied in the Constitution*, predicted the Sydney SUNDAY TIMES, *after all, women's affairs, which are mostly social, will concern only the States.*[7] (In the same column, the SUNDAY TIMES reported that *you can't tell what the natural color of the modern girl's hair is* and *Melbourne women are fonder of jewellery than those of any other part of Australia.*) A letter to the editor from 'X Ray' in the LAUNCESTON EXAMINER expressed an exasperated yawn. Surely the delegates knew that *people get tired of* the franchise question *being pushed down their throats on every possible occasion.* Furthermore, South Australia was manifesting *an abnormal amount of self-conceit* in assuming *the role of dictator to all the rest.*[8]

But around the country, women made their position clear. They would help campaign for Federation if, in exchange, the South Australian gold standard for adult suffrage was written into the Commonwealth Constitution.

There was no guarantee this bargain would be met. For one thing, the 1897 Adelaide convention was not going to be an urbane echo chamber of progressive opinion. *At the outset,* according to Deakin, it *possessed antagonisms...which needed little encouragement to discover their malignancy.* All of the delegates were, of course, pro-Federation, but each colony wanted to throw its weight around. Fortunately for the women of Australia, the South Australian delegation had some heavy hitters. Deakin's view was that *measured by all-round ability the South Australian delegation was undoubtedly the strongest.*[9]

There was Charles Kingston, *a Radical of strong opinions, strong physique and even stronger will,*[10] elected to the convention presidency amid what Deakin described as *fiery hatred and vehemence.*[11] There was Vaiben Louis Solomon, *the dark, well-whiskered, portly Jew speculator*—eccentric, but committed to women's suffrage. And most importantly, there was Frederick Holder. Holder was not a physically robust man—*as thin as a paling, dark, swarthy, narrow-faced and narrow-shouldered,* Deakin said; *he had one eye useless and a chest which seemed destined for consumption*—but he was cool-headed and whip smart.

Though the likes of Deakin, Barton and Parkes have become household names in Australian political history as Federation's celebrated fathers, the most critical negotiations were conducted by the unprepossessing Frederick Holder. It was Holder who ensured that what had started as a tactical cock-up in South Australia now came back to haunt conservatives in the other colonies.

⚓

On Maundy Thursday 1897, 15 April, while young Muriel Matters was basking in the glow of her BUNYIP review, Frederick Holder proposed to the federal convention delegates that womanhood suffrage should be written into the Commonwealth Constitution.

No doubt his wife Julia, ardent suffragist and best mate of Mary Lee, was watching. *Not an empty square foot remained in the galleries,* noted the Broken Hill BARRIER MINER, *South Australia, having womanhood suffrage, makes special arrangements for the accommodation of ladies.*[12] There had never been less than fifty women *in the gallery set apart for them*; *often it has overflowed.* Catherine Helen Spence had certainly been spotted there, *escorted to the Chamber by the Hon. Mr Charleston* (Nellie Martel's big brother). Spence was noted for *speeding along with that familiar little trot, her hair snow white now, but her voice full of cheerfulness.* Two delegates had *advocated her system* for proportional representation. No matter what happened to Holder's motion, at least she could be satisfied with that.

Tomorrow was Good Friday. The convention would not meet. It would reconvene on Saturday, but not Sunday (perhaps the Gawler Wesleyans were persuasive) and no decision had been made about arrangements for Easter Monday; suffice it to say the delegates were *so tired that they are not at all anxious to sit on that day, especially in view of the Onkaparinga races.*[13] The convention had spent over two weeks now debating everything from the gauge of the national railways to the composition of the Senate. Some deliberations had been nothing but legal *trumpery*; others going to the heart of what it would mean to be an Australian. Mary Lee might have noted *that those who had the least to say often took the longest to say it.*[14] It was late on Thursday night. Everyone was ready to go home.

It was at this moment that Frederick Holder now moved that *every man and woman of the full age of 21, whose name has been registered as an elector for at least six months, shall be an elector.*[15] Mr Bernhard Wise, delegate for New South Wales, *wished to know if it was prudent to venture upon an experiment.* After all, no other nation on earth had adult suffrage actually written into its constitution. Kingston jumped in, bovver boots first. He *strongly supported a uniform adult franchise.* Votes were taken. The motion failed 23 to 12.

Holder was not deterred. He and Kingston appear to have planned for this result. Now, in a crucial move, Holder played his trump card. He proposed *a compromise…and a very fair one* that would leave it to a future Federal Parliament to decide the extent of the franchise—but with one crucial proviso.

Let's watch the theatre as it played out:

> Mr. HOLDER: What I move is: To add to the clause 'And no elector now possessing the right to vote shall be deprived of that right.' That is to say that while the matter is left to the Federal Parliament no person who now possesses the right to vote shall be deprived of that right.

> Sir GEORGE TURNER: As I understand it Mr Holder wants to have this amendment passed in order that the Parliament when declaring the uniform franchise shall not be able to deprive any woman, who can now vote, of that right.

> Mr. REID: It will compel female suffrage.

> The CHAIRMAN: If I may, I would point out that it applies only to electors who now possess the right to vote.

> Sir EDWARD BRADDON: How can a uniform franchise be secured if this amendment is carried? It will bind the hands of the Federal Parliament.

> Mr. BARTON: As I understand the suggestion, it means that if the Federal Parliament chooses to legislate in respect of a uniform suffrage in the Commonwealth it cannot do so unless it makes it include female suffrage. It ties the hands of the Federal Parliament entirely.

With that sucker-punch amendment—*That no elector now possessing the right to vote shall be deprived of that right*—Holder and Kingston were in effect threatening that South Australia would vote against joining the Commonwealth if it meant its women would be deprived of the vote.

As the MAITLAND MERCURY put it: *in the course of the debate the delegates began to realise that the possession of the franchise by women in South Australia put federation in a very awkward position.* Unless the constitution safeguarded the right of South Australian women to vote for federal members, *South Australia would probably vote against the Constitution Bill when it came before them on the referendum.* This was a big problem. *The federal cause is not so popular in South Australia,* the MERCURY analysed, *that its friends can afford to run any risk of alienating the sympathies of the feminine voters.*

And if South Australia did not join the Federation, Western Australia was likely to opt out too. Western Australians distrusted the idea of a centralised federal bureaucracy on the east coast in any case. The colony had only been awarded its own constitution by Britain in 1890 and had already shown great reluctance to compromise its recently acquired self-government.

Holder's suffrage stand-off now frayed the tenuous thread of national kinship to breaking point. As the MERCURY assessed, *it is difficult to see what could otherwise be done without imperilling federation, for with South Australia standing out Western Australia could not very well come in.* Holder's proviso threw the federal ideal into disarray. Votes for Women, noted the American journalist Jessie Ackermann, would be *the political broom used to sweep the state of Western Australia into the Commonwealth.*[16]

The result was that Australia's future first prime minister, staunch anti-suffragist Edmund Barton, was railroaded *much against his will* into accepting a breathtakingly controversial constitutional amendment.

The vote was taken. The ayes prevailed by three votes. As the MERCURY realised, *the South Australian delegates, having been elected by adult suffrage, all felt themselves bound to champion the feminine cause, even at the expense of federation.*

Unbelievably, the winner-takes-all strategy had worked and Frederick Holder had effectively made women's suffrage the precondition of a federated Australia. It was like a bucket of ice thrown on the hot heads of Australia's politicians. Federation, it was now desperately apparent, would rely on the goodwill and participation of not only male voters, but female would-be voters too.

Although womanhood suffrage was not expressly written into the constitution, the South Australian delegates had extracted an irrevocable obligation to grant a national female franchise, something that would occur in the first Electoral Act.[17] What would eventually become section 41 of the constitution ensured that:

> No adult person who has or acquires a right to vote at elections for the more numerous House of the Parliament of a State shall, while the right continues, be prevented by any law of the Commonwealth from voting at elections for either House of the Parliament of the Commonwealth.

Devoid of the drama that led to its creation, section 41 appears an innocuous legal framework. But section 41 was not simply instrumental. It was existential.

⚊⚊

After the Adelaide federal convention wound up in late April 1897, second and third sessions were held in Sydney and Melbourne. There were heated debates, deals and compromises about such matters as the composition of the two houses, states' rights and the machinery of government. But there was no significant challenge to Frederick Holder's uniform franchise amendment.

By 16 March 1898, a draft constitution was agreed on. Electors in each state would now get their chance to approve the constitution by referendum later that year. Another great day loomed. As eligible voters, South Australian women—ambitious, independent-minded young women like Muriel Matters, as well as pioneers like Mary Lee, Catherine Helen Spence and Julia Holder—would have the opportunity to approve or reject the constitution.

By July 1899, they were joined by Western Australian women.

Western Australia's premier, John Forrest, who had been an explorer and killer of blackfellas before entering politics, was by no means a campaigner for womanhood suffrage. But he was a cut-throat pragmatist, and he knew how to find water in a crisis of thirst. When his government was threatened by the votes of the Othersiders—the large, predominantly male population of miners who had migrated from the eastern colonies to work on the Western Australian gold-fields—he saw a way to boost his core vote in the urban electorates: enfranchise the women. The strategy paid off.

Though votes for women had been advocated in Western Australia since at least 1875, parliamentary politics in the sparsely populated colony was exceptionally fluid, with no parties in place. The female franchise was therefore not high in the hierarchy of political needs. Even the most prominent women's organisation, the Karrakatta Club with its redoubtable member, Edith Cowan, did not think it *expedient* to campaign actively for the suffrage.[18] But when Forrest saw votes for women looming like an oasis in a wilderness of organised labour from the goldfields, the Karrakatta Club began to lobby in earnest, presenting a petition just as the bill was introduced to parliament. *A cat's-paw to carry a party measure* was how Jessie Ackermann described the winning of women's suffrage in Western Australia.

But the upshot was that women in two colonies would now get to have a voice in the creation of the nation. And if they (along with the menfolk, of course) voted for Federation, Frederick Holder's amendment would ensure that all adult women would get a say in the making of federal legislation, even though they might still not be eligible to vote in their own state.

Vida Goldstein played the politics of the moment. She urged the Victorian government to finally grant its women the franchise so that *on the consummation of federation, South Australian and Victorian women may stand on equal terms.*[19] Though a federalist, Vida hoped the colonial sibling rivalry would last long enough to tip her home parliament over the line.

But not all politically savvy women were pro-Federation.

Rose Scott, the most dominant member of the Womanhood Suffrage League after Dora Montefiore's departure, was one who looked at the prospect of a remote national legislature and saw a dangerous concentration of powers. Scott, a wealthy, unmarried fifty-something at the time of the Federation referendum debates, espoused the principle of political maternalism: the idea that women's experience as mothers instilled in them particular capacities for governing. These skills and endowments included care, righteousness and purity of heart and motive. *It is the mothers who make the nation*, Scott argued.[20] She envisioned *a Federation of men and women in all things…a socialism of Love.*

Scott believed that a centralised government, far removed from the centre of women's power—their homes—would alienate rather than truly enfranchise women. Women would have less access to the forums of decision-making, less face-to-face contact with decision-makers, fewer networks of influence. Scott feared the new nation would undermine women's close and collaborative way of doing politics, rather than empower them, thus limiting the scope for any virtuous feminine influence over the vice-ridden habits of the nation: drinking, gambling, prostitution. Indeed the federalists, in speculating on the fortunes of the colonies, were willing to *gamble away the freedom of the people.*[21]

Other anti-billite women (as those who rejected the Constitution Bill were called) held differently inflected concerns. When a Mrs Bateson hired the Perth Town Hall in July 1900 to hold an anti-billite rally, her advertisement read: *to keep Federation out as well as rabbits.*[22]

It was a classic political split: the female anti-billites worked in open opposition to other prominent women, including Maybanke Wolstenholme who, with Mrs Barton, had established the Women's Federal League in order to lobby men to vote yes. Drawing on the same maternalist rhetoric employed by Rose Scott, Wolstenholme asked: *Shall our children be Australians and of one family, or shall they be colonists and rivals? It is a woman's question, for from the home the national life must spring.*[23]

Belle Golding derided the WFL not as crawlers but something far worse: *politicians' wives.*

The anti-billite view did not prevail.

True, the first referendum on the Constitution Bill was defeated: New South Wales, though posting more yes than no votes, did not achieve the required majority. A technical knockout. But a second referendum was successful, this time with Western Australian women voting. (The recalcitrant Victorian upper house still did not buckle, despite Vida's vigorous arm-twisting.) On 9 July 1900, the bill received royal assent and the Commonwealth of Australia was proclaimed on 31 July. New Zealand did not join the federation, though some expected it might right up until the last moments of royal assent.

Henry Parkes, the putative Father of Federation, had a motto: *One People, One Destiny.* It was a fine sentiment, but when push came to shove, it turned out that the country comprised many people, not all with the same vision of the future. After all, not even the mothers of Federation could agree among themselves on its rightful course.

But the die was cast. A continent would become a nation, and women—for the first time in the world's history—had campaigned and voted to design a country's constitution.[24] In six short months, Australia would throw itself a jubilant birthday party, the new nation rising with the sun of the new century.

8

The Great Day

Melbourne, 1901

At last the great day arrived, the wife of South Australia's governor wrote home to her mother in England. Thursday 9 May 1901— the inauguration of the Commonwealth Parliament—and it was a howler. *It pelted with rain while I was dressing*, Lady Audrey Tennyson's letter continued, *but soon cleared again with a bitter wind.*[1] After the nation's birthday celebrations in Sydney five months ago, it was now Melbourne's turn to bring out the bunting. Twelve thousand people battled the bitter wind of a typical Melbourne autumn to attend.

It was still hard to believe that Queen Victoria—*a good woman, a good wife and mother*[2]—had been dead since 22 January, a grief that cast a pall over this year of festivities. But there would still be royalty to usher in the parliament of the world's newest nation: the Duke and Duchess of Cornwall and York.[3] The new King Edward VII's son and his wife, Mary of Teck, had made the journey out. Federation had not, after all, *cut the painter.*[4] Those uber-patriots who had advocated for a republic were minnows in a raging sea of imperial fervour.

Lady Tennyson was pleased to find that she and his lordship had *very good seats in* the Royal Exhibition Building, the only venue large enough to shelter the crowds. They were in the front row at the back of the dais, next to Lord and Lady Lamington. Tom Roberts' Big Picture of the occasion captures her there, head bowed, reading her prayer book. From this vantage point, she could discreetly observe the duchess, who cut *a beautiful figure* in mourning black, gussied up with *a very long necklace chain hanging below her waist of large single diamonds, a sort of muff chain, very magnificent.* It was quite apparent to Lady Tennyson that even though the duchess *has not much to talk about,* she was better at *saying little things* than the duke and *thoroughly enjoys it all much more than he does.*

From her superior position on the stage, Lady Tennyson could see the little cluster of parliamentarians' wives and daughters standing in front of the solemn duke. The strikingly tall, elegant Pattie Deakin with one of her three daughters, proud that Alfred was now Attorney-General of the Commonwealth.[5] Lady Barton, founding member of the Women's Federal League, now wife of the new prime minster. Queensland Labor MP Andrew Fisher's sweetheart, Margaret, was out there somewhere too, with her mother. They had made a special trip down from Gympie for the occasion, though not yet being married to Andrew she couldn't possibly stand at the front with the other MPs' wives. Lady Tennyson's ally, the Hon. Sir Frederick Holder was there, in his new role as Speaker of the House of Representatives. When Lady Tennyson had recently stepped out of her vice-regal capacity and petitioned Holder on behalf of the ill-paid and worse-treated sempstresses of Adelaide, he established a tribunal to improve their pay and conditions. No doubt Julia had a hand in that too.

If Lady Tennyson lifted her gaze from her prayer book, she could see the marvellous painting on the ceiling porticos of the Exhibition Building. Above the real women in the crowd, the allegorical women circled them like a halo. Britannia—regal, helmeted—at the apex of the arc, surrounded by her daughters, the former colonies, with their crested shields and downcast eyes. Lady Tennyson's illuminated invitation to this *tremendously important moment for Australasia* used the same chorus of idealised women to symbolise the idealised nation. Drawing on Kipling's verse for the Commonwealth inauguration day, the Old Queen and the Young Queen beckoned: Daughter Australia, astride a white horse, her head bowed, approaching Mother Britannia as a grateful supplicant.

Lady Tennyson shifted her focus to the duke's closing proclamation—*everyone was surprised at the strong voice coming from such a little man*—and finally came the only act performed by an actual woman.[6] Amid a *profound silence*, before thousands of awed spectators from around the country, the duchess *touched an electric button to announce it all over the world*. The first parliament of the Commonwealth of Australia was declared open.

All in all, it had been a memorable occasion, *very dignified, reverent and quiet*. The only *blot on the ceremony*, as far as Lady Tennyson was concerned, was the music; the orchestra played the Hallelujah Chorus *without voices*. That and the weather. It had been such *a bitterly cold day*. By the time all the formalities were over she *came back shivering*.

9

May 1901

A tableau

Nellie Martel was not among the thousands who came to watch the Duke and Duchess of York open the first parliament. On 9 May 1901, the ebullient Nellie was in Paddington, preparing to give one of her 'at homes', the monthly reception she had been hosting since rising to prominence as recording secretary of the Womanhood Suffrage League in 1897. At first, she and Charles hosted these lively affairs from their rooms at the Hotel Arcadia, where *the double inducement of a popular hostess and good impromptu music proved irresistible in making the visitors linger.*[1] When the couple bought a home in Paddington, purchased with the profits from Nellie's elocution and singing lessons, the fashionable crowd followed, eager to have their names recorded as guests by the AUSTRALIAN TOWN AND COUNTRY JOURNAL or the EVENING NEWS.

If Nellie was a stylish entertainer, comfortable with the froth and bubble of Sydney's middle-class elite, she was also proving herself a persuasive public speaker. As WSL recording secretary, she had become central to the *earnest work being done by the advocates of the cause.*[2] She took notes of the meetings, and took the punches when accused of *redundancy of expression*. One disgruntled politician suggested that Nellie was doing Rose Scott's dirty work—clearing the matriarch's *sooty chimney*—by censoring meeting notes to keep the league's reputation unsullied.[3]

By early 1898 she was ready to step out from the older woman's shadow. Was it significant that Nellie's mother had recently died?

The notice she placed in the SYDNEY MORNING HERALD paid tribute to *a noble life at rest*.[4] Perhaps Nellie thought of the life her mother hadn't been able to lead while raising twelve children on a blacksmith's wage. Whatever the impetus, the federal Constitution Bill provided Nellie's chance to test her own mettle.

The eighth WSL annual meeting in June 1899 debated the league's position on the bill—pro or anti—with anti-billite Scott declaring that if any of its members *chose to fight one way or the other, they might do so; but the League had nothing to do with it*.[5] The latest women's suffrage bill had again failed to pass the New South Wales upper house, and the meeting affirmed that suffrage itself was the main game, *the desired end* that must remain the league's sole aim, just as Dora Montefiore had intended.

Though she was re-elected recording secretary, Nellie was not present at the meeting. She was speaking at an anti-billite rally— *one of the largest, if not the largest held*—in Katoomba, in the Blue Mountains outside Sydney. The Mayor of Katoomba, who chaired the meeting, was congratulated for securing Nellie's services for *Mrs Martel is considered the best speaker on the side*.[6] The Katoomba MOUNTAINEER praised Nellie, too, reporting the audience's loud applause for her key objection to the bill: that New South Wales, as the most populous state-to-be, would *meet the whole of the burden* of financially supporting the smaller states. Nellie, warming to her subject with *a long and eloquent sentimental peroration about hungry women and children, appealed to the electors…[to] vote for their own country and homes and not allow their colony to be made a fish pond for the other colonies. (Applause)*.

She urged women to convince their husbands to wait for a better bill, one worthy *of the trust they had asked for* before rushing to Federation. And she exhorted the New South Wales government to follow South Australia's lead in adopting adult suffrage, for *here your women are cyphers*.

Nellie's speech was widely reported in the papers. The SYDNEY

MORNING HERALD noted that her address *met with remarkable success. She had a large and enthusiastic audience and a unanimous vote was carried against the bill.*[7] Whether it was the ovation or the influence that Nellie enjoyed most, the success of her anti-billite campaigning inspired her to take an even more audacious step.

Vida Goldstein, a long-term ally of Rose Scott, had always been conscious that Scott's class position gave her an unfair advantage. *Your independent means,* she wrote to Scott, *enable you to be the leader in NSW but I have to work hard for the barest living.*[8] Nellie, who had scraped her way to prominence, appears to have shared that perspective despite the bourgeois trappings of her Sydney life: that never-to-be-forgotten procession of London's East End workers continued to nag at her. Along with Annie and Belle Golding, she tried to steer the WSL towards a closer association with the labour movement, establishing branches in the industrial heartlands of Newtown, Glebe and Redfern. Scott resisted the push, holding firm to the citadel of her central Sydney branch.

By the end of 1900, with Federation imminent, the WSL was still pushing hard to win the vote in New South Wales. The upper house was still doggedly holding back the tide. TRUTH reported in December on the fate of the latest Suffrage Bill:

> Never before have so many women invaded the Legislative Council as on Wednesday night when [MPs] defeated the Suffrage Bill by the narrow squeak of three votes. Chirpy, chatty girls were there in evening dress; councillors' wives; Miss Rose Scott, looking tired and anxious; brick-haired Mrs Martell, [*sic*] and the prominent suffragists...the hopelessness of petitions were never more apparent.[9]

Frustrations were already mounting when, in 1901, Nellie and the Golding girls organised a deputation to the premier without Scott's knowledge. The shit hit the fan,[10] and members began to take sides.

Louisa Lawson stood firm behind Nellie. Mr Gundy, who represented the Australian Society of Social Ethics, told Scott that it was Nellie who was the problem, not the Goldings. If not for Nellie, he reassured her, the Goldings would be loyal to Scott but, swayed by *the artful elocutionist*, they had become *the party of lying and spying*.[11]

Brick-haired Nellie, her ample bosom and coiffed head held high, turned and walked.

Ten years after Dora Montefiore established the Womanhood Suffrage League in her home in Paddington, and with New South Wales women still not enfranchised, Nellie Martel founded her own organisation, the Women's Progressive Association, with herself as president. The Golding sisters followed her, as did Louisa Lawson.

The WPA would stand for more than the winning of the vote. It would champion a range of issues, talking political economy until the cows came home. At the first meeting, held in the School of Arts in Pitt Street on 28 September 1901, the object of the association was read to a large audience: *to educate women on how to vote, when they get it, and to expand the mind, enlarge the ideas, and familiarise the women with all progressive measures*.[12] From the stage, Nellie elaborated further:

> The object of the association [is] to bring a better state of social affairs than now obtained—better socially and politically…[We] intend still to agitate, first for womanhood suffrage, secondly for the federal franchise…then we want to do away with sweating and other evils attendant on it. We want women inspectors and police matrons…anyone in sympathy can join and help…though we would prefer workers.[13]

Nellie promised that despite her *large teaching connection*, she had never missed and would never miss a session in the House when a suffrage bill was being debated. She also indicated that the WPA would advocate for the postal vote, so that when women did eventually go to the ballot box on election day, *their husbands should not be put to the inconvenience of minding the children.* Indeed, husbands need not worry at all. *Not altogether is it a sex movement,* assured Nellie, *as it will be to the advantage of men also, on the theory that the elevation of woman means the elevation of man also.*

By the end of 1901, the WPA had established multiple branches and many respectable gentlemen, including members of parliament, had enrolled. *The Women's Progressive Association, Sydney, has risen, phoenix-like from the ashes of the discarded Women's Suffrage Bill,* reported the WORKER, organ of the union movement, preferring Nellie Martel's socialism of labour to Rose Scott's socialism of love.[14] The revolution would start now. But gently, so that no one might be inconvenienced.

⚓

While Mrs Nellie Martel was claiming leading lady status for herself, Miss Muriel Matters was pushing the boundaries that had previously constrained her ambitions. Since women had won their historic voting rights in her hometown in 1894, and Frederick Holder bent the other colonies over a barrel on the issue of women's suffrage in 1897, Muriel had been busy trying to figure out how she would make her own mark. After winning a scholarship to the Elder Conservatorium, she studied music for two years.[15] But university life didn't thrill her half as much as the public performances—benefit concerts, small-town plays—she continued to give whenever she could get a part. Muriel was particularly drawn to stage roles as heroic women, triumphant underdogs and sacrificial lambs.[16] Critics often noted the dissonance between her strong stage presence and her diminutive physicality. A *frail, pretty and essentially feminine creature,* noted one journalist, who leaves you *marvelling at the mettle.*[17] In 1897, Muriel was still too young to vote but, at eighteen, she was old enough to leave her family home and go test that marvellous pluck and determination.

Muriel left Adelaide in November 1897, bound for Sydney. There she languished in *exasperating* obscurity, trying to catch a break. It's unclear how, as an unchaperoned teenager, Muriel kept body and soul—not to mention reputation—together in the city, but she was never estranged from her large and close family, who appear to have supported her aspirations. Like Nellie, she may have given elocution lessons, teaching the daughters of Point Piper to enunciate.

After twelve months without so much as a hospital benefit to her name, Muriel stopped waiting to be rescued by some canny impresario and organised her own inauguration onto the Sydney scene. She arranged the publicity, apprising the press of her *debut* at the YMCA Hall on 20 October 1898. She chose a stage name, shoe-horning her mother's maiden name into her own for a touch of class: Miss Muriel Warburton Matters. Several newspapers announced the upcoming entertainment by *the popular young elocutionist from Adelaide* who promised to recite both *humorous and pathetic pieces in verse and in prose.*[18]

The media blitz worked. There was a large and appreciative crowd. *Miss Muriel Warburton Matters was rewarded for her enterprise in arranging such an excellent entertainment,* reported the SYDNEY MORNING HERALD, *by a numerous attendance.* A *bright example of an Australian girl*, they called her, showing *a special talent for depiction of boyish characters* and *touches of sly humour.*

The 'Australian girl' was not merely a description; she was a type. Vigorous and independent, brave and brash, the Australian girl appeared in literature and in melodrama as a deliberate counterpart to the withering English rose. Australian girls didn't get seduced by foppish gits or tied to railway tracks: they outsmarted the rascals and derailed the trains.[19] Muriel's impish charm perfectly suited the temper of the times.

Favourable notices kept coming, and soon Muriel no longer had to notify the press of her movements. The papers followed her, and not only in the theatrical columns. She also appeared in the social pages where her outfits were described as fulsomely as her acting. Miss Muriel (Warburton) Matters had arrived.

In September 1899, a year after she had plucked herself from anonymity, Muriel's impresario arrived. Robert Brough was an English actor-manager who had made his own illustrious debut on the Australian stage in 1885. Since then, he and his wife Florence had established one of the most successful touring companies in the country, producing all of the latest plays from London. Brough knew talent when he saw it, and he hired Muriel the following day. Ironically, her first performance as part of the Broughs' company was back in Adelaide. But no matter. Her name (minus the Warburton) was appearing on the playbills of this famous outfit. She was now *Miss Muriel Matters of the Brough Comedy Company* and she was off on *an extended tour through the eastern colonies, including Tasmania and New Zealand*, as the Adelaide QUIZ was proud to report.[20]

Adelaide newspapers were now reporting the success of their homegrown darling of the stage, but as the century neared its close, Muriel found herself restless again. After her eastern tour, she parted company with the Broughs and began *playing second lady* with George Rignold's company. Rignold, another English-born actor-manager, had a reputation as a serious man of theatre. Perhaps Muriel hungered for the gravitas of playing Princess Katherine to Rignold's Henry V; perhaps she was just tired of the lousy pay and conditions on offer in the Brough troupe. But by the time Muriel joined his company, Rignold was over sixty and past his prime—the BULLETIN complained of his *arrogance, slow-wittedness, unpleasantness back-stage with minor actors, impatience with stage-managers and interminable 'farewell' performances*[21]—and Muriel's association with him was brief. In January 1901, Rignold wound up his final farewell tour in Tasmania.

By May 1901, when Lady Tennyson of Adelaide was standing on a dais in Melbourne admiring the Duchess of York's diamond-studded muff chain, Muriel was back in Adelaide, teaching elocution. *Miss M. Matters wore a neat cream serge Eton navy skirt and black crinoline hat*, reported QUIZ.[22]

卐

If Muriel Matters was the epitome of the millennial New Woman—independent, mobile, self-governing, putting personal dreams before social obligations—another young artist was finding it more difficult to buck convention.

After her encounter with the New Zealand suffragists in 1892, Dora Meeson continued to travel, but still in the close embrace of her family. In May of 1895 the Meesons moved back to Melbourne, the place of Dora's birth, where she was accepted into the National Gallery of Victoria Art School, then a private fine arts college located behind the State Library in La Trobe Street. Eugene Von Guerard had been the inaugural master of painting. When Dora enrolled, Frederick McCubbin was drawing master. Tom Roberts had been a student at the school in the 1870s, and Arthur Streeton was another alumnus.

While Streeton and Roberts and their rugged Australian masculinity cast a long shadow over the reputation of the gallery school, a photograph taken of the class of 1895 reveals that not all, or even most, of the students were men. Of the cheerful faces surrounding a large replica statue of the Venus de Milo, over fifty belong to women. There are fewer than twenty men, all standing at the back hugging Venus. It is the women who overwhelm the foreground—buttoned and corseted (but largely hatless) though they be. Prior to the late nineteenth century, the idea of the professional female artist was anathema. Art could be a genteel drawing-room accomplishment, but not a calling. All this changed when public and private art schools around the world began enrolling women, who flooded through the open doors. Art became the avenue by which to pursue not only personal expression but also paid employment.

The gallery school class of '95 was a close one, known as *The Family*. Paterfamilias McCubbin, who sits at the front of the photograph surrounded by a sea of white linen and lace, was remembered by one of the students as that *dearly loved man…who* [along with *Mrs Mac*] *kept open house on Sundays to painters, musicians and senior students in their home in Brighton.* The 'children', with their family in-joke nicknames—'Mamma' was Agnes Kirkwood, somewhat older than the other girls and with *a motherly attitude to them*—comprised a collection of big, attractive personalities, including Percy, Lionel and Ruby Lindsay. But of all her charismatic classmates, Dora Meeson fell for George Coates, the family's 'Daddy': *a solemn boy and intensely interested in his work.*[23]

George was born in North Melbourne in the same year as Dora, 1869. Following the early death of his mother, he was largely raised by his two Irish grandmothers and according to Dora, had *much of the romantic and imaginative Celt in his nature.*[24] At twelve, George was sent to the North Melbourne Art School, and by fifteen was apprenticed to a stained glass firm. He was fit and athletic, with the body of a labourer and the tortured soul of an artist. If his fellow students found him *solemn*, Dora perceived something else in his bearing: *He had a woman's sensitive refinement along with his masculine strength.* George hated the *coarse humour* of other men and *was wretched until we got out of the hurly-burly* of crowds. In the equally serious, sober Dora Meeson, George had found a safe harbour. She sat for him, and, according to Dora, *a close friendship* formed. The two referred to themselves as *Coates and Trousers.*[25]

Like the rest of their art-school family, they *prided themselves on their freedom from conventionality in dress as a symbol of protest against the bourgeoisie who set store by these things*—and perhaps against her real family. Dora's father was an uncompromising disciplinarian; she had to fight for the right to a career. John Meeson, the proprietor and master of Hawthorn Grammar who had home-schooled his own children, liked to keep all his daughters' activities close to the family home. The Meesons had little social life.[26]

By September of 1895, still in her first year at the gallery school, Dora's future was looking bright. She won first prize in the

Chipman Art Competition, an honour reported in papers nationally and judged by the National Gallery of New South Wales, for the best picture of *Minerva, the Goddess of Wisdom*. The award was open to *all artists in Australasia*, and twenty-one designs were submitted. George entered too, with a painting expressing, in Dora's words, *his big Latin ideas*. Dora was more grounded; she painted her Minerva *from a tall, handsome barmaid in a hired gown*.[27] Dora's prize money of seventy-five guineas was not insubstantial, but the recognition of her talent was just as important.[28] The Minerva Company, a Sydney firm of manufacturing chemists—makers of the Minerva Pill, the Minerva Tonic (*the modern elixir of life...safe, speedy and effective*) and Minerva Wine—reproduced Dora's winning picture in black and white for its advertising materials.[29]

A month later, when *the French rage for artistic posters* had found its way to Melbourne, art students leapt at the chance to try their hand. *The aboriginal with his boomerang, the laughing jackass, the emu and the gum tree, were all popular local motifs to adapt for advertising purposes but*, noted TABLE TALK, the *designs suggest eccentricity instead of originality*. Miss Dora Meeson's work, however, was noted as *full of merit*.[30]

At the end of year annual exhibition of students' work, Dora's nude was singled out by the ARGUS as *conspicuously meritorious*, while George Coates' painting contained *plenty of promise*.[31] A pattern began to emerge in the critics' notices: Dora's work almost inevitably received higher praise than George's. Did it rile the serious young man when Dora received a long profile piece in the AUSTRALIAN TOWN AND COUNTRY JOURNAL two days after the exhibition opened, complete with biographical sketch of *this clever young lady*, a flattering portrait (Dora, usually noted for her particular melancholy expression, is almost smiling in the photo) and the headline *A Successful Australian Painter*?[32]

If George was put out, it didn't affect their friendship. And a year later, when the Christmas show of 1896 included a travelling scholarship, Dora was very pleased when George won. Only five paintings had been accepted in the competition, Dora's among them. TABLE TALK thought them all ghastly, with George's *faces homely to the verge of repulsiveness...realism without the spark of human feeling to make it appealing.*[33] (TABLE TALK judged Dora's painting *not without vitality but...clumsily done.*) Dora considered that the correct decision had been made in awarding the scholarship. *It was right he should have it*, she reasoned, *as the only other two likely winners were going home to England in any case.*[34] As it happened, one of those students was her.

John Meeson had decided to uproot his family and return to London. Dora, twenty-seven years old and at the start of a promising career, consented dutifully to follow. She and George *agreed to meet on the other side of the world.*

⚜

By May 1901, Dora Montefiore had been on the other side of the world for almost a decade. When she left Australia on her *study tour*, her two children were barely school age. Now Florence and Gilbert were teenagers, and knew London better than Sydney, the city of their birth. But Dora had not lost connection with the political awakening she had undergone when discovering she had no legal right to their guardianship. In fact, starting the Womanhood Suffrage League was but the beginning of her activism. And Dora had no ambivalence about where her allegiances lay. All women, as far as Dora was concerned, were outlanders—stateless—for without political rights they belonged to each other more than any putative homeland.

From Sydney, Dora had in 1892 sailed to Paris, where she would develop her lifelong passion for writing. In November her article 'L'Inspiritrice' was published in LE JOURNAL DES FEMMES, the organ of the French feminist movement. Fluent in several languages,

Dora had no trouble expressing her support for an article that had been previously published in the journal, *sur les questions brulantes de la cause feminine:* on the burning issues of the women's cause—one of which was the need to band together, particularly for the benefit of the most vulnerable in the community.

> *C'est pourquoi je voudrais fonder des confraternités laiques de femmes qui serviraient de refuges aux faibles parmi nous, a celles qui ne sont pas faites pour lutter dans le monde et qui se vendent souvent en mariage pour avour un chez eux.*

> That is why I would like to found women's [lay] communities, which would serve as shelters for the weak among us, for those women unable to do battle in the world, and who often sell themselves into marriage in order to have someone at home.

The idea that marriage was a socially acceptable form of prostitution was common among the Victorian-era feminists. Dora's experience of setting up the Womanhood Suffrage League had convinced her there was another way to keep body and soul together: associations of women, bound together not by charity, but by clarity of purpose and shared activism. She wanted to teach the women in these *confraternités*, particularly the young women, that it was good for a woman to work *for the community* and that her main purpose in such work should be to *develop what is best in her* rather than working *to please*, as women had been taught until now.[35] No longer a young woman herself, Dora had begun to find her voice.

By 1893, she was back in England and ready to join *my fellow-workers in the pioneer causes in which we [shall fight] shoulder to shoulder.*[36] Dora had no financial worries, with an income stream flowing from properties she still owned in Sydney, and soon established a base at Eldon Lodge in the Sussex village of Lindfield, about forty miles south of London. She sought out Millicent Garrett Fawcett, the leader of the National Union of Women's Suffrage Societies (NUWSS). A small woman with a huge capacity for work, Fawcett was four years Dora's senior and, like Dora, the daughter of a prosperous middle-class family that educated its girls as effectively as it boys. (Millicent's sister, Elizabeth Garrett Anderson, would become the first female doctor in the United Kingdom.)

Unlike Dora, Mrs Fawcett (as she was always called) had been radicalised while still a teenager. She'd seen John Stuart Mill speaking—a fine intellectual speech in which he advocated for women's suffrage—the year before the British Parliament passed the Second Reform Act of 1867. The first popular expansion of the franchise in England since 1832, the Reform Act liberalised, but did not abolish, the property qualification and resulted in the enfranchisement of male heads of households. But women were still excluded, a fact proved beyond doubt when almost four thousand Manchester women attempted to vote as householders, claiming that, by legislative precedent, the word 'man' in any Act included 'woman'. This claim was defended in court by socialist barrister Richard Pankhurst. He lost the case, but interest in the cause of womanhood suffrage was greatly stimulated.

Then in 1869 Mill published his influential essay THE SUBJECTION OF WOMEN, which he had developed with his wife, Harriet Taylor Mill, before her untimely death. The essay's call for *perfect equality, admitting no power of privilege on the one side, nor disability on the other,* was a profound challenge to the sexual politics of the day. A year later, Richard Pankhurst drafted the first women's suffrage bill. Borrowing Mill's language and sentiment, he called it the Women's Disabilities Removal Bill.

Unquestionably, Pankhurst's wife Emmeline would later write, *those pioneer men suffered in popularity for their feminist views.*[37] Yet they won the hearts of refractory young women. Emmeline Goulden was twenty-four years younger than Richard Pankhurst when they married in 1878. Millicent Garrett married J. S. Mill's fellow radical MP, Henry Fawcett, fourteen years her senior, in 1867. When Henry died in 1884, the widow Fawcett, only thirty-eight years old, started the NUWSS. Its aim: *to win the hearts and minds of our countrymen to the justice of our cause.*[38] Its platform: to win the suffrage on the same terms as men: that is, a limited franchise based on a property qualification. Accepting these terms, the NUWSS were *half-loafers*. In England, it was only a few fanatical *whole-loafers* who advocated adult suffrage, that which women in New Zealand and South Australia at the time enjoyed.

Dora Montefiore was a staunch whole-loafer, but the various local branches of the NUWSS represented just the sort of *confraternités* she'd had in mind in 'L'Inspiritrice'. She went to work for Mrs Fawcett, though she had to admit she found it *depressing work*. Twelve months of toil for the *annual Bill for the Enfranchisement of Some Women* culminating in its introduction to parliament by a sympathetic Liberal MP—when, invariably, it would be *talked out or laughed on* by the majority in the House. For the rest of the year, the loyal suffrage worker bees would go *begging for subscriptions*, organise public meetings (which went regularly *unreported by the Press*) and campaign for the election of Liberal candidates or re-election of Liberal MPs, *who then dropped the cause when elected*.

Dora had never before felt driven to sex antagonism—she had been personally well treated by her father, her husband and men like her mentor Sir George Grey—but she began to tire of the fellows who relied on women to be their political helpmeets but did nothing of value to secure womanhood suffrage. *Many of us felt rebellious*, she wrote of the moment the desire to please began to fade, *and realised that as long as we continued to help men into Parliament who did nothing to help us, we were simply wasting our time and our energies.*[39]

In 1896, worn down by the seeming futility of the NUWSS work, Dora returned to writing. The English feminist periodical SHAFTS published her blistering article, 'Why Women Need Woman Suffrage; and Why We Need It Now' in one of its earliest editions. (The cover of SHAFTS, whose themes included *vivisection, dress* reform, women's control of their sexuality, child care, and vegetarianism[40] featured a young barefoot woman in a Grecian gown, bow and arrow braced, the words Wisdom, Justice, Truth spurting from the tip of the arrow.) Dora's words belied her comfortable nursery upbringing and laid bare her current frustrations. England in the Belle Époque was being crushed under the weight of *the numbing soul destroying bonds of...materialistic luxury*, she wrote. *Commercial materialism... commercial Imperialism [has] won the day*. England needed *an Ideal*.

> It is the woman's role in life to keep alive and nourish the Ideal; for inspiration and spiritual life come to her in occult, subtle fashion through the pulsation of the young life within her own, which first teaches her the full lesson of her womanhood.

Just as the placenta feeds embryonic humanity, women's superior moral qualities would feed a higher spiritual life. So motherhood would provide the basis for the revolutionary internationalism that Dora had espoused since leaving Australia: *as long as her own motherhood makes her feel at one with motherhood all over the world, the soul of woman cannot be enslaved as her body is daily enslaved, cannot be prostituted as her body is daily prostituted.*

It was her experience in Australia that had alerted Dora to what fresh young life had to instigate in the ravaged body of the old. She wrote of *the colonies of England, who in the first flush of young inspired enthusiasm, are leading their Motherland on the upward path* and employed the military metaphors that would become standard usage for the suffrage movement to describe England's need to follow her daughters into *the social and political field of battle*.[41]

She wrote poetry, too: a volume entitled SINGINGS THROUGH THE DARKNESS contained two poems that harked backed to her years in Australia. 'One People, One Destiny', a sonnet about Federation demonstrating that she still had one eye on political affairs in Australia, and 'Christmas Morning on the Blue Mountains', written in Katoomba. The SYDNEY MORNING HERALD published a tepid review of the collection, noting the poems *of local origin* but complaining that *while the tone is sympathetic and the subjects are those that now engross the attention of thoughtful men and women, it can hardly be said that the verses make a decided impression upon a reader.* And the worst insult: *it is philosophy and philanthropy in metre.* The scribblings of a bored doctor's wife. Or a rich businessman's widow, as the case might be.

But Dora was hardly gripped by ennui. She was in fact developing some pragmatic solutions to the propaganda problems that plagued the NUWSS. She realised that *Our work as suffragists was to get our claims placed before the tribunal of public opinion, because it was impossible to obtain fair publicity in the Press.*[42] Women everywhere knew the truth of that. In 1887, American pioneers Elizabeth Cady Stanton and Susan B. Anthony noted in their history of the suffrage movement that leaders of the movement were *uniformly ridiculed, misrepresented and denounced in public and private by all classes of society.*[43]

But a new strategy for attracting attention was starting to brew in Dora's mind, a tactic that cut straight to the heart of democracy itself. In an inflammatory letter to the editor of THE WOMAN'S SIGNAL, Dora laid out her case for what she intended to do next:

> I cannot but think that now, when every argument against granting the suffrage to women has been met and answered, and when only privileged injustice prevents thousands of Her Majesty's taxpaying and qualified subjects from making their influence felt in the land, other measures...are required.

If the next suffrage bill was again talked out or shelved, *we women who believe in the justice of our demands should form a league, binding ourselves to resist passively the payment of taxes until such taxation be followed by representation.*

The last time the non-payment of taxes had been used as a political weapon in England was when the Quakers protested the payment of church tithes in the early 1800s. Dora knew what would happen: the bailiffs would be sent in. Non-taxpayers would have their goods and chattels distrained, confiscated—by force if necessary—and sold to cover the tax bill. She envisioned the spectacle of *five or ten thousand women* refusing to pay their taxes while all of England watched *as the goods of quiet law-abiding citizens [were] allowed to be sold at public auction*. This, she believed, *may convince the most sceptical* that the time had come to grant women the rights they so clearly wanted and justly deserved.[44] In Sydney, Dora had espoused education. Now, comfortable in her middle age, she advocated direct action.

But, as the nineteenth century drew to a close, the time was not ripe for Dora to raise her army of intractable tax-resisters. There was a real war waging, a war that tore at Dora's already burning distrust of materialism and its discontents. *Empire, I hate the word*, she wrote, *I know the misery that imperialism has always caused*.[45] Whether she was reflecting on the effects of imperial expansion on the original inhabitants of Australia is unclear. But it's certain that Dora kept a close eye on what was going on in South Africa. *We strain our ears in vain through the murky darkness*, she had written in Shafts in 1896 of the *trouble in Transvaal*. Now, with the outbreak of the Boer War on 11 November 1899, she had cause to pay close attention to the workings of empire.

The Boer War was nominally started over the grievances of British citizens who lived in the two Boer states, the Republic of Transvaal and the Orange Free State. These 'foreigners', or Uitlanders, had to pay tax but did not have a vote. The British government used the rationale of defending its subjects' democratic rights to fight a war against the independent states, ultimately annexing the republics as part of its existing South African colonial holdings, the Cape Colony and the Colony of Natal.[46]

For Dora Montefiore, Britain's justification for military

intervention in South Africa raised questions. In October 1899, on the eve of the declaration of war, she penned a pamphlet published by the Union of Practical Suffragists within the Women's Liberal Federation. The pamphlet was simply called WOMEN UITLANDERS, and her proposition was straightforward. England was still doing to half her population what she was accusing the Boers of doing in Transvaal. *We women*, she insisted, *are, in fact, Uitlanders as far as our political rights are concerned.*

Women were suffering because they had no share in the government of the day. Others were legislating on their behalf. Because they had no vote, women could not redress their grievances. It was exactly the same argument as was being made by the British government on behalf of their disenfranchised subjects in South Africa!

So, Dora asked, *how shall pressure be brought to bear on the men of England?*—men who were prepared to mount a military campaign in a foreign land to defend so-called British liberties. *If nothing but war will meet the situation, then war must be declared by women at all Parliamentary elections.* Women's *single weapon* in this now-declared war on the British Parliament would be the seemingly benign, but in fact incendiary, *Test Question*, which women would put to all parliamentary candidates before lending their help on the hustings in election campaigns.

The question was: will you support votes for women in the parliament? This question *shall in the end*, Dora was convinced, *prove as powerful as an appeal to arms*. The answer would determine whether women would be friend or foe.

Not all suffragists agreed. On the outbreak of the Boer War, Mrs Fawcett suspended the activities of the NUWSS. *Two fires cannot burn together*, she reasoned, privileging imperial obligation over domestic disturbance. She also had faith that the Boer War would in fact provide a fillip for the women's cause. *It has been observed again and again*, she wrote, *that a war or any other event which stimulates national vitality, and the consciousness of the value of citizenship, is almost certain to be followed by increased vigour in the suffrage movement.*[47]

From Dora's perspective, however, the Boer War was nothing but a hypocritical imperial folly. It would ultimately cost thirty-two thousand lives, including those of twenty-six thousand South African civilians, many of them children, who died of disease and starvation in British concentration camps. She would probably have agreed with the editor of the Australian REVIEW OF REVIEWS who concluded that *the revelation of waste, of unreadiness, of Titanic stupidity and mismanagement...will do much to destroy what may be called the Imperial prestige, if not to lessen the sense of pride and confidence in the Empire itself.*[48]

Dora Montefiore refused to pay her taxes for the duration of the war. Not only was she disgusted by the abuses of empire, but she would not fund a war *in the making of which I had had no voice.* It was a show of defiance against the leadership of Millicent Fawcett—and a mode of activism she would employ to astonishing effect in the new century.

By the time the Duchess of York pushed the button that signalled to the world that Australia's national parliament had opened, Dora was getting ready to drop a few bombshells of her own.

10

A Splendid Object Lesson

USA, 1901

On a frigid winter's day in February 1902, Vida Goldstein stood outside the door to the Oval Office in Washington DC. Here, in the newly built West Wing of the White House, she took a moment to reflect on the journey that had brought her to this spot. Outside there was snow, the first she'd ever seen. Inside, the setting was just as novel. Vida was about to meet Theodore Roosevelt, President of the United States of America.

It had been a whirlwind couple of months for the acknowledged leader of the women's suffrage movement in Australia. In December, four days shy of Christmas, Maggie Heffernan had finally been released from prison, a shell of the bush-born girl she'd been but a free woman nonetheless. Earlier that month, members of suffrage organisations from all states—as well as Trades Hall, representing Australia's working women—had voted to appoint Vida as the sole representative of Australasia at the upcoming First Conference of the International Woman Suffrage Alliance in Washington. *Objections had been raised in some quarters*, but in the end Vida's appointment was unanimously approved.[1]

Then there had been a big farewell dinner at the Austral Salon on 3 January, with all the usual trappings: speeches, music, recitations. Her colleagues agreed she'd *made a feeling and suitable reply*, which was just as well since it was their subscriptions that were paying for her passage to America. (Over £95 raised so far, with £30 coming directly from Miss Scott and the Womanhood Suffrage

League; other contributions from Dr Maloney, Catherine Helen Spence and Lady Forrest, whose husband, the former premier of Western Australia, had so recently become a convert to the cause.)

Finally, there was the emotional leave-taking at the docks the following morning, with Vida's sister Aileen agreeing to take over the editorship of the WOMAN's SPHERE in her absence. A week in Sydney, staying with Miss Scott at her charming home in Woolloomooloo, then the long passage across the Pacific to San Francisco on the US steamship SIERRA. At least the press seemed encouraging of her international endeavours. The SYDNEY MAIL published a striking photograph and informed its readers that *the young delegate...is a fluent speaker and her platform eloquence has brought her to the fore in the world of colonial women.*[2] TOCSIN called her *Australia's credentialed delegate.*[3]

Vida was less qualified for the sea journey: as she closed in on her thirty-third birthday, this was the first time she had left Victoria. After three days of seasickness, however, she discovered that *the rougher it was, the better I liked it.*[4] There were few passengers aboard, the SIERRA being a mail ship, so there was *not much chance of getting up any wild excitement.* An egg and spoon race with the crew provided the only entertainment. But the chance to be *quite alone* was not unwelcome after the torrent of activity in preparation for the Franchise Bill that went before the Federal Parliament in April. It was a pity not to be able to sit in the gallery to watch the debate—Vida never missed the opportunity to watch suffrage bills being debated in the Victorian Parliament, which they were, unsuccessfully, with alarming regularity—but she couldn't pass up the opportunity to represent Australia and New Zealand internationally. The trip had already been so interesting. Though they couldn't stop in at Honolulu, due to bubonic plague, she did go ashore at Pago Pago. *I wouldn't have missed it!* Never had she seen anything like the *native huts, curio shops and dances.*

It was almost as intriguing to pass through Salt Lake City en route from San Francisco to the conference in Washington. Vida billeted with a local family and had to admit she was *slightly disappointed* that *though I looked in every corner I did not see any more wives about*. She'd *expected dozens*. It was in her nature to be curious: *I am always on the qui vive for anything in the shape of an experience, and to be entertained by a polygamous family would have been an exciting experience*. And though she considered herself easygoing, Vida was shocked to learn that *the Americans are pre-eminently a nation of expectorators*. Their habit of spitting on sidewalks and in public buildings was *simply disgusting*. Cuspidors were everywhere. *I am a thorough going democrat*, she joked, *but I like a clean democracy*. She also ascertained that Americans *eat heartily*, especially at breakfast: grapefruit, fish, cereal *mush*, waffles, hot cakes with maple syrup, iced water and coffee. She would ask politely for dry toast, but receive it *hot buttered*.

If Vida had to learn fast about her American hosts, so she discovered they had a thing or two to understand about her. *Everyone thought I was travelling through America with my wedding cake*, she laughed. The acquisitive Americans couldn't understand that she was touring the country with only a small tin trunk the size of a hat box. She was also surprised to find that Americans knew so little about Australia or Australians.

> We have such a keen sense of our own importance that it came as something of a shock to hear the curious opinions they expressed about us and our country. Many were astonished to find I was white, others that I spoke English so well. 'Why, you speak it quite as well as an American' which seemed quite the highest praise they could bestow.[5]

But everyone she'd met so far had been *genial, lavishly hospitable* and *broad-minded*, if ill-informed. The cross-country trip had been nothing but a delight.

And now here in Washington, summoned to the White House

as something of a curiosity, Vida waited until she was bidden to enter. When the door opened, she saw the president sitting with his feet up on the desk. He rushed to greet her, grabbing her hand and pumping it up and down in a hearty grip. *I am <u>delighted</u> to meet you,* he shouted. *You're from Australia; I'm <u>delighted</u> to hear that.*[6]

Teddy Roosevelt told Vida Goldstein what fine people he thought the Australians were and talked warmly of the Australian soldiers he'd served with in the Spanish-American War. But the president was just as excited about the fighting spirit of Australian women. Roosevelt supported the principle of votes for women (though amending the American constitution to enfranchise them was going to be a hell of a struggle) and this was why he'd been keen to meet Vida. With Australia poised to legislate for the federal franchise, she had more political rights than any woman he'd ever met. It was a *great object lesson*, this antipodean experiment in equality. *I've got my eye on you down there in Australia*, the president of the free world told the watchful woman from Victoria.

And with that enthusiastic embrace, Vida Goldstein became the first Australian to meet an American president at the White House. She would be back in the West Wing before long.

⚚

The First Conference of the International Woman Suffrage Alliance opened on 12 February 1902 at the Georgetown Presbyterian Church—a much grander building than anything served up by Vida's own Presbyterian upbringing. In fact, the whole experience was overwhelming. The president of the American Suffrage Association, Carrie Chapman Catt, in her opening address before a packed audience of local suffragists as well as the delegates from Norway, Chile, Turkey, Russia, Canada, England and Sweden, warmly acknowledged the significance of Vida's presence at the conference:

> The little band of Americans who initiated the modern
> [suffrage] movement would never have predicted that...
> the island continent of Australia, then unexplored
> wilderness, would become a great democracy where
> self-government would be carried on with such enthu-
> siasm, fervour and wisdom that they would give lessons
> in methods and principles to all the rest of the world...
> Australia, associated in our memory of childhood's
> geography as the abode of strange beasts and barbarians,
> sends us a full, up-to-date representative woman, widely
> alive to all the refinements of life, and fully cognisant of
> all the rights of her sex.[7]

The world's newest nation had delivered the most stunning example of the New Woman: single, independent and, like her country, self-governing, 'civilised' and white.

The conference was declared open. Its purpose was to work towards establishing a permanent international suffrage association, and to that end a committee was formed for *the collection, exchange and dissemination of information concerning methods of suffrage work, and the general status of women in every country in the civilized world.*[8] The elder stateswoman Susan B. Anthony, eighty-two years old, was duly elected chairman and Vida, the youngest delegate, was elected secretary. Mrs Catt, the English delegate Mrs Fenwick Miller and Vida were chosen to draw up a constitution.

Vida's elevation to these prominent positions did not simply reflect the distinction of her country of origin. It was also deter-mined that Vida *possesses all the qualities in a statesman.*[9] This *dark, alert, slender girl from Australia,* as she was described in a Boston journal, captivated all she met. Even the NEW YORK HERALD, then considered *the greatest of American dailies,* published an interview with Vida, with accompanying portrait. She was not only the (hot buttered) toast of Washington, but of the entire country. Her diary was soon filled with bookings for a national speaking tour and she extended her stay in America for an extra three months.

Vida had so impressed her American counterparts that they invited her to make a submission to the select committee of the US Senate dealing with woman suffrage. Five senators would be present as well as a who's who of the US suffrage movement, including Susan B. Anthony, the Reverend Anna Shaw and Harriet Taylor Upton. At the hearing on 18 February, Anthony noted that this was the seventeenth Congress in thirty-three years to be addressed by American women in the hope of amending the constitution.

One after another, women brought forward the usual arguments: *taxation without representation is tyranny*; *municipal housekeeping is simply housekeeping on a larger scale*; *even criminals, if they be men, may assume the prerogative of the franchise*. Lashings of heavy-handed metaphors of motherhood and birth swamped the testimonies. *A great reform never had spontaneous birth, but exists in embryo, often for years, waiting for the fullness of time when it shall be born*, ventured Lucy Hobart Day. *Share and share alike—the lesson our mothers taught us in infancy*, tried Mrs Lucretia Blankenburg.

Finally, Susan B. Anthony got up to announce her star witness: *Miss Vida Goldstein, of Australia, where women vote*. Vida took the stand.

> I am very proud to think that I have come here from a country where the women's suffrage movement has made such rapid strides as it has in Australia...women to-day are struggling here for what we have had in Australia for years and years.

Warming to her subject, she pressed further. If women in South Australia, Western Australia and New Zealand were the world's guinea pigs, they had not only survived the experiment, but:

> proved all the statements and arguments against women's suffrage to be utterly without foundation... The women have not raided the platforms; they have not neglected their homes; they have not gone away and left their babies.

Vida had collected testimonials by leading men in New Zealand—lawyers, clergy, educators and MPs—to attest to the positive effects of women's suffrage in that country, where women had now had the vote for nigh on a decade. Their conclusion? It had *raised the tone of political life.* The only change, Vida insisted, was that *they manage to get alterations in the laws that previously they had been asking for years.*

And there was more. *We now have a federated Australia*, Vida lectured the (potentially geopolitically unwitting) senators, pointing out that it was none other than the female electors of South Australia and Western Australia who *helped to frame our great Australian Commonwealth.* Why, within a matter of months, the Federal Parliament would have to pass voting legislation *on the widest franchise existing.* And in case the good senators didn't appreciate the full extent of that victory, Vida would spell it out for them: because of South Australia's franchise, all Australian women will *not only vote but have the right to sit in Parliament.* Vida wished the senators to know, too, that this was *the result of years of hard fighting*—in case they also subscribed to the 'one fine day it just happened' school of political progress.

Like the seasoned platform orator that she was, Vida had built her case with rational precision. Now she mounted her final, heartfelt finale:

> I want to say to you that if Australia, that land tucked away in that far corner of the world, can trust its women with a vote, why can not you American men do the same. You trust the Indian, you trust thousands and tens of thousands of ignorant, illiterate foreigners who arrive on your shores every year. I am proud to have the privilege of coming to-day to plead with you to trust your women. You will find your trust is not misplaced.

The American women in the audience were thrilled. In the past, Anna Shaw noted, all they'd had to back up their claim to the suffrage was *theories*. But with Vida's testimony, *we now have proof*.[10] Reverend Shaw ordered that a transcript of the proceedings be made immediately and that copies be distributed as a matter of urgency. Ten thousand copies would do for starters.

⚲

After the conference in Washington wound up, Vida started off on the lecture circuit, addressing huge audiences on the topic of The Australian Woman in Politics and attracting press coverage wherever she went.[11] The most celebrated Australian woman in America since Nellie Melba, Vida herself used Melba's fame to dispute one of the favourite arguments of the Antis: that women would be degraded by voting. There was nothing degrading about the polling booth, countered Vida, *nothing like so objectionable as elbowing all sorts and conditions of men in a scramble for tickets for the theatre, or a Melba concert, or the races*.[12]

One of Vida's themes was that campaigning for women's suffrage was what she termed a *Policy of Concentration*. She saw the parliamentary vote as *the right that covered all other rights*, and decried *the futility of working piecemeal for the emancipation of women, without the vote*.[13] Only the vote, Vida argued, would ensure *the protection and prevention of degraded womanhood*. Only the vote would unravel the vast web of legal, economic and social disadvantage that ensnared women and girls the world over. Furthermore, she told her rapt listeners, women should enter Parliament, something South Australian women alone in the world were entitled to do—but for which, by the time she returned to her native shores, she too would be eligible in the national legislature.[14]

I have always maintained that wherever there are women's and children's interests to be considered, she argued, *women should be there to consider them*.[15] Such a simple premise; such a revolutionary idea.

All the world will be wondering, Vida knew, *how the experiment answered—what exactly was the result of this bold recognition of the principle of democracy—government by the people—in the political affairs of a continent.*[16] She was fully aware of the leadership role she had been asked to play in presenting this prized object to the world. *Woman suffrage is with us to stay,* she told a crammed house during her address to the 34th American National Suffrage Convention in Washington in March, *and that our success may hasten the day when you American women will stand before the world as political equals of your menfolk is the earnest desire of the countries which have sent me here to represent them at this great conference.*[17]

Her authority was given a boost, when, on the eve of her New York speaking engagements, the Federal Parliament passed the Franchise Bill. *The most significant political event of the century is the enfranchisement of 800,000 women of Federated Australia,* reported the CINCINNATI COMMERCIAL TRIBUNE in an article that was syndicated throughout the United States.

> This is the first time in the history of the world that a whole nation has enfranchised its women, and the object lesson will help the cause of human liberty throughout the earth. [This]…is the greatest victory ever won for woman and ensures the establishment of woman's complete equality in the near future throughout the Southern Hemisphere.[18]

As a proud currency lass, Vida was chuffed to know these sentiments were being shared around the country, consumed at the breakfast tables of Americans along with their waffles and coffee: Australia being lauded as the world's exemplar in human progress. *These people are attacking and solving the complex governmental and social problems that have baffled the great nations of the earth,* the COMMERCIAL TRIBUNE article went on. *The triumph of human liberty echoes from Australian shores…Australia, the infant in the family of nations, leads the van, and is an object lesson to the world.*

⚵

Throughout her topsy-turvy journey from the enfranchised South to the retrograde North, Vida kept a travel diary that doubled as a sort of autograph book. It was a peculiar nineteenth-century fashion, the autograph book, where people met along the journey would scrawl aphorisms, offer romantic platitudes and cite poems and Biblical verse. In her book, Vida collected the wellwishes of admirers like journalist Elizabeth Hauser, who scribbled:

> To Australasia all the world gives ear
> Youthful, audacious, unrestrained and free
> No immemorial bonds of time's decree
> Shackle her progress nor excite her fear.[19]

Social reformer William Lloyd Garrison Jr wrote in a similar vein, harking back to earlier Australian novelties of democratic reform: *Australia gave us safer ballots, wiser laws. Armed with the record of your land's great deeds. Welcome light-bringer from the Southern Cross.*[20]

Mary Garrett Hay joined in the chorus:

> We are glad 'Little Australia' crossed the waters to see us, and now we will look for great things from across the sea. We love Australia more because we have known you. God speed the day when women are free in every way.[21]

Vida was not a silent witness to all this hero worship. She was growing into her role as an ambassador and representative, her confidence increasing daily. Photographic portraits reveal the nervous eyes of an accomplished but unworldly activist replaced with a steely glint. Vida was an inveterate note-taker as well as a speechmaker, scrawling aide-mémoires in her looping copperplate. After visiting Washington DC, her note to self reminded her to advise Alfred Deakin to think of the great American city when he was planning the new federal capital site on the bush acreage that would become Canberra.[22]

Vida also had her own homilies to add, spoken in the captivating, *essentially womanly* voice for which she was always noted.[23] Never one to be patronised, she cheekily parroted Teddy Roosevelt's own words to her:

> The [Australian] Federal Franchise Bill is the greatest step in the direction of political equality that we have yet seen, and must be a *splendid object lesson* [her emphasis] to every civilised country in the world.[24]

This speech was reported by the WASHINGTON POST, with none of the caustic disdain that was generally reserved for women who knew not their rightful place.

The Australian press also tracked Vida's progress. *Victorians are very proud of Miss Goldstein*, reported the QUEENSLANDER, *she has captured the hearts of the Americans, not omitting that of President Roosevelt*.[25] The Sydney DAILY TELEGRAPH headed its report of her tour *The Superb New Woman*. In sharing details of her tour, it noted one of Vida's most rousing speeches:

> Citizens of no mean country, let us enter the new international alliance, and never rest until we have obtained for the women of other lands the same privileges which we enjoy in Australia.[26]

TABLE TALK enjoyed reporting the boast of one Victorian senator *that their delegate must have been the most intellectual and best looking at the convention*.[27] To be fair, it also conveyed one of Vida's descriptions of a prominent American she'd met, *a self-made man, in love with his maker*.[28] Apart from noting that Vida was *really a smart, pretty girl, the very opposite to what one unconsciously expects in a woman's suffrage advocate* and her attire (*a skirt which clears the ground, and rather a tailor-built style, but for dress occasions always very prettily and stylishly gowned*), the papers also regularly commented on her voice: *fluent, mellifluous, womanly*.[29]

But Vida was not so seduced by her diva's reception that her own critical faculties were blunted. Her notes contained some disparaging remarks about her host country, which she would later share with Melbourne audiences in a series of lantern-slide lectures designed to recoup her expenses. (The subscriptions collected before her departure had not covered the unexpectedly extended stay.) *Most of us regard America as the most democratic and advanced country politically in the world*, she logged. *Instead it's as conservative as a country can well be. A democratic form of government does not necessarily mean that the people rule.*[30] Vida offered an analysis of the root cause of the hypocrisy: *Their written and hidebound constitution [has] played directly into the hands of moneyed and unscrupulous politicians.*[31]

The AGE published her *American Notes*, including the observation that *among the many social problems that the United States is confronted with, the negro problem is by no means the least.* She confided that *the feeling of race hatred is so bitter that the Southerners will hesitate at nothing to accomplish their desire to disenfranchise the negro.*[32] If Vida perceived any parallels between the citizenship status of African Americans and Indigenous Australians, she kept those thoughts to herself.

On the eve of her return voyage, Vida penned and published an *Open Letter to the Women of the United States* thanking her *Dear Friends* for their *lavish hospitality* and *unnumbered kindnesses*, acknowledging that *we women in the land of the Southern Cross are reaping what England and America has sown.* For this reason, she vowed *to help our English sisters and American cousins in their struggle for freedom.*

Vida promised: *Our chief care will be to so use our right of suffrage that the men of other nations will soon want to follow the example of the Australian champions of woman's enfranchisement.* And, with respect for the decades of effort of *dear Miss Anthony* and her noble warriors, Vida offered some advice. *You want, and must have,* she declared, *the support of the rank and file of working people...Of this I am convinced. That is how we got it in Australia.* The labour movement and the woman movement were *both working for a better social order.* She predicted that there would be *a big smash-up between Capital and Labour in the United States*. It would be *the trusts* and *your political machines* that would be the major roadblocks to suffrage. *But take courage*, Vida reassured her American readers, *our own recent victory in Australia will help you, and the united forces of Labour and Women will enable you to surmount every obstacle*.[33]

If Susan B. Anthony was offended by Vida's audacity, she didn't show it. Before Vida's departure on 24 July, the venerable old woman made a gift of her momentous HISTORY OF WOMAN SUFFRAGE. On the dust jacket, Anthony inscribed these words of respect and affection for the trail-blazing Australia:

> From her disenfranchised friend in the city of Rochester, county of Monroe, state of New York, Country of the United States of America—the Land of the *Free*—who has worked, to the best of her ability, for fifty years and more to get the right for women to vote—and will continue to battle for it to the end of her life.
>
> With congratulations that the new world of *Australia* has given to her women all the rights of citizenship equally with men, and with the love and esteem of her friend.
>
> Rejoicing that you have gained the national franchise...while we of the United States of America struggle on—no one can tell how long—to get the right to vote.[34]

Vida sailed home from San Francisco in the heat of July, with the hefty volumes in her little tin trunk and the weight of expectation on her slim shoulders.

11

The Question of How White

Melbourne, 1902

On her arrival in Sydney on 18 August 1902, Vida was greeted at the wharf by a breathless Rose Scott and the exclamation: *We've got it! Isn't it lovely?*

Vida didn't immediately understand why her friend and mentor was so animated. The Federal Franchise Act had passed in July; she knew that already—she had celebrated the victory all over America. But this news of Scott's was hot off the presses. The bullish New South Wales Legislative Council had finally passed one of the suffrage bills that the lower house regularly sent up: New South Wales women now had adult suffrage. It did not yet include the right to stand for parliament, but surely the scales had been irrevocably tipped. It was only a matter of time before Vida's own state of Victoria enfranchised her women too.

That night at a meeting of the Womanhood Suffrage League Vida congratulated Scott on *adding one more star to the suffrage flag.*[1] The gathered women were *cheerful almost to the degree of hilarity*, reported the DAILY TELEGRAPH.

Almost. Vida was not so certain that victory in New South Wales made adult suffrage in Victoria a lay-down misère.

In fact, there had not even been anything inevitable about the passage of the Federal Franchise Act, despite section 41 of the constitution. After all, it was not womanhood suffrage that had been enshrined in the founding document, just the promise that no citizens would lose their existing voting rights in the federal arena.

This assurance sounded admirable in the making, but had proved complicated in the enacting, as Vida could now read in HANSARD.

The first parliament, inaugurated on that great day in May 1901, had pledged to *introduce at an early date a measure to concede the Federal Franchise to women*, as Louisa Lawson happily published in THE DAWN.[2] Edmund Barton was on side. Originally an Anti, Barton had been outmanoeuvred into accepting adult suffrage at the constitutional convention in Adelaide in 1897 and, by the time he was sworn in as Australia's first prime minister, he had completed a full U-turn, having publicly changed his tune in his election speech at Maitland on 17 January 1901.

The suffragists, having learnt from bitter experience not to take such commitments at face value, put their shoulders to the wheel of Barton's new bandwagon. In early 1901, Vida Goldstein wrote to him seeking clarification of his position as prime minister of the new nation. Would he *kindly give us an assurance that the Bill will be introduced in the first session of the Federal Parliament...?* Rose Scott amped up the pressure in March, writing to enquire whether Barton would *advocate the immediate and uniform enfranchisement* of women? The Equal Franchise Association of Brisbane expressed its expectation *that you may succeed in striking the political shackles from a class which is half the world and Mother of the other half.*

Countering the barrage, Mr P. J. Gandon, Honorary Secretary of the Anti-Suffrage League, urged Barton to reconsider his stance and *recognise that the evils underlying such an extension of the Franchise are both insidious and far-reaching.* It was only *a few women who agitate for votes...a mere handful of ladies with masculine ambitions.*[3]

Barton did not renege. The Franchise Bill was scheduled to be introduced in the second session of parliament. The business end of legislation came first: the Consolidated Revenue Act (nos 1 and 3), the Acts Interpretation Act (no. 2), the Audit Act (no. 4), the Customs Act (no. 6): the *machinery measures*. But after they were out of the way, the path was clear to introduce bills that would regulate the lives of citizens rather than the processes of government.

No time was lost, noted William Guthrie Spence, a Scots-born union organiser and the Labor member for Darling, *in tackling the big measures*—immigration, adult suffrage and the deportation of Pacific Islanders from Queensland. Integral to all three measures, was *the question [of] how white the Federation is to be*, as the Perth WESTERN MAIL bluntly stated.[4]

The first of the acts that would determine this question was the Immigration Restriction Act, designed to implement what was known at the time, and has been known ever since, as the White Australia Policy. There was no gilding the lily about its intentions and no perceived need to obfuscate the desired result. As Spence wrote in his history of the labour movement, AUSTRALIA'S AWAKENING:

> *The exclusion of alien and coloured races gives a chance*
> *for the development on the Australian island continent of*
> *a great nation of the white races...that ideal has come to*
> *stay.*[5]

It was Australia's special destiny to *make brighter the lives of the masses*, and to thinkers and policymakers like Spence, 'bright' meant untinted white.

The unambiguous top plank of the Labor Party platform was from the start a White Australia. *The party stands for racial purity and racial efficiency*, explained Spence, *industrially, mentally, morally and intellectually*. It was not only that brown or black men must not be allowed to do the jobs of white men for a lower wage, and thus degrade the living standards of Australian families. It was also about *national character*: maintaining the necessary *high standard* required that there be no *admixture with the white race*.

As Methodist lay preacher William Judkins wrote in the Australian REVIEW OF REVIEWS, *Our contiguity to Asia, with its teeming millions of dusky and yellow people ever on the look out for fresh fields in which to settle, constitutes a menace*. The highly politically loaded word 'protection' referred, then as now, not just to certain levers that could be pulled to regulate the Australian economy—as in tariff protection. It also implied control of Australia's population: border protection. The White Australia Policy, Judkins argued (articulating a generally held opinion), was based not on *animosity to coloured people* but on *an ideal of life which can only be realized by means of a living wage.* This ideal pertained to material prosperity, to be sure—but a prosperity that rested on the bedrock of unquestioned racial superiority.

> We hold Australia in trust for the white race, with its nobler ideals of religion and social culture…that indefinable pride of race, which, like a family tie, holds us to all the traditions of the past.[6]

A family that could abide no strangers coming to dinner. A table at which there was room for only one race: the British 'race'.

White Australia was already a well-established Australian doctrine and practice by Federation, with the various colonies having decreed restrictions against non-Europeans and Chinese migrants since the 1840s.[7] The Immigration Restriction Act simply affirmed the principle in federal law. It was also a way for the new upstart nation to publicly pronounce its undiminished loyalty to the mother country. Nationalism would not interfere with imperialism, for the racial blood tie—*the crimson thread of kinship*—inextricably bound Australia to Britain. Indeed, some contemporary commentators, like expat Australian author Florence Gay, argued that the imperial movement was *practically inaugurated by the Commonwealth's Act of Federation in 1901.*[8]

If the Labor Party nailed its (monochromatic) colours to the mast of racial purity, so too did Australian liberals. The need for the Immigration Restriction Act *is the one matter on which the Commonwealth is united*, reported the London MORNING POST in September 1901; White Australia was *an article of the national faith.*[9] Alfred Deakin's election platform included *fiscal peace and preferential trade for White Australia*, binding the issues of tariff protection and racial self-protection in one.[10] Deakin even claimed that Australia's national ideals *were* Liberal ideals: *the ideal of the Constitution is equality and uniformity in all national matters…a white man's country from north to south.*[11] Liberals like Deakin saw themselves as the natural progressives, and cast Labor Party members in the role of reactionary obstructionists.

This division emerged in the debate of the Immigration Restriction Act in that first parliamentary session. Though all sides of politics agreed with the policy (Conservatives completing the triangle) the mechanisms for exclusion were contested. How would impure aliens be detected at the border? After all, many British subjects in the Crown colonies and protectorates were decidedly *dusky*.

An *education test* was the preferred method, out of consideration for English fears and prejudices. William Spence explained the Liberals' approach:

> If the person desirous of entering Australia is considered undesirable the department finds out some language which it knows he does not understand, and then dictates fifty words to him. Of course he fails, and is then deported back to where he came from.

Labor didn't approve. *This is a round-about and mean sort of way to accomplish the end sought*, argued Spence. It also depended too much on customs officials *who may not in all cases be in sympathy with the spirit of the Act itself.* No, it was better to say *straight out that we didn't want any other than the white race here.*[12]

⚕

The question of whiteness—of purity and danger—did not end at immigration, the regulation of who could come to Australia's shores and under what circumstances. It also infused debate in the Franchise Bill, regulating the rights of those who were already Australian. For it was this piece of legislation that would determine eligibility for the fundamental right of citizenship: the right to vote for those who make the laws that bind us.[13]

It was not only women who were now being considered for citizenship status. If the new nation had *a higher aspiration for a pure-bred population capable of full citizenship*, as the MORNING POST correspondent read the situation, who would make the grade of purity?[14] Who would qualify, or be disqualified? *The ideally fair basis*, said the WESTERN MAIL, *would be to recognise no colour line inside the Commonwealth, however much stress may be laid on it in dealing with new immigrants.*[15]

But politics is rarely 'ideally' anything, as the women's suffrage debate in Western Australia had shown. There, just three years earlier, *women were given the right to vote by a Parliament to whom the idea had been abhorrent*, as the KALGOORLIE MINER, the mouthpiece of the miners, knew only too well. Could the obverse now be true? Could a house of fair-minded liberals shoot itself in the democratic foot?

From its inauguration, the Federal Parliament contained more than its share of progressives. Political reactionaries were in the minority, as might be expected in a uniquely representative institution elected on the basis of 'one man, one vote' in four states, and 'one adult, one vote' in two. Except for matters of the tariff, which were hotly contested, broad democratic rights were not a source of contention. As the KALGOORLIE MINER put it, *the anti-democrats in either Federal Chamber are too few to make a decent fight.*[16] The issue was more to do with what complexion of democracy Australia wanted.

The root policy question to be determined by the Federal Parliament was not who would qualify for the franchise (all adults), but whom to disqualify. It was like a game of citizenship Kerplunk: pulling out democratic planks and watching which marbles might fall through the gaps.[17]

On 10 April 1902, Bill no. 8 of 1902 was introduced into the Senate by Richard O'Connor, a native-born New South Welshman, and a member of Barton's ministry.[18] It was autumn in Melbourne, where the Federal Parliament was still squatting in the sandstone buildings of the Victorian Parliament while the new capital was built, and the days were getting shorter. The Franchise Bill was succinct too. It had only five sections.

The principal one was section 3, which in its original draft form provided for *one man one vote*.[19] By the time it reached the Senate, the bill provided that *all adult persons not under 21 years of age, whether male or female, married or unmarried*, could vote in a federal election. The qualifications were: such adults must be born in Australia (*natural born*) or be a naturalised British subject; they must have lived in Australia for six months continuously prior to the election and be on the electoral roll of any federal electoral division. It was section 4 that began pulling out the planks and sending the marbles tumbling.

Some disqualifications were universally agreed: those *attainted of treason* or under sentence for an offence punishable by more than one year's imprisonment *in any part of the King's dominions*, or *of unsound mind* were automatically excluded.[20]

The clause that stirred debate was this: *No aboriginal native of Asia Africa or the Islands of the Pacific or person of the half blood*. These were the words of the original bill. Subsequent amendments saw the word *Australia* inked in after Asia, *person of the half blood* crossed out, and an exemption made for Maoris, so that the clause as it was finally debated read: *No aboriginal native of Asia Australia Africa or the Islands of the Pacific except New Zealand*.[21] One other important rider was added: *unless so entitled under Section 41 of the Constitution*. This provision would save some Indigenous Australians from what was about to happen next.

On the question of the female franchise, most members were in favour—at least on the constitutional grounds of uniformity if not on the principle of political equality. Labor senator for

Queensland Thomas Glassey dubbed it *a Bill of no mean order.*

> I believe that when the history of the Parliament of the
> Commonwealth comes to be written, the conferring
> of this immense boon upon so many people, not as a
> privilege, but on the grounds of justice and equity, will
> receive the commendation of the historian.

Not all believed that the parliament was on the right side of
history. Senator Edward Pulsford (Free Trade Party, NSW) tried
to have the word 'male' inserted as a qualification. *This measure is
being forced upon us against the general feeling and against the general
tendency of legislation in Anglo Saxon countries*, he barked.[22] As a point
of order, Senator Higgs reminded his colleagues that section 41 of
the constitution prohibited such an amendment, whereupon Pulsford
suggested that Western Australia and South Australia *may in their
wisdom consider it to drop woman suffrage and then the franchise would
be uniform.* (He was dreaming.)

Senator Major Albert Gould (Free Trade, NSW) was also
against the measure. He put the very fact of the bill's existence down
to *the persistency of certain ladies*—there was no doubt *the community at
large* did not want it. John Downer (Conservative, SA) said he would
only vote for the bill because he believed that women of independent
means should have the right to safeguard their property interests.
All other women would simply vote *just as their husbands, fathers,
brothers or sweethearts vote.* It was not a progressive bill at all, Downer
corrected, but rather a highly conservative measure which he would
vote for *solely on that account.*

James Stewart came to the same point from a completely
different direction. *The opposition to the female franchise*, held the
Queensland Labor senator, *comes from the rich.* Women going down
coal mines because *male labour is too dear*, now that is *degrading*, he
argued; voting was not. And another *stupid assertion*: that women
would *neglect their homes. Election day is one out of every three years*, he
scoffed.

Does anyone imagine that in the interval between one election and another a woman will interest herself in nothing but politics—that she will devote her mornings and her noons and her evenings to politics! politics! politics!—nothing but politics? Do they believe that when her husband gets up in the morning, instead of his breakfast, she will give him Hansard?

And as for the ridiculous proposition that women would only vote for young and handsome members, well, *the honourable senators returned from South Australia do not number a single dude amongst them… all fine, big, rough, upstanding men, but not particularly handsome.*

Stewart had the last say that night, before the Senate adjourned at 10.20 p.m.:

I hope that the Bill will become law very speedily [so] that every man and woman on this continent will be invested with full political power; that in this matter Australia will show an example to the whole civilized world.

⟁

Lofty sentiments. But would every man and woman in Australia really get a vote, or only the so-called 'civilised' ones?

Senators of all stripes—Labor, Liberal and Tory, Free Trade and Protectionist—were simply apoplectic at the idea that Australia's Indigenous inhabitants might be considered in the democratic catch-all: *all adult persons not under 21 years of age, whether male or female, married or unmarried.* It was not simply that Aboriginal Australians were considered racially inferior. In the thinking of the day, the Aborigines were an historical anomaly.

Little more than a hundred years ago, wrote the MORNING POST correspondent, expressing a near universal sentiment, *Australia was a Dark Continent in every sense of the term.* There were no white men and the native population—*as black as ebony*—was *sparse* at best. Now there were at least sixty thousand Aborigines but, *in another century, the probability is that Australia will be a white continent with not a black or even dark skin among its inhabitants...the yellow, the brown, the copper-coloured are to be forbidden to land anywhere.* The Aboriginal race had *died out* in the south and were *dying out* in the north and west, even though *most gently treated.* [23] It was an existential anomaly to legislate for the citizenship of people who barely existed now and would soon cease to do so at all.

The debate was passionate, fiery and breathtakingly candid. It was Scots-born, Harrow-educated Western Australian senator Alexander Matheson, 3rd Baronet, who introduced the amendment to add Australians to the list of debarred aboriginal natives. *It appears hardly credible*, he reasoned, *but apparently it is a fact, that in South Australia any aboriginal is entitled to be placed upon the roll.* And by 'any', he meant the shocking fact of 'every': *so far as I can judge any lubra or gin is entitled to the same privilege.*[24] Matheson asked the South Australian members in the Senate whether any such person had *taken advantage of this privilege.* Senator Playford reassured him that it was rarely the case, except for *one or two natives who have become civilized*, by which, he clarified, they had acquired property and been educated by white men.

Matheson conceded that under section 41, no federal legislation could retract the rights of Indigenous South Australians. But, he demanded: *why go out of the way in our federal legislation to give rights to aborigines which they do not possess today?*

> Surely it is absolutely repugnant to the greater number of the people of the Commonwealth that an aboriginal man, or aboriginal lubra or gin—a horrible, degraded, dirty creature—should have the same rights, simply by virtue of being 21 years of age, that we have, after some debate to-day, decided to give to our wives and daughters.

Apart from the prospect being repugnant and absurd, Senator Matheson believed the enfranchisement of the Aboriginal population was illogical, as section 127 of the constitution, which provided for boundaries and quotas for electoral rolls, expressly excluded Indigenous Australians. *In reckoning the numbers of the people of the Commonwealth*, Matheson cited, *aboriginal natives shall not be counted.* If they did not count for the purposes of the electoral rolls, reckoned Matheson, how could they possibly count as voters?

And if Indigenous Australians were counted—if the sixty thousand-odd Aborigines of Western Australia were registered as citizens—why, it would entitle that state to have an extra representative in the House, surely a subversion of the democratic process. Not only that—Matheson turned to the problem of the feudal outback—if Aborigines had the franchise, there would be no stopping the mischief of the *real old crusted conservatives*, the squatters of Western Australia. These money-grubbers would *put every one of these savages and their gins upon the federal rolls.* The nation *will be swamped by aboriginal votes.* It would be the same in Queensland and the Northern Territory, *which swarms with the most active aboriginals.*

Matheson's views were echoed, slightly less luridly, by other senators. *While I believe in the widest franchise possible for people of our own colour, race and civilisation*, began Stewart, *I draw the line very strictly at uncivilised barbarians like the aborigines of Australia.*[25] It was all very well for the southern states to shine liberal largesse on the Aborigines, he argued—they were states *which in a very great measure have got rid of the black evil.*

It was Senator Miles Staniford Smith (WA) who drilled down to the real heart of the issue. *It would be a travesty on our legislature*, he bellowed, *to give the aborigines votes and put them on the same plane of citizenship as ourselves.* Aborigines were simply not equal: how could one treat them as such? Further, given women's imminent eligibility to stand for parliament, if Aborigines had the vote there would exist *the possibility of their sending to the Senate or the House of Representatives a black gin!*[26]

'Ladies with masculine ambitions' was a bitter enough pill to swallow. Black ladies with the legal capacity to emulate white men was a bridge too far.

There were those in the Senate who strenuously opposed inserting the word *Australia* in the disqualification of aboriginal natives. One of the more heated exchanges serves to illustrate the complex notion of sovereignty. South Australian Senator Playford defended the rights of *the unfortunate aboriginal, whose forefathers were here perhaps tens of thousands of years before we came here.* To exclude them from the franchise would be *a heartless thing...and it is absurd that we should say we are so frightened of the original inhabitants of this continent that we dare not allow them the right to vote.* To this preposterous notion, Senator Matheson had one thing to say:

> MATHESON: Cannibals.
>
> GLASSEY: What progress have the aborigines made?
>
> PLAYFORD: That is no reason why we should take away from them what is their right.
>
> GLASSEY: Simply because they have been here for a number of years we are asked to enfranchise them.
>
> STUART: If he was an intelligent man, I should be the last to refuse him the franchise, but he is not.

Senator O'Connor, who had first introduced the bill into parliament, shook his head in shame. He rose to defend the principles of the Commonwealth as it was envisioned by those who had thrashed out the constitutional accord:

> It would be a monstrous thing, an unheard of piece of savagery on our part, to treat the aboriginals, whose land we were occupying, in such a manner as to deprive them absolutely of any right to vote in their own country,

simply on the ground of their colour and because they were aboriginals...surely we are not going to apply this doctrine [of] a white Australia, not only with irregularity but with a savagery which is quite unworthy of the beginning of this federation? It is a monstrous and savage application of this principle of a white Australia.[27]

The nation would remain white, but it must uphold that which was right. Aboriginal Australians had a claim to citizenship on the grounds of natural justice.

On that note, the Senate voted, and on 10 April, by a tally of twelve noes to eight ayes, it rejected including the word *Australia* in the list of aboriginal exclusions. The nation's borders would be protected, but so too would the rights of its original inhabitants.

Temporarily. The amendment was not dead, and when it was debated in the House of Representatives two weeks later, it was the Western Australia problem that had the most purchase. Labor MP Chris Watson (later prime minister) argued that the Aborigines of Western Australia and Queensland were *practically the slaves of those squatters*. They could be used to *turn the tide of an election. Savages and slaves* would be *running electorates*. Hugh Mahon, the Labor member for Coolgardie (WA), argued it would be *distinctly dangerous* to allow the squatters of Western Australia to *muster up their niggers and drive them to the polling booth to vote*.

If the democrats in the House were confronted by this language, they didn't express it. Henry Bournes Higgins, one of Victoria's most celebrated liberals, argued that it was *utterly inappropriate to grant the franchise to the aborigines, or to ask them to exercise an intelligent vote*. There might be a duty to extend the suffrage to women but there was no similar *constitutional obligation on the community for a uniform franchise for the aborigines*. Isaac Isaacs, a fellow Victorian member and key participant in the 1897 federal convention, agreed with Higgins. He sided with Senator Matheson's constitutional argument, that being excluded from counting on the rolls was *an intimation that it was intended to exclude natives from participating in power.* And he queried whether the Federation Fathers' vision of 'One Nation, One Destiny' could be fulfilled if aborigines voted. *How, for instance,* he asked, *would these blacks vote on the question of a white Australia?* Tasmanian Edward Braddon, the oldest member of the House at seventy-one, remarked that the only thing worse than conceding the female franchise was *the giving of it to any of the numerous gins of the blackfellows...it can even less be claimed that the gins would give a vote which would be intelligible.*

Vaiben Louis Solomon countered this argument with experience. *In South Australia,* he averred, *the aborigines have a perfect right to the franchise and they exercise it.* But Braddon was having no truck with the contention that the aborigines either deserved or were owed the franchise.

> As an argument for including Australian aborigines within the provision of this measure, we are told that we have taken their country from them. But it seems a poor sort of justice to recompense those people for the loss of their country by giving them votes.

Certainly the Aborigines would not be asked for their opinion on that.

In the end, when the House divided on the proposition that *the word to be inserted be so inserted* the ayes had it: twenty-seven to five.[28]

When the bill returned to the Senate a month later, O'Connor reaffirmed his *strong view against* depriving Aborigines of the franchise, but he conceded that the House of Representatives had decided otherwise. *The prospect of our giving the franchise to the half-wild gins living with their tribe,* he owned, *seems to have startled some of our friends in the other House.* That vision did not so startle O'Connor, but he wasn't prepared to die in a ditch for it. *We cannot have ideal consistency in this world...It is not worthwhile, for the sake of this particular provision, to stand out for our own way and so run the risk of losing the Bill.*[29]

He would not sacrifice the most pressing issue of the day—womanhood suffrage—for the sins of the past or untold consequences in the future. In the end, the Senate accepted the House's amendment. The Commonwealth Franchise Act was voted in without a division in the Senate, and by twenty-nine votes to six in the House of Representatives.

Commentators noted the small proportion of the seventy-five members of the House who were present to vote on the bill. Barton was absent. Deakin was paired. *This is significant,* noted the KALGOORLIE MINER, as *showing that the victory for the rights of women was a foregone conclusion.* The division was taken late at night, and many pro-suffrage members had gone home, *not thinking it necessary for them to wait to vote, as the motion was certain to be carried.* The MINER considered this an indication of *the marvellous advance in public opinion.*[30]

The Commonwealth Franchise Act received royal assent on 12 June 1901. It was now race, not gender, that defined the limits of Australian citizenship.[31] If any of the women present in parliament to witness their historic victory were uncomfortable with the racial sting in the tail of this exceptional democracy, they were keeping mum.

12

The World Fairly Stood Aghast

An interlude

By the time the first parliament closed on 10 October 1902, thirty-eight acts had been written into the statute books and sixteen bills had been withdrawn or shelved. It required sixteen thousand-odd pages of Hansard, bound in twelve volumes, to contain all the words spilled in putting the new government in motion and setting the Commonwealth on its course.[1]

Henry Gyles Turner, assessing the first decade of the Australian Commonwealth in 1911, argued that the Immigration Restriction Act was the piece of legislation *that most directly affected the workings of the Australian community*. New Zealand statesman William Pember Reeves remarked that *the grant of the suffrage by the Parliament of the Commonwealth in 1902 was chiefly noteworthy for the absence of any sort of alarm, fervid advocacy, or strong repugnance.*[2] Feminist journalist Bella Halloran celebrated the attainment of *equal rights of women in politics* but observed *how silently the great fact has been accomplished*: she noted a distinct lack of *clamour* in the press. More attention was being given to the prime minister's trip to England for the forthcoming coronation of Edward VII.

Nothing to see here.

But the Commonwealth Franchise Act had a significant impact on the international reputation and standing of the new nation. Like Teddy Roosevelt, the rest of the world had its eyes trained on Australia. For there was something to see, and it was remarkable.

Australia's world-leading status was soon touted by woman

suffrage campaigners around the world. Millicent Garrett Fawcett's NUWSS published a propaganda pamphlet intended to demon-strate to the British public, and recalcitrant members of the British Parliament, that the female franchise was neither a passing fad nor a quixotic thing of the future. The enfranchised woman, assured contributor Pember Reeves, is *a triumphant, a real, an irrevocable she!*

> Female suffrage is an Anglo-Saxon institution of to-day; not a story of Utopia or the planet Mars or of some coming race, but one of the ordinary, every-day matters of political life amongst people who speak your language, who belong to your blood and race, and who are the subjects of Queen Victoria and citizens of the British Empire.[3]

This *she!* was not to be feared. She was no different from any British mother, daughter or sister. *Because they have become citizens,* verified Pember Reeves, *they have not ceased to be women; their clothes still fit them well; their manners have not lost their feminine charm.* The argument went that these *two venturesome colonies* had done the world a great favour, putting a toe in the great Southern Ocean and finding that the whole leg was not chewed off. Pember Reeves urged not vigilance, but valour.

> I feel convinced that the boundless British courage which enables the male Briton to build up empires…to confront foes, to face savages…will enable them to meet even so alive and terrible a person as the Enfranchised Woman—when she comes.

Just as President Roosevelt had wanted to meet an enfranchised woman in person—and got his chance with Vida Goldstein—now Pember Reeves, only somewhat tongue in cheek, urged British men to have the balls to confront the enemy unflinchingly.

Sir John Cockburn, in a speech to the NUWSS reprinted in Mrs Fawcett's pamphlet, described his arrival in London from South

Australia in terms of time travel back to *the mediaeval ages.*

> I come from a country where the women have enjoyed
> the exercise of the franchise for some years past, and
> we have so got used to it that it is quite strange to come
> to a country where one's wife has not got the vote.
> (Laughter)

Cockburn's self-referential aside was greeted with mirth, but his remark was strategically pointed. *Why should your colonial sisters be privileged to come here and parade their plumes before the women of the old country? Why should you not have the advantages which the women in the colonies possess?*

If reason would not work, perhaps sheer peacock pride would inspire the women of Britain to greater action.

Other commentators were similarly bemused that it was Australia, of all places, that had breasted the tape of female sovereignty first. Edith Palliser, an Irishwoman who was the co-secretary of the NUWSS and editor of its organ WOMEN'S SUFFRAGE RECORD from 1902–04, expressed the common disbelief that America was not leading the charge.

> In the new world, the English colonies have granted full
> political rights to women, while America, which was
> the first to formulate the claim of self-government for
> all, still denies political rights to its women.[4]

American pundits were just as perplexed. One Boston journalist wrote in 1902 that *psychologically, it is a curious problem that a phase of evolution so natural and logical* as women's suffrage should not have been first adopted in America...

> a country which is a synonym for progress, liberty
> and enlightenment, and where resistance to taxation
> without representation is a historic slogan...while in a
> comparatively new country, which owes allegiance to a
> monarchy, the emancipation from the Oriental ideas of
> woman's place is established without difficulty.[5]

How odd that *the great Commonwealth at the antipodes* should turn the tables and arrive on top! The characteristically self-satisfied Americans had to concede their democratic malfunction. *The United States should have been the first nation to enfranchise its women*, admitted the Commercial Tribune, *but we failed to live up to our principles.*[6] Some were not so much confounded as obliged. The Californian State Suffrage Association sent a letter to the Women's Council of Australia, expressing its profound gratitude: *Australia's recent enfranchisement of her 800,000 women with eligibility to the national Parliament has given great encouragement to those of California.*[7]

If Australia's advances inspired activists, they also provided data for cold hard research. The burgeoning academic field of sociology was particularly interested in the *social experiment of Australia*. Australian sociologist Clarence Northcott, who was educated at the University of Sydney and later did a PhD at Columbia University published as Australian Social Development, was quick to realise that his native country would attract *considerable attention* and be studied by *men with careful research training in the social sciences*. Australia, proposed Northcott, *has worked out a unique and interesting experiment in democracy*, one that revealed a characteristically *reckless optimism*. Northcott concluded from his extensive research that, while the *psychology of a people* was noteworthy in determining its social resourcefulness, it was more important to understand

> such concrete factors as climate, rainfall, and the quantity and distribution of minerals…Only a country with potential wealth of natural resources widely distributed and fairly accessible can afford to conduct democratic experiments.[8]

Northcott further determined that Australia's world-leading standing was due to the character of its women as well as its underground wealth. *They have an instinctive desire to count*, analysed Northcott, *somewhere in the social process as an integer*; that is, a thing complete in itself, an irrevocable she. Australian women, Northcott

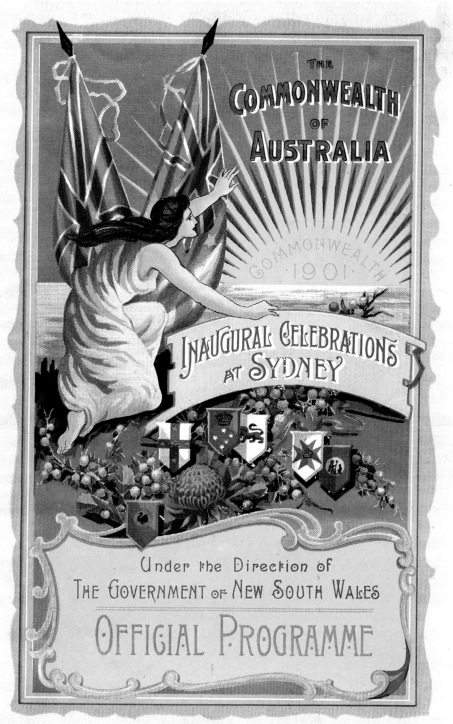

The dawn of a new century and a new nation. Daughter Australia graces the front cover of the Sydney birthday party celebration program, January 1901.

Above: A young Dora Montefiore.
Date and place unknown.

Top right: Nellie Alma Martel,
elocutionist. Sydney, 3 April 1902.

Right: Aspiring actress Muriel
Matters, c. late 1890s.

Right: Portrait of Dora Meeson accompanying the *Australian Town and Country Journal* article that announced her prize-winning artwork, *Minerva*.

Below: Britannia and Minerva flank the invitation to the Great Day, 9 May 1901.

THE TOWN AND COUNTRY JOURNAL.

AN AUSTRALIAN ARTIST.

MISS DORA MEESON,

WINNER OF THE FIRST PRIZE (75 GUINEAS) IN THE MINERVA ART COMPETITION.

(See letterpress on this page.)

A Christmas Song.

IN CELEBRATION OF THE OPENING

PARLIAMENT of the COMMONWEALTH of AUSTRALIA

To meet Their Royal Highnesses The DUKE and DUCHESS of CORNWALL & YORK

His Majesty's MINISTERS of STATE FOR AUSTRALIA have the honor to invite

to an Evening Reception at the Exhibition Building MELBOURNE, on the 9TH of May 1901, at 8 o'clock.

Vida Goldstein's
Senate campaign
portrait, 1903.

argued from his empirical sources, and presumably his personal experience, show *a general reluctance to enter into any relationship which is not free, in which they cannot stand upon a basis of economic and personal independence.*[9] He ascribed much of this female tendency towards autonomy to the particular circumstances of Australian girlhood, one lived in the open air, the physical environment contributing to *her fearlessness, her grit and her entire absence of artificiality and diffidence.* Both Australian men and women were *intolerant of special privileges* and consequently had transformed English institutions into ones *stripped of their traditional conservatism.*

Alice Zimmern, an English scholar whose research culminated in her influential 1909 book WOMEN'S SUFFRAGE IN MANY LANDS, confronted the widespread impression that American women were the freest in the world. Yes, she admitted, they were enrolled in universities, entered professions and pursued a wider range of callings than women anywhere else, but for political freedom—the ultimate goal of *awakened* women everywhere—one had to cast the eye south. *In Europe and America we may watch the struggles and aspirations after freedom, but we must turn to the Antipodes to see the achievement.*[10] Australia, argued Zimmern, was *reaping the reward of having responded to the unanswered appeal of justice.*[11] Unanswered in all parts of the world other than Australasia.

The REVIEW OF REVIEWS, a suite of monthly journals established by British liberal journalist William Stead which operated from three international offices—London, New York and Melbourne—took particular interest in the Australian precedent. *Women*, it reported,

> now have a larger and more direct share in the public affairs of the Commonwealth than in those of any other civilised State. What may be the effect of this cannot as yet be imagined, but sooner or later the effect must make itself visible, and it may well give a totally new complexion to Australian politics.

If outcomes were not yet apparent, one thing was crystal clear: *The experiment will be watched all over the civilised world with curious interest.*[12]

Whether it was through journalism, books, suffrage networks or social science reports, intelligence of Australia's experiment in equality was broadcast globally. Jessie Ackermann summed up the tenor of the reporting.

> When the spirit of democracy seemed to seize the people of Australia...the various States became the great experimental stations of the world [and]...the world fairly stood aghast.[13]

⚓

What did Australia make of all this attention? Did the new nation enjoy having its name up in lights?

The Review of Reviews certainly held that the southern states were enjoying their day in the sun.

> If there is one thing about which all Australia and New Zealand are cocksure, it is that the purest type of democracy the human race has ever known flourishes today beneath Australian skies. From the eminence of that delightful conviction we look down with wild pity upon the rest of mankind who have not yet reached our level of political beatitude.[14]

To Percy Rowlands, an English-born teacher who worked in Queensland as a headmaster at the turn of the century and wrote two books on the Australian nation, such *'blow'*—skiting—*remains a prominent Australian characteristic.*[15] Rowlands observed that the Australian was particularly *sensitive to criticism of his country and somewhat vain of both its physical charm and of the mental and moral excellence of its inhabitants.*[16] His evidence of Australia's mental and moral excellence: its record on women's suffrage. That, *and the great national self-conscious act of Federation.* It was in the Australian child that the tendency to forward behaviour, as befitting such forward thinking, was most noticeable.

> They look you as frankly in the face as the stars of a
> Southern night—no tremor of self-distrust, no shadow
> of fear or doubt, marring the open glance of those alert
> young eyes.

Rowlands noted the *humourlessness* of most of Australia's public men, a trait that was particularly remarkable given the *resourcefulness and cheerfulness* that was the *most striking characteristic* of its women. All in all, he summed up, *what a nation of nations the Commonwealth has it in her to become!*[17]

It was for all these reasons that Vida Goldstein believed that Advance Australia really was the most fitting motto for her home-land. *We Australians*, she wrote, *have good reason to glory in the advance of our country, which, in granting women absolute political equality with men, has reached a position unique in the world's history.*[18]

There was no shying away from the fact. In the eyes of the world, and in her own self-estimation too, Australia was no longer merely facing the dawn, waiting expectantly for the light to shine upon her. Australia was now carrying the torch, and marching boldly forth to ignite the flames of other political lanterns across the globe.

The New Woman was now, at least where Australasia was concerned, a voting woman. She had more than rhetoric and a bent umbrella on her side. And in the Commonwealth of Australia, she could be a legislating woman too. All it would take to put a woman in parliament was to find someone with the courage to throw her bonnet in the ring.

13

The Modern Eve

Victoria, 1903

This ball is at your feet. So began Vida Goldstein's pitch to the voters of Korumburra.

It had been an arduous journey to get here, 120 kilometres from Melbourne; an inconvenient swamp made it a circuitous route up through the Strzelecki Ranges. But Vida wouldn't spurn an invitation to tell the women of this small South Gippsland dairying and coal-mining community that it was time to pick up the political football and run headlong at the forthcoming 1903 federal election. They had never possessed such a marked home-ground advantage. *The hoary Tories are now kow-towing to the women's associations*, as Vida put it, abandoning the sporting metaphors but warming to her subject. The electoral roll contained seven thousand more women than men. They—the voters—could do the maths.

The numbers cut straight to the heart of something Dora Montefiore had said to Rose Scott over a decade before, when starting the Womanhood Suffrage League: *Women will never get laws past* [sic] *to help the cause of purity* <u>until</u> *they have the suffrage. A vote means power and those who have power also have to be conciliated.*[1]

It was so true. Women in England had been lobbying to get a vice suppression bill for almost a century. Such a measure would make it a crime to seduce a woman with the promise of marriage, such as had led Maggie Heffernan to her ruin. But why would men ever concede their licence, except through pressure at the ballot box?

Now, in Australia, that pressure could be applied. Even the Citizens Reform League was plumping for the women's vote—*and if ever there was rank Conservative Body*, Vida told Korumburra's burghers, *it was the Citizens Reform League*. (This statement *created uproarious amusement* among those who had put aside their milking and mining duties to come see the lady candidate. The chairman of the meeting, who had invited Vida to speak, also happened to be the chairman of the local branch of the Citizens Reform League.)

But gaffes aside, the fact that her speech at Korumburra on 14 October 1903 was reported as far afield as the Tasmanian NORTH WESTERN ADVOCATE AND THE EMU BAY TIMES was music to Vida's ears. Her campaign for the Senate was a novelty, yes, but it had tongues wagging. And now, on 23 November, the good people of Korumburra had invited her back to address the much larger crowd of electors who had piled into the Mechanics Institute Hall.

It's possible her father was there—Major Jacob Goldstein managed the state-funded Labour Colony at Leongatha, just down the road—but Vida had not seen much of him in the past few years. Her mother, Isabella, had effectively kicked him out, preferring to live with daughters Vida, Aileen and Elsie (and Elsie's husband, socialist publisher Henry Hyde Champion) in their spacious Bourke Street apartment. Vida and Jacob had not seen eye to eye on much recently. In the lead-up to Federation, Jacob publicly opposed women's enfranchisement, speaking at meetings on behalf of anti-suffrage women who were happy to gather petitions but felt it inappropriate to take to the platform.[2] He even made a few jokes at his high-profile daughter's expense. It was a slap in the face to all the Goldstein women, for whom getting the vote was just as much a spiritual calling as the Christian Science faith to which they now adhered.

The Korumburra crowd had gathered despite Vida's insistence on charging a silver coin for entry. *She was not a moneyed woman*, she explained, *and she had firmly determined that she would not, as some candidates had done, get into debt*. But even the people who simply *came out of curiosity to see the terrible person who was to be nominated for the Senate,* seemed inclined to think they'd got their money's worth.

While she had her audience captive, Vida dealt with various rumours that had been circulated. No, she was not *a believer in free love.* Neither was she an advocate of *easy divorce,* though she knew this view was unpopular among some women. But no, she had not become *an out-and-out conservative.* Nor was she *a disciple of Mr Tom Mann,* the British socialist and trade union organiser. That too was *a cowardly insinuation* designed to injure her chances of election. And yes, *women's sphere was the home. But so was man's. (Cheers and laughter) It was a sphere, too, that he had often neglected.* She would be the first to admit that she might not make the ideal member, but *I am perfectly certain that I could not do worse than some of the men you have sitting in Parliament. (Loud cheers).* Voters would also come to realise, *as the Americans quickly discovered,* that Vida was *one of the most home-loving and womanly of women.*[3]

Now that was out of the way, she had something to say:

> Government of the people by the people for the people, without respect to property, person or sex. That, I say, is what the Federal Parliament has made possible. Thus far we have not had democracy—only male democracy.

And finally, Vida asked something of the gentlemen who had come to see her today. She wanted them to cast their minds back, not to last week or last year, but to thousands and thousands of years ago. *Yes, back to the garden of Eden. (Laughter).* Remember how peace and love reigned supreme? Remember how happiness abounded, until woman tempted man, and *he did eat the apple of discord?* Now, bring your minds back to the present, coaxed Vida. *I am a modern Eve. I offer you an apple—but an apple of a different kind—the apple of harmony—the idea of a woman going into Parliament.*

Take and eat of it, she dared, *and you will find you will develop a relish for more apples of the same kind.* Vida looked out at the crowd. *Loud laughter,* perhaps prompted by apprehension as much as jest.[4]

⚓

Having risen to public prominence—a young, beautiful, intelligent single woman with guts and determination—Vida Goldstein quickly became a national symbol of the new dawn of women's potential. *Every woman*, proclaimed Vida, *unless she be a household drudge, an industrial slave, has time and opportunity to inform herself concerning great public questions...A woman must be a citizen to know how to train citizens.*

The test of that citizenship was now upon them. At the beginning of winter 1903, the first election of the Federal Parliament after the passage of the Franchise Act was called. 16 December 1903 would be a red-letter day, Vida wrote, for this was *when, for the first time in the world's history, the women of a nation* would take part in *the making of a National Parliament.*[5] That these auspicious electors would be white women went without saying.

Vida had long argued that that a woman must not only cast her ballot, but also represent other women in the supreme cauldron of democracy—the parliament. She believed that *the interests of the home should be directly represented as are the manufacturing, farming, mining and labouring interests.*[6] All legislation in some way affected women and children, she contended, so there should be a woman in the legislature to consider their interests. Not because men were innately evil or incompetent but *because owing to the different sex, men cannot understand such questions from the woman's point of view, and injustices creep in in spite of their most earnest efforts to forestall them.*

Moreover, the all-male parliament meant women wasted countless hours in the *often Herculean task* of educating MPs to recognise those blind injustices. Lord knows, Vida had devoted enough of her own time to sitting in the gallery studying the passage of legislation and barging in and out of MPs' offices to lobby them on some matter of male bias or prejudice that would ultimately affect women and children. *We had to tramp around getting petitions signed*, she recalled, *we had to write to the press. It was always hateful work.*

The solution was simple: *Let a woman of great mental power combined with executive ability enter Parliament and she will make surrounding nations stare*, wrote Vida in a widely circulated essay.[7] Not all women would be suited to the task, she conceded, but neither were all men. (Even some of the men who had been duly elected!) *But once you get the right woman, or women, there*, she reasoned, *the people will ask themselves 'why on earth didn't we try this experiment before?'* And by the spring of 1903, Vida reckoned this woman—the right woman—was her.

Earlier that year, Vida had started the Women's Federal Political Association to educate women in the exercise of their new citizenship rights. One of the standard arguments against women's suffrage was that women would just vote the way the male members of their family instructed them. Vida didn't believe this for a minute, but she also knew that not all women were versed in politics, or the political process. They would need to be taught, just as they were taught to darn or cook or ride a bicycle. With assistance to understand the issues and assess the candidates, *the women of Australia are unlikely to cast an unthinking vote…they will do their thinking for themselves.*[8]

If they cast a ballot at all. Voting was at this stage voluntary, so part of the task for Vida and the WFPA was to convince women of the importance of enrolling.[9] It was a great responsibility to have the vote, argued Vida, noting that *American women looked with envious eyes upon their Australian sisters as in this respect 'the salt of the earth'.*[10] Would Australian women *give a good account of themselves, when the eyes of the world would be upon them*, as Vida urged them to do?[11]

Vida's view of the upcoming election as a focus of world politics was not an exaggeration. *As it will be the first time in history that a Parliament will be returned on a basis of adult suffrage*, wrote academic C. J. Martin in a British journal, *it is perhaps not too much to say that the eyes of the civilised world will be upon [Australia].*[12] Martin reported that the campaign cries were *Educate! and Organise!...teaching and learning, learning and teaching, day by day.*

Education was the key, and though she hoped women would support her candidacy, Vida was sincere when she said *I would sooner see women educated in views diametrically opposed to mine than not educated at all.* She vowed to lend a hand in the process of schooling the electorate. The WFPA would canvass federal candidates on their views regarding issues of importance to female voters—including equal pay, age of consent legislation, pensions, maternal and child welfare, improved industrial conditions for the thirty per cent of women who earned their own living, child labour, sweated labour, restrictions on gambling, drinking and vice—and publish findings in Vida's journal, WOMAN'S SPHERE.

It would gather evidence from New Zealand and South Australia that would demonstrate the influence of female voters on public policy and social relations in the five-odd years that women in those colonies had been going to the polls. There was plenty of supporting data. In New Zealand, pubs were now closed on election day. Women were treated with more respect and not as *a mere afternoon tea machine.*[13] New Zealand's labour laws were now, according to its premier, Richard Seddon, *the most advanced in the world.* In South Australia, testified Sir John Cockburn, *all questions of social, sanitary, industrial and domestic legislation now receive much more careful and earnest attention.*[14] The WFPA would also use the occasion of the federal election to draw attention to the fact that Victorian women like Vida, while now national voters, were still disenfranchised at the state level.

The WFPA was politically astute but party neutral. In fact, it was non-party, believing that party politics and the *machine ticket leads to disastrous consequences.*[15] Vida owned that labour should represent labour, as women should represent women, but she was hostile to the *log-rollers*, feeble candidates who had been trundled into parliament purely because they were on a party's ticket. Such men could often be found *intoxicated* in parliament, *men of doubtful character, men whose social life is a scandal.*

One of the chief aims of the female franchise was to *purify politics*. Vida adopted a light-hearted way to describe the need for women's direct parliamentary representation: *man seems to be constitutionally unable to keep things tidy*. Playing to the four-fifths of the crowd at her election rally meetings who were female, Vida joked that it had always been woman's lot to tidy up after men—*He leaves the bathroom in a state of flood, his dressing-room a howling wilderness of masculine paraphernalia, his office a chaos of ink and papers*—and this disorderly boor was equally *untidy in the nation.* No wonder the *national household* was in such *a terrible state of muddle!*[16]

Such gendered metaphors and gendered stereotypes were not challenged by women's rights advocates. It was a later generation of feminists whose demand was to be liberated from the role of 'angel of the hearth' or spiritual redeemer—God's police. The feminists of the early twentieth century proudly accepted their natural function as civilisers of the civilisers. They simply wanted the political power to make the white man's burden woman's burden too.

Women cherished their feminine virtues and saw themselves as morally and spiritually superior to men. As Jessie Ackermann put it, men in power had *selfish aims* and a *greed for gain. The advent of women into national life*, she argued, *would mean clean politics.* As mothers taught their children to share and play nicely, so women would take a principled approach to *national housekeeping.*[17] Their votes and their parliamentary presence would clean up individual men's acts, and clean up the nation too.

Vida may have considered that female voters would be astute judges of character, sniffing out the stench of avarice, sloth and vainglory, but she was neither a political prude nor a gender separatist. *We are not advocating a political nunnery for women*, Vida clarified. The WFPA welcomed, as member or supporter, any man who wanted to assist in women's campaigns for justice, equality and social reform.[18] Indeed prominent male public figures, including Alfred Deakin and Charles Kingston, appeared on the stage beside her at meetings.[19] Vida was ever at pains *to give honour where honour is due: To the men of Australian, who have grown so far in democratic sentiment that they can tolerate the idea of living with political equals.*[20]

Despite her conflicted relationship with her own father and her vow to remain unmarried, sex antagonism was never a motivation for Vida's activism.

When, in August 1903, the WFPA nominated Vida as 'the woman's candidate', not all greeted the novel occasion with pleasure or sympathy—not even all women.[21] The Victorian Executive of the WCTU publicly declared its opposition to female candidates (contradicting their organisation's own motto: 'No sex in citizenship'). They felt it was too early in the franchise experiment to countenance such an extreme move, one that would ultimately *prejudice the interest of the women's cause.*

Nonsense, retorted the Australasian WCTU in its journal OUR FEDERATION. *Women have never won any improvement in the condition of their sex by sitting down to wait.*[22]

The GIPPSLAND TIMES greeted Vida's candidacy as *a welcome sign of the times.* It praised the WFPA's prudence: *a better choice could hardly be made. Miss Vida Goldstein has a remarkably clear insight into politics, and will soon outshine our second and third rate male politicians.*[23]

But if Vida herself was seen by some as an optimal pick, others disparaged the whole notion of 'Petticoats in Parliament'. *Hon. Members will have to debate, so to speak, in kid gloves when a lady is an actor in the fray,* tutted journalist and clergyman Dr William Fitchett, *while a lady will probably have a quickness of wit and an incisiveness of speech which male politicians will find disconcerting.*[24] Which was it then? That grown men would be forced to behave as if there were children in the House? Or that grown women would beat them at their own game? The reasoning was unclear. The anxiety was palpable.

Vida opened her hair-raising campaign in the Western District town of Portland, the place of her birth. If she expected a hometown welcome, she was disappointed, at least as far as the conservative ARGUS newspaper would have had readers believe. The meeting was crowded, noted the ARGUS, *but the audience scarcely seemed to take her seriously.*[25] Still, she laid out her platform briskly, as she would in dozens of town halls and mechanics institutes around the state over the following three months. She stood for the principles of democracy; so far in Australia it had been *government for the people by the men*. On the tariff issue, *although rather inclined to call herself a fiscal atheist, she was a protectionist*. In this regard, she aligned with leading Liberals like Alfred Deakin. But the 'Fiscal Question' was *not a very vital one from her standpoint*, as the social evils which she primarily stood to eradicate could be found in free trade England as well as in protectionist Germany. She was in favour of compulsory arbitration and conciliation, a position more consistent with Labor policy. She was opposed to the federal capital being built any time soon. *We [are] only four millions of people*, she reasoned, *and why spend millions on a capital in the bush*. She approved of the Commonwealth taking over the state railways, but wanted to hold off the building of the transcontinental railway—*a wild-cat scheme*—for the time being. (Like the capital, it would cost too much money to service too few people.) She wanted to see the nation develop a proper system of water conservation, as well as a 'squatter tax' on unimproved land value and better mining laws, *which are no credit to masculine government*. She was not averse to the federal government taking over state debts. She favoured an Australian navy.[26]

On the key social and political issue of White Australia, Vida heartily approved of the Immigration Restriction Act. She made it clear that she believed in *the principle at the root of this legislation*—in her interpretation, that Australia should be protected against the cheap labour of other countries—but feared that the operation of the law had *resulted in palpable absurdities and injustices to others of different blood from ourselves.*[27] Ultimately, she believed, it would be the principle of equal pay for equal work that would provide the best protection for the Australian economy and labour force, not the principle of racial exclusion. Her beef was chiefly with capital, not colour.[28] She was against *alien pauper labour*, but would consider some skilled migration. She also deemed it *a hardship* to insist on the deportation of some of the *imported kanakas [who] were very much civilised.*

But, like most suffragists (and progressives), she still held that unrestricted immigration was unwelcome, due to *its dangers to health and morality.* This view, she confided, had been formulated during her trip to America, when she *saw the thousands of foreigners that were landed there and whose children were foisted on to the state.*[29] Central to immigration restriction was an assertion of Australia as a self-governing dominion, able to make its own choices and set its own standards. (A concept that dovetailed with Vida's orthodox feminist argument for sexual sovereignty: that *woman wanted herself to herself.*[30])

As a patriotic Australian native, Vida was in synch with the almost universal acceptance of the theory and policy of a white Australia. Just as white women had been complicit in the process of colonialism, so white women abetted the process of creating and perpetuating a racialised nation.[31]

At the end of her Portland address—as at Prahran, Fitzroy, Horsham, Benalla, Hamilton, Stawell, Bendigo, Ballarat, Korumburra and wherever she went—Vida addressed the various criticisms put forth by the newspapers of women's suffrage in general and her candidature for parliament in particular. She answered questions from the audience with patience, grace and humour, *her sparkling dark eyes...very much on the alert.*[32] She assured them that, should they favour her with one of their four votes for the Senate, *the world would not come to an end.*[33]

And through it all, as the BENALLA STANDARD noted, she managed the crucial balancing act of *getting off a slap at the other side without in the least descending from the pedestal she as a lady stands on.*[34] Ever the womanly woman, even in open battle.

14

She Loved Politics

New South Wales, 1903

Vida, however, was not the only gladiator in the arena. Three weeks before the election, another woman announced her candidature and this time the nomination came from Sydney, for one of the New South Wales Senate places.

If Vida was down to earth, sober and chaste, the new candidate was bold, brash and fresh from controversy. If Vida looked to win over voters with the force of reason, the new contender would seek to bowl them over with the force of her personality. If Vida represented all that was pure and good and modest about Australian womanhood, the new contender was a perfumed pugilist with the scent of notoriety wafting around her extravagant millinery and gaudy jewellery.

The new candidate was Nellie Martel.

By the winter of 1903, Nellie was burning the candle at both ends. She was a working woman, running a successful business as an elocutionist out of her home studio on one of the busiest corners in the city of Sydney.[1] Her advertisements in the Sydney press were equally conspicuous: *Mrs C. Martel, Professor of Elocution, Voice Production and Dramatic Art in all its Branches. Out of SEVEN pupils sent to Young People's Industrial Exhibition, SIX took medals.*[2] Nellie was introduced in press reports of her activities as *the well-known elocutionist of Sydney.*[3]

It seems likely that Charles was not faring as well as his high-profile wife; there are no corresponding advertisements for Charles' services as a photographer or any other creative or mercantile calling.

Nellie's dance card was copiously filled with her well-attended concerts, recitals and student exhibitions. But throughout 1902 and 1903, her days and nights were also jam-packed with political engagements. Winning womanhood suffrage in New South Wales was a great milestone. *Words cannot describe*, wrote Nellie, *the joy which fills one's heart at the realisation of one's life work.*[4] Like Rose Scott, with whom she'd parted ways on the issue of working women's access to the WSL, Nellie was *thoroughly happy* with the victory. It had taken their band of activists eleven years to achieve the result that Dora Montefiore had set in train—*in getting political freedom*, as Nellie put it. She had never stopped believing it was *our absolute right*.

But during that eleven years, Nellie had also worked for the removal from the New South Wales statute books of laws *which were a disgrace to any country*: questions of municipal reform, regulation of the liquor trade, female sanitary inspectors, provisions for state wards, equal pay and anti-sweating among others. This work didn't miraculously stop when women won the state and federal franchise. In fact the vote upped the ante, as MPs were more likely to pay attention to what the women had been saying for over a decade. So, in her dual roles as the honorary secretary of the Women's Progressive Association and the president of the Women's Liberal and Reform Association, Nellie kept up a gruelling schedule of public lectures and private deputations.

Her pet topic was age of consent legislation. In New South Wales, the legal age at which a girl was considered capable of consenting to sexual intercourse was fourteen. After that, Nellie protested, any man could *rob a girl of her good name*. And this was not all he could take.

> Should he succeed in coercing, intimidating or bribing the child into saying she had consented to her own ruin, the law allowed that man to go free, even though he were a father of children of the age of his victim.

The law protected a woman's property for longer than her chastity, Nellie pointed out: it considered a woman *not yet wise enough* before she turned twenty-one *to know how to dispose of her land or property* but perfectly able to sign away her virtue. For Nellie, the question was one of class equality as well as sexual equality. *Protect the poor girls' good names*, she demanded, *at least as long as you protect the rich girls' property*.[5] Like other women's rights campaigners, Nellie wanted the age of consent raised to seventeen. She spoke on this issue at countless deputations, trying to convince politicians that the protection of women's bodies was no different from the protection of the nation's borders. The nation's purity, like women's sexual integrity, required *a vigilant effort to keep out* foreign intruders.[6] Just as it was the uniqueness of women as mothers and homemakers that had been germane to suffrage campaigners' justification for the vote, so it was Nellie's mission to prove that female electors bore the ultimate responsibility for safeguarding the nation's virtue.

By the time the federal election was called in August 1903, forty-eight-year-old Nellie was burnt out. She had been skipping WPA meetings since April, citing illness. *We are sorry to hear that Mrs Martel is not so well as usual*, reported THE DAWN in its August 'News and Notes' column.[7] Perhaps it was the flu, but THE DAWN obliquely suggested Nellie might have collapsed in exhaustion: *Contented women who enjoy the privileges of the day little know what their busy sisters endure to gain them for them.*

It was not only relentless activity that wore the campaigners down. *We were subjected to ridicule, contempt, abuse and to anything but flattering cartoons*, 'brick-haired' Nellie pointed out. One particularly nasty caricature of Nellie in TRUTH painted her as *a lady of fascinating frocks and irreproachable jewellery...the ornamental and oratorical figurehead of a narrow-minded political sect*. The accompanying line drawing showed a flat-faced woman with a large hat and a cruel scowl.[8] Yes, the vote was the chief privilege of the day, but its attainment had come at a price.

Still, sacrifice or not, Nellie was in demand, as a Western Australian newspaper was eager to note on 2 October:

Women in Politics: A Lady Candidate

Sydney, 9 a.m.

At a meeting of ladies yesterday afternoon, a motion was carried—That Mrs C. Martell [*sic*] be asked to become a candidate for the Senate at the next general election.[9]

Perhaps Nellie was assessing her health; perhaps she was being realistic about her chances of success. Perhaps Charles, though supportive of his wife's suffrage activities, thought a berth in parliament an act of overreach. Whatever the cause of her reluctance, it took Nellie a full month to consider the invitation. On 31 October, the Sydney TELEGRAPH reported:

Mrs Martel for the Senate

Mrs C. Martel, at the request of a large number of her friends and supporters, has consented to stand as a freetrade candidate for the Senate.[10]

Consent did not guarantee consummation, however. Unlike Vida, who got her campaign off at a gallop and never slowed down, Nellie's race looked like it might not leave the stalls. *Mrs Martell, [sic] who threatens to become a candidate for the Senate*, reported one paper on 21 November...*is a sister of Senator Charleston, of South Australia.* Wouldn't it be curious, asked the reporter, *to find a brother and sister both in the Senate?* Clearly, less than a month before election day, Nellie had still not completely made up her mind whether to run. As Nellie, like Vida, would run as an independent, her candidature would only serve to split the *Freetrade Senatorial vote.*[11] The press was informing readers that any attempt would be *ill-advised...she has not the slightest show of being elected.*

♆

But whether the fiscal question would be jeopardised by Nellie's candidacy was possibly the last thing on her mind that nervous November: she was involved in a legal and verbal stoush of epic proportions.

Earlier in the year, *a particularly nasty piece of scandal* did the rounds of Sydney's progressive circles. The story went like this: Nellie Martel had overheard a conversation between a fortune teller called Madame Sassoon and a policeman. They were talking about a woman incarcerated in Bathurst Gaol who was boasting— as Madame Sassoon had learnt from one of her clients, a female warder—that she would not serve her term because she knew a thing or two about Sir John See, the premier of New South Wales. He was, she said, *none too clean himself.* Afterwards, Nellie repeated the claim at a suffrage meeting, without Madame Sassoon's authority.

The story leaked, and for months the gossip swirled. *Someone holding a very high position* was in a very compromised position, an insinuation *comprehensive enough to leave every public man in the city under the shadow of a cloud.* With the facts of the case unknown, the scandal had *ever since been travelling around in secret corners, and through key-holes, and behind curtains, and leaving a large leaven of unwholesomeness in its trail.*[12] In August, matters came to a head and the premier let it be known that he intended to take out a writ of criminal libel against Mrs Martel.

Annie Golding, the secretary of the Women's Progressive Association, waited upon Sir John and *induced him not to take action.* In return, he convinced her to read a private detective's report into the minutes of the next WPA meeting. It's unclear exactly what the contents of the report revealed, but the reading was duly done. At this point an anti-Catholic Sydney newspaper called the WATCHMAN entered the fray. Outraged by the public reading of the detective's report, which it called a *budget of obscene literature,* it cast aspersions on Golding and Martel's ability to run the organisation along proper lines of accountability, and accused them of making false statements in the minute books. Annie Golding promptly announced her intention of suing the WATCHMAN for libel, claiming £1000 in damages. While waiting for his day in court, the newspaper's editor, William Dill Mackay, accused the WPA of internal *squabbling* and reckless *scandal-mongering*.[13] He denounced the Golding sisters as *the hidden hand of Rome* and called the WPA an outfit *so quiet, dark and dirty that it gropes in the moral sewer for subsistence*.[14]

Nellie, who was embroiled in the scandal up to her bejewelled neck, watched impatiently as the libel case against the WATCHMAN was postponed through adjournment after adjournment. By late November the court date had still not been set. Nellie had still not published her election manifesto. And the WATCHMAN was still sniping at the presumed papists that ran the WPA.

After weeks of accusations that she was a Catholic, Nellie decided enough was enough and wrote a fiery letter to, of all places, the WATCHMAN. It published the letter in full, perhaps hoping to give the loquacious 'lady candidate' enough rope while indulging in some sidelong Catholic-bashing.

I may state first most emphatically that I have never been anything but a Protestant, Nellie began. To suggest that she was anything but was *a most malicious move on the part of my enemies, the Roman Catholics*. What could be the result of this *plot*? Why, to turn her Protestant brothers and sisters against her. And why would the Micks want to do that? Obviously, because *I have fearlessly advocated the inspection of industrial homes ruled by them, and the inspection of convents*. She had pursued *this unpopular path* because *my sole desire is to see the condition of the women and children of the fair land made better and freer. And because they know I am strong on the side of freedom, liberty and truth, their motto is to 'crush her'*.[15]

The WATCHMAN was so far the only outlet on the public record to reveal the 'hidden hand of Rome' pulling Nellie's strings, but this illogic seemed not to concern her.

*

Despite all this, Nellie eventually did announce her Senate candidacy, and it was good old-fashioned competitiveness that pushed her over the line. Two more women announced their intention to stand as independents for federal election to New South Wales seats—author Mrs Mary Moore-Bentley in the Senate, and twenty-four-year-old Miss Selina Anderson in the House of Representatives—and Nellie finally got her skates on.

True to form, she was immediately embroiled in controversy. Nellie turned up at an election rally in Balmain for Selina Anderson. Though nervous, the young woman had made a fair fist of her first public speech but then Nellie, seemingly unable to allow the younger woman her moment in the limelight, literally upstaged her. As Anderson herself informed the DAILY TELEGRAPH the next day:

> The facts, briefly, are that Mrs Martel took the liberty of ascending to the platform unasked, and announcing to the audience her own candidature for the Senate regardless of the fact that she, though a freetrade candidate, was using a protectionist-labor advocate's platform for the purpose.[16]

Unaware or heedless of her misjudgment, Nellie *boasted of her thirteen years' experience* as an advocate for the cause of womanhood suffrage. She also took the opportunity to tell the audience that she was *a perfectly proper pure Protestant.*[17]

Poor Miss Anderson was indignant, noted the TRUTH, always happy to have a women's rights advocate to mock. But it was true. Here Selena Anderson had paid for the hall to deliver a Protectionist speech, but found herself having to accommodate a Free Trader because she was a fellow suffragist. *One would naturally expect,* sniffed Selina, *that those thirteen years would have taught Mrs Martel something of the etiquette that should prevail at a public meeting.* The BALMAIN OBSERVER was cheered to note that its suburb had been blessed by the local appearance of *two aspirants for political honours.* And that *a good deal of mirth has been created at their expense.*[18]

Unlike Vida, who made friends and converts wherever she went, Nellie had now managed to alienate the old guard of Rose Scott's circle and insult the young Turks of Selina Anderson's stable—not to mention being at loggerheads, somehow, with both Catholics and anti-Catholics. There was no doubt about Nellie. As the TRUTH proclaimed, she was *extremely well provided with nerve.*

⚲

A week after the Balmain debacle, Nellie formally declared her election manifesto at her own meeting in Newcastle. In front of two hundred electors, half of whom were women, Nellie spoke from a balcony in the hall, like Juliet. (Just two months earlier she had played Desdemona, *with a hint at maidenly tenderness, rising in a crescendo of rapture.*[19]) Nellie began by noting *she loved politics.* She countered the argument that parliament was not a fit place for women. *If such were true*, she said, *women should be sent there to purify it, and it certainly required cleansing.* She openly denounced certain members of the state parliament, and the whole of the Labor Party which, she argued, *with their boasted legislation for the masses, had not benefitted women.* Wages for domestic servants had actually gone down since she'd been in this country. When a member of the audience cried out to ask whether she was running for state parliament, she shifted to federal matters.

She was opposed to preferential trade and government bonuses to industry. The land should be unlocked for the people. Women should be paid an equal wage with men (and then more men would be employed and their wives could stay at home). She advocated the teaching of two languages in schools, in addition to English. She wanted water conservation and free ports. She wanted to see good laws made for women by women. Women had suffered long enough through laws passed when *half the members were present, and the other half were intoxicated.* Nellie spoke for over an hour and was well received.[20] THE DAWN published a letter from 'Elector' endorsing Nellie's candidacy. *She is a healthy little woman*, wrote the elector, *and her principles are sound. She should have the support of all having the welfare of women at heart.*[21]

The following day, whether by scurrilous design or rotten luck, the Watchman v Golding libel case finally went to court. The plaintiff, Annie Golding, was asked about Mrs Martel's political position on the tariff. Though it bore no direct relation to the case, it went to her possible motivation for ruining the reputations of certain public men. As to the obscene literature, did Mrs Martel try to stop the reading when they came to *some hot and strong part*? No, she did not. But neither, it turned out in a sensational twist, did Golding: *[I] wanted the report read in order that they could call upon Mrs Martel to resign as president.* Golding admitted that she and her sister wanted Martel out to clear the name of the WPA *which rested under the imputation of spreading the scandal.* Golding let on that since the scandal, prominent men had ceased to give lectures for the WPA. As the case continued, and more witnesses were called, the details became grubbier. TRUTH finally revealed the dirt the woman in prison had on Sir John See, the accusations that lay at the heart of Nellie's slander: the woman now *languishing in gaol* had been *procuring young girls for him...shy young girls.* TRUTH had a field day with the case, just the sort of combination of low gossip and high politics it lived for.

The tables were turning fast on the woman who just that week had promised to purify the parliament if elected. *From what can be gleaned*, jibed TRUTH,

> it would appear that MRS MARTEL IS AN 'ADVENTURESS' at present, posing as a teacher of elocution, but is described as a 'charlatan' in the profession and as being a formidable orator very much given to defamatory loquacity. Her husband is an invalid at present at a private hospital at Newtown, and it is said has willed some house and land property at Randwick over to his wife.[22]

There was enough contained in that character sketch to hang, draw and quarter Nellie. She was a vindictive poser and liar, living off the assets of a sick husband whom she didn't even care for at home, and might possibly dispose of to secure her inheritance. The term *adventuress*, while not a direct euphemism for prostitute, carried connotations of advancement through immoral means. For good measure, TRUTH republished the cartoon portrait of Nellie looking like a spiteful bulldog. And there was one final piece of evidence to damn Nellie for all eternity: a witness *said that she was a Roman Catholic*. If the editor of the WATCHMAN was the defendant in Golding's libel action, you wouldn't have known it from the nation-wide news reports. Nellie Martel was the only villain in the piece.

On 8 December, eight days before the federal election, the Supreme Court judge delivered the verdict. The jury found for the plaintiff. Annie Golding was awarded £50 damages. In his summing up, the judge noted that Miss Golding had been humiliated by Mrs Martel.

The jury said it was *perfectly satisfied with Sir John See's inno-cence*. It was not the premier who was on trial.

15

The Greatest Day
That Ever Dawned

Australia, 16 December 1903

> The sun rose on the morning of the sixteenth upon the greatest day that ever dawned for women in Australia.[1]

So wrote Louisa Lawson on 1 January 1904, three years to the day after Australia became a nation and two weeks since the first election in which all white adult Australians could vote. Though the primary votes of the three parties were almost equally divided, the newly expanded citizenry of the Commonwealth had returned the incumbent Protectionist Party. The Protectionists, led by Alfred Deakin after Barton's resignation to join the recently constituted High Court of Australia, were able to form government with the support of the Labor Party, led by Chris Watson. George Reid's Free Trade Party remained in opposition. The Protectionists had lost five seats in the House, while Labor had picked up seven. Frederick Holder retained his seat as an independent.

For Louisa Lawson there were two reasons to celebrate the recent elections, despite the fact that she had not voted for any of the candidates representing the three major parties. First, the female voter was able to enjoy the sheer *pleasure of exercising the just privilege so long denied her.* And second, for someone who was better known as the mother of a famous poet than the political pioneer she was, the Australian woman had the *blessed satisfaction of being seen as she is—not through the glasses of those interested in her suppression.*

Press, public and parliament alike had to admit that the great experiment had been a success. Female electors had come out in great numbers. There had been no discord at polling booths, and no more than usual in homes. Women had voted in about the same numbers (proportionately) as men, which was *not as exhilarating as it sounds*, Vida Goldstein had to admit, given there had been a small voter turnout:[2] 1.7 million voters had registered on the rolls, and only nine hundred thousand went to the polls.

To the relief of many men, despite *the great scale of the women's vote* (including those seven thousand extra votes in Victoria), female electors had not been *moved by some great impulse* to cast their ballot in a block and hence *sweep the polls*.[3] Women had largely voted along class lines, not gender lines. It was widely acknowledged that the women's vote had increased the Labor vote, setting up either heady anticipation of the coming domination of the 'working man and voting woman'—or profound fear, depending on one's political persuasion.[4]

Vida *personally observed* that there was an increase in political sentiment among *so-called labour ranks*. That is, women who earned their own living and women in country areas were far more likely to actually vote compared to the city toffs who were *notoriously ignorant*. The monied women of Melbourne, noted Vida, were too preoccupied with *social matters* to even bother to enrol. She deplored political apathy in anybody, but reserved her particular contempt for lazy, entitled (enfranchised) women.

Though women hadn't voted en masse—*no cataclysm, no sudden revolution*, as one observer put it[5]—their presence as electors had changed political culture irrevocably. Male candidates had now to address women at their campaign meetings. Alfred Deakin, in his opening policy speech in Ballarat, frankly acknowledged that women were part of the federal electorate, about to *cast their virgin vote*. He added 'women' to his standard salutation: 'Men of Australia'.[6]

Others observed that not only was the language of citizenship more superficially inclusive, but some politicians had also needed to quickly change their policy stripes. *It was amusing to observe how some candidates who had fought against women's suffrage with all their might*, noted Lady Julia Holder, *tried to show their supreme regard and esteem for the voters whose rights they had previously refused.*[7] Edmund Barton wasn't the only politician to do a sharp U-turn in his campaigning, if not his fundamental thinking.

It was not only Australian election watchers who took stock of the situation. The results of the federal poll were reported around the world, and the lessons analysed and debated. Ida Husted Harper, reporting for the WASHINGTON POST, noted that what Australia had just witnessed was *the most important event in the history of the world movement towards women's suffrage.*[8]

Tom Mann, with whom Vida had been accused of being in secret cahoots, reported the result for an English readership. *Women were quite as keen to exercise their votes as the men*, he wrote, aware that one of the most persistent arguments against women's suffrage in Britain was that the majority of women did not want the vote. What's more, the monotony of many a political meeting had been relieved by women, *or men on their behalf*, reminding candidates of their previous position on women's suffrage then *watching them wriggle.*[9] Mann was categorical in his conclusion: *fate has decreed that these Australian States shall be the forerunners in a really triumphant democracy.* The outcome of the election had demonstrated that this democracy would not be on the lines set forth by Mr Andrew Carnegie, the exploitative American industrialist, but along lines that would raise the standard of living of workers. He predicted that Australia would soon be enjoying a collectivist regime, with the common ownership of raw materials. (Mann expected the first nationalised industry to be tobacco, followed by iron and steel manufacturing.[10])

There was another keen observer of the Australian experiment in England. From her home in Sussex, Dora Montefiore penned an essay on 'Women Voters in Australia' which she published less than two weeks after the election in the journal NEW AGE. *Once again,* she began,

> have our Australian sisters vindicated through their vote the opinion [that] if you educate and enfranchise women, and give them equality of opportunity with men, you will be making giant strides towards progress in its best and most evolutionary form.[11]

The real victor at the 1903 election, Dora wrote, was the labour movement—and the labour victory was *attributed largely to the women voters.* This was a valuable lesson to the socialists in England who remained indifferent when successive Conservative governments failed to recognise women's rights. Could the British Labour Party now fail to see the *expediency (not to say justice)* of enfranchising women? She was sick of *the ill-conceived hostility of the men-comrades in their organisations* and hoped they would finally see reason. Dora noted too the *great amusement* caused by watching former opponents of the cause *now taxing their brains as to how to secure the votes of women.* All up, she was most heartened by the actions of all female voters, no matter which party they voted for: *their independence was shown and the right to do exactly as they pleased was freely claimed and acted upon.*[12]

If the election results directly affected Australian voters, they also had a profound influence on global wannabe voters. In Britain prior to 1903, opined English author Brougham Villiers, the case for women's suffrage had been confined to *obscure corners* of journals and drawing rooms. Now *the question of women's emancipation has suddenly become the most insistent political problem of the day.* Even tariff reform and labour politics were less discussed in the press.[13] The Australian experiment had proved that *the denial of citizen rights to women is more than a mistake in detail; it is a blasphemy against the spirit of democracy.*[14]

*

But there was one step that had not been taken in this *forward march of humanity*, as Villiers termed it. For all their independence and freedom, Australians had not elected a woman to parliament. Of specific concern to the feminists, Australian women had not voted for one of their own sex.

Nellie Martel had barely got a look in. She gained just over 18,500 votes, coming eleventh of the twelve candidates. Mary Moore-Bentley, who was a complete unknown compared to Nellie, polled four hundred more votes, possibly because she drew the number one spot on the ballot paper. Either of them would have needed ten times these numbers to win a seat. Supported by trade unionists, Selina Anderson polled almost eighteen per cent of the vote for her House of Representatives electorate, enough to save her £25 deposit.

Louisa Lawson took a dim view of these results. *Woman has allowed her birth right of freedom to be wrested from her*, she declared of female electors' refusal to support the female candidates. She had *hushed her voice—which ought to have resounded through the earth*. Louisa was particularly indignant about the treatment of Nellie. *We supported her*, she noted, but *Mrs Martel suffered much misrepresentation from an action in which her enemies for interested reasons unduly involved her*.[15] The uncomfortable truth was that some of those enemies were former friends. It's not known who Annie and Belle Golding voted for.

Vida Goldstein was characteristically upbeat and dignified, despite her election loss. She considered the 51,497 votes she had received *a veritable triumph*.

> I polled magnificently in spite of all the odds against me...I stood for the sake of a cause, the cause of women and children. I stood as a protest against the dictation of the Press and against the creation of the ticket system of voting.

This latter goal, she conceded, was an *unpopular crusade*. Her chief aim in running had been *educational*, she claimed, and that objective had been roundly successful. Some women remained non-party aligned, as she advocated, others *broke away* and acted as organisers for women's branches of political parties. She didn't recommend this strategy if the elevation of the status of women and children was the ultimate goal of political activism, but she had to concede their right to follow it. Indeed, the *chief lesson* of the election was the *necessity of organisation*. The Labor Party had been the best organised, and the most effective at mobilising the women's vote. Though she would never think to stand as a Labor candidate, abhorring the party machine, she believed that the labour cause deserved as much support as the women's cause because the two were closely aligned. Both, in the widest sense, were the *cause of humanity*. Labour represented the material wing of this dove; woman the spiritual. Both looked to change the social order forever.

Ultimately Vida was proud of her achievement and not shy to trumpet her self-defined victory. The press had predicted the *humiliating insults* that would be hurled at her. But she had found nothing but courteous and warm support wherever she went. The press had predicted her physical breakdown but she *stood up to the campaign trail* better than most men. After a month on the hustings, others' voices were *tattered and torn*. But *mine was fresh and clear the night before the battle as it was when I started skirmishing three months previously*. And she knew she had changed minds: about women in parliament, about the social and industrial injustices faced by women, about sex prejudice in general. Her conclusion: Veni, Vidi, Vida. *They came, they saw, I conquered.*[16]

Even Nellie Martel, who'd had three weeks, not three months, to marshal voters and who had been subjected to far worse than humiliating insults, was, in due course, confident that the direction of women's emancipation had been set and there was no turning back.

> It is coming like the mighty roar of the ocean, this great voice of the People...our movement is on the *crest* of that great wave and *no* power can stop it!

PART 2

COURAGE

The cause which does not advance
cannot remain stationary, but slips back
into the limbo of forgotten things.

SYLVIA PANKHURST

*The Suffragette: A History of the Women's
Militant Suffrage Movement*, 1912

16

The Fateful 12th May

London, spring 1905

At 12 p.m. on Friday 12 May, 1905, the afternoon session of the Imperial Parliament at Westminster was about to begin when it was noticed that there were not enough members in the House of Commons to commence public business. No one could blame the weather for the members' sudden truancy. It was neither unseasonably hot nor unbearably cold; rather a mild spring day in London. Light north wind; 61 degrees Fahrenheit. Cloudy in the morning clearing to *bright sunshine*. But inside the House, there were two bills on the agenda for debate before today's 5.30 p.m. adjournment and *not forty members present*. After a further seven minutes, *a scouring of the House brought in thirty-nine* more members, whereby the deputy speaker counted himself as one and *business proceeded.*[1] Mr Bignell moved the second reading of the Vehicles Lights Bill.

Three hundred women had gathered in the Strangers' Lobby outside the Commons that day and, for them, the flagrant no-show was a most dispiriting sign. Many of them were from the Women's Co-operative Guild: working women who had sacrificed a day's pay and courted retribution to be here. A fortunate few had received a ticket to watch proceedings from the Ladies Gallery and would at least have a seat, if not a clear view of the wearisome proceedings.

Many of these women had, over the years, spent *night after night* behind the metal mesh bars that enclosed the high, narrow windows of the gallery so that they could see into the Commons but not be seen. Most of the time they came to listen to debates of legislation like the Contagious Diseases Act, which, as Dora Montefiore now reflected from her seat in the gallery with Emmeline Pankhurst, *raised questions that concerned their sex as much, if not more, than they did that of the men who were discussing them.*[2]

The Vehicles Lights Bill was not in that category. It was a ruse to delay debate on a bill that concerned women more than any other: the third reading of the Women's Enfranchisement Bill.

It would be the eighteenth time in thirty-seven years that a private member's bill had been presented to parliament for the enfranchisement of women. For much of the previous twenty years, the United Kingdom had been governed by a coalition of the Conservative and Unionist parties. This women's suffrage bill was the first to be read in eight long years.[3] Since 1902, the Tories had been led by Prime Minister Arthur Balfour, whose government held a massive majority. It fell to Liberal Party men like Bamford Slack, a brickmaker's son and Methodist lay preacher who had been elected to the House only the previous year, to introduce bills for women's suffrage. Slack's sister, Agnes, was a high-profile temperance activist, the British secretary for the World Woman's Christian Temperance Union. Agnes believed in political equality for women. Slack believed in supporting his sister and, by extension, her 'sisters' in the movement. The suffragists themselves had long maintained as an article of faith that *men and women will advance with equal steps towards their common destiny.*[4] The conviction was pragmatic as much as pious. Only men had the vote, and only men were MPs, therefore only men could change the laws.

Each parliamentary session the suffragists lobbied potential allies to convince one who had been successful in the ballot for a private member's bill to devote that place to women's suffrage. In February this year, Bamford Slack had won a ballot place and the tiny white-haired suffrage pioneer Elizabeth Wolstenholme Elmy had persuaded him to give his place to the suffrage bill.[5] The bill was duly drafted by Keir Hardie, the Independent Labour Party member, and approved by Emmeline Pankhurst's Women's Social and Political Union.

Could the time now be ripe for a victory? In 1897, when the last bill went up, Christabel Pankhurst was aged seventeen. Now she had a law degree, if not the legal capacity to be admitted to the bar. Last time, Australia was not even a nation, much less a nation where universal adult suffrage was a cornerstone of the constitution. New Zealand's women had been voting for over a decade by 1905. Surely times had changed.

Over and over again, the suffragists had mounted the stairs to the gallery with high hopes, only to slump back down again having watched their bill crushed by ridicule, contempt and parliamentary game-playing. One of the favourite tricks of the government was to refuse to give the bill 'facilities'—that is, a slot in the session in which it could be debated. Sometimes facilities would be granted, but other business left no time in the parliamentary session to get to the suffrage bill. Or the bill might be 'talked out'—filibustering, the Americans called it—in which case opponents would stretch out debate for so long that there was no time left to call for a division.

On seventeen previous occasions, such obstructionist tactics had prevented British women from receiving their rights, or even getting their arguments across. Last year, however, on the second reading of Slack's bill, a division had been taken—and *carried by a large majority*.[6] To avoid going to a division was the object of the opponents who had bothered to turn up today.

Which was why the men were now droning on about how, in some English counties, every moving vehicle needed to carry a light, while in other counties *a slow moving cart, or a cart standing by the roadside, need not carry a light at all*. Did Mr Bigwell intend to extend his bill to sheep? What of bicycles? Parents were afraid to let their children on the street...The Tory MP Mr Labouchere rose to say he *supposed he would be accused of talking on this bill in order to keep off* the Women's Enfranchisement Bill, but *totally dissociated himself from this charge, although he had strong views, both on the ladies and the lights.* On it went, member after member. For four hours. A division was called; the Vehicles Lights Bill was narrowly defeated.

It was 4 p.m. by the time Bamford Slack was called to introduce his bill. In doing so, *he regretted the extraordinary abuse of the House which had been indulged in.* But he would waste no further time. His bill was a modest one. It proposed *no new-fangled franchise.* It merely called for an extension of the existing franchise of this country to women. *It would give a vote to every woman,* he explained, *who under the present register would have had one if she had been a man.* He proposed nothing so outlandish as adult suffrage, which, of course, was not yet available to British men, let alone women. His bill was *simple, fair and workable.*[7] The enfranchisement of women was *a necessary factor in our modern social progress.*[8] It was *unconstitutional, inexpedient, mischievous and unjust* to continue to deny women the British liberty for which the parliament surely stood.[9]

The motion was seconded by Sir J. Rolleston. Then Mr Labouchere stood. He had voted for women's suffrage when John Stuart Mill raised the issue thirty-seven years ago, he began, and regretted it ever since. With every passing year he had realised how constitutionally unfit women were for political rights. *After all,* he reasoned, *there was a difference between men and women, physically and intellectually. (Laughter).* She could not be a soldier. She could not be a policeman. Women had *little sense of proportion.* And when you try to argue with them, well, *everybody knows.* As the STANDARD reported, this he said *shrugging his shoulders, and sending members into a whirl of laughter.*[10]

> Let them think what would happen if they turned this Parliament into a promiscuity of the sexes. It would not be safe…the intelligent Ulysses closed his ears not to hear the song of the sirens…I am an old man, but even I refuse to see ladies who come to the lobbies of the House of Commons to cajole members to vote for

Female Suffrage, for fear I would succumb. (Laughter)
But there are younger members than myself…there will
be political flirtations in the lobby.

On went the pantomime, with Mr Labouchere *entertaining the
House* while some of the women stood at *the little peep hole by the side
of the folding doors whence in turn they could watch Mr Labouchere, with
tongue almost obviously in his cheek.*[11]

Just before half past five, a *blushing* Bamford Slack moved to
extend the session so as to take a division. The deputy speaker denied
the motion and allowed the bill to be talked out. Mr Slack *stalked the
floor, an outraged man.* The House adjourned at 5.35.

⚓

With Slack prowling like an angry tiger, the women in the gallery
were more akin to a tribe of irate monkeys. They were offended,
humiliated and indignant. They had seen it all before—Labouchere's
worn-out platitudes had been refuted over and over—but there was
no doubt that this government was getting worse. More retrograde,
more reactionary. Why did women have to prove themselves worthy
of the franchise when men like Labouchere were so patently unworthy
of running the affairs of the nation?[12] And how could the Imperial
Parliament be so conducted as to devote four hours to such a slight
proposal as the Vehicles Lights Bill?[13] Yesterday at least the order
of the day had been a matter of importance: imperial defence. But
whether a cart needed to carry a light on a dark night on a country
road…?

These shenanigans—the talking out, the keepings off, Mr
Labouchere's *feeble jibes* and *obscurantist prejudice*—would get a fair
run in the London papers. But what happened next went unreported.
One woman saw the fury and disgust on the faces of those leaping
down from the Ladies Gallery and, knowing there were hundreds
more waiting in the Strangers' Lobby to hear the fate of the bill, she

decided that something must be done.

Let us protest, the woman determined. She proposed an impromptu demonstration and led the infuriated suffragists outside to the statue of Richard Coeur de Lion. The police moved them on. A sympathetic Commons clerk led them to the 'Sanctuary', along Parliament Square. And there, under the woman's guidance, they drafted a declaration of no confidence in the government.

> Your petitioners view with indignation and alarm the exacting procedure of the House of Commons, which reduces legislation to a mere game of chance, and permits the repeated and insulting postponement of the first claims of women to citizenship.
>
> Your petitioners therefore humbly pray that your honourable House will so reform your procedure as to secure in future fair consideration of public questions with some regard to their relative importance.

The woman was requested to read it, *which I did*, and it was carried unanimously. Elizabeth Wolstenholme Elmy signed the declaration and pledged to give it to Keir Hardie, who was her contemporary and friend. He would table it in the Commons the next day. Satisfied, the group *retired to the tea room and wrote other resolutions, and they have been broadcast over the land*. The woman later wrote to her friend in Australia:

> It would have done your heart good to have seen the old workers, the wronged workers, the independent and the dependent workers, the strong and the weak, the learned and the less advanced, all joining together, irrespective of position, asking for justice for their sex...The women are not cold when wronged in England any more than in Australia.

And she signed off her letter to her old mate Louisa Lawson: *With hope for our future work in Sydney...NELLIE A. MARTEL.*[14]

⚓

The aftermath of Nellie's election loss had been grim. Where respect for Vida Goldstein's intelligence and integrity was elevated by her campaign and result, Nellie's reputation copped a beating. Not only did she forfeit her £25 deposit, but she lost the high moral ground of sex superiority. *Who is THIS MARTEL WOMAN who prates about personal purity in politics?* asked the TRUTH a few months after the election, when Nellie tried to engage in a heated public debate about the falling birth numbers in New South Wales.

> Is she herself such a model of marital and maternal propriety and perfection that she should pose as a paragon prophetess on personal and political purity?
>
> ...The irresponsible wagging of the tongue of this Martel woman as to the personal 'purity' of one of our most highly esteemed public men led to an action for libel very properly taken against the wild, wanton 'Watchdog' by Miss Annie Golding, a highly competent school-teacher.[15]

The Australian press was playing favourites, and Nellie was decidedly not the flavour of the month. She threatened to launch a libel action of her own, but did not follow through. Instead, she wrote letters to the editor trying to express her opinion (including that Australian women were *remarkable amongst the women of the world for practising prevention and abortion* to limit their family size16) only to be slapped down in counter-letters. She continued to work as president of the Women's Liberal and Reform Association and the press continued to parody her. One journal reported Nellie addressing a meeting of working-class women and *punctuating her political promises and premises with a glittering forefinger the diamonds on which would have meant warmth and nourishment...for many months.*[17]

By midwinter 1904, Nellie had found a reason to retreat from the front line. *Mrs Nellie Martel has left Australia,* announced TRUTH on 21 August, *my informant says she has taken her husband, who is a very aged man, to his people in England. The exact date of Mrs Martel's return is not known.*[18]

Like much of what TRUTH passed off as news, only parts of the story were true. Charles, who was fifty-six, had left for England in February that year, six months before his forty-nine-year-old wife. The exact date of Nellie's return was unclear, but she happily told anyone who asked that she planned to return next summer to continue her suffrage work in Sydney.

Nellie travelled to London via South Africa, where the NATAL MERCURY published an extensive interview with *the inveterate and ruthless talker*, details of which were freely published in newspapers across Australia.[19] The Sydney EVENING NEWS feared that *this feminine bearer of evil tidings will repeat her story of misfortune, losing nothing by repetition as she pursues her wordy way.*[20]

Nellie's reputation as a crank and a whinger was not entirely misplaced. In her NATAL MERCURY interview, she criticised Australia for the political chaos that reigned, though she claimed the bedlam had nothing to do with female voters. Instead, *the labour party are really at the root of the whole matter.* Nellie was an enigma: a *lady agitator abroad* who decried the *socialistic laws* that, for many, were part of the progressive spirit that had ushered in womanhood suffrage. Contradicting the message that Vida Goldstein was sending to the world, Nellie was adamant that *the women of Australia are not supporters of the labor party.*[21] The Australian press had its answer to this puzzle: *No sensible person ever took Mrs Martel seriously.*[22]

If the Australian press continued to make Nellie a pariah, in South Africa she found a new audience. In 1904, South Africa had just seen its first organised women's suffrage association, but there were many women advocating women's rights, even during the Boer War. One of the most vocal of these, English South African Olive Schreiner, in fact linked the two causes. *Many a one [woman] had taken her place in the trenches during the late war*, argued Schreiner, proving their fitness for citizenship.[23] Schreiner was not only pro-Boer, but a republican who argued for a federation of the South African colonies along Australian lines. Many South African suffragists believed that, following the Australian precedent, if women *helped bring about federation they should be given the suffrage*. Australian women's agency in nation-building had been observed from afar, and now Nellie was on hand to offer her advice and experience. Far from rushing to be with her husband and his people, Nellie stayed in South Africa for three months.

She arrived in London in November 1904, just as Emmeline Pankhurst was considering starting up a London branch of her Women's Social and Political Union. The WSPU had been founded in the Pankhursts' home in Manchester in late 1903 by a small group of women who were aligned to the Independent Labour Party. The WSPU was a half-loaf organisation: resigned to the property quali-fication, never aiming to achieve the franchise for all women. If at least some women had the vote, Pankhurst believed, then social reform could be achieved for all women. The initial strategy of the WSPU was to convince the ILP to include women's suffrage in its party platform, just as Mary Lee had convinced South Australian Labor over ten years earlier.

Though the Manchester-based WSPU had some success in raising the profile of the cause, Nellie couldn't help but notice on her arrival that its membership was small: only thirty people.[24] So far, convincing Bamford Slack to devote his ballot place to a women's suffrage bill was Emmeline Pankhurst's greatest political achievement.

Dora Montefiore had also become attached to Emmeline's small retinue, despite the differences in their view of the franchise. Dora was a voracious whole-loafer, but you had to admit that Emmeline Pankhurst had something Mrs Fawcett, her rival at the NUWSS, lacked: *gentleness and charm*, as her daughter Sylvia noted, *but also steel strength in her determination to fight to the end*.[25] The glint in her eye was magnetic.

In London, Nellie lost no time in making her presence felt. By April, the Sydney SUNDAY SUN noted in its gossip column that *Mrs C. Martel, of Sydney, has been lecturing and addressing meetings in London.*[26] Dozens of them, by Nellie's reckoning, particularly the Women's Co-operative Guild. *The dresses, the fine linen, the pretty knick-knacks,* Nellie told them,

> all these little luxuries that make the home pretty, often have been made with the life-blood of our sisters. I am thankful that I have made my home under the Southern Cross [where] we give them the interest of the labour which made the wealth of the country.[27]

Nellie criticised the disgraceful poorhouses which were *a blot* on English society. *Such conditions as the people are living under here,* she argued, *can never happen in the country where women have the vote.*

The London press began tracking her, and on 3 April she was afforded an interview by the DAILY NEWS, one of London's most highly circulated papers. *How We Won the Vote: Australian Lesson to English Women* screamed the headline, followed by a lengthy interview that was circulated throughout Britain. Nellie had evidently learnt from her South African experience that pulling some of her punches, or at least redirecting them, might be in her long-term interests. Instead of criticising Australia, she decided to claim it as the feminist utopia the world clearly wanted it to be. *The Woman's Suffrage Bill is coming before your Parliament in a few weeks,* noted Nellie. *What surprises me—pains me, in fact—is to find here much division of opinion on the subject.* Did you expect to find all classes of women in agreement about the vote in England? asked the journalist.

> I expected to find at least something of the spirit that guided us in Australia. We fought for eleven years through one society alone—a society of which I was recording secretary before we won the vote in New South Wales.

Nellie's answer was equal parts sanctimonious and self-aggrandising. But she had found her groove, and she stuck with it.

> I am inclined to attribute the indifference of the Parliament [to womanhood suffrage] to the deplorable lack of agreement among Englishwomen on the subject. In Australia we were united as one in our agitation for the franchise. Conservatives and Liberals, Protestants and Catholics, Socialists and Labour people, or whatever else women called ourselves individually, made not the slightest difference to our movement for the vote… What on earth is the use of women belonging to this political party or that until they have a vote?[28]

Nellie admitted she was politically aligned as a Free Trader, but insisted that such battles as tariff reform could only be fought once the vote was secured. The same went for adult suffrage.

Let Englishwomen get the vote, Nellie concluded. *They will then cease to be simply voices crying in the wilderness.* Her advice was not a suggestion. It was a challenge.

⚓

Christabel Pankhurst would later write about the *fateful 12 May*, claiming that *Mother* called the protest meeting outside the House of Commons, ably supported in her defiant action by Elizabeth Wolstenholme Elmy, *the aged pioneer*, and Mrs Martel, *the woman voter from Australia*.[29]

But Emmeline herself—never one to hide her light under a bushel—didn't make herself the heroine of the story. She later called the events of 12 May 1905 *the first militant act of the WSPU* but claimed no personal credit.[30] Sylvia Pankhurst split the difference. In her account, when the police insisted that the women move from the Richard the Lionheart statue, Emmeline, with *tremulant voice and blazing eyes*, cried out *where could we meet then; where could poor women voice their indignation?* It was to Nellie that Emmeline looked for the answer. *Mrs Pankhurst called on Mrs Martel, as an Australian woman voter, to lead us and, joined by a single MP, Mr Keir Hardie, we marched with the police to Broad Sanctuary.*[31]

It was there they drafted the resolution that Nellie read to the crowd. It was also Nellie who brought the Women's Co-operative Guild workers, a fact not disclosed in her own account to Louisa Lawson. Sylvia wrote that the co-op women had been *brought thither by Nellie Alma Martel...in high spirits, believing that they were to witness a brilliant victory.*[32] That triumph was not to be. But it was significant that the potential passage of the first Woman's Suffrage Bill in eight years had attracted not only members of the various middle-class suffrage societies, including the WSPU, but working women as well. *This day began the fusion of classes*, stated Mrs Elmy, *for women [who] have left the wash-tub to come to the House walked hand in hand, side by side with fashionably dressed ladies.*[33]

It is Sylvia Pankhurst who gives Nellie the credit for first crossing class lines.

> Amongst the rest was a large contingent of women Co-operators, accompanied by Mrs Nellie Alma Martel, of Australia, who had helped to win votes for women there, and had afterwards run as a candidate for the Commonwealth Parliament, having polled more than 20,000 votes.[34]

A newcomer to the London suffrage scene, Nellie claimed an authority based on her prior experience, prominence and presumed success in the Australian movement. (In England, twenty thousand votes were *enough to return half a dozen men to the British House of Commons*, as Louisa Lawson pointed out.[35]) She had something new to offer, something that had already been road-tested, and when Christabel Pankhurst called her 'our Australian friend', it must have been nice for Nellie to know she had some.[36]

Up until now, the campaign strategy of the suffrage societies had been entirely 'constitutional': raising petitions, lobbying members, sending deputations, holding meetings, publishing and disseminating written propaganda. The approach had been a softly-softly one, suitably genteel and ladylike. Win the support of Liberal members. In turn, help them win their election campaigns. Educate the general public, and women themselves, in how to argue for female enfranchisement and refute the dire predictions of its antagonists. The suffragists had been trenchant, but not transgressive. Argumentative, but not agitators. They worked to raise consciousness, but never Cain.

But this compliance hadn't got the suffragists anywhere in close to forty years, had it? With *these militant tactics commenced on May 12, 1905, outside the House of Commons*, reckoned Nellie, *we have hit on a magnificent plan of campaign.*[37]

Women were *awake at last*, rejoiced Emmeline.

> They were prepared to do something that women had never done before—fight for themselves. Women had always fought for men and for their children. Now they were ready to fight for their own human rights.[38]

There was not only anger in the air that pleasant spring evening, but excitement too. Something had shifted, something was changing. It was as the editor of the women's page of the DAILY NEWS wrote that May: *everyone is trying just now...to live 'half a hundred different lives'...at a sort of motor-speed.*[39] And there were suddenly new drivers behind the wheel.

If Dora Montefiore—who had left the New South Wales Womanhood Suffrage League before Nellie joined but had kept a watching brief on antipodean affairs since her departure from Sydney over a decade ago—was suspicious of 'the Australian woman's' integrity or intent, she was smart enough to keep it to herself.

17

No More Peace

London, autumn 1905

By late 1905, the beleaguered Nellie Martel had been joined in England by another Australian renegade. This one, however, was not fleeing ignominy. Quite the opposite: Muriel Matters was at the top of her game.

Where the Adelaide press poured scorn on Nellie, despite her brother's status as a South Australian golden boy who had risen through the local political ranks to become a federal senator, Muriel was universally adored. On the eve of her departure for Europe on 22 July 1905, the Northam Advertiser sang the praises of the *gifted dramatic artiste*.[1] (The best the Adelaide Critic could do for Nellie was refer to her as someone who, though she *speaks well, provokes opposition which often takes a personal turn*.[2]) Two states wanted to claim Muriel: South Australia, where she was born and raised, and Western Australia, where Muriel's mother had moved, taking eight of her children, in 1903 after separating from John Matters.

The estrangement was a gift of sorts for twenty-six-year-old Muriel, whose relationship with her overbearing, rage-filled father was strained. She had pursued her acting career against his wishes.[3] The marital break gave her the opportunity to stay in Adelaide, alone, and nurture not only her flourishing business as an elocution teacher but also a budding romance with Bryceson Treharne, a fellow music student from her days at the Elder Conservatorium. Treharne was a difficult man and a divisive figure, whom the musical fraternity in Adelaide initially embraced but soon shunned when he proved himself to be a snob and a prat. Though she had *always been a democrat*, Muriel might have forgiven Treharne's elitist views about music. But she simply couldn't abide his reactionary stance on one of her core beliefs: women's equality. Treharne considered women inferior in most regards, including their musical abilities, and alarm bells went off for the little woman with big dreams. She was mindful of her favourite literary anti-hero, Ibsen's Nora, married to a bully and trapped in a domestic cage which she herself had locked. Muriel had first read A DOLL'S HOUSE at fourteen and it made a lasting impression on her. *I shall never forget my joy in finding that the sentiments I had always vaguely but keenly felt had been put into words, forcible, majestic, dignified.*[4]

Muriel decided to trail her family west.

But despite rave reviews and an ever-expanding repertoire, she was restless. Her favourite brother, Leonard, had gone to serve with the South Australian Imperial Bushmen Contingent in South Africa, sparking his lifelong taste for travel and adventure. Muriel too had a wanderlust. After just over a year treading the boards in Perth, she decided to throw caution to the wind and sail to London. There she could spread her wings and try her luck on her own terms. In Australia, her fortunes had been tied to the dictates or fancies of a series of men: her father, Robert Brough, George Rignold, Treharne. Why not ride the wave of expectation that the New Woman, and the 'Australian girl' in particular, could move mountains?

By 1905, when Muriel was ready to take flight, the Australian girl represented modernity and independence, qualities aligned with the new nation.[5] Australian girls enjoyed a cultural free pass not yet accorded European women, signifying and embodying a young democracy, unburdened and unbound by old world traditions. If Stella Miles Franklin could write about Sybylla's brilliant career, Muriel could live it:[6] life mimicking art mimicking life. Making the nation had been a deliberate act of political production that intimately involved women. Making an Australian national identity was just as active a process, and women were similarly conscious of their role as producers of a character type. Muriel was tired of playing the deuteragonist, albeit a feisty one. It was time to be the heroine of her own story.

Muriel arrived in London in October 1905, just five months after Nellie had led the longstanding, but somnolent, English suffrage movement into its first public demonstration. She was met at the docks by an old pal from Australia, baritone Frank Robertson. Like Robertson, she soon discovered that what passed for a big fish in Adelaide or Perth was but tasty krill in London. There was a whole school of failed Australian actors living together in cold and cramped boarding houses in London's outer suburbs.

Fortunately for Muriel, she didn't have to join them. She had arrived with letters of introduction from British actors whom she'd met touring in Australia, including *a push on* to George Bernard Shaw. She even had lodgings with one such couple in their *charming flat* in Russell Square, at the heart of the metropolitan action.[7]

What was the key to Muriel's good fortune? Her winning personality? Her niche talent as an elocutionist? Or sheer good luck?[8] Muriel had been advised that even with her many gifts, it might pay to disguise her identity as an Australian if she wished to be successful. *The Australian must not expect any of the sentiment which he himself feels for England to be felt by the Englishman for Australia*, warned a journalist friend from Perth. It was not that the English disliked their colonial cousins, but that the Australian performer could not *expect to go such a long distance and secure a preference [when]...we have hundreds of our own people.*[9]

Muriel needn't have worried. Within a month of her arrival— and without having to modify the *lazy vowels* that *speak of kyke for cake*—she had a stage engagement in the West End and press plaudits began to roll in.[10] She'd signed up with a theatrical agent and was receiving a variety of *tempting offers*, including a tour of the

Netherlands. For ready cash, she appeared at recitals and 'at homes', gave lectures on literary topics and tutored Shakespearean actors on the finer points of enunciation and projection. She was even *indulging in journalist work*, interviewing Prince Kropotkin, the exiled Russian socialist, and other *interesting personalities*.[11] Muriel was on her way. Not yet Melba, but not squashed into a miserable sardine can with a sorry lot of other Australian hopefuls either.

By the new year, Muriel was appearing on the society pages in two hemispheres. She'd lined up an engagement at the Royal Court Theatre through a management company, *which produces chiefly plays by Ibsen and Bernard Shaw. With such a future*, predicted the ADELAIDE CRITIC on 24 January 1906, *it is not surprising that Miss Matters has no present intention of returning to Australia.*[12]

⚓

Middling success—neither supernova nor space debris—glittered brightly enough on the outside. But it was not long before Muriel realised that the core of the metropole was red hot, molten bullshit. She described the problem in more discreet terms: *an antagonistic social environment*. Everything in England *conspired* to drag one down: the cold, damp mist and fog of November; the extremes of wealth and *bitter black poverty*; the rows of *squalid awful lodging houses;* and the endless beggars that *tugged at one's heart strings* on every street corner. All who have *eyes that see and hearts that feel* cannot but be affected, wrote Muriel. At the heart of the rot was hoary old English conservatism, especially easy to perceive for one *coming from a younger country, where the tides of life run high and pulses beat more strenuously*. Where Australians were risk-takers, prepared to gamble on a brighter future, the English lacked the capacity for optimism.

> Into the very bones and marrow of this sea-girt people
> has entered that insularity which although the cause of

so much that is admirable, breeds likewise the sincere
belief that what is, must continue ever to be.[13]

As an *onlooker* to the pain and suffering of others, Muriel
felt her democratic temper arc. But it did not flare and force her to
become a *combatant* until she witnessed first-hand the exploitation
and degradation of other actresses working in London's theatres,
where theatre agents were unregistered and therefore had licence
to operate on the dark side of decency street. Many such agents,
she quickly realised, were *decoying young English girls* to Europe.[14]
Once marooned in these foreign ports and cities, the aspiring
actresses soon became 'actresses', their bodies, souls and reputations
in tatters.

Around the time Muriel realised the fate that could befall girls
with less luck, charm or skill than her, a fateful and suitably dramatic
encounter changed her life. Performing for Prince Kropotkin one
night, Muriel looked into the revolutionary's deep, searching eyes and
saw her future. *To what end? To what end?* she saw Kropotkin silently
implore her. *A personal career. A name in the world of art!* Suddenly, in
this moment of dramatic transference, it was not enough to entertain
an audience. She must use her talents to move them, to mobilise
them.

As Vida Goldstein had consciously eschewed marriage and a
family to work for the betterment of all women and children, so
Muriel realised that individual success was nothing compared to
serving an ideal.[15] The veil had been torn from her star-struck eyes by
the penetrating gaze of a mysterious Russian prince. *I had to cross the
line to discover myself as an active agitator in this movement*, she would
later reflect.

Before too long, she had organised *a little circle of women* she
called the League of Light, a support network for young women in
the theatre world who were being abused. *Ever since I have started to
think*, confided Muriel, *I have felt that it is terrible, so many women
must sell themselves to live; that something must be done to enable a*

woman to possess her own body…so that she may not have to barter one in the marriage market and lose the other in the streets of cities. The league's symbol was a lighted beacon, its MO simple.

> The object of the league was to go quietly among the girls—chiefly girls of the stage and studios—and let them know where friends were to be had if they wanted them. We wanted to try and prevent immorality being forced on women and girls through the exigencies of their having to earn a living.[16]

Whether Muriel's own safety or dignity was ever compromised by an unscrupulous agent is impossible to know. How often had she been seduced, groped, mistreated? How many times had she looked the other way, in order to guarantee her own place in the company, while a fellow actress was abused? How many times had silence been her surety? The record gives no answers to these intimate questions. What is evident is Muriel's immediate sense of commitment and responsibility once she determined that the purpose of her art would no longer be personal achievement but social reform.

> Believing from the start that the present social and industrial structure was inimical to the well-being and development of the masses of this people, it was but natural that within a short time of my arrival I should be taking part in the women's agitation for political freedom.[17]

Through the league, Muriel attempted to lobby the home secretary to register theatrical agents for the protection of women in the theatre industry. But when *Mr Gladstone said that nothing could be done in the matter,* Muriel realised she was going about the business of reform all wrong: *putting the cart before the horse.* Without the vote—something she took for granted, having already voted in a state and a federal election—Muriel realised that there was nothing she could do for the women of the West End. Only the vote could *remove stumbling blocks which lie across the path of women.* Only the vote could grant women the opportunities *denied them to-day by their economic dependence on men.*[18]

Within weeks of Muriel Matters' arrival in London, her world had turned inside out. She was no less ambitious, but her aspirations had changed. Muriel had needed to travel to the other side of the world to realise just how lucky she had been at home. She would not rest until she had helped British women win what Mary Lee and Catherine Helen Spence—her feminist foremothers—had helped win for her. The ticket to her freedom. The vote.

⚜

The fire now burning in Muriel Matters' belly was not the only political hot spot in London in the autumn of 1905. Until that fateful year, the women's suffrage campaign was *like a beetle on its back*, according to prominent suffragist Emmeline Pethick-Lawrence. Every avenue for reaching public opinion had appeared to be closed: the press was hostile and impenetrable, the parliament obdurate and obstructionist. But the unprecedented events of 12 May suggested a new way forward: a younger generation of women now looked *to political and social ideas that were alive.* It was the beginning of *a great movement*, wrote Pethick-Lawrence, *the uprising of British women.*[19]

From her new home in Hammersmith, Dora Montefiore watched the spot fires igniting around her. Elizabeth Wolstenholme Elmy stayed with her whenever she was in London, and together the polyglot widow and the little white-haired warrior kept each other informed of events. Dora learned from Mrs Elmy that the WSPU had *flared up like a torch in Manchester*, under the charismatic leadership of Emmeline Pankhurst and the *clear and logical mind* of her daughter Christabel, who had a gift for practical politics.

On 13 October, Christabel and another young activist, Annie Kenney, went to a Liberal Party meeting held by Winston Churchill and Sir Edward Grey in the Free Trade Hall in Manchester. It was customary for members of the public who had obtained a ticket to the meeting to send questions up to the stage for the candidates to address. Emboldened by the new spirit of defiance slowly catching light, Annie Kenney put forward a novel query: *If you are elected, will you do your best to make Woman Suffrage a Government Measure?*

It was a valid line of questioning. The Liberal Party was hoping for an historic victory at the January 1906 election and had pledged to uphold *people's rights against the powers of a privileged aristocracy.*[20] Indeed, its election motto was *trust the people.* Many Liberal members were privately committed to women's enfranchisement. Would they make it a party platform? An election issue?

Neither Churchill nor Grey answered. Instead, Christabel and Annie Kenney were forcibly ejected from the meeting—but they were not prepared to go quietly. They physically resisted their removal and were charged by police with *disorderly behaviour and causing an obstruction.* In court the next day, faced with a fine, Christabel saw the opportunity to score a publicity coup, just as Nellie Martel had attracted press attention when defiantly marching the contingent of women at the House of Commons to the Broad Sanctuary instead of dispersing when moved on by police. Christabel and Kenney refused to pay the fine, thus incurring short prison sentences: a week and three days respectively.

The stunt had the desired effect. The press was instinctively drawn to the *extraordinary incident* where two primly dressed young women *caused an uproarious scene by their attempted advocacy of the cause of women's suffrage.* Insisting their question be addressed, *the women both mounted a seat in the body of the hall and yelled and shrieked to the utmost of their powers*, reported the MANCHESTER GUARDIAN. When removed from the hall, *Miss Pankhurst spat in the faces of Superintendent Watson and Inspector Mather, and also struck the latter on the mouth.* Asked to explain her unladylike behaviour in front of the police magistrate, Christabel said *I am only sorry that one of them was not Sir Edward Grey.* Christabel assured the magistrate she had nothing against the police. *Her action was meant as a protest against the present position of women*, she said, *who, as they had no votes, could not help creating disturbance.* While the magistrates were absent considering their decision *the defendants, who were seated in the body of the court, fixed a small banner bearing the words 'Votes for women' on the rails of the dock.*[21]

From the press point of view, it was gold. *Ladies of education* acting like *women from the slums*, as the magistrate said himself. The coverage went viral, reported throughout England.

The WSPU took the bit between their teeth. Another feisty young suffragist, Teresa Billington, wrote a letter to the MANCHESTER GUARDIAN revealing that Pankhurst and Kenney had waited quietly for over an hour to get their answer. When, towards the close of the meeting, they rose to ask the question again, *they were howled down by the liberty-loving Liberals, the champions of free speech.* They were then brutally removed by *four or five burly men...Passive resisters, temperance advocates, and Liberal officials shared in the glorious work of dragging two slight women from their seats and flinging them from the hall.*

Not one of the fine Edwardian gentlemen rose to stop the brutality. Rather the crowd of Liberal men *cheered the sight of this indignity.* The greatest consolation in the whole sorry affair, wrote Billington, was that the Liberal position regarding the *rightful demands* of women had been *publicly exposed* and, in the process, *the cause of the emancipation of women has received an impetus which is immeasurable from the action of the two brave women whom we are proud to call our sisters.*[22]

Like moths to a flame, the public meeting to welcome Kenney and Pankhurst's release from prison attracted not only the press, eager to follow this beguiling he said/she said story, but also a host of new suffrage recruits. From that day forth, announced Emmeline Pankhurst from her base in Manchester, *there should be no more peace until the women's question was answered.*[23]

This was the news that Mrs Elmy passed to Dora Montefiore. For her part, Dora kept her northern friend *au courant with what was going on in London*. She reported that the WSPU was marshalling its forces for a metropolitan branch under the leadership *of a group of women, myself included, who undertook to attend political meetings and question speakers about their intentions towards the enfranchisement of women*. The tactics of their northern sisters were duly noted: *if necessary, holding up proceedings until an answer was obtained*.[24] In Australia, Dora had faced mockery but little active resistance when she and other members of the WFL requested a deputation upon MPs, and even the premier himself. But in England, they could not even get a foot in the hallowed doors of Westminster, such was the stubborn refusal to abide women's suffrage advocates.

This *original band* of women now mustering in London included Nellie Martel—*the woman voter from Australia*[25]—who, having *inaugurated the militant movement*, as one press report noted, had a leadership role to play. They made it their mission to attend Liberal rallies and put the question, over and again, though they never received an answer. Ex officio, Liberal members would pledge their personal support, but in public they refused to speak on behalf of the party. The duplicity was galling.

As a single-issue organisation, the WSPU made its position transparent: the vote, and only the vote, would end its campaign. *The cross on the ballot paper is a symbolic act of citizenship*, explained new recruit, Cambridge-educated barrister Frederick Pethick-Lawrence, *as the band on a finger is the symbol chosen by law for marriage*.[26] Just as a lover could only legitimately exercise his conjugal rights if he put a ring on it, so the voter is *exercising his sovereign rights as one of the rulers of the country*.

For a rising generation of New Women, it was becoming clear which symbol of domination she most aspired to own. Though the leaders of the movement were older—married women and widows like Emmeline Pankhurst, Dora, Nellie and Mrs Fawcett, born in

the 1850s—the new recruits were Christabel's contemporaries, girls
born in the 1870s and '80s. The experience and vision of the mothers
was complemented by the energy and ambition of their daughters.

After Annie Kenney's release from prison in Manchester, she
joined the London squad, only to be just as violently treated when
she again put the question to aspiring Liberal leader Herbert Asquith
at a meeting at Queen's Hall. Dora had obtained tickets for Annie
in the orchestra, and for herself in the stalls. The crowd had been
in *excellent humour with itself,* reported Dora, *for it smelt victory and
knew that the spoils of office were within the grasp of Liberalism.* But
the merriment turned sour when there was a *prolonged scuffle in the
orchestra punctuated with cried of 'Votes for Women,'* and finally Annie
Kenney was carried out.

With Annie removed, it was now left to Dora to implement
the program of deliberate disruption.

> It was then my turn and at the next opportunity that Mr.
> Asquith gave when rehearsing the Liberal programme,
> I rose to my feet and asked if the Liberals were returned
> to power, what they were going to do for the emancipa-
> tion of women. A gasp of outraged surprise filled the
> stalls and people round me asked me to sit down, but
> I insisted: 'Will the speaker tell the audience what the
> intention of the Government is about the enfranchise-
> ment of women?'

Dora never received an answer to her question, but neither
was she manhandled away from the meeting. Perhaps it was her
age—Dora was fifty-four compared to Annie Kenney's twenty-six.
Perhaps she chose to beat a more dignified retreat, realising that
if the movement was going to have forward momentum it would
require a constant, reliable presence in the engine room.

For all around the country now—in Wigan, Liverpool,
Brighton—the word was catching on. Women turning up to Liberal
meetings and popping the question. Women standing on chairs or

sitting in balconies, draping bright banners embroidered with those three little words: Votes for Women. One fledgling suffragist wrote to Dora explaining the significance of her guidance:

> please take good care of yourself, for the world cannot do without women like yourself, they are very scarce. I have been very much encouraged since knowing you and reading your pages in the NEW AGE. It has helped me you will never know how much, and I am not the only one.[27]

In one of those articles in the NEW AGE, entitled 'Women Voters in Australia', Dora had encouraged readers to join the WSPU and *strengthen the hands of those who are uniting to demand the sweeping away of sex injustice*.[28] When Annie Kenney arrived in London in late 1905, it was Dora she first went to see. Kenney had lost her own mother earlier that year, an event that scattered the family. Personally untethered, she looked to Dora for guidance.

In another NEW AGE article commenting on the effect of the woman's vote in the 1903 Australian federal election, Dora argued that women's *independence was shown and their right to do exactly as they pleased was freely claimed and acted upon*.[29] How alluring these words must have sounded to a generation of women who had been educated, then intellectually confined to the drawing room. Or to a legion of working women constrained by a different set of stifling conventions and stunted opportunities. Whether chained to the wheel of industry or to the pedestal of gentility, women longed to break free.

As Jessie Ackermann observed of the Australian experiment, *within democratic citizenship is enfolded the hidden possibilities of a new social order*.[30] The immediate goal was the vote. But the ideal was to change the world.

Forty years of ladylike methods, according to Frederick Pethick-Lawrence, ended in 1905. The new wave of suffrage campaigners concluded that decades of patient argument and entreaty had failed: failed to sway public opinion, failed to attract the attention of the press and failed to achieve even a modicum of political reform. The adoption of militancy was *the outward sign that [women] have at last abandoned this false and pernicious doctrine of submission*. If they could not persuade, then they would coerce. They would disrupt, heckle, annoy, irritate, aggravate, demonstrate, provoke and incense.

If no other way is open to win their liberty, warned Fred Pethick-Lawrence, whose wife Emmeline was moving into the inner circle of the WSPU, *even revolution will not be eschewed*. He could see that for centuries men had treated women as an *inferior and subject race*. But the *awakening of women* was daily occurring. No one should be anything but convinced that this new breed of warrior woman would take by force what was rightfully hers as a proud, freeborn Briton and sentient human being.

A war was coming and, surprisingly, the arch nemesis was not the antediluvian Tories, whose number was surely up. The enemy was the Liberals, who preached enlightened autonomy for all but delivered trumped-up tyranny to women.[31] Prejudice was one thing; hypocrisy was worse.

Our army is growing, growing daily, announced Nellie Martel of the swelling ranks of the WSPU. *We are fighting for Liberty and Freedom*.[32]

And there, in those last eye-opening months of 1905, watching for her cue, was Muriel Matters. Star struck by a new cast of characters—a real life company of players on what now seemed like the biggest stage she could imagine—Muriel began attending WSPU meetings. This troupe even had its own stage name now, courtesy of Charles Hands, a journalist for the popular DAILY MAIL newspaper: he had dubbed the WSPU women *suffragettes*. He meant the term to be offensive, a way to distinguish *that modern absurdity, the suffragette* from the conventional, non-politicised term for women and men the world over who campaigned for the vote, the suffragists.[33] Soon all the papers were running with the word and rather than suck up another form of derision, the WSPU leadership chose to embrace the free publicity, proudly adopting the nomenclature. As Fred Pethick-Lawrence said, *In a war of armies the immediate tactics of one side are determined by the tactics of the enemy.* Call us names, and we'll adopt them as our sticks and stones.

Muriel had witnessed women in Australia achieve their citizenship rights without such tit for tat. The leaders of the suffrage movement had worked hard for their political inheritance—Vida Goldstein was still moving heaven and earth to tip the Legislative Council over the line in Victoria, the only state yet to adopt adult suffrage—but they had not gone to prison, let alone gone to war.

Yet simply asking the British government to regulate the theatre industry had come to naught so, Muriel now realised, *womanhood suffrage is not just an asking for the vote.*

> The movement is the awakening of women—their demand for light. In order that they may have light there must be social, economic, and political equality of the sexes; in order that there may be social, economic and political equality women must have the vote.

It had taken the ocular kiss of a prince to wake Muriel from her slumber. She knew it would take more than that to shift the torpid giant of British prejudice. *The movement for womanhood suffrage is not ephemeral and local*, she decided, *but universal and gathering strength.*

In this roiling forward motion, being Australian would not be a hindrance, as her actor friend had warned. Being Australian would be an asset. Being Australian would cast the spotlight on Muriel, as it had already shone on Nellie Martel. She just needed to find the right time to make her entrance.

18

The Siege of Fort Montefiore

London, summer/autumn 1906

It was not quite the view from the Octagon, but Dora Montefiore, standing at the second-floor window of her Hammersmith home, could see directly to the river. Perhaps it didn't sparkle like Sydney Harbour; nonetheless the Thames, with its endless, mesmeric passage of barges and water traffic, pulsed with a life of its own. And now that it was May and the interminable London fogs had started to lift, there was promise in the air.

Imagine. A landslide victory to the Liberals at the recent election—the Conservatives losing more than half their seats, including Balfour's own seat in East Manchester—with the biggest swing in the history of British elections. An unbelievable 125-seat absolute majority for the Liberals, and the Tories so reviled that even the Labour Party had picked up twenty-nine seats.

Dora wished she could share the buoyant spring mood of England's populace. But it had not taken long for the high hopes that Dora and her compatriots held for Henry Campbell-Bannerman's government to fade. The prime minister had turned a deaf ear when a deputation, including Dora and her friend and fellow socialist Selina Cooper, waited on him at Number 10 a week ago. They represented over a quarter of a million voteless women, including fifty thousand textile workers like herself, Selina had told him: *women who produce the wealth of Lancashire.*[1]

Campbell-Bannerman was sympathetic to the women's cause, he said, but his cabinet, particularly Mr Asquith, the chancellor of the exchequer, was opposed to introducing a suffrage bill as a government measure. He could make no pledge. His advice was threefold: *go on pestering*, cultivate *the virtue of patience* and *educate Parliament a little more*. Nag. Wait. Educate. Good grief! As if the politicians had not heard every claim for and counter-claim against women's suffrage rehearsed ad infinitum. Poor Mrs Elmy. At seventy-three, she had witnessed fourteen parliaments, *but has never seen a Cabinet so inimical to Woman's Suffrage as the present.*[2]

Campbell-Bannerman's condescension was all Dora needed to cement the course she had set herself on here today. Patience was not an option. Resistance was the only route possible. And *pestering*? That she could do. She would make the weak-willed prime minister rue the day he issued those foolish words.

On 24 May 1906, with the bailiffs who had come to either *effect an entrance* or *starve her out* surrounding her home, Dora stood at her bedroom window. Holding the railing of her balconette with one hand and her little terrier with the other, she regally addressed the crowd gathered outside.

> The women who are refusing to pay their taxes are taking this course in order to advance the education of the cabinet ministers. Those of us who are conducting this campaign are determined to obtain our indisputable rights. The cabinet ministers who oppose the movement are marked men. The Chancellor of the Exchequer is an assassin. He stands in the way of the advance of the women's movement. Ladies, I suggest you break the windows of Mr Asquith's house. I would do so myself, if it were not for the fact that I am engaged in defending my residence against the tax collectors.[3]

This was a 'harangue', according to the WASHINGTON POST's London correspondent: *Leader of Woman Suffragists in London Harangues Crowd*. But Dora knew she was neither berating nor lecturing the hundred-strong body of women who had rallied outside. She had their complete support. Many had come with food and were now throwing it over the high front wall, upon which they had draped a banner: *We Demand the Vote this Session*. One woman had even brought a pot of marmalade which she passed over the wall to a maid: *to succour the garrison*, she said.[4]

Dora called for a megaphone but none was forthcoming. Instead she shook the marmalade and raised her voice. *My action is against the injustice that in New South Wales I am a voter*, she explained to her friends, *here I am a political nonentity*. (Mrs Martel, who had recently been appointed as a paid organiser for the WSPU, was standing on a chair also *haranguing the crowd*, as one of the twenty-two reporters present noted with a certain lack of originality.[5])

Dora had come a long way from her Sydney days as a vulnerable young mother and widow, aghast at the threat posed by her legal subordination. Now, she was a mature woman, independent financially and intellectually. She was employed as a columnist for the radical journal NEW AGE; she owned her home and drew an income from properties in Australia, where her grown son Gilbert was once again living.

She had what the Lancashire mill workers did not: options, security and citizenship. She could join Gilbert in Australia at any time. Indeed, she frequently encouraged young British women to emigrate to *the land where the woman Uitlander has ceased to exist… for there only and in the neighbouring colony of New Zealand are women really free citizens; and there only can a mother boast of being the free mother of free sons and daughters*.[6] In that land that knew no fog, Dora had family connections and friends in Labor circles. But right now, Britain needed her. She would stay and fight.

Feeling a tickle in her throat, Dora tucked a cocaine lozenge under her tongue and continued her 'harangue'. The Siege of Hammersmith had begun.

♆

The perfidy of the new Liberal government might have been the trigger for Dora's present action, but her tax resistance was a tactic she'd been experimenting with over the past two years. In July 1904, she'd made headlines for her 'Widow's Heroic Stand', in which she had refused to pay her tax bill, *because she has not a parliamentary vote*, and waited to see what would happen.

What happened was that *an unsympathetic collector thereupon put in an equally unsympathetic bailiff*. The bailiff barged into the Hammersmith house, seized a sideboard, six chairs, a dressing table and *a lady's bicycle* and handed them over to an auctioneer. The sale was well advertised—*mostly by Mrs Montefiore and her friends*, noted the Brisbane TELEGRAPH as Australia watched the proceedings from afar—and by the time the sale of her distrained goods proceeded, the auction room was crowded not only with furniture but also with unrestrained *suffragists and advocates of female rights*. Dora's principled stand had turned out to be a brilliant publicity stunt.

The auctioneer, flustered by the sudden popularity of his rooms, decided to express his regret at seeing that *anyone bearing the honoured name of Montefiore had refused to pay the King's taxes*. Dora could sense that his speech was *somewhat resented by those present*, and seized the opportunity to take the high ground. Since the auctioneer had thought to mention her name, she would hasten to remind the crowd that *the name belonged to a family which had always fought for liberty on behalf of the race to which it belonged.*[7] A reference to her dead husband's Jewish heritage was the perfect segue to her own oppression.

When the time came to sell Dora's goods, the auctioneer permitted her to make a speech. It's not clear he had any other choice. *I stand here on liberty*, Dora began.

> The government has a large majority…but we women can be neither in the majority or the minority. We are outsiders—we are Outlanders. We ought not to be forced to obey laws we did not help to make. Therefore

I feel it incumbent on me to show in every way that I
stand for liberty.[8]

The auctioneer, keen to move on and clear his rooms of
goods, chattels and suffragists, *led the applause* and declared that
female enfranchisement was only a matter of time. But Dora wasn't
finished. *In Australia*, she went on, *a woman can give her vote, but here
in England, voting is denied her. I am ranked with convicts, children and
lunatics. That is the difference between England and Australia.*

Perhaps the colonial 'blow' didn't go over so well with Dora's
supporters. Her possessions were knocked down at prices that
covered the tax bill of just over £12—but they weren't bought back
for her by her friends, as she expected. In fact, her friends didn't place
a bid at all.[9]

If Dora was irked by the pinchpenny response of her wealth-
ier supporters—there were present in the room women from the
Primrose Society, drawn from the same ruling class in which she'd
been raised in Surrey, as well as the socialist organisations to which
she'd been drawn since becoming politicised in her forties—she
didn't express it. She had learnt through bitter experience that it was
imprudent to make enemies in high or low places. For though the
plump, matronly widow did not look like a femme fatale, she had in
fact been embroiled in a high-profile sex scandal.

In 1899, Dora began a relationship with George Belt, a former
brickie's labourer thirteen years her junior, who was working as a
paid organiser for the Independent Labour Party. They met while
travelling together in the Clarion Van, a touring party of socialist
propagandists funded by the left-wing CLARION newspaper. George,
described by solicitors in the ensuing court case as a *well built, good
looking man of the artisan class, active, energetic, keen*, was married to
a factory worker, with whom he had four children, when he fell for
Dora.[10] Their attraction appears to have been based on a mutual
interest in economic theory, class struggle and social justice, ideas
they shared with others in their circle: William Morris, George

Bernard Shaw, Keir Hardie and Eleanor Marx among them.

But there was a clear romantic connection also. 'Satyriasis'—uncontrollable sexual desire in a man—was the term used to describe George's attachment to Dora.[11] Dora herself called it *a muscular bond* and saw the relationship as consistent with her wider political principles, including her commitment to free will and free thinking. *I do care for liberty*, she wrote to Keir Hardie when the scandal first broke, *my private friendships no one has a right to control or question*. But her socialist peers did not see it that way. When the affair became public, Belt lost his job and Dora was forced to take a back seat in her role in various socialist organisations.

The court case was in fact initiated by Belt, who sued the wife of ILP leader Ramsay MacDonald for libel. At the centre of the case was a letter written by Dora, described by defence lawyers as a *remarkable letter for a lady of good social position to write to a bricklayer's labourer*. The case revealed the complex, socially conservative sexual politics of the labour movement, as well as the need for the women's movement to be seen to be beyond moral reproach. It also gives an idea of the extent of Dora's resources and her nerve: though Belt was technically the plaintiff, there is no doubt that Dora bankrolled the litigation. A thoroughly peeved MacDonald eventually settled out of court for the not-insubstantial sum of £120, but Dora may have been the real loser. She not only feared reprisal from Labour cronies but also worried that the respectable matriarchs of the women's movement would not take kindly to her indiscretion.[12] Purity—of body, mind and purpose—was critical to the sex superiority claimed by suffragists.

So Dora knew that she was, as one WSPU member noted, *not everywhere well received, there having been heterodox passages in her private life which people resent*.[13] Dora played by the rules of social convention, taking care not to openly criticise any but her sworn political enemies. But political precepts were another matter. When tax time rolled around in 1905, Dora (who was still involved with

Belt, despite the public disgrace) once again refused to pay her bill. In an article written for the New Age to explain her stand, she made it apparent that having her goods confiscated was not her ideal punishment for non-compliance. *If the choice were possible*, she wrote, *I should prefer going to prison to purge my offence of rebellion against an unjust law, rather than suffer a financial loss which I can ill afford.*[14] Dora was evidently not so comfortably well off that she was happy to keep replacing the furniture.

This time around, the bailiffs took the silver. Perhaps because there were, by late 1905, many more suffragette skirmishes to tempt the press or perhaps because the auction occurred on a Friday night three days before Christmas, only one newspaper reported the sale. Again, Dora made a speech in front of a small but devoted crowd. Some men who were present in the auction rooms uttered cries of *Shame* and *Hear, hear* at appropriate moments in her address. When her silverware was knocked down for £13, more than the amount of her tax bill, Dora queried the auctioneer. He told her not to be concerned. The buyer, he informed her, *was someone representing her.*[15] Dora would eat her plum pudding with her own cutlery. But it would not be the last time she failed to receive a Christmas card from the Crown.

⚵

The residents of Hammersmith all seemed to be walking in the same direction on the afternoon of 27 May 1906: towards the plain red brick house at number 22 Upper Mall. *There was nothing to distinguish the house from its neighbours*, noted the Observer, *save a banner stretched across a little summerhouse in the corner of the raised garden.* Dora's hand-stitched banner was bright crimson with white lettering upon it, bearing the motto:

> Women should vote for the taxes they pay and the laws
> they obey.

Otherwise, the house was a simple three-storey villa tucked behind a high brick wall. The window above the front door had a small semi-circular railing enclosing its panes. And it was to this balconette, big enough to fit a stout woman and a small dog, that the gathering crowd now looked. It was clear that there was to be no quick fix for the trouble at *Fort Montefiore*, as the WSPU had taken to calling the otherwise unassuming house where the *Siege of the Suffragette* was entering its third day.[16] But so far there had been no sight of the intractable landlady or her *wire-haired terrier*.

It had been rumoured that Miss Kenney and Miss Billington would be arriving today with a contingent of women from Canning Vale and Bow to hold a demonstration in the garden. Dora had shared her plan—to barricade herself in her home when the bailiffs arrived, knowing that, by law, they were only allowed to enter via the front door during daylight hours—with Kenney and Billington. They agreed that the publicity such an action would generate would be a boon for the WSPU. Sure enough, a procession of women was now approaching, *banners flying*. A pair of steps was fetched for the leaders to scale the wall. Annie Kenney, wearing a green tam o'shanter cap and a dark blue cape, tripped when landing in the flower-bed on the other side of the wall, causing some titters among the casual onlookers. The rest of the women stayed back and sang 'Keep the Red Flag Flying', no doubt to warm the cockles of Dora's socialist heart and as a pointed reference to the crimson banner hanging over the summer house.

Teresa Billington (in a *light brown ulster and green velvet picture hat*, for there was no context too earnest for the annotation of women's fashion) opened the outdoor meeting. *Whatever weapons we are obliged to use*, she said, *we shall use them and continue to use them without stop or stay until the government...*But the rest of her sentence was drowned out by a passing coal wagon which *wedged its way through the crowd*. Billington *eulogised Mrs Montefiore* for her protest, and urged every woman to refuse to pay taxes until she got her vote.

A group of boys from St Paul's School, directly across the river, had swelled the throng after their 3 p.m. dismissal. One looked up to the house and noticed that the old lady and her dog were sitting at the open window. When Miss Billington had finished eulogising, Mrs Montefiore stood up to speak (white blouse, black tie) and was *received with a round of hearty cheers from her supporters in the garden and on the roadway*. Dora explained that her present action was a direct response to the prime minister's advice a week ago to educate the parliament. So here she was, *giving them an object lesson*. She had tried quieter methods of getting her message across, but the time for reasonable means was over. *We women don't like publicity [but] we are obliged to go against the deepest tradition of our nature*, Dora exhorted, somewhat disingenuously, *and go down and fight as men fight for our rights*. The cabinet members had had enough *abstract teaching*, she continued, *now a little concrete teaching may do them good*.[17] Dora was candid about her circumstances, telling the press:

> My income is derived mainly from property in Australia where for many years I resided. It is taxed over there, and taxed again in this country. I never objected to paying taxes in Australia, because there women have votes both for the State Parliament and for the Commonwealth. There women are not disqualified from sitting in the Commonwealth Parliament. One lady at the last election, although unsuccessful, polled over 20,000 votes.[18]

Nellie Martel, take a bow.

More cheers, followed by more speeches from other suffragists present, followed by a resolution denouncing taxation without representation as tyranny and calling upon the government to enfranchise women, followed by a show of hands for the motion. All raised their hands except the schoolboys. Finally, Miss Billington called on those gathered to make a monetary contribution to the cause and stood back from the wall as people flung their small change into the garden. Miss Billington closed the proceedings by announcing there would be a meeting every Wednesday and Saturday, unless, she added ominously, *the siege is raised in the meantime*. For the meantime, the WSPU would make Fort Montefiore the centre of its London operations. The crowd dispersed. Those taking an evening stroll by the river in the cool spring air would see only *an uninteresting house front*, a dozing policeman and the odd spectacle of a parcel of household goods being piffed over the wall.[19]

And so it went day after day, week after week, as May turned into June, spring into summer. All over England, suffragettes were invading Liberal Party meetings, disrupting proceedings with their questions, unfurling banners, and being *forcibly ejected* by annoyed politicians. David Lloyd George, the *victim* of one such action in Liverpool in June, declared he had always been a supporter of women's suffrage and would continue to be *whatever some silly women might do*.[20] Some of those suffragists who had been working for the franchise for decades through the auspices of Mrs Fawcett's NUWSS began to worry that political reform might be *actually handicapped rather than assisted* by the conduct of *the extreme suffragists*. To these anxious onlookers, Dora Montefiore's action was seen as but *the latest exhibition of eccentricity*.

One Australian journalist covering the London proceedings for the Adelaide ADVERTISER noted with some consternation the change in Dora's tactics. He had been present in her drawing room in Sydney at the very first meeting she convened of the WSL in 1891. *I could not help contrasting the methods then adopted*, he wrote, *with those now being pursued by the militant section of the woman suffragists in England*.

> The programme we formulated on that occasion was based on moral suasion and was purely educational in its scope. It aimed at convincing the male electorate of New South Wales by argument that equal electoral rights at the ballot-box belonged equitably to women as much as to men.

It had taken time to achieve that aim, but after the vote was eventually won, the journalist noted, all men agreed with the women's claim that *the agitation had been conducted throughout with ability, honor and dignity.* It was a matter of *profound astonishment* to the journalist that with *Australia's experience to guide them*, the suffrage advocates in England had resorted to such *indiscreet* methods, an approach sure to fail in its object, just as militancy would have failed in Australia had it been tried.[21]

It was of no concern to Dora that fellow suffragists, and the Australian press for that matter, disproved of her methods. People had asked her, was she mad? Yes, she was mad, was her sharp reply, *in the sense that Americans used the expression* to mean *thoroughly stirred and angry.*[22] But she wasn't crazy. Sane people kept their distance from crazy people, but look what was happening here in Hammersmith. Each day, at about noon, a contingent of supporters would arrive, joined by assorted street waifs and *riverside loungers.* There was always a solitary constable on duty to guard the house and keep the peace, but his services were never required.

Dora would sit at her bedroom window, stroking her Irish terrier. Women would bring her a basket of strawberries, a jar of cream, a bunch of flowers, two cottage loaves. Tradespeople made deliveries, including her freshly laundered white shirts. Her mail was delivered—*shoals of letters…a few sadly vulgar and revolting, but the majority helpful and encouraging.*[23] Each day she would address those present from her window, noting that her object was to demonstrate *how a woman feels when she has to pay taxes without the right to vote.*[24] (A Lancashire mill worker, who also had to pay tax, might have quipped that it appeared to feel quite restful, thanks all the same.)

One Australian paper noted that *in the state of open war* between the suffragists and the government now at play in England, the Siege of Hammersmith was *the most picturesque incident of the struggle so far.*[25] Dora's wellbeing was never threatened, but she refused to have her action trivialised.

> I explained in all my speeches and writings that though
> it looked as if I were only asking for Suffrage for Women
> on a property qualification, I was doing this because the
> mass of non-qualified women could not demonstrate in
> the same way, and I was to that extent their spokes-
> woman.

There was no doubting her sincerity. It was Dora who had marched a thousand destitute women from the East End slums to Westminster to lobby Balfour over the Unemployed Bill. (Balfour had notoriously *protected himself with a scent spray from the smell of their poverty.*)[26] And it was Dora who had introduced Annie Kenney to the East End women she was now recruiting to the WSPU. Adult suffrage was as important to Dora now as it had been in Australia; in this much her outlook had not changed since Sydney. And in this way her ideology differed from the WSPU.

By the beginning of July, the authorities had had enough of the performance. It was time to move the circus on. The mad widow had been *a self-made prisoner* for six weeks now. With all the strawberries and cottage loaves going over the wall, there was no starving her out. The police obtained a warrant empowering them to forcibly break into the house. The great oak gate, set into the brick wall, would prove *a rather formidable obstacle* for the bailiffs, but they would break it down if need be.

The OBSERVER predicted a showdown in its coverage on 1 July—*Mrs Montefiore's house to be taken by storm*—but when the bailiffs eventually broke through her blockaded front door two days later, it was more like a sun shower than a tornado. Dora wasn't even there. She had slipped out to go to a demonstration protesting the arrest of Annie Kenney. She simply requested that they leave the furniture and take the silverware, as much *as may be required to settle the debt,*[27] and left it to her maid and her dog to greet the bailiffs. They stayed true to their mistress's aim of *passive, non-violent protest* and let the bailiffs take the spoons.[28]

Unlike the previous two occasions when Dora's goods had gone up for sale, the Crown supplied twenty-two police officers to guard the auctioneer. But all the king's men were not required *because again we agreed that it was useless to resist force majeure when it came to technical violence on the part of the authorities.* A young Indian lawyer who was in London at the time studied this instance of non-violent civil disobedience closely. His name was Mohandas Karamchand Gandhi; he was later more commonly known as Mahatma.

⚵

The stand-off at Fort Montefiore had proved that passive resistance to unjust laws could attract considerable attention, fulfilling at least one of the prime minister's exhortations: to *go on pestering.*[29] The press was still scurrilous in its bias and misrepresentations, but public opinion might start to side with the suffragists if the justice of their case became more visible, especially if their 'rational' male antagonists became more flustered. But would that sway the judgment of those in power? Would the Liberal government's cabinet ministers agree to introduce a suffrage bill at the next sitting?

In the autumn of 1906 the WSPU, which had recently moved its headquarters from Manchester to London, requested a meeting with the prime minister ahead of the opening of parliament for the autumn session on 23 October. Campbell-Bannerman refused to see them, on the grounds that he'd already informed the WSPU leadership (and the public) that as long as the cabinet was divided on the issue he could not introduce a Women's Suffrage Bill. On 3 October, twenty suffragettes, including Nellie Martel, Dora Montefiore, Annie Kenney, Emmeline Pankhurst, Christabel Pankhurst and Emmeline Pethick-Lawrence, led a 'raid' on the House of Commons, determined to seek an audience with the prime minister. They rushed the lobby of the Commons, stood on chairs, heckled and shouted 'Votes for Women', refusing to leave the building when police tried to eject them. Nellie and nine others were arrested for using *violent and abusive language* but not charged.[30]

On 23 October, *the importunate women* repeated the whole scenario.[31] Thirty suffragettes, including Nellie and Dora, assembled in the lobby of the House of Commons. *Women were daring to voice their wrongs in the very sanctuary of male exclusiveness*, declared Dora.[32] In *violently worded speeches*, they declared that women were entitled to the franchise and would *no longer be slaves*. They *waved flags and banners*, and when police intervened, the women linked arms and formed a cordon around the leaders, who, *mounted on a bench, continued their harangue*.[33] Emmeline Pankhurst was dragged off the bench by police and thrown to the floor. More police were summoned and a scuffle broke out. Dora was caught in the centre of the action: *My arm was twisted up against my back by a very strong-muscled policeman.* The women *scratched and fought until they were overpowered*. Dora was thrown down the steps of Westminster Hall. Some were carried out into the street *kicking and screaming hysterically 'Cowards! Do you call this freedom?'*

Once outside, the women refused to go home quietly and started another meeting instead. Ten suffragettes, including Nellie, were arrested on the charge of using *threatening and abusive language. Take Mrs Montefiore [too]*, bellowed Inspector Jarvis, *she is one of the ringleaders*.[34] As Dora was led away to Cannon Row police station, her hair down and her clothes torn, Nellie told police that as an enfranchised woman of Sydney, she had the right to enter the lobby of the parliament. Nellie reminded those who had gathered to watch the fracas that she had polled twenty thousand votes as a candidate for the Commonwealth Senate and warned that *if she were not admitted to the lobby, she would dispatch a cablegram to Australia, intimating that she had been excluded*, and then *'the Ministry will soon see that Australia supports me'*. [35] So far, being an Australian had worked as a propaganda tool. Her status as an enfranchised woman gave her authority and credibility. But would it keep her from ending up behind bars?

In court the following day, *the fair-complexioned, middle-aged Australian* made a scene widely reported in the British and Australian press under headlines like *A Sydney Suffragette Arrested* and *An Australian Implicated*.[36] Nellie *shouted and gesticulated*, and repeated her claims of the previous day. The court magistrate was not intimidated by her claim that her conviction would be a diplomatic disaster. The suffragettes were each fined £10 and bound over to keep the peace for six months.

As a group they decided on the strategy of refusing to pay the fine, electing to go to prison for two months. Dora explained that the charge was *farcical*; they had not used any abusive language, only proclaimed 'Votes for Women'. *A shameful outrage by a Liberal Government*, shouted supporters from the court. Teresa Billington, who was among those arrested, made the point that *as well as these women rebels, we gathered about us also a great number of working women, earnest, unlettered and poor, having nothing to give but personal service and sacrifice and giving these willingly*.[37]

Bolstered by the incendiary mood of the courtroom, the convicted suffragettes, who included Sylvia Pankhurst, her younger sister Adela, Annie Kenney and Billington, refused to leave the dock. *We have come to the conclusion*, announced Sylvia, *that it is a question of harassing and persecuting the Government until they will, for the sake of peace, concede women the franchise*.[38] Mrs Cobden-Sanderson, daughter of a famous British statesman and neighbour of Dora in Hammersmith, claimed she was *at war with the State as at present constituted*.[39] Eventually, when it was clear that there would be no end to the verbal barrage, the women *were forcibly dragged out and rem*oved to the *cells*.[40] Among those so delivered to Holloway Prison was Dora Montefiore, who had finally received the gaol term that her tax resistance had failed to deliver. When asked her religion by the wardess on her admission to prison, Dora replied *Freethinker*.[41]

*

Emmeline Pankhurst now had two daughters in prison. She called a meeting at the WSPU's headquarters at Caxton Hall, requesting funds for a war chest. Mr Cobden-Sanderson immediately pitched in £100 and Fred Pethick-Lawrence promised £10 a day for every day his wife was in prison.[42] He didn't need to dig deep. On 28 October, after four days in Holloway, Emmeline Pethick-Lawrence was released due to illness.

The following day, Dora too petitioned for her freedom. According to Sylvia Pankhurst, Dora was *horrified to discover her head infested by lice, owing to the lack of precautions against the spread of vermin in prison*.[43] Tensions had been brewing between Dora and Emmeline Pankhurst—two powerful, commanding women, one of whom would infamously broach no rivals—and the Pankhurst daughters fell in behind their cutthroat mother. Dora accused Sylvia of deliberately misrepresenting her: she claimed her early release was due to illness. Whatever the truth, Dora was released with an undertaking to keep the peace for six months. She didn't remain in prison long enough to enjoy Emmeline's moral victory over the authorities: her successful petition to have the suffragettes transferred from second division, where the common offenders were housed, to the more comfortable first division, where political prisoners traditionally were sent. *We are at last recognised as a political party*, Emmeline proclaimed, *we are now in the swim of politics, and are a political force*.[44]

If the incarcerated Nellie expected a sympathetic response from the country whose high democratic standards she claimed to uphold, she would be disappointed. The Australian press continued its longstanding attitude of demeaning *the lady (?)* and questioning *her sudden interest in the world of politics…where ladies fight policemen, scratch them and leave their hair behind*. The Brisbane TELEGRAPH claimed that *poor Miss Rose Scott* entirely rejected the *absurd fusses* of the suffragettes and was *exceedingly upset at the commotion in England*, in which her former associate was now playing such a prominent part.[45] Nellie's old nemesis, TRUTH, reminded its readers that the 'lady', who had *posed as an elocutionist*, had *straw-coloured hair and a very artificial complexion, and showed her neck*. But what was revealed by *the English trouble* (a common description of the suffragette *outbreak*) was something more sinister than Nellie's refusal to *wear collars*. Nellie was not only masquerading as a respectable professional, but she was also impersonating an Australian.

> We in Sydney who know Nellie and her pearl-cream
> hide and dyed herbage, smart violently when she poses
> as a distinguished Australian, and tries to shelter herself
> behind our brand-new Southern Cross flag...she isn't
> Australian, and her haw-haw speech betrayed her.[46]

For her part, Nellie was unfazed by yet more bad publicity in Australia. In fact, the events of 1906 nailed her colours all the more firmly to the imperial mast. In a letter to a friend (probably Louisa Lawson) written from prison and reported in the Australian press in September, Nellie revealed that she had decided to extend her temporary stay in England indefinitely.

> There is so much work to be done in London, so many
> evils to remove, so many weak to defend, we shall never
> do anything in England till women have votes, so I give
> my all to that aim.[47]

Nellie's request for diplomatic assistance from the Australian government had fallen on deaf ears, but it didn't stop her appealing to the women of Australia for support. Nor would the TRUTH's denunciation of her claim to belong to the tight white family under the Southern Cross deter her affiliation. In December, she penned 'An Appeal to Australasia', which was subsequently published in Australian dailies.

> I appeal to you, my free sisters of Australia, to do all
> you can to back up the women of the Mother Country
> in their terrible struggle for political freedom. You
> cannot realise the awful position of the English women
> workers; many have to toil seventeen to nineteen hours

a day for the sum of one shilling per day, and a penny an
hour is looked on as a fair wage in this country, which
boasts of being the freest country of the world.

Nellie claimed that the women with whom she was currently
imprisoned were all there to prevent a continuance of sweating, a
problem with which Australian women did not have to contend due
to the country's more enlightened industrial and social conditions. *I
therefore appeal to you all*, she wrote, *to do all in your power to awaken
Australian sympathy in the justice of the women's demand.*[48] Nellie
remained in prison until all her compatriots were released, ahead of
their two-month sentence, in early December.

By this time, Dora had broken off her affiliation with the
WSPU and the Pankhursts. She could no longer tolerate the organisation's undemocratic structure under Emmeline's tyrannical rule,
nor its hostility to full adult suffrage. And she had no stomach for
the increasingly pugnacious turn of the WSPU's activities. *We should
always be able to control our voices and our actions and behave as ladies*,
Dora shouted into the gale of an increasingly militant movement.
She did not lack courage, but she couldn't abide violence.

The British press dubbed the action in the lobby of the House
of Commons as *hysterical hooliganism*. But as far as public opinion was
concerned, remarked Teresa Billington, the suffragettes went into
prison as *freaks* and came out as *heroes*.[49] The government had gone
too far. Through its pompous obstinacy and aggressive use of force,
it had allowed a new vocabulary to slip into the public discourse.
We should, Billington noted, *by our revolt, be awakening women to
see, rousing them to rebel, undermining the superstructure of servitude
by sapping at the roots of women's acquiescence in her own subjection.*[50]
The imagery of slavery—unshackling chains—had always been part
of suffragist rhetoric. Now, added to resistance, were two new Rs.
Rebels. Revolt.

If there was a turning point in the British campaign,
23 October 1906 was it.

19

Electrify the House

London, winter 1907

After Dora Meeson left Melbourne with her family in 1897, agreeing to meet George Coates *on the other side of the world*, she kept her promise and so did he. They met up in Paris, where they both enrolled at the prestigious Académie Julian, a private art school favoured by international students for its fine tutors, progressive values and willingness to enrol women in an environment of amiable collegiality. Coates was unwell that first year in Paris, the result, thought 'Trousers', of *too much drinking—for bad French wines were cheap—and not enough eating*. But Paris itself was *at its zenith*, with Monet, Manet, Renoir and Degas all still living, still pushing the boundaries with the animated power of their impressionism.

Dora and George agreed, however, that the Parisian art world was particularly cruel to women. They both watched in horror as their fellow French students *threw over* their mistresses and left them *penniless and stranded*, these girls who had *given them their all*. Dora admired that Coates had *the greatest pity and tenderness* for these women, and for the prostitutes who so often served as artists' models.

In Paris, the couple competed at the Salon. Trousers won a prize. They studied the great masters at the Louvre. They worked constantly, and soon realised that each had a very different relationship to light. George preferred to work with the blinds half-down, but Dora's Australian childhood had instilled in her a love of sunshine. *That which is fair light to one*, she mused, *is a glare to another.*[1] But they *both favoured a full brush* and by 1900, when the Meeson family moved to London and took their eldest daughter with them, Coates and Trousers were secretly engaged.[2] They suited each other.

John Meeson was apprehensive about a prospective son-in-law who was not *making a steady income* but eventually the couple wed, with the patriarch's grudging consent, in a modest ceremony in July 1903 with only Dora's parents for witnesses. They honeymooned in Rye, where they gave painting lessons in exchange for room and board. They were both thirty-four years old.

With the £100 a year stipend from Meeson that was customary for middle-class Victorian-era parents, they were able to live frugally on herring, bread and oatmeal in their Wimbledon studio, and paint.[3] They posed for each other to save money—the cost of a nude model was out of the question—and pawned Coates' gold medal from the National Gallery competition regularly. The couple had long decided that *our pictures were to be our children*. It was a moral as much as pragmatic choice. *I had no sympathy*, Dora explained, *with people who brought children into the world to starve or to be kept by other people*.[4] There was a less high-minded reason for their deliberate childlessness too. Dora's grandfather was an alcoholic, and she took the concept of *racial fitness* seriously.[5]

Despite small commissions and local exhibitions for each of them, these first few years in London were a string of *endless disappointments*, particularly for Coates, who took rejection harder than his phlegmatic wife. He was *forever striving*. He *could never paint anything insincere or cheap*, and, with his *high ideals*, nothing *came easily*. He hated *the Jew in art*: *the flaunting and extolling of your own goods, in order to sell them well*. So loath to play the art-world game was Coates that he even eschewed titles on his paintings. He believed the art should *announce itself*. Sometimes Dora had to admit that her husband was too much of a *stickler*, a *perfectionist* who lost commissions because he took too long over them. Her pet name for her husband was *Boy*.

As a couple, they were well matched, complementary: one crisp and tight, the other looser, more able to go with the flow. But as artists, their habits clashed. For one thing, there was George's preference for painting in the half-light. Dora longed for a huge sky. He didn't *understand my struggle to express light and colour*, she worried, *but always wanted me to lower my work in tone, whereas I would urge him to lighten his*. Sometimes Dora would have to flee to the river or the docks: *the crampedness [sic] of painting and living in a studio drove me out to study the river and the multitudinous forms of water.*[6] And it was troublesome when art dealers came around. They almost invariably preferred Dora's work, even the Thames landscapes that challenged the feminine ideal of domestic art.[7]

If ever the couple were able to leave their family compound in Ealing, they would head to Romney Marsh, the sparsely populated wetlands of Kent and East Sussex. Coates loved it there. *It was there*, he would say to his wife, *that he escaped from the sense the English country always gave him of being enclosed in a tidy garden*. Or they would visit Rye Harbour, where *he felt the openness of big distances as in Australia*. They both, at times, longed for *the vastness of the Australian country… the land of light!…the _free_ unbroken Bush…where Time is not*.

In the Wimbledon studio, time and history closed in on them. Coates was congenial, but didn't enjoy social gatherings. As far as his wife could tell, he was not like the other Australian men in London, *noisy, blatant fellows*. After three years of penury and isolation, they needed a change.

A spare room opened up in Chelsea, at number 9 Trafalgar Studios, just off the King's Road and close to the river, where a number of Australian artists were already in residence—Charles Conder was just down the hall at number 6. The rent for the unfurnished studio was a fairly hefty £50 per annum and it wasn't fancy: nothing but a pink muslin curtain across the bedroom window, the floors scattered with dirty socks and everything covered in dust and grime. But the space was up to date and pleasingly *bohemian*;[8] above all, thought Dora, it had *splendid light*. They snapped it up. George made furniture out of some old doors and, *like all George did*, beamed his wife, *they were solid and strong*.

It was not so much that their material or artistic lives changed with the move to Chelsea, but the social setting could not have been more different. Coates joined the Chelsea Arts Club, where Tom Roberts, Arthur Streeton and George Lambert were already members. Dora was teetotal, but she gave George a two-shilling drinking allowance to go to CAC meetings. In Melbourne, the Victorian Artists' Society was co-ed, but here women were not allowed as members.[9] It irked her. The inequality was particularly galling given that the Chelsea Arts Club was practically an Australian Club[10]—and weren't the Australians supposed to be more enlightened than the English on such matters? *It is the women artists, not the men, who welcomed us as new-comers to Chelsea*, noted Dora.[11]

Then Florence Haig invited her in for tea at number 4.

Florence was the well-heeled daughter of a barrister, eleven years Dora's senior. She had hair down to her ankles and could *paint a better portrait than a great many men*, according to Coates. Dora found her *hospitable and sincere, like the true Scotswoman she is*.[12] But Haig had not invited Dora in to discuss portraiture. She was hosting a meeting of the WSPU. Emmeline Pankhurst was to be the speaker. Another prominent suffragist, the playwright Cicely Hamilton, was already in Haig's studio. Hamilton, *a fair-haired, Celtic-looking woman with a strong, handsome face*, was arranging chairs. Dora offered to help her and while the two women were organising the furniture, the novice expressed her private fear that *if women got the vote in England, it would only strengthen the Conservative Party*. Hamilton turned to Dora impatiently. *I'm a Socialist myself*, she replied with restraint, *but even if they did all vote Tory, I would give them the vote in common justice*. It was at this point that Dora intuited what later she would know for certain: that Cecily Hamilton, and other suffrage women she would come to know, were *rare people with a big heart as well as a big brain*.

From that moment, Coates and Trousers were hooked: *We both threw ourselves heart and soul into the suffrage movement.* Coates cared little for politics but he was keen on fair play. It suited his democratic temperament to support a campaign that worked to grant *the same facilities to women as to men*, as well as to *improve the condition of the masses*. He even joined the newly formed Men's League for Women's Suffrage, as a show of support. This could not be said of all husbands.

At thirty-seven years of age, Dora was finally in a place where she could begin to separate herself, psychologically and politically, from her conservative upbringing and her sometimes suffocating marriage. She longed to stretch her wings—to throw open the window and let in the light—and here, here at Trafalgar Studios, she had the chance.

So now it was 1907 and already her life had become so full, so rich, so…she had to admit it…so exciting.

In January, she had helped found the Artists' Suffrage League with the extraordinary Mary Lowndes. Mary was twenty years older than Dora but with so much energy it was hard to keep up. She was a painter who had been exhibiting at galleries and at the Royal Society since the early 1880s. Since 1897 she'd been running her own business, Lowndes and Drury, a firm making stained glass. She lived with her companion, Barbara Forbes, who was now the secretary of the ASL.[13] Lowndes was the chairman. Other artists joined the committee, including Violet Garrard and Bertha Newcombe. They met at the ASL's headquarters in the stained glass studios at Lowndes and Drury, just a stone's throw from the Coates atelier. In fact, it was a feature of the ASL: all the women lived within walking distance of HQ.[14]

New friends, drawn together in this, the first of the societies of professional women that would pop up like mushrooms in spring rains. The intransigence of the Liberal government had provided fertile ground for activism. Soon there was the Actresses' Franchise League, with Cicely Hamilton at the helm, and the Writers' Suffrage League. The WSPU said that what was needed to *wake up the nation* was propaganda. Information and posters and badges, banners and essays and plays. A speech was one thing, and lord knows the suffrage leaders made hundreds of those. But something to hold in your hand, or wear at your breast, was another. They needed merch.

The members of the ASL could illustrate the speeches, leaflets and pamphlets and sell them both to educate and to raise funds. They could come up with new designs and motifs that would capture the spirit of the age: construct their own meanings and make sense of their own circumstances. They didn't need the always-intransigent press to tell the public what to make of the sudden insurrection of women: the open-air meetings, the demonstrations, the interruptions of parliament. They could contest the representations of women—flighty, frivolous, too emotional, too sensitive, too unworldly—that were used to keep them out of public life and deny them the franchise.[15]

There was so much work to do, and suddenly, after all the dragging years, the waiting years, so little time in which to do it.

Dora soon learned that many of those drawn to the ASL had been politicised by the attitudinal or institutional obstructions they'd faced as female artists.[16] For whatever reasons—Coates' support, or the co-ed camaraderie of the gallery school in Melbourne—she had never felt the sting of overt discrimination. Still this feeling of solidarity, belonging and sisterliness had given her a whole new outlook.[17]

In our unromantic age, our unromantic land, wrote one social commentator, *a great popular movement has at last arisen, a movement of revolt, not less heroic than those of more distant times and nations.*[18] Dora was eager to be part of that movement, that great romance of the times. She tended to agree with Annie Kenney, who said that *no companionship can ever surpass the companionship of the militants.*[19] There was a kind of mateship there, among these new women passing in and out of her studio, with whom she was discussing ideas, talking politics, planning events and making art. She even began to dress differently, throwing out the corsets and long skirts of her girlhood and adopting more tailored, roomier garments.[20]

And there were suddenly so many things to do. The NUWSS (Mrs Garrett's organisation still had its adherents, over fifty thousand of them, although the WSPU was getting all the new recruits) was planning a big demonstration for February. It was a protest march to coincide with the opening of parliament for the winter session, and the ASL had agreed to help make it a visual masterpiece. The NUWSS had another novel idea too: an original poster competition. There would be a six-guinea prize for *the best poster in favour of women's suffrage, for use at Parliamentary Elections.*

Dora Meeson Coates hadn't decided which of the two big organisations she wanted to join—the NUWSS, with which Mary Lowndes was affiliated, or the WSPU, which had Florence Haig's loyalty. What she did know was: she wanted to win this competition.

⚓

If the NUWSS had had Nellie Martel in its ranks while planning its February march, it might have asked her advice on the organisation—for Nellie had become something of an antipodean oracle.

In late 1906 she had published a pamphlet under the auspices of the WSPU and its imprint, The Women's Press. THE WOMEN'S VOTE IN AUSTRALIA sold for a penny, and became so popular it ran into multiple printings. Nellie's advice came to be prized as much as her actions, her message strong and abiding:

It is because I am sure of the great good Votes for Women

will bring about that I shall devote the remainder of my
life to this work. Come and help, you British women, to
work out your own salvation. May God speed the day
when you shall be truly free.[21]

On 9 February 1907, British women turned out in droves to
come and help by joining the NUWSS's march. Led by Lady Frances
Balfour, Lady Strachey and Mrs Fawcett, three thousand women
trudged their way from Hyde Park Corner to the Exeter Hall in
the first mass demonstration of suffragists London had witnessed.
(High-profile members of the WSPU including Mrs Pethick-
Lawrence and Annie Kenney marched, but in an unofficial capacity.
It was the NUWSS's day.)

One journalist, who put the number of marchers at five thousand, described the procession as *the first really great women's franchise
demonstration.*[22] It was also the first public open-air meeting of the
non-militant suffragists, an indication that the times had changed.
By early 1907, 140 militant suffragettes had been sent to prison,
including a collection of *Australian agitators.*[23] (This, in *free England*,
spat Nellie Martel.) Now those pledged to moral suasion had veered
towards the militants with a strategy that was more dynamic, more
visible and more inclined to attract publicity.[24]

And indeed, the procession was a spectacle. There were massed
bands, a red and white colour theme, and the white silk banner
of the NUWSS with its motto stitched in scarlet: *The Franchise
is the Keystone to Our Liberty.* Other banners were raised by affiliated suffrage unions with mottos reflecting the carefully calibrated
tone—purposeful but not strident—of the constitutionalists: *Gentle
but Resolute*; *Failure is Impossible*; *Justice not Privilege*; *For Hearth and
Home.* (Emmeline Pankhurst had adopted the more strident *Deeds
Not Words* for the WSPU, to convey the militant message that the time
for talking was over.) Thousands of onlookers lined the route. Some
cheered. Others hurled insults at the women. Most commentators,
including the MANCHESTER GUARDIAN, agreed that it required real

courage for a woman to step out of her drawing room into the street to take her place in a mixed throng for a cause…and to see herself pilloried in the newspapers next morning.[25] Cartoon depictions of the day did indeed satirise the marchers as *well mannered and well bannered*, including an image of two women trying valiantly to right their flailing banner against a stiff wind. *Oh Maude*, read the caption, *be careful and do hold it up.*[26]

But respectable women's supposed distaste for notoriety was only one of the obstacles that the *high-born dames*, factory hands, writers and artists who turned out for the demonstration had to overcome. As it happened, it rained cats and dogs on 9 February. The women had to slog through fog, slush and sleet. Photos from the day show them rugged up in long black overcoats, fur stoles and warm hats tied to their heads with scarves. The spectators had to hide under awnings or be drenched in the storms. Passing under barebranched trees and past policemen in sturdy rainwear, the procession looks more like a funeral cortege than a fete for freedom.

The event soon became known as the Mud March. The term alliterated nicely, and, given the overall success of the day, was an affectionate appellation. But mostly the name stood as a warning. If you've got an axe to grind in London, don't hold your procession in winter.

At the opening of parliament three days later, on 12 February, it became clear that the King had not been swayed by the marchers' sodden fortitude and that his speech would contain no reference to the granting of the vote. The WSPU held a crisis meeting. How would they respond to the King's insult? One of the WSPU organisers had a plan.

> Mrs Nellie Martel, an Australian lady, urged the meeting to 'go to the House of Commons. Defy every one. Never mind the police, not even the mounted police. Never mind anybody or anything. Electrify the

House, so they will be obliged to grant women's suffrage in the coming week'.

Three hundred suffragettes followed Nellie and the other leaders down to Westminster, where *a tumult closely approaching a riot* broke out in the lobby. It took an hour, a deployment of mounted police and fifty-seven arrests to quell the *feminine assault and battery*. But wave after wave kept arriving at the House throughout the afternoon, only to face the same scene. One paper noted that *the more warlike of the suffragettes* staged a five-hour *disturbance. The women all take themselves terribly in earnest*, wrote the London correspondent for the ADELAIDE OBSERVER,[27] and he was not wrong: London's women were wide awake, and the fight was on.

20

The Social Laboratory

Australia, 1907

The women of England, observed Nellie Martel from her place in the front ranks of the WSPU leadership, *have looked on the younger colonies of the Empire, and have seen that where women have the vote social laws and their industrial position have greatly improved*. They could no longer close their eyes to their own continued subjugation: *Seeing this, a holy discontent seized the women of Great Britain.*

And now there was even more to be envious of. In 1907 it was ten years since the federal convention in Adelaide that had ensured a distinctive, world-leading constitutional equity. It was five years since the Franchise Act had made Australian citizenship sexually inclusive, if racially and ethnically exclusive. And in this year, there was another international milestone, one that demonstrated just how far the English liberals lagged behind their Australian counterparts on social and industrial policy.

In 1907 the principle of a *fair and reasonable wage*—a *living wage*—for a married working man with children was established in Australia when the Harvester Judgment was handed down by Justice Henry Bournes Higgins in the Commonwealth Court of Conciliation and Arbitration.[1] The judgment abandoned the traditional wage system, which depended on *the laws of supply and demand*, as Prime Minister Alfred Deakin noted. Instead a minimum wage was fixed by law, using a calculation based on *the normal needs of the average employee, regarded as a human being living in a civilised community*.[2]

To come to his standard of wage arbitration, Higgins had

amassed *exhaustive evidence* through *minute enquiries* into the cost of living among the working classes, those likely to benefit most from the decision. His research was largely based on reports provided to Higgins by Vida Goldstein, who was a close friend of his sister, Ina.[3]

The Harvester Judgment, lauded for both its audacity and its humanity, was dubbed the 'New Protection'—because, according to Deakin, no industry which could not afford to pay *fair wages* could afford to receive his government's protectionist duties. Groundbreakingly, workers and their families would be as sheltered by fiscal policy as their entrepreneurial, acquisitive bosses. *Probably no strike*, Deakin boasted, *could have accomplished this result and certainly not as quietly and inexpensively.*

Two expressions entered the vernacular when it came to describing the particular breed of democracy being reared in the world's newest nation: *Working man's paradise* and *social laboratory*. Under the heat lamp of the southern sun, Australia had become *a valuable testing shop for all sorts of political and social experiments*, as one British newspaper put it.[4] The theory of politicians, lobbyists and social scientists was that *as much may be learned from Australian failures as from Australian successes*. But to date, there hadn't been much failure.

The extension of the franchise was the experiment most closely observed, particularly since the outbreak of hostilities on 'the woman question' in Britain in 1905. Various commentators—from American feminist journalist Jessie Ackermann through British radical authors such as Brougham Villiers to Australian statesmen like Sir John Cockburn—wrote accounts of the Australian experience of adult suffrage, accounts which campaigners eagerly mined for evidence—proof of concept—to use in their propaganda. Apart from the goldrush, wrote Jessie Ackermann, *the first genuine interest taken in the country was due to the glaring innovations along the lines of democratic, not to say socialistic, legislation.*[5] Commentators pointed to a range of progressive and protective measures as concrete markers of the impact of female citizenship: along with wage fixation there were pure food laws; tighter controls on drugs, alcohol and gambling; welfare reform; and a marked decrease in infant mortality rates.

Nellie Martel, in her WSPU pamphlet, bragged particularly loudly about Australia's introduction of old age pensions. *In the country where men and women are political equals*, she wrote, *they share equally in the distribution of the interest of the wealth which they create. With old-age pensions*, argued Nellie, *go citizenship, liberty, honour.* She described England's Poor Law system with its network of poorhouses, by contrast, as a *disgrace* and a *blot.*[6]

And she was quick to draw the connections: *Such conditions as these people are living under here*, she lamented, *can never happen in the country where women have the vote.* As evidence, she cited the unprecedented legislative advances made in South Australia since women became voters there in 1893: Married Women's Protection, Gaming Suppression, Indecent Advertisement Suppression, Police Pensions, Opium Amendment, Affiliation (Illegitimacy), Legitimation of Children, Married Women's Property, Workmen's Wages and Compensation, State Children's Protection, Factories Amendment and Early Closing, as well as the Age of Consent legislation that had been her own personal mission.

Women had campaigned for all of these reforms, Nellie explained, for years without success prior to gaining the vote. Afterwards, miraculously, the bills were suddenly taken seriously and passed by MPs eager to please a volatile extended electorate.

The stats didn't lie. Since the passage of legislation to protect illegitimate children in New South Wales, the deaths of ex-nuptial infants had decreased from 240 per thousand to less than 100 per thousand, as Nellie documented. The new bill also allowed an unwed mother to name the father of her child, forcing him by law to raise the funds *to carry her through her trouble* and provide for the child until she reached a certain age. Not only had infant deaths gone down, but fewer children were born out of wedlock. It was these changes that addressed precisely the kind of trouble poor Maggie Heffernan had found herself in less than a decade ago.

As Nellie Martel spruiked the Australian example from platforms across England, other suffragists began to incorporate her evidence into their own speeches and publications. British feminist journalist Alice Zimmern cited a raft of state and federal reforms (wages boards, children's courts and welfare measures, new marriage and divorce laws—even, soon, equal pay within the Commonwealth public service) concluding that *within a few years of their enfranchisement, Australian wives and mothers have received a measure of justice for which women in England are still asking in vain.*[7]

Australia's international reputation as a world leader in political, social and industrial reform was beyond doubt. (Zimmern worried, however, that credit might not be given where it was due. *Perhaps it is not always realized*, she wrote with a prophetic eye for historiography, *how much of this social legislation was helped on by women.*)

Just as significant as the example of what had happened in Australia was what had not. As William Pember Reeves put it, the antipodean experiment *not only proves a good deal, but disproves a good deal more.*[8] The anti-suffragist argument leaned heavily on prophecies of doom. If women could vote there would be marital discord; an end to the family; a degraded race of manly women and womanly men. Indeed, there was an interesting tension brewing for the WSPU, which wanted to attract young and energetic women to its ranks with the excitement and adrenaline of staging a revolution. Yet most suffrage propagandists were at pains to demonstrate that in Australia there had, in fact, been no such cataclysmic upheaval. A leaflet published by the People's Suffrage Federation assured readers that, if the antipodean experience was anything to go by, the *Prophets of Revolution* would be disappointed.

We can show the highest marriage rate of any European

or English-speaking country except Hungary; higher birth rate except Italy, the Netherlands and two Australian states and the lowest infant mortality in the world.

The women's vote does not cause any revolution, the pamphlet's anonymous author (presumably a New Zealander) argued, *though it steadily improves the condition of life for the women and children and thus ensures a strong, intelligent progressive people.*[9] Other commentators, like Jessie Ackermann, believed that the only thing the Australian example proved was that women could not possibly *remedy the results of centuries of bad legislation.* There would be no wondrous transformation of the social order. No breathtaking makeover of the political system with the hoary toad of male tyranny miraculously turning into the prince of British liberty.

Woman, regretted the pragmatic American, *possesses no magic wand.*[10]

⚕

Vida Goldstein might have regretted her lack of fairy godmother powers, but she made up for it with prodigious energy. Not content to rest on the laurels of her respectable Senate campaign, she now found every inch of her elegant body was itching to be *up and doing*, as Mary Lee had exhorted the women of South Australia all those years ago.

Vida had decided not to run for parliament at the 1906 federal election that saw the Australian Liberals retain government and Alfred Deakin become prime minister. She knew from experience what singular focus and commitment a campaign required. The travel, the long hours, the expense—she was still paying off her 1903 campaign by giving illustrated lectures about her American tour—and the constant, microscopic attention of a largely hostile press. Nor did she attend the International Woman Suffrage Alliance conference in Copenhagen, though the IWSA's president, Carrie Chapman Catt, urged her to do so. *My heart*, lamented Catt, *yearns for a genuine voting Australian woman!*[11]

Not that Vida was daunted by the hard work, the vilification or the time-consuming travel to Europe; but she had a battle to fight closer to home. Victoria, the place where universal suffrage was first mooted and home to the first women's suffrage societies in Australia, was the only state of the Commonwealth yet to enfranchise its women. A singularly reactionary upper house and a notoriously truculent premier, the corpulent and (true to his name) corrupt property developer Sir Thomas Bent, saw to that.

It was galling to Vida that she still had to argue the case for women's suffrage when the rest of the country was enjoying its benefits. Victoria *at one time led the way in every form of progressive legislation*, she repeated endlessly, but *was now content to go lazily on in the wake of the other states.*[12] Two votes would have swung it: only two more votes and the Legislative Council would pass the women's suffrage bill that was presented almost annually. But, Vida lamented, Victoria did not *possess a Premier with sufficient strength of character to compel its Upper House to bend to the popular will.*[13]

The jovial premier smirked in rejoinder that Miss Goldstein was a *very nice young lady possessed of great ability.*[14] Mired in the quagmire of Victorian politics, it would take all of the nearly forty-year-old Vida's considerable gumption to maintain her dignity and fight Tommy Bent.

But Vida had always been international in her outlook, an Australian patriot with a strong sense of her nation's evangelical mission. After Nellie's appeal to her *free sisters of Australia* to come to the aid of the embattled women of the mother country, she hit on an idea that would help out the British movement while she was welded on to the Victorian political terrain. One of the questions that curious onlookers from England posed to the Australian crash test dummies was *How do the men like the change?*[15] Vida decided that the best way to answer that query was to ask the men.

On 12 April 1907, Vida Goldstein wrote a letter to members of the Commonwealth and state parliaments of Australia in her capacity as president of the Women's Political Association. *Dear Sir,* her letter began,

> We Australian women who have had our right to political liberty granted by the National Parliaments and by every State Parliament save one, have been appealed to by the International Woman Suffrage Alliance to help our less fortunate fellow women in other lands, where it is urged by those in authority that the enfranchisement of women means social and political disaster.[16]

And she pressed the statesmen, many of whom she knew personally, to write testimonials about the successful workings of full adult suffrage in Australian political and social life. She was obliged with an avalanche of letters, including responses from Prime Minister Deakin, as well as ringing endorsements from the federal attorney-general and postmaster-general and from state premiers. Even former opponents of women's suffrage, like Thomas Waddell, the colonial secretary of New South Wales, testified that women *exercise the franchise wisely and I feel sure that their influence in public life will be all for good.* Vida was able to forward a thick wad of sanguine, self-important letters of validation from respectable and influential men to the campaign leaders at the IWSA. *The replies bear gratifying testimony to the good results of woman suffrage,* Vida summarised for her *less fortunate fellow women* abroad.[17]

They were put to good use. Alice Zimmern cited the testimonial of the Bishop of Tasmania to close her 170-page book, WOMEN'S SUFFRAGE IN MANY LANDS: *Australia is thus reaping the reward of having responded to the unanswered appeal of justice,* quoted Zimmern, adding: *surely these words sum up the whole case for women's suffrage!*[18]

Vida herself had always emphasised that Australian men were

core to the solution, not part of the problem, of women's political emancipation. Indeed, it was a feature of the Australian suffrage campaign that made it *radically different* from any other country, this *readiness of our men to admit that our cause was a just one and entitled to immediate recognition.* To Vida's mind, it was not male privilege that held Victoria back from being *the last link in the electoral chain that encircles Australia*, but class privilege. In the lower houses, where one man, one vote was the standard, it was relatively *easy* to get suffrage bills through. It was the propertied class of the upper houses that choked the life out of democracy, she argued: the gatekeepers of privilege *who, in Australia, are always against reform.*[19] This was why she believed the Victorian example offered *the most curious and interesting parallels to the movement in England.*

Her one personal word of advice to her British colleagues was this: *to concentrate on working for the right that covered all other rights—the right to the parliamentary vote.* This was the *secret of our comparatively rapid progress.* It was a *waste of time* to expect reform on any other matter without first attaining the vote. *As long as Suffragists do not put the foundation stone of social reform—political principle, the vote—above every other question*, Vida preached from the altar of experience, *they have none but themselves to blame for the delay of which they complain.*[20]

⚓

If, by late 1907, the state of Victoria and the British government were both stuck in their reactionary slough, there'd been a seismic shift within the suffrage movement itself over the northern summer. Dissension within the ranks of the WSPU had been rising since Emmeline Pankhurst relocated her organisation's headquarters from Manchester to London the previous year. Her despotic management style was one thing. Coupled with her tendency to play favourites— both towards her daughters and between them, with Christabel being the pet, young Adela positioned as the black sheep and Sylvia the sensible centre—it sorely tested the sisterly alliance. Teresa Billington-Greig[21] summed up the problem: to Mother Pankhurst, *all outer criticism is abuse; all inner criticism is treachery*. The charismatic leader required *fanatical loyalty at all costs* and ruled through *a conspiracy of silence*. For many women, who had joined the movement as *a gateway to liberty* and a means to find their own voice, the price of solidarity was too high.

Two factions began to emerge. One group was led by the unlikely pairing of thirty-year-old Billington-Greig and sixty-three-year-old Charlotte Despard, a high-born Anglo-Irish suffragist, author, vegetarian and childless widow who had devoted her life to the welfare of the poor. The other group stayed loyal to the Pankhurstocracy. There were ideological and strategic, as well as personality differences. The mutineers wanted to run the WSPU under a democratic constitution. The Pankhursts, supported by the Pethick-Lawrences, worried that monocratic control was essential to the success of the militant campaign: that too many (popularly elected) cooks would spoil the broth.

In September, Emmeline Pankhurst halted the infighting by declaring that the WSPU would henceforth be governed by a committee appointed by herself. Three days later, Charlotte Despard steered the disgruntled democratic faction towards a new association, which, by November—after precisely the sort of representative wrangling that drove Emmeline Pankhurst spare—members voted to call the Women's Freedom League. The WFL declared itself an unashamedly militant organisation committed to using any means that did not injure person or property to achieve the vote for women on the same terms as men. While many of the WFL's leaders were themselves aligned to the Labour Party, the organisation was committed, like the WSPU, to oppose any candidate for election who did not canvass on a platform of Votes for Women. The WFL's beef was not with the WSPU's combative tactics, but its domineering organisation. *I am a feminist, a rebel and a suffragist*, announced Teresa Billington-Greig, who was voted the WFL's first honorary organising secretary, *a believer, therefore, in sex equality and militant action*.[22] Billington-Greig's platform was suitably lofty and inspirational:

> I seek [woman's] complete emancipation from all shackles of law and custom, from all chains of sentiment and superstition, from all outer imposed disabilities and cherished inner bondages which unite to shut off liberty from the human soul borne in her body.

To Billington-Greig, the movement was not just about political freedom but *personal emancipation*. Rejecting Vida Goldstein's advice, Billington-Greig made it clear *it was the revolution for which we gathered*. The vote was but *a preliminary concentration*. It was not just the franchise that drew young women out of their homes and studios and onto the streets; women who had *proved their powers in science, art, letters couldn't tamely submit to exclusion from social status, public life and personal liberty*. The energy of militancy, argued Billington-Greig, came not from political impotence alone, but from an ineluctable desire to *cast off her immemorial chains of correct behaviour*.[23]

Australian women had called for political citizenship in a new and flexible nation. They wanted to help make the rules. British women cried freedom and found *the abandonment of the worship of propriety the great cause for rejoicing*. They wanted to break the rules.

Despite the mobilisation of great numbers of women—including Dora Meeson Coates, who joined the WFL, won over by its promise of both democracy and insurgency—and the new-found visibility and venom of their actions, the movement found its situation at the close of 1907 invidious.

Journalist Brougham Villiers summed up the problem: *It is still perfectly possible that the largest Liberal majority for generations may do nothing for women; it is almost certain that it will do nothing unless compelled by outside pressure.* Even with a fact bank of information about the successes of suffrage from the Australian and New Zealand experiments, and ambassadors from those parts to guide and inspire, the British government would not listen to reason. *Fortunately,* recognised Villiers, after forty years of pleading in vain, *this outside pressure is now being applied and that in a number of ways hitherto unattempted.* The ground had been prepared over the long course but *the electric spark was needed which should turn woman the suppliant into woman the rebel.*[24] That spark was militancy.

21

Trust the Women

London, spring/summer 1908

1908 was a leap year—in more ways than one. The world seemed to be bounding ahead, ascending to new planes of possibility, and at unfathomable speed. In 1908 Henry Ford produced his first Model-T automobile (price tag: $836) in Detroit. The first around-the-world car race, from New York to Paris via Alaska and Siberia, was held to wild acclaim. Wilbur Wright flew an aeroplane in France, demonstrating powered flight in Europe for the first time. Not to be outdone on home soil, French aviator Léon Delagrange made the world's first flight with a female passenger, his girlfriend Thérèse Peltier. A long-distance radio message was transmitted for the first time from the Eiffel Tower, and, as if humanity recognised its terrifying hubris, the SOS distress signal became the international standard for calling for help.

Technological progress was shattering perspectives—one could see the ground from the sky, the centre from the outmost periphery—and so was human advancement. Elizabeth Garrett Anderson became the first woman in England to be elected as a municipal mayor. Edith Morley was made professor of English at University College, Reading—the first woman appointed to a chair at an English university. At Fort Myer, Virginia, Thomas Selfridge became the first person to die in a plane crash. (His pilot, Orville Wright, was injured but escaped from the wreckage.) Cincinnati Mayor Mark Breith stood before city council and told his constituents that *women are not physically fit to operate automobiles*, while New

York City by-laws made it illegal for women to smoke in public. And demonstrating that tectonic shifts always have their casualties, an earthquake struck Messina, Italy, killing nearly eighty thousand people.

The world turned—crazing, cracking, racing forwards, crawling back. Welcome to the Belle Époque, what one historian has called 'the long summer garden party of the Edwardian afternoon'.[1] Or a Mad Hatter's picnic, depending on your point of view.

⚜

Dora Meeson Coates was pleased with her entry to the NUWSS poster competition. She had seized the political and cultural moment, finding a way to express—in terms that made complete sense to her—the place of women in the home, the community, the state and the empire. Her entry illustrated both her broadbrush analysis of the British political landscape in which she was now a player, and also her own fine-point experience of measured independence, beginning to break free of the roles of dutiful daughter and loyal helpmeet she had always (willingly) played. Paradoxically, the central figure in her poster was a mother: the one female responsibility she had never undertaken. Dora wove into her image all the 'repressions, anxieties, projections and desires' of her life as a woman and her position as a pseudo-citizen. Her poster was a 'political argument in a visual form', as the art historians might one day put it, the aesthetic embodiment of 'social and psychic needs'.[2]

Her entry was called 'Political Help'. A woman, plainly dressed in blouse and apron, her hair swept up in a simple bun, stands upright. Commanding, almost disdainful. She stares down at six little boys, if not her own children, then certainly her charges. She is dishing out the dinner from a huge bowl, on which is written *Political help*. The boys are holding out their bowls to her, pleading, please ma'am, can we have some? On their little white bibs are the names of those groups beseeching the woman—all women—for more political assistance: the Primrose League, the Independent Labour Party, the Women's Liberal Association, the Social Democratic Federation, and the Trade Unions. The Liberal Federation is closest to the woman, with his hand on her arm. She stares him down. Along the top of the poster in large lettering, the caption: *Mrs John Bull. 'Now you greedy boys. I shall not give you any more until I have helped myself'*. The woman holds her own bowl against her hip. On the side is etched *Votes for women.*

It was one of the first times that a political woman had been depicted in realist terms: neither allegorical—a goddess, a nymph, a fairy: tropes favoured by the suffragists—nor a parody—the misogynist 'humour' long pursued by the Antis, where women demanding their rights were represented as fat (or skinny), gossiping, ugly and aggressive.[3] In simple, elegant, straightforward black and white lines, Dora had reproduced a real woman's opinion of her compromised situation from a real woman's perspective.

The fact that Dora had used an idealised mother as her central motif was of its time: the concept of motherhood was absolutely germane to the suffrage cause. Socialist Ethel Snowden wrote that the point of the struggle was not to cast off maternal duties but to incorporate the *glorious responsibilities and deep suffering of motherhood* into the idea of citizenship.[4] Motherhood was a political concept, a radical, life-affirming, transformative concept that would improve and enrich humanity, rather than hold back half the population. The suffragist claim was not simply for equality along conventional liberal lines, the inherent right of the individual in a democratic state to a share in governance. They believed their vote would make the world a better place.[5] It was precisely the 'mother-heartedness' of women—their spiritual purity, their righteous regard for the value of life—that made them fit to be citizens.

Suffragists were quick to point out that 'mother' was defined in its broadest sense: the term was a signifier, not an embodied proof

of reproductive function. Mrs Bramwell Booth, in charge of the
Salvation Army's evangelical work in England from 1904, explained
the notion in a speech entitled 'Mothers of the Empire':

> [Any woman] whose heart yearns to protect the weak, to
> instruct the ignorant...to rear noble characters amongst
> the youth of our nation...though she may not, herself,
> have brought children into the world...is a mother.[6]

There was a defining difference between men and women,
argued the feminists, and that was women's ability to create, nurture
and express love. Love was key to the advancement of humanity, *the
solution to the needs and sins and sorrows which cry aloud for relief and
remedy*, as Mrs Bramwell Booth put it. This was the public motherhood, the civic motherhood, that would purify and redeem the world.
Through their innate sex superiority, mother-citizens would create
love where there was hate, peace where there was war. They would
also cleanse the world in a racial sense, enlightening the 'ignorant',
turning that which was black pearly white.[7]

That was the politics. There may also have been a psychological dimension to the cult of the ideal mother. Olive Banks, an
early feminist sociologist, observed that women drawn to the suffrage
movement often had emotionally precarious relationships with their
own mothers, feeling them to be cold, distant and discouraging of
their daughters' ambitions. 'Rejection or perceived rejection' of the
mother, concluded Banks, played some part in their identification
as suffragists.[8] Banks found that the psychic impetus towards political activism was more likely to be a rebellion against a forbidding
mother than an autocratic father. Except in the case where feminist
mothers raised feminist daughters, it was the disapproving mother
that created a 'drive for independence'. It may have been patriarchal
social, political and legal structures that confined women as second-
class citizens, but it was often women themselves who policed the
boundaries of acceptable female behaviour.

Dora Meeson Coates' depiction of the groundbreaking moment

when England's women put their own need for political sustenance above the nourishment, happiness and expectations of those who had traditionally relied on their steadfast assistance was a hit. She took out first place in the poster competition. The artwork was reproduced in the NUWSS journal, WOMEN'S FRANCHISE, on 30 January 1908. Shortly afterwards, Dora would be invited to co-illustrate a book to be published by the ASL. BEWARE! A WARNING TO SUFFRAGISTS was written by Cecily Hamilton and illustrated by Mary Lowndes, Hedley Charleston and the woman signing her work as DMC. The book was told in rhyme, with a striking moral coda: winding up in Holloway for the crime of suffrage activism was no worse a fate than being sentenced to *Sit at home from morn to night / and cook and cook with all your might.*[9]

But it was to the WFL, not the NUWSS or the WSPU, that Dora had pledged her allegiance. She set up the Kensington branch of the WFL and lent her studio to Charlotte Despard for meetings, while visiting the studios of other artists she now met through *the movement,* recruiting them for the ASL. In particular, she made friends with Emily Ford, a Quaker-raised woman almost twenty years her senior. Ford had been campaigning for women's suffrage since the mid 1880s, and her home had long been a meeting ground, as Dora realised with delight, for *artists, suffragists, people who did things.*[10] 'Trousers' was fascinated by the older woman's *huge canvasses…Michelangelesque in conception.* Ford combined her large, soaring images of Pre-Raphaelite heroines with smaller-scale works, drawings that could be used for suffrage propaganda. Ford's work demonstrated that Dora didn't have to make a choice between her oil painting and her graphic design: both could be put to good use.

But it wasn't enough, Dora came to realise, for an artwork to be hung in a drawing room and admired by a coterie of dilettantes. It had to move people, mobilise people, enrage and inspire people. And to do that it must be seen. But, at a time when the chief media—the mainstream press—was largely controlled by the vested interests of property and privilege, how to broadcast the message?

An army of volunteers was deployed to advertise the various meetings and demonstrations of the WSPU and WFL. They stood on street corners and at tube stations and distributed handbills. They chalked announcements on pavements. They posted bills on walls and public infrastructure. They hired boats and rowed down the Thames, holding up posters and placards.

Dora was up for this activity, but *avoided doing anything really militant* because Coates *would have been so upset had I landed myself in prison.*[11] Coates was only risk-averse, however, not tyrannical. He supported his wife's involvement with the movement, so his compromise was to accompany her on nocturnal missions rather than either forbid them or sit at home worrying. *The most risky thing we did together*, confessed Dora with perhaps a hint of regret, was pasting notices on public hoardings and pillar boxes in Chelsea under the cover of night, *he holding the paste and keeping watch, I rapidly doing the pasting.* It was *a dark deed done at midnight*, and quite futile. The posters were invariably taken down by morning.

Dora recognised that she was fortunate. She was aware that the other Chelsea men artists were *always conservative* and therefore not partisans of the suffrage movement. *In this*, she lamented, *they did not differ from the average male.* And her husband—usually *too dreamy and wrapped up in his art* to be much of a practical person—even managed to surprise her. Joining her in support of Mrs Despard at one of her regional speaking gigs, he responded to hecklers with an uncharacteristic desire to *punch the interrupters who jeered while we were speaking.* (When Mrs Despard was *stoned by hooligans*, even Dora's father was converted to the woman suffrage cause. How could he deny *a fine type of woman* like Mrs Despard a vote while giving it to stone-throwing hooligans, he wanted to know?)

⚲

Summer. Every occasion of note in England happened in summer. The Ashes started at the end of May. The Derby was held at Epsom on the first Saturday in June, and then there was Wimbledon. This year the Olympic Games—still in 1908 a fairly new institution—would be held in London in July. The many Australians living in London knew why. For all but a few months of the year, the weather was nothing but dreary grey skies or short days of peasoup fog. (The literal and figurative *fog of pessimism* under which the British existed—their *general readiness to be gloomy*—inspired Lady Eugenia Doughty, a Melbourne journalist living in London in 1907, to write a self-help book entitled THE CHEERFUL WAY.[12] It was her attempt to imbue her English neighbours with the optimistic temperament that days, months and years of unbroken sunshine, she believed, had instilled in the Australians.)

This summer the NUWSS was off the bit. The Mud March had merely been a prelude. The next event would be a public relations triumph. An event that Londoners could enjoy; not simply a curiosity, but a performance, a grand entertainment. The English loved pageantry. State rituals were always well attended; the labour movement put on parades, with their marvellous trade union banners and marching bands. It was the government that the suffragists were contesting, not the people. If the people wanted cake, why not give them lashings of lovely rich, moist, colourful cake?

A date was set: after the spring rains; before Wimbledon and the Olympics. (The Ashes were being played in Australia in 1908, so there would be no competition for spectators there.) The Great Procession of the NUWSS would be held on Saturday 13 June. Not to be outdone by Mrs Garrett's old stagers, Emmeline Pankhurst announced that the WSPU would hold its own 'monster meeting' the following week, on Sunday 21 June. The Olympics would not be the only games in town.

⚓

In April 1908, a passing of the political baton made the need for action all the more pressing. On 3 April, Henry Campbell-Bannerman retired from parliament due to ill health. He had recently become the longest continuously serving member of the House of Commons, earning him the title Father of the House. Three weeks later, the political patriarch died. He was succeeded as prime minister by Herbert Asquith, with David Lloyd George taking over as chancellor of the exchequer. Thirty-four-year-old Winston Churchill was promoted to the cabinet.

The reshuffle did not bode well for the suffrage movement. Asquith, as the suffragists knew only too well, was *a lifelong opponent of our cause*.[13] American suffragist Alice Ives predicted that with Asquith at the helm, Britain was about to endure *one of the firmest, rock-bottomed, steelriveted governments on earth*.[14] Dora Montefiore dubbed the new prime minister Balsquith, for it mattered not *whether he figures at the head of a Liberal or Tory Government*.[15]

But Asquith's ascendancy was a catalyst as well as a curse. *Will the Liberal Party give votes to women?* was the question on all radical lips that summer. *From an impotent moan*, observed Ives across the Atlantic, *it became a battlecry*. If Asquith was deaf to the demands of disenfranchised women, then those women would just have to shout louder.

It may have been Mary Lowndes who first proposed the idea of fusing the mediaeval pageantry the English public adored with the women's political demonstrations to which they were becoming accustomed.[16] As much of a washout as the Mud March had been, it had made clear the value of the procession as political tool: a PR double-whammy. Huge numbers could witness the spectacle of women marching for their rights, but even more would read about it in the days that followed, as the press was spellbound by the event.

The new technology of press photography synched perfectly with the new tactic of visual display, so it was a win–win: the dailies sold sensational copy and the women sold their message to a larger audience than could ever be reached by placards and handbills. Even more potently, photography meant that the suffragists could be seen for who they were—young, old, modest, flamboyant, professional, respectable—not as the press had conventionally caricatured them.

Perhaps most importantly, the procession could be outright fun. If suffrage meetings were prone to be dull and worthy—long speeches followed by the earnest passing of resolutions—the procession would be joyful, exuberant, light-hearted and thrilling. The chance for women to 'experience their collectivity in the process of presenting it to the public gaze'.[17] As English novelist Rachel Ferguson wrote, *the Suffrage Campaign was our Eton and Oxford, our regiment, our ship, our cricket match.*[18] In their activism the women found mateship. In mateship they found their collective voice.

The government had issued the challenge: show us a general demand for suffrage among ordinary women. Even Asquith had promised to withdraw his opposition if it could be shown that large numbers of women wanted the vote. The procession, then, would be like a walking petition that took hours to deliver (and for the NUWSS it went without saying that the method of delivery was designed to be peaceful). If all went to plan, a procession could both reflect and influence public opinion.

For the 13 June march, the skills of female artists would be utilised as never before. The women of the ASL set to creating a magnificent war chest of embroidered banners, drawing on traditional feminine handicrafts but putting them to devastating political effect. Mary Lowndes spurred the members of her league to use their *dignified womanly skills while making unwomanly demands.*[19]

Political craft was not new to women, of course: they had designed and made the trade union banners that were a feature of late-nineteenth-century public demonstrations. But in that case, male union representatives were using women's creative labour to produce male narratives of power and dominance. Political help.

And now, rallied Lowndes, *into public life comes trooping the feminine.* If the union banners had demonstrated unity, the suffrage banners would showcase diversity. The five hundred banners stitched and sewn by the ASL members that spring displayed the full miscellany of women's regional, occupational and historical identities. On silk backgrounds appliquéd with fine thread were the names of urban, provincial and rural suffrage organisations (Manchester, Cardiff, Newport), professional affiliations (Writers' League, Potters' Guild, Midwives' Association) and historical role models (Joan of Arc, Jenny Lind, Lucy Stone). In their magnitude and multiplicity, the banners would demonstrate both the broad base of the support for the suffrage, and give every woman her place.

Some time in that spring of 1908, Dora Meeson Coates decided she would not only assist in the ASL's group work of cutting and cross-hatching—she would also contribute her own banner to the procession. But how to reflect her place in the parade of female endeavour and aspiration? As an Australian woman, she had the vote that her English sisters coveted. Could this be her way of fitting in and standing out? Could she make a heroine banner, but one that reflected her place as an outlander in the land of outlanders?

In the end, Dora realised that everything she needed was already in her professional, emotional and national tool kit. She would design and paint *a very large banner for the Commonwealth.* She would stretch the motif of political help in a different direction from her previous depiction of the maternal provider. One element of her winning poster would remain the same: the figure of a 'mother' would be central to the composition and the message. But this time there would not be greedy 'sons' but an uppity 'daughter'. For this work, she would not use a realist black-and-white illustrative style, but adopt the allegorical motif that was so popular in contemporary painting.

In Melbourne in 1895 she'd won a poster prize with her

depiction of Minerva painted from a tall barmaid in a hired gown. But this new work would not be a fly-by-night poster, to be pasted on a hoarding and ripped down by dawn. It wouldn't be reproduced on a postcard and sold for a penny. This artwork would be on a magnificent scale, like those she saw in Emily Ford's studio. And it would also be practical, able to be put to use: a great warhorse of a painting. Dora rejected Mary Lowndes' advice that the banners should be no more than four feet six by six feet six (1.4 x 2 metres), which was as large as Lowndes presumed a woman could carry *should there be any wind.*[20] She also flouted Lowndes' edict that the banners should be *less of a painting and more of a flag.* Dora's banner would not be stitched and sewn: it would be magnificently, proudly painted. She would go one step further than the ASL banners that used traditional feminine skills to challenge the terms of femininity. She would appropriate a male artistic paradigm—oil painting—to make her argument about female desire.

If the scale would be grand, the materials would be necessarily frugal. She found a bolt of hessian, coated it in an olive green paint (green—symbolic of hope), lined it with red woollen twill and cut the bottom edge into three points, a mirror of the trident that would be held by the tallest of the two figures in the piece: Britannia, England, Mother. Beside Britannia, leaning forwards, her arm outstretched, open-palmed, towards the stony-faced, resolute woman, would be Minerva, Australia, Daughter. Take my hand, Mother, join me. I'll show you the way.

Dora's design rejected the ever-present assumption that she should recoil from her colonial background and accept the superiority complex of empire. It had taken her a while, but she saw now that she had something unique to offer. She need not follow Lowndes and Ford, Despard and Hamilton. She could lead them. She need not listen to Asquith. She could speak to him. Her banner would be beautiful, but challenging. A celebration of imperial affinity, and an uncomfortable reminder of the topsy-turvy affront of colonial pre-eminence. Distinctive, but appropriately so, given its message:

> *Commonwealth of Australia. Trust the Women Mother As*
> *I Have Done.*

Dora might not have it in her nature or the limits of her marriage to stand on a balcony before a cheering crowd, or on a bench in the lobby of the Commons, and trumpet the achievements of her homeland, as Nellie Martel and Dora Montefiore had done. But she could, in one short line painted above the figures of two inextricably bound goddesses, tell the Liberal Party of Britain everything they needed to know.

Australia has done it—so should you. You hypocritical, arrogant bastards.

⚵

Women and the vote. Great march through London. Procession of 10,000 Women. Huge Albert Hall gathering.[21] The headlines said it all. Saturday 13 June 1908 was a tremendous success for the NUWSS. In glorious sunshine, thousands upon thousands of women (one observer put the number at fifteen thousand) turned out to march *shoulder to shoulder* from the Thames Embankment to the Albert Hall, where with *music and flying colours, a proud and victorious army* swung into the hall, *conquering and to conquer.* Banners lined the walls (Dora's among them) and bundles of summer flowers were deposited at the feet of Millicent Garrett Fawcett *until I was almost buried in them.*[22] Mrs Garrett thanked Mary Lowndes for the stunning array of banners, whose *design, correct heraldry and arrangement* had been the centrepiece of the procession. Lowndes had also decorated the Albert Hall so that it was *a fairy place of beauty.* It was the mistake of the press, she said, to think that *abuse and misrepresentation* can kill a movement. The procession had been a triumph of management, artistry and ardour. *We converted the scoffing,* concluded another participant, *we won over the half-hearted. We successfully appealed to those who must see the beauty in a principle before they accept its truth.*[23]

It was true that the press was charmed. The MORNING POST allowed that the typical man on the street—fair-minded, even-tempered—would, *if consulted, readily admit that the demonstration was one of the best organised, most orderly and most picturesque that has ever been seen in the Metropolis.* The procession was a study in precision and planning, *no rambling excursion of the 'shrieking sisterhood'.*[24] Another paper declared it was:

> unanimously voted a splendid success not only by the ten thousand women who participated in it, but also by the hundreds of thousands of men and women who witnessed the procession in the streets.[25]

All reports devoted columns of print to describing the banners that had been the centrepiece of the day's proceedings. Leading the procession were Mrs Garrett, Lady Balfour (wife of the former Tory prime minister) and Mrs Ethel Snowden (author and wife of a prominent socialist MP), marching behind the NUWSS banner which bore the inscription: *The franchise the keystone of our liberty.* Behind them were the alphabetically arranged provincial branches of the NUWSS, followed by the professions and working women, arranged by occupation, including Ladies of Title, Doctors, School Teachers, Power Loom Weavers, Actresses, Barmaids, Typists, Clerks, Home Makers and Journalists. University graduates wore their academic regalia. The Women's Freedom League walked en masse, led by Charlotte Despard, Edith How-Martyn and Teresa Billington-Greig. They marched behind a banner bearing the name of Holloway Prison and the sentence *Stone walls do not a prison make.* It was undeniably a unique procession, wrote the POST, noteworthy, in particular, for its *sane and vigorous appeal to the intellect* as well as *feast for the eyes.*

Almost every report made special note of one banner in particular. *The representatives of the daughter colony of Australia,* noted the MORNING POST, *presented an appeal founded on practice. 'Trust the Women, Mother, as I have done'*. From the picture gallery on display at the Embankment, the PARINGDON ADVERTISER singled out *The Commonwealth of Australia, with a most effective motto*. The LANCASHIRE DAILY noted the *striking banner depicting Australia appealing to Britannia to 'Trust the Women, Mother, as I have done'*.[26] A number of outlets reported that a *numerous body of women* marched behind the Australian banner.[27] One paper gave the Australian banner its own subheading within a full-page report: *Commonwealth Advice*. Noting that the procession was *world-wide in its scope*, the paper remarked on the *Australian delegates* who *held aloft a flag with the legend: 'Trust the Women, Mother, as I have done'*. The Australian section was followed by the League of Self-Supporting Women of New York. (The only other foreign contingents to be named were *the Indian ladies in their native costumes*, the Irish Suffrage Society and the Edinburgh Society.[28]) The SUNDAY OBSERVER reproduced images of six of the banners: the WFL's Holloway banner, four of the historical heroine banners—Florence Nightingale, Black Agnes of Dunbar, Elizabeth Fry and Sarah Siddons—and the Commonwealth of Australia banner. *The application of this banner and its text*, explained a caption, *is that in Australia Women's Suffrage is in vogue*. The TELEGRAPH used another interesting wording: *from the Commonwealth of Australia was sent a handsome banner depicting young Australia appealing to Britannia to 'Trust the women, mother, as I have done'*.[29] Another paper put it this way: *Australia, which gives votes to women, sent a banner expressing the hope that England will follow in her footsteps*.[30]

Thus Dora Meeson Coates' personal contribution to the pageantry was transformed into a diplomatic missive. Did she squirm in this limelight? Was the responsibility of representing her nation welcome? Had she, perhaps, been asked to craft a nationally representative banner by someone with one foot in government? Sir John Cockburn, who had been on the suffrage journey since the 1897 federal convention, had been living in London as a sort of unofficial ambassador since 1901.[31] So...perhaps. Dora did later say she made the banner *for the Commonwealth*.

Whatever else we did or did not do on last week's famous Saturday afternoon, wrote 'One Who Marched' in a report to the WOMAN WORKER journal, *we women won the heart of a great city.*[32]

In creating a distinctive and disruptive banner that spoke to and from her own experience, Trousers had not set out to win any prizes. But she did anyway. In a competition held after the procession, Dora's work was selected as one of the six most popular banners. *The banners named on the winning card*, WOMEN'S FRANCHISE announced, *were Cambridge Alumnae, Elizabeth Fry, Artists' League, Australia, Holborn, Scriveners'*.[33] Australia: the People's Choice. Dora Meeson Coates was now someone in London who counted.

22

Force Majeure

London, summer 1908

Suffrage Saturday, as 13 June became known, was an unmitigated coup. Glorious weather. A huge turnout. Jubilant participants. Captivated crowds. A converted press. The NUWSS had proved that the organisation was still relevant and could be influential, despite the more eye-catching escapades of the militants. Could the WSPU's Women's Sunday a week later live up to the success of the NUWSS procession, as well as its own propaganda?

For weeks, WSPU volunteers had been handing out leaflets, bill-posting, house-to-house canvassing, sandwich-boarding, pavement-chalking, advertising in VOTES FOR WOMEN and otherwise promoting Sunday 21 June as the breakout event of the militant campaign. Emmeline Pankhurst had taken British Liberal stalwart and statesman William Gladstone's *force majeure* theory of political reform very seriously. Change, advised Gladstone, could only occur when crowds of tens of thousands gathered to demonstrate the will of the people. He also held that *of course, it is not to be expected that women can assemble in such masses*; Pankhurst was determined to prove him wrong.[1]

Hyde Park was the chosen venue for the WSPU's monster meeting. The largest demonstration in Hyde Park for the Reform Bills extending the male franchise in 1832, 1867 and 1885 had attracted seventy-two thousand people. The suffragettes expected to get thirty thousand in the march, but hoped that hundreds of thousands would come to Hyde Park: that was many, many more than had attended the NUWSS event. But the difference between the two events was that the WSPU rally would draw its participants from all parts of England, not just London. Thirty trains would bring suffrage campaigners in from seventy towns. It would also ensure that not only *upper and middle-class elements predominated*, as the papers had reported of Suffrage Saturday.[2] As the London TIMES noted, the gathering was advertised as one *in which the masses as distinguished from the classes will demonstrate in favour of 'votes for women'.*[3]

Women had been asked to wear white. It was a colour appropriate to the season, *effective from a spectacular point of view*, able to be purchased inexpensively, and, importantly, *a ready means of enabling the procession to present a uniform appearance symbolical of their united demand.*[4] And as an innovation for Women's Sunday, Emmeline Pethick-Lawrence had devised a colour scheme for the WSPU of white, purple and green. It was by 'the colours' that each suffrage society would be recognised. (The NUWSS had adopted red and white in 1906.) By giving the organisation its own colours—white for purity, purple for courage, green for hope—the WSPU had devised an ingenious way to both brand its members and market its message. Selling WSPU merchandise, realised the publicity-minded and financially canny Mrs Pethick-Lawrence, would be good for the coffers. The idea of the colours was born in the middle of May, noted Sylvia Pankhurst, and by June *they were known throughout the length and breadth of the land.*

Suitably attired and easily identifiable, the marchers would be organised into seven columns, each proceeding from a different direction in the city, all carrying banners (over seven hundred in total) with a band at the head of each section. Each column would set out from its starting point (Paddington Station, Regent's Park, Trafalgar Square and so on) and parade through the major thoroughfares of London, converging on Hyde Park via designated gates, where a meeting would be held from 3.30 to 4.45 p.m. At the end of the meeting, a bugle would sound, indicating the time for *a united shout by the assembled multitude of 'One, two, three. Votes for women, votes for women, votes for women!'*

For the meeting section of the event, the WSPU organisers—chief among them Frederick Pethick-Lawrence, who planned the logistics of the day down to the last footfall—had invited twenty of its finest speakers to occupy a platform in Hyde Park. From their platform, each speaker would simultaneously address the crowd. Photographs of the speakers were distributed on postcards and handbills, and immense posters of thirteen by ten feet (four metres by three) were pasted on hoardings in London and the regions, making the speakers instant celebrities.[5] Emmeline, Christabel and Adela Pankhurst were among the speakers, as were Annie Kenney, Mrs Pethick-Lawrence, Jennie Baines and Mrs Flora Drummond, known as the General.

So too was Nellie Martel, *our Australian friend*: one of the WSPU's deadliest weapons. The propaganda power of Nellie's message of hope and success—that the Australian example proved the Antis wrong—could not be underestimated. Moreover, having Nellie at the rally underscored the WSPU's credibility. They were not just a domestic insurgent rabble, but the principled extension of an international movement for change. As Mrs Snowden had written in her book THE WOMAN SOCIALIST in 1907, neither liberty nor equality, for men or women, would be possible until the establishment of *a great co-operative commonwealth in which the good gifts of the earth shall be enjoyed by all the sons and daughters of humanity.*[6] Nellie was the living, breathing embodiment of both that little-c and the big-C commonwealth.

Nellie's allotted position on platform seven—next to Christabel at eight—was A-list territory and an opportunity too good for any prima donna to refuse. But Nellie also knew from first-hand experience the dangers of speaking in front of large public crowds. The knowledge was not gleaned from her election campaign in Australia—where audiences were as polite as the press was vitriolic—but from her tour of rural England with Emmeline Pankhurst earlier in the year.

Following the election of the turncoat Liberal government, the WSPU had begun a strategy of targeting parliamentary candidates at by-elections. The plan was simple: publicly pester the Liberal hopeful on his position regarding votes for women. Would he support a government bill—yes or no? The tactic was modelled on Parnell's Irish home rule campaign: no support for any government candidate, no matter which party formed government, until victory for the cause had been won.

For the WSPU, the benefits of the by-election manoeuvre were two-fold. Not only did it test the commitment of the candidate to the liberal values of freedom and equality he supposedly held dear, but it gave the suffragists the opportunity to take their message to localities outside London and the major industrial centres. Emmeline Pankhurst believed that although the government was *all-powerful* and *consistently hostile*, with its rank and file MPs *impotent*, the problem also lay with the countryside, where voters were *apathetic* and women *divided in their interests*.[7] The WSPU's by-election policy was therefore both educational and insurgent.

After the split with the WFL, it was Emmeline Pankhurst herself who undertook the majority of the by-election campaign work. Though still consulted on policy issues, Emmeline was content to leave the day-to-day organisation of the WSPU to others: Christabel ran operations, Mrs Pethick-Lawrence was in charge of finances and Fred Pethick-Lawrence managed the logistics of outdoor demonstrations. They were known as *the triumvirate*.[8] Emmeline had justified the fact that the WSPU had no constitution or rules by claiming her workers were *simply a suffrage army in the field*.[9] At fifty, Emmeline was proud to be the field marshal and content to live the life of a gypsy, travelling by train from town to town with only a suitcase and an address book crammed with the names of friends and supporters with whom she could billet. With her haughty charm, quick wit and personal magnetism, Emmeline—like the pied piper—was a most effective recruiter.

In January 1908, Emmeline was bound for the Newton Abbot by-election in Devon, where the sitting Liberal member had resigned to take up a judgeship. True to its policy, the WSPU was campaigning for the Conservative challenger over the favoured Liberal candidate, even though the Tory was an opponent of women's suffrage. The government had a comfortable majority in the seat, which it expected to retain. Emmeline chose as her companion for the uphill battle Nellie Martel, who was also without fixed address at this time. According to Annie Kenney, Nellie *had a habit, having no settled abode, of taking her luggage wherever she went, which meant that hotel porters had always to go to the station for her belongings.*[10] Unlike Vida Goldstein, Nellie did not travel light.

The winter of 1907–08 had been a bitterly cold one, making the duo's reception in Newton Abbot even chillier than it might have been given that they were there to *wake up the country* with a merciless *heckling campaign.*[11] For days, Emmeline and Nellie woke up the public with the ringing of bells, public speeches delivered on rickety chairs in the open air and constant interrupting of the Liberal candidate's campaign meetings—hurling questions at him *calculated to spoil his arguments.*[12] The women's meetings were invariably *smashed up*, as Sylvia Panhkurst described.[13] Emmeline and Nellie were pelted with vegetables, stones and snowballs. *Dried peas hurt*, as Emmeline observed stoically.

On the morning of 18 January, polling day, Emmeline and Nellie woke to severe frosts. It was a foul day, yet a joyous one. Their campaign had worked. At the declaration of the poll, the Conservative candidate was announced the winner, recording some five hundred more votes than the Liberal incumbent.

The Liberal voters of Newton Abbot were apoplectic. A

mob of *vanquished Liberals* besieged the Constitutional Club, headquarters of the local Tories, and broke every window in it.[14] It was *an extraordinary scene of riot*, as the press duly noted. But the venom of the mob was not confined to the conquering Tories. Word was conveyed to Emmeline that she and Nellie should *hurry away and leave the town at once.* Emmeline laughed off the warning. *I have never yet been afraid to trust myself in a crowd*, she reassured her anxious suffragist informant.

Then, on their way back to their lodgings, Emmeline and Nellie were confronted by *a procession of young men and boys wearing the Liberal colours.* The lads had just come from work in the nearby clay pits and heard the election results. One of them pointed at Emmeline and Nellie, and shouted: *Those women have done it*, and the pit workers set upon the two blockaded women. The attack must have been a premeditated ambush, for the boys proceeded to pelt Emmeline and Nellie with *a shower of rotten eggs*, clay and snowballs laced with rocks.

The women ducked into a grocer's shop, while a burly drayman, who had witnessed the scene, stood in the doorway and *fought their assailants off until they were safe.* Emmeline and Nellie escaped out the back door of the shop into a narrow lane, only to be run down by some of the lads who had anticipated the dodge. Nellie was caught by one, who grabbed her by the throat and *began to beat her about the head.* The shopkeeper's wife and Emmeline managed to drag Nellie away from the boy and into the shop's yard. Just as they were bolting the gate, Emmeline copped *a heavy blow on the back of the head* and fell. The boys set upon her, grabbing her coat and wrists and flinging her onto the muddy ground. She lost consciousness for a time, waking to feel the *wet mud soaking through her clothes.* A ring of *puny half-grown youths* surrounded her. *Are there no men here?* Emmeline hissed, with what was left of her strength.

Just as she was sure the taunt would be her final words, a policeman entered the laneway and the youths scattered. Two hours later, when the rubberneckers and press surrounding the shop had cleared, Emmeline and Nellie were escorted out of town in a police car.

The attack left Nellie with a permanent scar on her neck. With a severely injured ankle, Emmeline was unable to walk for *some considerable time*, and limped through the pain as she went about her subsequent by-election work. No arrests were made, despite multiple witnesses to the attack, and, as Sylvia Pankhurst pointed out, *scarcely a word of regret for the violence which had been done to these two women ever appeared in the Liberal newspapers.* The Conservatives took full credit for their upset win in the by-election, with only one paper, the MANCHESTER GUARDIAN, admitting that *the Suffragettes did influence votes.*[15]

As a *souvenir* of the Newton Abbot triumph, a win that could easily have turned to tragedy, Nellie kept a blood-stained motor veil.[16] So yes: she knew that accepting a platform at the Hyde Park rally would not be without potential risk to life and limb. But she was *a brilliant speaker and keen debater,* as the newspapers readily testified, *smart and most convincing…a vigorous and clever champion of the cause.* Nellie possessed *a happy way of putting her points and riveting the attention of her hearers.*[17] How could *the Australian suffragist*, as she was routinely called, fail to take her place in this historic event? Would she ever have a more prominent stage from which to publicise the cause that had now consumed the best part of the last fifteen years of her life?

If we must fight, Nellie determined, *we are all ready, we will stand with our backs to the wall and fight to the finish!*[18]

⧲

The largest political demonstration ever held in the history of the world. That's how Fred Pethick-Lawrence described Women's Sunday, the event he'd lovingly orchestrated.[19] It was a mighty claim, but even the conservative press put the number that gathered at Hyde Park that afternoon, under radiant sunshine, at a whopping five hundred thousand. *Half a million in Hyde-Park. Remarkable scenes. Processions through the streets.* These were some of the headlines that trumpeted the appeal of the event. *Its organisers had counted on an audience of 250,000,* noted THE TIMES, never one to give the suffrage campaign a leg up. *That expectation was certainly fulfilled and probably it was doubled, and it would be difficult to contradict anyone who asserted it was trebled.*[20] *All of London,* it seemed, had come out to watch as London's streets became *a bustle of curiosity.* What was truly remarkable was that *scarcely a jeer was heard.*[21] People leaned out of balconies, windows and the tops of buses, cheering and waving as if at an army returned from a war, not a legion of women going into battle against a belligerent government.

Journalists noted that the procession had *nothing of the high dignity* of the Suffrage Saturday march the week before, and yet there was a certain splendour in *watching plain working women from Lewisham, Woolwich and Plumstead* walk together with *women in academic gown and hood,* the scarlet Labour banner (*the world for the worker*) beside hundreds of women in the *uniform of the cause*—a white frock with a Votes for Women sash in the WSPU colours. So mesmerising was the scene that thousands of onlookers followed the columns of marchers down to Hyde Park, where they were greeted by the sight of thousands more who had come from other directions. There were also coffee stands, costermongers (fruit stalls) and hawkers selling badges and programs in the purple, white and green. *It was a gay and beautiful as well as an awe-inspiring spectacle,* sighed Emmeline Panhkurst.[22] *It is probable,* wrote the DAILY EXPRESS, *that so many people never before stood in one square mass anywhere in England.* Every inch of Hyde Park was shadowed by people. You couldn't see a blade of grass. The assembled mass was *not black, as crowds usually are,* noted Sylvia Pankhurst, *but coloured, like a great bed of flowers.*[23]

*

Was this a dream? Standing on her platform at *this great historic demonstration*, looking out across an ocean of spectators, the sea of hats unending, Nellie had to agree with the journalist who remarked that *it was a wonderful sight. Banners had been furled. A hot sun shone down on hundreds of thousands of straw hats and summery millinery.*[24] Nellie summoned all her elocution training to steady her nerves and project her words above the din.[25]

In my own country, she began, *I am a voter and, therefore, as a British subject, the peer of any man present.* She knew her lines. She had rehearsed them at many an open-air meeting before this one.

> Before the Australian women had the franchise the minimum wage for women was 5s a week. Now it is 16s a week, and labour is regulated so that if they work longer than eight hours a day they are paid an extra wage in proportion. This has been done by the power behind the vote, the key to all reforms.[26]

Women asked for nothing more than their due. But they needed assistance in getting it. *We ask for help in the great effort we are making to win constitutional liberty for women of the nation.* There was nothing to fear, no calamity to forestall. Did men *really think that women would use the power of the vote to do harm to their men folk?* Most men were good and kind, *better than the laws would have them to be*, but when a man was unjust *the woman could be made to suffer the most outrageous wrongs.* (Was Nellie speaking from experience or observation? Had Charles hurt her, or was she perhaps referring to the editor of the WATCHMAN, and all the journalists of Sydney who hauled her good name through the mud just as the clay-pit boys dragged at her body?)

She would not get personal. She knew that *John Bull likes Truth and Justice*,[27] and even more than abstract concepts, the British liked facts. Evidence, not argument. Well, she had plenty of proof to give them.

In Australia, as soon as the women received the vote, old age pensions became law, and every aged man and woman was entitled to 10s a week, without losing the rights of citizenship...Women's votes in New Zealand and Australia were...the lever which removed the sweated home labour, the voice which wiped out opium traffic, the power which made it easier to be more moral, more temperate, more progressive...the experience of women's suffrage in Australia has convinced me that it makes for better mothers, the children are better fed, better housed, and better educated. In fact, the country is taking a higher spiritual as well as a higher moral standard. That would be the effect when the women obtained the vote in this country.

Nellie told the crowd that together *we are killing prejudice and winning support...Men and women are awakening to the injustice done to the mothers of men...John Bull's daughters are not lacking in the noble qualities any more than John Bull's sons.* All it would take was more pressure on the government, more messages from the electorate to Westminster, more interference and influence at by-elections and then *votes for women will not be 'talked out'.* She was now orchestrating her crescendo:

We do not want protection, we want justice; nothing else will satisfy us. We fear your protection. It may be, indeed is, the kind of protection wolves give to lambs, covering and devouring them. No! like the Chartists of old, we will take no promises of reforms—we will have the vote, and work out reforms and salvation for ourselves.

Hallelujah.

It is quite possible that no one but those closest to the platform heard a word Nellie said. It would require a Nellie Melba, not a Nellie Martel, to pitch her voice across the din of five hundred thousand people. Such was the hullabaloo of the massive crowd that *it is very doubtful if her words were heard half a dozen yards away.*[28] Over at platform six, Mrs Masey was trying to speak over *the noisy element...a crowd of young fellows trying to drown the voices of the speaker by singing music hall songs and other ways.*[29]

Fortunately, the purpose of Women's Sunday was to create a spectacle, not compete for elocution prizes. The event passed off peaceably enough. Mrs Pankhurst was jeered and pelted with *little bombs full of unpleasant smelling stuff* and a few fights broke out between men in the crush of the crowd. A policeman copped a gash in the head from a stick. The *roughs* had had their fun, but there were no arrests. Nellie had stuck her neck right out in the fray, but she would have no new scars to add today.

And the press, for once, was noticeably impressed. Journalists had gone along expecting to find *hooligans* and *fooligans* and *unsexed women* but instead were surprised by the sophistication and eloquence of the speakers. *I am sure a great many people never realized until yesterday*, reported the DAILY MAIL the day after Women's Sunday, *how young and dainty and elegant and charming most leaders of the movement are.*

> And how well they spoke—with what free and graceful gestures; never at a loss for a word or an apt reply to an interruption; calm and collected; forcible, yet, so far as I heard, not violent; earnest, but happily humourous as well![30]

The combined effect of the NUWSS procession and the WSPU's Hyde Park rally had been a PR masterstroke, attracting mainstream attention and massive public support. And an Australian woman had been central to both: one allegorical, one actual. Nellie Martel exhorting John Bull's daughters to rise up and claim their rightful inheritance, demonstrating that only good could come of it. Minerva, Daughter Australia, goading Mother England to follow the righteous path laid out for her by her youthful offspring. Both told a duplicitous government, whose party's guiding principle was to trust the people, that to keep faith in a changing world it needed to trust the women.

Would Asquith listen? Would he be persuaded by argument? Impressed by evidence? Stimulated by strength of numbers or provoked by colonial precedent?

Or would he simply turn his back on the overwhelming crowds, the vaulting public opinion, the passing parade of silk and sentiment, and row merrily against the tide?

As the DAILY MIRROR asked—perhaps naively, perhaps scornfully—*It has been a day of sunshine, of thunderous cheering, of music, of colour and of immense good will. But what has it done for the women's cause?*[31]

23

A Generous Feeling of Solidarity

England, summer 1908

They simply couldn't believe it.

Our wonderful demonstration, lamented Emmeline Pankhurst, *had made no impression whatever on him*.[1]

Following the Hyde Park demonstration, Christabel had written to Prime Minister Asquith forwarding the resolution framed and passed by the mammoth crowd on the day: that a women's enfranchisement bill be passed at the next session. Had there ever been more popular support, more publicly demonstrated, for a government reform? Christabel asked *What action the Government would take in response to the demand?*

Asquith's response was swift and characteristically stalwart. On 23 June, only two days after the demonstration, Asquith replied: he had *nothing to add* to his promise of a reform bill made in May. The proposed bill would not include a womanhood suffrage clause, but would be worded in such a way as to *allow an amendment* if any member of the Commons chose to move one and if the public proved desirous of one. Nothing, in Asquith's mind, had changed since May. The people have been *contemptuously ignored*, declared Sylvia Pankhurst. As far as the WSPU was concerned, the Hyde Park demonstration had proved, once and for all, *the uselessness of peaceful propaganda*.[2]

The constitutionalists—the NUWSS—had tried to win the

hearts of the government through their ladylike display of fine artwork, marching bands and tens of thousands of well-behaved women striding shoulder to shoulder through London's streets.

The militants—the WSPU—had replicated the spectacular procession a week later, and upped the ante with a public outdoor demonstration attracting hundreds of thousands of people, the size of which England had never seen before for any political reform movement.

Together, they had followed Home Secretary Gladstone's advice to the letter. *Power belongs to the masses*, he had told Emmeline, *and through this power a Government can be influenced into more effective action than a Government will be likely to take under present conditions.*[3] Well, present conditions now included that *force majeure* by which men had already won a popular widening of the franchise. But still Asquith would not make good on his own undertakings. It made no sense. He was an avowed social reformer and self-proclaimed man of the people. The House of Commons had now approved four women's suffrage bills by majority consent since 1870—the most recent in February 1908, by a resounding 271–92—only to be stymied by government obstruction.[4] This was understandable, if infuriating, under Tory governments but Asquith's personal vendetta against the cause was seemingly inexplicable.

What was to be done? What could possibly change the mind of a man so two-faced as to see 360 degrees, and yet be entirely blind to reason?

⚓

Muriel Matters had not participated in either Suffrage Saturday or Women's Sunday. The Australian actress, now thirty-one years old, had chosen to align herself with the Women's Freedom League under the leadership of Charlotte Despard. Like Dora Meeson Coates, Muriel responded to the WFL's brand of democratic activism, identifying herself as a 'militant suffragist' rather than a 'suffragette'. Perhaps the organisation suited her bush-bred temperament. The WFL was more adventurous than the NUWSS, but less dogmatic than the WSPU. Despard herself had described the sweet spot between the two dominant organisations: *Militancy to the WFL is an elastic weapon. We can use it or we can refrain.*[5]

There was another factor in Muriel's allegiance, apart from the question of tactics. As her sister-in-law, Mrs Leonard Matters, noted: Muriel had *a keen sense of humour, a quickness of repartee and in everything a deep and convincing sincerity.*[6] The WSPU, under the Pankhurst family's iron fist, was dynamic but dour. Muriel wanted to fight against the *established order of things*, but she had an abiding playfulness, as well as an outsider's capacity to look at things from another angle. *First of all she is an Australian*, reckoned her sister-in-law, *with all of the Australians' incapacity of understanding why the people of England should not do as the Australians do in matters political.*[7] If Asquith's motivations were incomprehensible to the English, his unwillingness to see the future in the eyes of the young made even less sense to the culturally confident Muriel.

After its formation in late 1907, the WFL had adopted Dora Montefiore's trademark tactic as its first campaign strategy: tax resistance. Members would refuse to pay their tax bill on the grounds of conscientious objection and have their goods seized by the bailiffs, to be purchased back at auction by other WFL members. It was a merry lark. Other strategies included sandwich-boarding in prominent London locations and handing out leaflets championing not just the suffrage issue, but also the wider purpose of social and industrial liberation for working women and their communities. This too suited Muriel, who always felt her calling to the cause was linked with a wider social critique. Like many Australians, Muriel had been shocked by the level and visibility of poverty in London, where the *white slave trade*, including *girl slaves*, was rife.[8] *Believing from the start*, she reflected,

That the present social and industrial structure was inimical to the well-being and development of the masses of this people, it was but natural that within a short time of my arrival I should be taking part in the women's agitation for political freedom.[9]

The WFL's motto was *Dare to be Free*. Muriel instinctively understood that courage was the key to freedom. The women's movement was *but a phase* of the greater *evolutionary and spiritual* movement taking hold in the world. It was human rights, not merely the vote, that would ensure universal uplift.

It did not take Muriel long to make her mark in WFL circles. Physically attractive, diminutive but with an actress's gift for commanding a space, *the little Australian*, as she soon became known, was an enormous asset to the nascent organisation.[10] *We debated how best we could use her gifts*, remarked Marion Holmes, a member of the WFL national executive, *her enthusiasm, her eloquence, her wonderful, magical voice—for the cause.*[11]

Muriel was first put to use in a by-election campaign; the WFL had adopted the same policy as the WSPU of targeting Liberal candidates at regional by-elections. In April 1908, Muriel travelled to Manchester to participate in one of the highest-profile of these spoiling campaigns, this time aiming to stymie the re-election of Winston Churchill. Churchill had won the seat in the landslide Liberal election of 1906, but was forced to recontest when he was elevated to a cabinet position after Asquith's ascendancy. The WSPU were also targeting Churchill, but Muriel added a novel twist to the now-familiar by-election tactic. She casually approached the mayor and asked whether a woman could nominate for election. No one had thought to ask this question before, and for a time, no one could furnish a response. It was all a bit of fun, with no concrete outcome other than a media scrum that followed Muriel around for the rest of the pestering campaign. The COURIER remarked favourably on the WFL's *feats of derring do*. Churchill was defeated.[12]

Later that month, ever-mindful of the plight of vulnerable actresses, Muriel participated in a workplace relations dispute at a restaurant in central London, supporting striking waitresses who had no union support to achieve better pay and conditions. The protest attracted huge publicity, and large public donations—resulting in the waitresses opening their own restaurant, run by the women as a co-operative. By the summer of 1908, Muriel was recognised in press reports as one of the *very prominent members of the Women's Freedom League*.[13] In Muriel, the WFL knew it had found *a recruit of rare courage and initiative*.[14]

In May, while the WSPU and NUWSS were preparing for their upcoming processions, the WFL took a different tack. Instead of bringing suffragists to the city, centralising the movement in a spectacular tour de force of colour and movement, why not quietly take the suffrage message to the regions? This would achieve two purposes: for one, it would potentially attract members to the newly founded and cash-strapped league.[15] The NUWSS had built its financial capacity as an umbrella organisation for a phalanx of local suffrage societies. Conversely, the WSPU was bankrolled largely by a handful of wealthy, well-connected members like the Pethick-Lawrences.

But it wasn't only about the money. Gladstone's original advice to suffrage leaders had been not just that women needed to assemble in great numbers, but that they needed to do it *all over the country*— as male agitators for political reform had done in the 1830s, '60s and '80s. The WFL needed to take its message out of the metropolis. And going by rail, as the protesters did when they attended by-elections, would not suffice. Travelling station-to-station bypassed the women of England's backblocks: the millions of potential voters who lived in the counties.

It's not clear who came up with the idea of a horse-drawn covered wagon that could tour the regions for months at a time, but it was an excited Muriel Matters who put up her hand to play the gypsy for a season. She would 'go vanning' with Mrs Lilian Hicks, a veteran suffrage campaigner almost twice Muriel's age: experience and audacity teaming up. Their caravan, painted in the WFL's new colours of green, white and gold, covered in Votes for Women slogans and fitted out with two little beds, set off in mid-May, pulled by a dawdling horse called Asquith. Destination: the densely populated southeastern counties of Kent, Surrey and Sussex.

The van proved enormously popular with passing crowds, a travelling circus offering plenty of sideshow voyeurism. Cyclists would on occasion ride alongside the caravan, adding to the holiday mood. When Muriel and Lilian pulled in to towns and villages, they held meetings and rallies, *bringing the gospel of the need for women's enfranchisement* as Muriel put it.[16] At Hastings, they staged a meeting at the Fish Market, *amongst the weather-beaten old sailors and fisher folk.*[17]

Some audiences were hostile, blowing whistles, shouting insults, releasing rats and mice at meetings (on the assumption that women were afraid of rodents) and generally putting Muriel and Lilian's safety at risk. The attack on Nellie Martel and Emmeline Pankhurst in February had proven that being an activist for the cause could have potentially fatal consequences. Eggs and mice were one thing, but fists and fire were another. The little wooden van wouldn't stand a chance against an arson attack in a distant field. The women could be roasted alive in their beds, with only Asquith to provide a whinny of warning.

But they pressed on regardless, speaking from the back of the van at open-air meetings or booking town halls with the help of local suffragists. In her speeches, Muriel took a leaf out of Nellie Martel's book, playing 'the Australian card' to great effect. *I know the power of the vote*, she would begin, *I know how in Australia, the status of women went up immediately they had it. And they used it well too.*[18] She reeled off the various improvements that had been made to women's and children's lives through social legislation passed since

1902. She made it clear that it was for these equivalent advances in the well-being of the British masses that we are *making ourselves objectionable.*[19] The end of her speeches contained a request, half plea, half gibe: *if you want to be on the right side then come over and join us.*

Though the meetings sometimes descended into chaos, Muriel was mostly heartened by the reception. She was particularly pleased when:

> in some small town, an Australian would come forward and, after my speech, add a few words to champion our cause. Sometimes it was only an encouraging 'coo-ee' to let me know I had friends nearby.[20]

As May turned to June and then to July—a notoriously hot summer for the English but simply *pleasant* for an Adelaide girl— Muriel had no trouble finding friends. The *Caravan Campaign* was *strenuous and laborious* but, as Lilian Hicks reported, from Godalming to Haslemere, from Grayshott to Petersfield, the women made *many kind friends who help us on our way…their helpful sympathy and pecuniary support will be long remembered.*[21]

Muriel reported back to WFL HQ that beyond those ruffians who *rang the inevitable bell and dispersed strong smelling chemicals there was no trouble.*[22] Converts recruited. Literature sold. Collections taken. *Everything promises well.*

⚓

Dora Montefiore was not in London for that steamy summer of discontent either. She was not even in England. From 15–20 June 1908—the week between Suffrage Saturday and Women's Sunday— the globe-trotting socialist possum-stirrer was in Amsterdam for the third biennial congress of the International Woman Suffrage Alliance.

She was not there as a delegate of an Australian suffrage organisation. No one was, not even Vida Goldstein. The IWSA accepted only delegates from national organisations, and Australia didn't have one. Although the Australian suffrage societies were arguably the most successful in the world, they had remained constituted along colonial then state lines. But Dora did not attend as the WSPU's delegate, either, as she had the two previous congresses in 1904 and 1906. Had she renounced internationalism, then?

No way. She had, in fact, given up on the WSPU. In 1907, Dora parted ways with the militant society she had helped to establish in London, having become desperately unhappy with its organisation. Elizabeth Wolstenholme Elmy, with whom Dora was close, saw the trouble brewing as early as October 1906, on the eve of Dora's short-lived imprisonment.

> Whenever she and I...were alone, it was one continuous wail of discontent against everybody else. Everything other people did was wrong, everybody slighted her—nothing she did was recognized or acknowledged... she did nothing but find fault all the way with every-body and everything connected with the W.S.P. & U. Movement. They undertook to do things but left all the doing to her. [23]

Mrs Elmy was driven nearly round the bend by all this *fault finding and blaming of the absent*. It hadn't always been this way. Dora had been fierce and never suffered fools, but *she was not thus self-absorbed, and egotistic and pathetic of old*. Mrs Elmy recognised that there had been *an awful change in her*.

Four elements, perhaps, contributed to the sudden shift in Dora's demeanour from heroic to pathetic. One was the arrival in London in 1906 of Emmeline Pankhurst. Both Emmeline and Dora liked to be queen of the castle. Their thunderous person-alities probably clashed at close quarters. Second, some time in 1906, Dora's affair with George Belt ended. Perhaps she believed that, at fifty-five, her days of enjoying a *muscular bond* with a man were over. Third, Dora was concerned about the effects of her militant actions on her children. Florence was married by 1907 but was *not at the moment in very good health.* Gilbert was working in an engineering business in Rochester *and I also wished to save him from more trouble than I realised he was bound to have on my behalf.* She had asked neither her daughter nor her son to come to the court during her trial or visit during her imprisonment, *not wishing to add to [their] sufferings.*[24]

But Mrs Elmy wondered about another reason for Dora's personality swing. A mutual friend told her that to his mind Dora's *awful change* was *due to her extravagant use of cocaine lozenges.* Dora claimed to take the lozenges for a persistent cough but, as Mrs Elmy knew, the popular remedy *easily becomes quite as dangerous and demoralizing as the 'morphia' habit.*

In the first decade of the twentieth century, cocaine was the over-the-counter drug of choice, readily recommended by doctors as a remedy for sore throats, haemorrhoids, indigestion, teething and fatigue. It was used, unregulated, as an ingredient in soft drinks, wine and cigarettes. In 1900 a Belgian pharmacy marketed cocaine drops and lozenges as *indispensable for singers, teachers and orators.*[25] It would be no surprise if suffragists, who could speak at up to fourteen meetings a week, became cocaine addicts.

Mrs Elmy confided the likelihood of Dora's affliction in a letter to a fellow suffragist—not as gossip but from a desire to get Mrs Montefiore *medically warned of the danger.* The WSPU leadership was less sympathetic. For them it was not about the lozenges, nor the *old scandal*; they simply would not *have her on any terms. Self aggrandisement seems to be inseparable from her. While she can lead an admiring entourage all goes well.*[26] Perhaps Dora jumped from the WSPU before she was pushed. Certainly, a final meeting with Emmeline after her release from prison *was heated* and Mrs Pankhurst *spoke plainly—as she can!*

Dora retired from the WSPU before Charlotte Despard packed up her own bat and ball and started the WFL. But she didn't join the new league like fellow expats Dora Meeson Coates and Muriel

Matters. Instead, Dora Montefiore held to the one political principle that had always truly separated her from the WSPU regardless of any personality clash: adult suffrage. As early as 1901, Dora had written that she preferred the term adult suffrage to woman suffrage; it was not only *less open to misunderstanding* but also *a necessary part of a democratic programme.*[27]

Dora believed absolutely in votes for women, but she was first and foremost a socialist. She toured Europe regularly, speaking on behalf of a variety of associations, including the Socialist Democratic Front and the Adult Suffrage Society. At the Socialist International Congress in Stuttgart in 1907 she had made the acquaintance of Frederick Engels, with whom she discussed the *colonial question* and the dilemma of *our proletariat being necessarily, and to some extent unconsciously, fellow exploiters with our bourgeoisie of our coloured colonial dependencies.*[28]

The WSPU's acceptance of a property qualification for the female franchise was always a stumbling block for Dora. Some of her stauncher socialist comrades snubbed her for having joined the WSPU at all; she was certainly well aware that *beneath the suffragette skirt peeps the cloven hoof of extension of political power to property and privilege.*[29] But she'd initially been open to the WSPU's argument that a campaign for the franchise on the same terms with men was the most likely to succeed in conservative England. Now she feared that democracy was less important to the suffragettes than equality for wealthy white women.

So, no: Dora had not lost any of her commitment to the internationalism that had encouraged her eager acceptance of the WSPU's invitation to represent it at the 1904 and 1906 IWSA congresses. It was only that now, in this summer of 1908, she went under her own steam.[30]

At the Hague, she was met by Mrs Madge Donohoe and Mrs Emily Dobson, official delegates of the Australian government, which had paid for their expenses. Though Australia still did not have a viable national women's organisation, Alfred Deakin's government had seen fit to appoint women to represent its national interests. Vida Goldstein had also been invited to represent Australia, but had once again declined, due to her ongoing battles with premier Tommy Bent in Victoria.

And of course Australia was the international poster child for woman suffrage, along with Finland (then still a grand duchy of the Russian Empire). Women had won the vote there in 1906 and the following year nineteen of them had been elected to the legislature.[31] At a reception where the flags of Finland and Australia were *conspicuously placed in the centre, that especial honor might be done the full suffrage countries*, Dora listened to speeches praising her former home.

The delegate from the Cape Colony, for example, revealed that the Australian experience shaped South African women's sense of the possibilities when it came to the union of its four colonies. South African suffragists were considering *the same understanding that the women of Australia had with their men, that if they helped to bring about federation they should be given suffrage.* It was not only Australian women's act of good faith that guided this strategic decision. *The men of Australia kept their word*, said the Cape Colony's delegate, *and we believe the men of South Africa would do the same.*[32]

Carrie Chapman Catt expressed the *appreciation* that was *due to our Australian and New Zealand sisters* who had *come from the antipodes…to help the women of the less favoured countries.* Their selfless actions showed *a generous feeling of solidarity* against a common enemy, concluded Catt, *whose name is not man, but conservatism.* It was against this foe that *our international army* was fighting.[33]

Vida couldn't be there at the Hague in 1908 with Dora Montefiore, whom she'd never met, and Carrie Chapman Catt, with whom she'd spent many stimulating days in Washington. But Vida did send a report, containing her heartfelt advice. Don't worry about your enemies. Concentrate on your supposed friends. Spend the conference talking about tactics, Vida counselled, *of laying down a clear, definite election policy.* This strategy would be of more practical good than the endless discussion of principles or even the outcomes of suffrage. She had learnt this from bitter experience in Victoria, where suffragists had decided:

> they would sooner have a hundred parliamentary oppo-
> nents to deal with than enjoy the gelatinous support of
> a hundred members who, on the platform, prate about
> the eternal justice of women's suffrage, but who, in the
> House, never give the slightest evidence that they mean
> business.[34]

Convincing theories, convincing results, even convincing majorities—none of these things counted a jot in the face of wobbly politicians.

It didn't matter what colours peeped from beneath your suffrage skirt. According to Vida, all MPs, regardless of nationality or party, were the same: *the Ins want to stay In, and the Outs don't want to stay Out.*

24

Chain Gang

London, autumn 1908

October 1908, and Muriel Matters, back from vanning, was concealing something beneath her garments that no one expected. The conception had been sharp and painful. Some saw it coming; others smirked. It was inevitable, they said. It's a wonder it didn't happen sooner. As Muriel stood outside the House of Commons, waiting to enter, she had only a moment to pause and reflect on the origins of her secret.

Sunday 11 October. The summer had been a protracted and fiery one, by English standards at least, with temperatures reaching into the eighties Fahrenheit (high twenties Celsius), and the heat continued well into autumn.[1] *Truly our British climate plays strange freaks*, wrote the COVENTRY EVENING TELEGRAPH on 30 September of the *abnormal heat wave*.[2] Emmeline Pankhurst remarked that the summer was one of *the most oppressively hot seasons the country had known*.[3]

And the citizens were getting not just sweaty but toey. At the end of June, a hundred thousand people had gathered outside parliament to no avail. That evening, a suffragette threw a rock through the window of the prime minister's residence at 10 Downing Street. (*The smashing of windows*, remarked Emmeline Pankhurst, *is a time-honoured method of showing displeasure in a political situation*.[4])

No one was more impatient than Emmeline. She was waiting for a reply to a respectful letter she'd written to Asquith asking whether his government was planning to debate a Women's Enfranchisement

Bill in the autumn session of parliament. The bill had been before the Commons for nearly a year, since late 1907.

On 9 October, Emmeline received her reply. To no one's surprise, Asquith nixed the bill.

A plan of action was ready to go. Women, Emmeline warned the government, would enter the House *to plead their cause in person.*[5] If they could not vote, the women would have no other recourse than to assert *the essential justice of making women self-governing citizens.*[6] Speaking in the Commons was, technically, the last constitutional means open to them.

Emmeline now called a mass public demonstration for Sunday 11 October. She, Christabel and a pregnant General, Flora Drummond, rallied the troops from the plinth of Nelson's monument in Trafalgar Square, a traditional place to vent communal unrest. The three suffragettes exhorted *Men and Women* to join them to *Rush the House of Commons* on 13 October. If they could barge their way in en masse, someone could exercise *the oldest of political rights… the constitutional right of the subject to petition the Prime Minister as the seat of power.*[7]

They didn't make it as far as the front gate of Westminster, let alone the seat of power. Police had been taking notes at the Trafalgar Square rally, and the following day all three—Emmeline, Christabel and Flora—were arrested on a charge of 'inciting to riot'.

Christabel represented the trio at the ensuing show trial. The magistrate denied her request for a jury. Christabel decided they might as well make it a real celebrity circus and subpoenaed Gladstone and Lloyd George, who had both been present at the Trafalgar Square demonstration. In her cross-examination, Christabel pointed out that it had been the home secretary himself who had advised the women to take matters into their own hands.

The press devoured her brilliant show of legal nous, with one paper calling her *London's Lady Lawyer. Miss Christabel Pankhurst would have been a barrister had the man-made rules of Lincoln's Inn allowed her to eat her dinners there*, said the Willesden Chronicle, *and the indications she gave the other day show that it is a profession in which she is likely to have achieved fame.*[8] All three women were found guilty nonetheless.

It was a result the Pankhursts had anticipated. *I may not see you again for six months*, Emmeline wrote to Elizabeth Robins, head of the Actresses' Franchise League, *for I have a feeling that the magistrate means to give us as long an imprisonment as the law allows him.*[9] She was right, and wrong. All three women were to be incarcerated in Holloway, Emmeline and the General for twelve weeks, Christabel for ten. Before being taken away, Emmeline addressed the magistrate:

> I want you, if you can, as a man, to realise what it means to women like us. We are driven to do this, we are determined to go on with this agitation, because we feel in honour bound. Just as it was the duty of your fore-fathers, it is our duty to make this world a better place for women than it is to-day...We are here not because we are law-breakers; we are here in our efforts to become law-makers.

With that, the magistrate sent the women—mother, daughter and expectant mother—to gaol, not with the status of political prisoners, but as common criminals, *to be treated as pickpockets and drunkards*, as Emmeline lamented. There they joined scores of other suffragettes who had chosen prison rather than paying their fines for window-smashing, using insulting language, failure to move on, obstructing the pavement and other petty crimes of protest.

Asquith had locked up many of those who had thrown their bonnets in the ring for the cause; now he had the ringleaders. Nailing the Pankhursts was the cherry on top.

⚓

So on 28 October, there was Muriel Matters: standing outside the House of Commons while the Trafalgar Three awaited their sentence. She had no intention of rushing anything. She would execute her purpose steadily, with systematic calm, knowing that her secret weapon was safely concealed beneath her clothing. Fortunately, the autumn days had finally cooled, so it was not conspicuous that the woman showing her ticket to climb the stairs to the Ladies Gallery was bundled up in a heavy coat.

When Teresa Billington-Greig conceived of the plan to show the government that suffrage militancy could be fought on many flanks simultaneously, Muriel had eagerly volunteered to execute it. Another young WFL member, Helen Fox, agreed to accompany her. On the morning of 28 October, according to Sylvia Pankhurst, *all the world had awakened to find little placards posted on every hoarding.* (It is quite possible that this is one occasion when Dora and George Coates tiptoed around at midnight, paste pot in hand.) The posters read: *Proclamation. Women's Freedom League Demands Votes for Women This Session.*[10] The stage was set.

At 5.30 p.m., the actors took their positions. Muriel and Helen were escorted to the eyrie of the Ladies Gallery by Stephen Collins, the well-meaning MP who had unwittingly agreed to provide two gallery tickets to a pair of curious 'public servants'. Muriel, costumed in her heavy coat, carrying a book of Robert Browning poetry and a box of chocolates, mellifluously thanked Mr Collins and entered the small, airless chamber. She saw that the other WFL members had already arrived—there was her dear friend Violet Tillard, a Votes for Women poster obscured beneath her cloak. The gallery was surprisingly full of MPs' wives, considering that it was a banal licensing bill that was being debated.

Muriel took a seat in the second row and waited. For three hours she waited. *The minutes dragged, then flew, alternately, according to the beats of my heart,* Muriel later recalled.[11] Finally, it was the droning of a Tory MP, the Dickensian Mr Remnant, that gave

Muriel her cue. At 8.30 p.m., a woman in the front row abandoned her seat and Muriel darted to take her spot.

She was now sitting within spitting distance of the despised metal screen that separated the Ladies Gallery from the floor of the House below, that *vile grille behind which women have had to sit in the House of Commons for so many years*.[12] Though Muriel had only been in England for three years she well understood, as she later explained to Australian readers, that to suffragists the grille was *one of the symbols of man's conventional attitude towards women.*

> The House of Commons represents men's opinions solely. The actual building plainly demonstrates this. All kinds of men are admitted freely to various parts of the House, but to women is allotted only a small, remote gallery in an obscure corner with a heavy iron grille in front, quite an Oriental custom.[13]

Reduced to a faceless blur in a distant harem behind the nine panels of iron lacework, women could neither see nor be seen. There was only one thing for it. *These stupid conventions, founded on and nourishing inequalities, must be broken down.*

There were two exquisite ironies in what happened next. The first was that the woman who volunteered to symbolise the rebellion—*to emancipate myself*—was already a politically enfranchised woman. The second was that she used the symbol of servitude—the chain—to execute the revolt.

Muriel Matters, *an Australian suffragette*, as the papers made sure to note the next morning, now stood, reached beneath her coat and unfurled the heavy link of chain she'd wrapped in muslin to stop it clinking and giving the game away. She had a leather belt around her waist and, around that, one end of the chain was securely fastened with a keyed padlock. The other end she quickly bolted to the grille with a self-locking Yale padlock. Snap! Muriel had travelled thousands of miles to reach London and now she wasn't going anywhere. *It was over*, she realised exultantly, *over in a second.*

Dora Meeson Coates' very large banner for the Commonwealth,
painted in her Chelsea studio in the summer of 1908.

A meeting of the WSPU inner sanctum at Emmeline Pethick-Lawrence's apartment, 1906. From left: Christabel Pankhurst, Annie Kenney, Nellie Martel, Emmeline Pankhurst, Charlotte Despard. The photo was taken by Sylvia Pankhurst.

Up, up and almost away. Muriel Matters in her rented airship, February 1909.

Above: Nellie Martel braves the threat of eggs and peas to front a jocular all-male crowd. Place and date unknown.

Right: Dora Montefiore 'harangues' the crowd from her window at 'Fort Montefiore' during the Siege of Hammersmith, June 1906.

THE STEEL LINK IN THE WOOLLEN WRAPPING: SUFFRAGETTES CHAINED TO THE GRILLE BEING REMOVED BY ATTENDANTS.

The action of the two Suffragettes in chaining themselves to the grille of the Ladies' Gallery, and then demanding votes for women, had at least one curious result that does not seem to have been much noticed. When the grille is in place, the ladies behind it are not technically within the House, but so soon as the grille is removed they are in the House. Thus the two Suffragettes in question were actually placed in the House by the attendants of the House. The chains used by the ladies were bound with wool, that no noise might be made while they were being fastened round the grille.

The London Illustrated News's depiction of Muriel Matters—the Heroine of the Grille—a media sensation in the autumn of 1908.

But that was only the start of the performance. Muriel had a speaking part and now, over the tedious oration of the unsuspecting MP on the floor of the House, she began to recite her lines, her flat Adelaide accent modulated by years of elocution training.

> Mr Speaker, members of the Il-Liberal government. We have sat behind this insulting Grille for too long. It is time that you ceased to legislate merely on effects, it behoves you to deal with primary causes. You are discussing a domestic question, and it is time that the women of England were given a voice in legislation which affects them as much as it affects men. We demand the Vote.[14]

Now for the chorus. In the commotion, Helen Fox had similarly fastened herself to the grille. *The women of the country demand the vote*, she roared, her lips poking through the grille like a child trying to taste ice on a lamp post. Violet Tillard jumped to her feet and pulled out the poster she had hidden beneath her cloak, the same as the ones *all London* had woken to that morning. Violet pushed the poster through the lacework of the grille, whence it unrolled to reveal the 'proclamation'.

Now a diversion. Someone stood up in the Strangers' Gallery. *I am a man*, Thomas Simmons cried out, *and I protest against the injustice to women*. The Strangers' Gallery was elevated, but not obstructed by an iron screen. Simmons tossed a sheaf of pamphlets over the simple railing, showering the House with suffrage propaganda.

There was now no doubt as to what was occurring. It was an ambush. While the leaders of the WSPU were anxiously awaiting their fate in court, the press hanging off every detail of the trial, the WFL had swooped in to launch a surprise attack. It was, wrote the league's Stella Newsome, *a red letter day in the history of the women's suffrage agitation*[15]—the particular genius of the action being that it was now incumbent on the politicians present to decide what to do next: a choose your own political adventure. Adjourn the session, or ignore the ruckus in the gallery and continue with business as usual? Valiantly, Mr Remnant prattled on while the parliamentary SWAT team went to eject the insurgents.

But when the attendants burst into the gallery to apprehend Muriel and Helen, they soon discovered the women were immovable. Where was the key? they demanded. (The key was in fact tucked down the back of Muriel's dress.) *You cannot get me away,* Muriel laughed defiantly, and she was right. One man tried to rip Muriel from the grille, jerking her head back violently and knocking her into a chair. Another grabbed at her mouth, attempting to muzzle her with his hand. A WFL accomplice sitting in the gallery jumped on the man's back, and it was on for young and old. *Cowards, bullies,* shouted the remaining women in the gallery.[16]

Since they couldn't remove the women—who were still *crying continually in shrill voices their demand for immediate votes for women,* according to the NOTTINGHAM EVENING POST the next day[17]—from the grille, they would have to remove the grille from the gallery. *In sheer desperation,* the HAMPSHIRE TELEGRAPH reported, *the guardians of law and order had to wrench the panels of the grille from their sockets and bodily convey ladies, grille, chains, and all out of the gallery.* THE TIMES described the scene as a *farcical procession,* as the women were dragged, carried and pushed out of the gallery and down the staircase, still attached to the panels of iron trellis. Muriel was taken first. One of the policemen had his hand around her throat. The gallery had been cleared of women, who now formed an impromptu honour guard for Muriel and Helen's journey along a corridor to the committee rooms. They cheered the women and jeered the police. Mr Remnant, determined to be the last man standing, continued to expostulate on *the position of the Licensing Commission and its attitude in relation to the assessment of compensation.* He could barely be heard over the din coming from above. Many MPs left the House to get a front row seat in the committee room.

Inside the room, a legion of police waited for the two malcontents and their iron appendages. A blacksmith filed through the chains. Muriel fully expected to be arrested, but to her surprise, she and Helen were escorted from the premises and released via a back entrance.

By now, crowds had gathered around the front at the St Stephen's entrance. In part, the crowd was composed of spectators who had come to see what the morning papers would call *Extraordinary Scenes in the House of Commons*.[18] The sea of intrigued onlookers was swelled by a scrum of reporters vying for a scoop. But there was also a vocal group of WFL members who had staged a co-ordinated demonstration inside St Stephen's Hall, leading police in *another game of tig* when the long arm of the law tried to move them on. Finally ejected from the building, some women mounted the statue of Richard I, near where Nellie Martel had begun the first open air protest on *that fateful day* of 12 May 1905. Almost three and a half years later, with no victory in sight, the women could do little but hang on for dear life as police tried to rip them bodily from the statue.

It was here, as one protester *clung tenaciously to the legs of Richard's horse*, that a battered and bruised Muriel finally achieved her aim. From the centre of the crowd, she demanded admission to *The House of the People*, shouting: *It is as much a House of women as it is of men*. With these revolutionary words, she was arrested for 'wilfully resisting police', and taken to Cannon Row police station.

Sylvia Pankhurst later assessed that, although the grille was soon restored, *even the temporary dismemberment of a fixture which seemed so strikingly typical of the long enslavement of women was widely regarded as a triumph*.[19]

And this was the beauty of Teresa Billington-Greig's plan. The poetry of protest. What attracted so many women in such great numbers to the movement, she realised, was not suffrage per se, but insurgence, insurrection: to *cast away these chains*.

It was women crying to the masculine sovereignty: 'You do not only deny me the right of self-government, you deny me the right of rebellion against bondage, against the worst servitudes, against every manifestation of your control. This first right I take. I disavow your authority. I put aside your cobweb conventions of law and government. I rebel. I claim my inalienable right to cast off servitude. I emancipate myself. And the liberty I have claimed and taken you shall register in the writings of your law.[20]

I rebel. Je suis prêt. I am ready. And so is she. And so is she. By such logic is an army raised. Particularly when there is a valiant leader, also equipped for action.

25

Rowdy and Repellent

Australia, spring 1908

The name of Muriel Matters, surmised WFL member Stella Newsome, *may not go down to future ages, but her deed will never be forgotten.*

Certainly, the grille incident was not soon forgotten and there is no doubt it made Muriel's name in London. *The Suffragette Scene in the Commons* was the publicity stunt of the year, outstripping Suffrage Saturday and Women's Sunday for press coverage. Muriel, the *Heroine of the Grille* as she was now known, had managed to turn heads in a way that half a million people gathered in Hyde Park had not. *Amazing Women. Riotous Scenes In and Out of the House. Padlocked Women's Vain Protests. The Suffragette Nuisance.*

The more sensational the headlines, the more copies sold. Muriel's speech from the Ladies Gallery was characterised as the first time a woman had spoken in the House of Commons, a history-making moment. Not only was Muriel's pleasingly alliterative name splashed across newspapers the length and breadth of Britain, but so was her *striking, pretty face*. Newspapers were largely illustrated at this time, press photography being rare, and papers revelled in producing lavishly detailed pictures of Muriel chained to the grille, like a damsel in distress tethered to the railway tracks (although not, since the *noisy creature* was herself driving the train).

What followed Muriel's arrest was not as historic, nor as histrionic, but equally fascinating to a rapt British public. *The Police Court Sequel* was how the SHEFFIELD EVENING TELEGRAPH titled its

coverage of the subsequent trial of the fourteen WFL members and
one man who were arrested on the night of the 28 October. (Helen
Fox was not among them.[1]) Charlotte Despard, Edith How-Martyn
and Teresa Billington-Greig were all in court to watch the proceedings, *wearing the colours of the League—yellow, white and green*. The
police magistrate said it was *one of the most disgraceful and disorderly
scenes* that had occurred during the votes for women campaign. He
then proceeded to fine the one man on trial, Alfred Cutler, twenty
shillings. Cutler's offence was telling the police to *Leave the women
alone* when they were being dragged off the plinth of Richard I.

Then it was Muriel's turn. The SHEFFIELD EVENING
TELEGRAPH reported thus:

> Miss Muriel Matters, an Australian lady, one of the two
> who chained themselves the ladies' grille, and who was
> afterwards arrested for disturbance in the street, asked
> for an adjournment. The Magistrate said he would be
> willing to grant the request if the evidence were to
> be produced, but not if the defendant desired only to
> prepare a speech. He said that he would be glad to have
> an expression of regret from the lady and the assurance
> that she would go back to Australia, where she could
> vote.
>
> Miss Matters: No; while I am here I must do my abso-
> lute best to improve the condition of the women in this
> country.
>
> The Magistrate: Pay £5.
>
> Miss Matters: What—no option?
>
> A month's imprisonment was then stated as the alterna-
> tive.[2]

The magistrate told Muriel she should go back to where she
came from; Muriel told the magistrate where he could stick that
helpful suggestion. (She would have enjoyed the banter—she was
always complaining that the English had no sense of humour.)

And then she gladly accepted the stated alternative. A sketch in the NOTTINGHAM EVENING POST shows Muriel being escorted by two moustachioed policemen to the Cannon Row station. She is wearing a long white coat and a beatific smile. There is no depiction of her being taken to Holloway to join the thirty other suffrage prisoners presently housed there.

Back in Australia, Muriel's headline-grabbing antics didn't go unnoticed. *Most South Australians who read daily of the eccentric and athletic behaviour of the Suffragettes in London*, proposed the Adelaide GADFLY, *will be surprised to learn that an Adelaide maiden is among the most strenuous clamorers for the cause.*[3] It was with a measure of both pride and bemusement that GADFLY reported Muriel had gone beyond chalking pavements and *now draws crowds like the most hardened of veterans.* And why wouldn't the suffragettes be eager to recruit *the gifted Muriel*, chuckled the journalist—she possessed *a quantity of charm, besides what is known in high and culchawed circles as 'the gift of the gab'.*

The Perth papers were also happy to claim Muriel as their own. Under the headline *Miss Muriel Matters to the Front*,[4] the WESTERN MAIL praised Muriel for pouring her *heart and soul into what seems to be becoming a burning question in England.* Listening to the stories of her *marvellous courage* in the face of hostile crowds, where she risked *life and limb* touring the regions, it was *difficult to realise that one is living in the prosaic and commercially inclined 20th century.* England was patently stuck in the dark ages: as far as the WESTERN MAIL was concerned, those against the suffrage movement *are simply in the position of stopping a clock in the vain hope that the passage of time will thus be delayed in its flight.* Womanhood suffrage had been positive for the state; Western Australia had remained on the right side of modern history—and the English would surely realise that *the franchise for women is bound to come in time.* Muriel could be forgiven for helping to convince the knuckle-draggers to get with the program.

In the eastern states, the press was less kind. The AGE pointed out that Muriel Matters, *the Australian girl who has been a prominent agitator among the suffragettes in London, displayed no interest in politics here.*[5] (The editor, having failed to crunch the numbers, did not concede that Muriel had indeed been only a girl when South Australian women won the vote, and barely over voting age at the granting of the federal franchise; or that, at thirty-one, she was now entitled to be called an Australian woman.) According to the AGE, Muriel's attention-seeking—her *love of notice*—had gone largely unheeded in her homeland, but she had now found a way to *bring down the house* in England. If *the English editors admit that Muriel matters*, the Age was not going to return the favour.

The Melbourne ADVOCATE published a letter from a Victorian living in London, written on 1 November, who lamented that *the militant 'Suffragettes' of London are verily becoming more and more rowdy and repellent in their manners and methods. They are in real danger of completely unsexing themselves.*[6] The correspondent, who claimed he had *thrice voted for female suffrage*, confirmed the common perception that most of the English agitators were *feather-headed young women, actuated more by the craze for notoriety...than by any burning zeal in the cause of female enfranchisement.* The gentleman concluded his letter with a report of the grille incident in which *Miss Matters, who described herself as an enfranchised Australian lady...and a lecturer by profession* had elected to go to prison rather than pay her fine. *With the help of Miss Matters*, he concluded, *our would-be lady voters have certainly been making matters lively.*

Apprised, perhaps, of the way the press was making light of her actions, Muriel wrote a long and graphic account of the grille incident and forwarded it to the Perth MORNING HERALD. It was subsequently republished in papers around the nation. Muriel stressed the violence done to her—*ruthlessly was my head jerked back upon a chair*—and concluded that with so much attention drawn to the cause, *the grille has at last been used to some good purpose.*[7] Perth's

TRUTH newspaper, a gutter rag not known for its progressive tendencies, asserted that Muriel Matters was *a worthy Westralian* and a martyr *in the cause of votes for women.*

> Miss Matters has earned fame for herself and women's cause as the gallant young Australienne who addressed the members of the House of Commons from the grille, for which offence against the sacred laws of that august assembly she was sent to Holloway prison.[8]

The sarcasm was, for once, directed not at the protestor but towards the object of protest. It was the politicians and their *bluecoated minions* who deserved scorn, not the *Westralian woman* who addressed the House *coolly, calmly and collectedly.* Winning over Australia's conservative press was conceivably Muriel's finest achievement yet.

⚜

It was a feat Nellie Martel certainly hadn't accomplished.

The MOLONG ARGUS seized the opportunity to take a swipe at *ex-Australian agitator…Mrs Nellie Martel—a bouncing blonde, who was the chief rival of Miss Rose Scott when the movement was in full-swing in this State,* even though Nellie had nothing to do with the incident they were reporting on their front page. (The piece was on the incarceration of Constance Clyde, an Australian journalist working in London, for her part in a suffragette protest in 1907.) To the ARGUS, the suffragettes were *busy-bodies, frenzied females* and *raving lunatics seeking martyrdom.*[9]

Of the riotous scenes at Newton Abbot, the ADELAIDE OBSERVER noted that, following the defeat of the Liberal candidate, Emmeline Pankhurst and Nellie Martel (*sister of the Hon. D. M. Charleston of South Australia*) were *rolled in the mud* by a *party of roughs.*[10] TABLE TALK similarly hurled mud at *our old friend Nellie Martel* after the Newton Abbot affair.[11]

> Nellie of the peroxidised locks must be a proud woman
> to-day. She has been arrested in the street for rioting,
> she has waved the scarlet flag through the 'grille' in the
> House, and been carried out kicking in the arms of a
> stalwart policeman, she has, when attired in a fashion-
> able yellow, satin blouse (per cable) through the streets
> of London at the behest of 5000 women, shouting for
> freedom and equal rights with man...and now she has
> rolled in a slushy gutter, where the mud was 10 inches
> deep: Could devotion go any further? We felt like
> cabling Bravo.[12]

Had the journalist done so, Nellie might have retorted that she
and Emmeline had not started the riot but had nearly been killed in
it.

After the grille incident, the Adelaide REGISTER bundled
Muriel's *unseemly antics* together with Nellie's lawbreaking to make
a case for the way the intervention of Australian activists in British
domestic politics had *rais[ed] doubts in the slow-moving Anglo-Saxon
mind regarding the superior wisdom and meekness of the fair sex in South
Australia*. British progressives looked to Australia as politically
superior, the pace-setters, but women like Nellie and Muriel were
kicking own goals, knocking Australia off its carefully constructed
pedestal. The REGISTER was scathing of the suffragettes' *exceedingly
foolish* methods, yet equally critical of the response of authorities.

> The idea of sending women to gaol because they are
> endeavouring to obtain a share of democratic powers
> is as repugnant to British ideals as the unfeminine
> demonstrations which are thus punished.[13]

Regardless of Nellie's keynote on the platform at Hyde Park
in front of half a million people, TRUTH was still obsessing about
her peroxide straw-colored hair and three layers of perle blanc—despite
which vanities the British sheilas still appeared to have taken to
her.[14] It seemed that no matter how much favour Nellie gained in
London, *becoming quite a personage among the English suffragettes*

as TRUTH conceded, her reputation in the Australian press would remain tarnished.

But the TRUTH article, published on 10 January 1909, turned out to be the last time Nellie was mentioned in the Australian press—or, for that matter, the British press. Some time in late 1908, and certainly by early 1909, Nellie followed Dora Montefiore's example and split with the WSPU. Unlike Dora, she did not divert her activist energies elsewhere: she simply disappeared from public life.

What happened? Was there an incident that forced her exit from the organisation she had helped to establish in London five years earlier? Or did relations slowly go pear-shaped, as they had with Rose Scott and the Womanhood Suffrage League in Sydney, or with the Golding sisters in their breakaway organisation? Did Nellie jump ship just when the WSPU was reaching full sail; or was she pushed? There are no clear answers, but a few clues.

After the success of the Hyde Park rally, Nellie continued with the WSPU's propaganda work around the country. In September, she was in Liverpool, where scores of women *listened to the brilliant address of the 'invader' as Mrs Martel was called on the Liverpool posters the day following.*[15] The event was so successful that a band of women followed Nellie on her tour of New Brighton and surrounding districts, shouting *Shame on a British Government who imprison women* at her meetings. Some time in September Nellie either was ditched from, or stepped down from, the WSPU Committee, meaning she probably ceased to be a paid organiser too.[16] In October, despite her demotion, Nellie toured Yorkshire, often speaking at two meetings per day. In November, her addresses to audiences in the north of England were favourably reported in the MANCHESTER GUARDIAN. *There were thirteen men hanged before the men present were entitled to a vote*, she told one meeting. *Was the Government going to demand from women the same price as men paid for their liberty? (Applause).*[17] And with that ovation, Nellie dropped off the radar of the British

press too. Her last appearance in the WSPU's journal VOTES FOR
WOMEN is 6 January 1909.[18] Her penny pamphlet, THE WOMEN'S
VOTE IN AUSTRALIA, ceased to be listed on the WSPU's Women's
Press publications list soon after. [19]

Was there an insurmountable personality clash that led to
Nellie's departure not only from the WSPU but from public life?
Evidence about how Nellie's fellow campaigners regarded her
suggests so. In 1907, Elizabeth Robins wrote a novel called THE
CONVERT, about a rich society beauty who becomes caught up in
the militant suffrage cause. The characters in the book were based
on women Robins had met in the movement, the dialogue based on
their actual speeches. Robins gave a draft of the book to Emmeline
Pankhurst to read. *I like it all immensely*, Emmeline told her, *the only
thing that jars is Mrs Martel.*

> She is such a good soul really, and I fear she will recognise
> the portrait. I would not have her hurt for worlds. She
> is horribly sensitive under that surface that repels you.
> Is it too late to cut her out or alter her beyond recogni-
> tion? I'd rather see her cut out. She is a good fighter and
> came to our side when we had so few friends. In spite of
> her little ways which sometimes made me squirm, I am
> very fond of her and I don't like to think of her being
> wounded.[20]

It is possible that Robins followed Pankhurst's advice and cut
Nellie's character out, given that the novel was published in 1907
and there doesn't seem to have been a reaction from Nellie. Another
suffragist comrade, Rebecca West, gives a clue to Nellie's reputation:
I was agreeably surprised with Mrs Martel, she wrote to her sister. *She's
a dear old soul in spite of her hair, and takes the crowd tremendously.*[21]

Nellie was clearly a divisive figure: brash, flamboyant, outwardly
confident but ultimately insecure. She *repelled* people (who apparently responded with freely exercised condescension). Her *little ways*
could jar with even her closest allies. Nellie's personality was a useful

weapon in a guerrilla war of irritation and pestering, but perhaps she exasperated and infuriated her allies as well as her enemies.

Or perhaps the years of campaigning had taken a toll. She'd suffered a spell of exhaustion before leaving Sydney, and after five intense years of public speaking, outdoor demonstrations, by-election campaigns, propaganda meetings, writing essays and pamphlets, fund-raising and hell-raising, she could have been in poor health, mentally and physically spent. Possibly she needed to care for Charles.

In any case, she doesn't appear to have made a philosophical break with the movement. Some time in 1909, Nellie wrote a letter to suffragette Mary Ann Rawles, scribbled on leftover WSPU letterhead. Rawles was one of the four hundred textile workers who had travelled to London to speak at the deputation to the prime minister in May 1906, where Nellie was speaking. *Sorry to learn you are still suffering from the rough handling you received*, Nellie wrote, *but my heart leapt when I read your spirit was not damped. Bravo! With such women to help on the Cause, we* _must_ *win.*[22] Nellie had also applied, unsuccessfully, to visit three prisoners in Holloway. *We shall go on asking*, she told Rawles, *and give them [the visiting committee] extra work to reply to us.*

From the sound of it, Nellie had lost none of her fight, and she still identified with the movement that had given her life in England purpose and solidarity since 1904. She also—and perhaps this was one of her *little ways* that could rile—took implicit credit for the current strength of the campaign. *England will not go to the walls*, she wrote, *whilst her women are so brave and loyal as we have proved you to be.* It took Australian women (*we*) to push English women (*you*) to the limits of their courage and perseverance. Perhaps the WSPU leadership were sick of having Nellie rub their noses in her sweet-smelling, pearl-encrusted, upstart Australian ascendancy.

In early 1909, as Nellie bowed out of public life, Ethel Hill published a book called GREAT SUFFRAGISTS AND WHY: MODERN

MAKERS OF HISTORY. Her entry on Nellie Martel concludes: *No woman has played a more prominent part in this great and vital question.*[23]

When she wrote the manuscript, Hill could not have known that her words would be Nellie's valedictory epitaph.

♆

On 20 August 1908, two months after 500,000 people crammed into Hyde Park to witness a full-throttle Nellie and the spectacle that was Women's Sunday, the same number of Sydneysiders turned out to watch a very different event. The US Navy's 'Great White Fleet' was sailing into Sydney Harbour. It was the largest crowd ever seen in Australia, far larger than the one that came to celebrate the birth of the nation seven years earlier. The sixteen-strong fleet would take its show of maritime strength to ports around the globe, but no other country would welcome the Americans as jubilantly as Australia.

It was a triumphant moment for Prime Minister Alfred Deakin, who had defied the British Foreign Office in making a unilateral invitation to President Roosevelt to host his navy. When Roosevelt had met Vida Goldstein six years earlier, he told her that he had his eye on Australia; Deakin clearly had his sights set on America too.[24] Britannia no longer ruled the waves as she once had. Why not court the Americans?

Vida was a patriotic proponent of an Australian navy and an admirer of both Deakin and Roosevelt. But she was not focused on the visit of the shiny American troopships. There was a hand-to-hand land battle going on in Victoria in the last four months of 1908, one that required all her strategic capacities. Victorians would go to the polls in December, and Vida was determined that this would be the year that those two recalcitrant Legislative Council votes for women's suffrage would finally be snared.

She had always believed that education was the key to political reform: change minds, and those minds would organise to change laws. But the continued delay of Victoria in gaining suffrage—the sheer *political drudgery* required to keep up the pressure—was starting to test her faith. With Tommy Bent behaving much like a bovine version of the pig-headed Asquith, she was no longer so sure that peaceful propaganda was the way through the logjam of prejudice. In 1908, she reported to the IWSA conference in Amsterdam, *we find ourselves crushed between our straight-out opponents and our professed friends. None of them likes the practical working of women's suffrage; each Party thinks that it lessens its party influence.*[25] She would take a leaf out of the suffragettes' book if she had to. *Sensationalism is everything*, Vida wrote in her diary in 1908, *and so the suffragists have had to make sensationalism the chief motif of their educational work.*

In the spring of 1908, a member of the Labor opposition introduced yet another Adult Suffrage Bill to parliament. Vida tried to lure Bent into a public meeting where he would be forced to answer questions from the audience. Why would the premier not make adult suffrage a government policy? He agreed to a meeting, but banned questions.[26] Inspired by the twin summer suffrage processions in London, Vida considered holding a public march through Melbourne's streets. *They must be made to feel that women are in earnest*, she wrote, *and English women have shown the world how that can be done.*[27] Instead, she convinced male supporters to form a Men's League for Woman Suffrage, another English innovation. And she tried speaking to Bent again. To Vida's surprise, he agreed to talk to one of the two uncooperative MPs. By September, the corrupt old curmudgeon started to drop sly hints that the women might have his support. On 7 October, three weeks before Muriel Matters fastened her reputation to the grille, Bent renounced his former position and, without a hint of contrition or irony, announced that he would introduce a government bill to replace the Labor bill. The Bent bill was introduced a week later, though Vida wasn't there to see the historic moment when Victorian women's forty-four-year struggle to win the state franchise neared its end: Bent had closed the public galleries to women.

On 18 November, however, Vida was looking on from the gallery (another Bent flip-flop), as the bill passed its second reading in what she termed the *House of Obstruction, constitutionally known as the Legislative Council.*[28] As a division was not called, Vida defied the parliamentary rules that forbade visitors taking notes in the gallery and wrote down the names of the noes. She considered it an opportune moment *to do some mild 'suffragetting' on my own account.* Victoria, *the first colony to demand political freedom* in 1869, was the last state *to see it realized.*[29]

That December, Vida sent a card to the National American Woman Suffrage Association.

> This is the Christmas mail to the United States, so you can imagine I have lots of cards to send off. I have only time to let you know that on November 18 our suffrage bill passed the Council by 23 to 5, and was a glorious victory. We never expected such a tremendous success. I can scarcely believe yet that the struggle of years is absolutely over…I want you and the good suffrage friends in the State to know how happy we are.[30]

When it came time to register to vote, Vida Goldstein was literally the first in line.

The *glorious victory* meant more to Vida than simply the end of an exhausting era of intellectual and organisational brawling. Her newfound political emancipation at home was matched in other, more personal ways. Vida was now unshackled from her domestic obligations, able to take wing and stretch the limits of her statecraft. *We are thankful to be free,* she wrote to both the NUWSS and WSPU leadership, *because of our own self-respect, because of the power it gives us to help in making Australia a great nation, and because we shall be freer to help our sisters in other lands to win their political liberty.*

Failure is Impossible.

26

Fight and Flight

London, winter 1909

The grille incident had been spectacular, but the next stunt Muriel Matters was planning might be catastrophic—and it was definitely going to be cold. It was 16 February 1909, and the weather was predictably frigid. Even in a thick woollen coat, several layers of clothing, gloves and an aviator's cap tied under her chin with a big white scarf, Muriel wouldn't be snug at 3500 feet.

But she was undeterred from her brazen plan: to travel by air— in a hired dirigible—from the Welsh Harp Reservoir near Hendon down to central London and around Big Ben to Westminster, timing the flight so as to drop fifty-six pounds (twenty-five kilograms) of handbills on the state procession of the King to open the winter session of parliament. The powered airship wouldn't attempt to land in London; rather, Muriel would shout down to the crowd through a megaphone as she passed, and then land in the downs near Epsom. A carload of WFL members led by Edith How-Martyn would follow the course of the airship by road and pick Muriel up at the other end of her journey. Strategic masterstroke or sheer madness?

The plan was devised to thwart the restrictions placed on the WFL's activities after it claimed responsibility for the tumult in parliament the previous October. The WFL was barred from distributing leaflets in the streets, the public galleries of the House remained closed and security was on high alert, with police surveillance trailing the suffragettes' every move. But no one was expecting an attack from the air. Only a handful of people, let alone women, had ever been up in a flying machine. (The risk was considerable, although perhaps not solely of plummeting to one's doom. If medical men in the 1890s discouraged women from riding bicycles with warnings of *bicycle face*—a permanent distortion of the facial features due to the strain of pedalling—and reprised their concern with predictions of *automobile face* when women began driving cars in the early twentieth century, they might have had something to say about 'airship face'.)

In any case, what could the police do when they did catch wind of the plan and saw the snowstorm of Votes for Women leaflets? Chase her? Even if their police horses could magically grow wings, *their regulations do not extend up there*, Muriel pointed out: *You see, there are still some limitations to man's authority.*[1]

There was only room for one passenger in Henry Spencer's airship, and Muriel had made sure it was reserved for her. She had been released from prison on 5 December, surviving the ordeal of Holloway in reasonable shape, even though she frequently *gave sauce* to the matron.[2] The Heroine of the Grille was now free to become the Heroine of the Skies. It was just as novel a part, pleasingly showing her range. In the first performance, Muriel shackled herself to the obdurate bars of tradition. Today, she would unleash herself upon the great open promise of the future.

At least one man accepted that the winds of change favoured rather than froze women's independence. Mr Spencer not only let the suffragettes paint a huge *Votes for Women* sign in black lettering on one side of his airship, and *Women's Freedom League* on the other. He also allowed them to attach forty-foot streamers from the airship in the WFL colours, and volunteered to be Muriel's aeronaut for the day. And all for £75 for the expected two-hour journey.

It was cold but fortunately it was not raining. The skies were clear and a small crowd had gathered in the field to watch the peculiar happenings: a cheerful lady in a green coat being lifted into the wicker basket of the airship; a pile of pamphlets being loaded in;

the pilot trying to start the engine. Another try. And another. This was not a dress rehearsal. There could be no repeat performance. The King's carriage would be making its way down the Mall. Other WFL members would be bobbing about on the Thames in a gondola, waiting for Muriel's arrival to speak to the royal-watching crowds from a megaphone. It was 1.30 p.m. Time for lift off. How could she calm her nerves while Mr Spencer fiddled about with the thirty-five-horsepower engine that would somehow push this cigar-shaped balloon through the air? Perhaps she could recite the witty little poem that a fellow had composed after the grille incident.

> They regard us at home as a lunatic crowd,
> In Australia they know us as 'hatters'
> But let women-enfranchised Australians please
>   note,
> We've got with us Miss Muriel Matters
> Some may regard us unequal to man;
> Such folly a suffragette scatters,
> While importunate widows continue to fan
> The flame lit by Miss Muriel Matters.[3]

The engine sputtered, then sparked, then purred. At 2 p.m. they were off, soaring upward as a laughing Muriel waved to the ever-receding crowd.

⨸

The latest move of the militant suffragists was a balloon raid on St Stephen's, reported the NORTHERN DAILY TELEGRAPH,[4] but unfortunately for them, *the elements were unpropitious*.

It was true, Muriel's airship had been heaven-bound, but the conditions were not heaven-sent. The winds gusted more sharply than expected, pushing the airship off course. It was a difficult beast to steer at the best of times. At one stage, Spencer climbed out of the basket and onto the wire-and-rope rigging. *I was afraid that he would say at any moment, 'Just climb out there and see to the ballast'*, Muriel later recounted to an audience eager for thrilling details. *Of course I should have gone had I been asked.*[5] They were now at 3500 feet (a thousand metres)—too high for her megaphone to be any use. And instead of tracking south towards Westminster, they were over Hyde Park: they had drifted too far west and would miss the parliament buildings altogether. They were floating over Chelsea now—somewhere down there fellow WFL member Dora Meeson Coates would be in her studio, painting—and with Big Ben falling away into the distance, there was no time like the present to unload the leaflets. Down they fluttered, hundreds of yellow, green and white fliers. *The leaflets and the shrill cry of 'Votes for women' wasted themselves upon the desert air*, wrote The Times. All that was left was for Mr Spencer to get them safely to ground. The great balloon had now coasted beyond London's southern suburbs, over soft green pastures such as South Australian farmers could only dream about. Never mind Epsom; Spencer brought his craft down in the borough of Croydon, landing somewhat inelegantly in a hedge. It would take another hour and ninety kilometres of helter-skelter driving along the trail of handbills for Muriel's companions to reach her.[6]

The escapade wasn't a waste, of course; far from it. The press went wild. London had never witnessed an extra-terrestrial political protest. Nowhere had. *A Lady Who Cannot Be Kept Down*, shouted the headline in the Daily Mail the following day. *Masterful, ingenious*, were words used to describe the plan, if not the execution. It was a particularly modern act of resistance, harnessing a new technology to announce the topsy-turvy power of the New Woman, a detail which did not go unremarked by the press.

> 'I think we can say now we are well up to date,' she observed. 'If we want to go in the air, neither the police nor anyone else can keep us down, and if we could throw handbills we could easily throw anything else.' Miss Matters is Australian.

To be 'up in the air' no longer meant to be debatable or uncertain. It now meant to be 'up to date'. Fresh, prevailing, enlightened and forward-looking, like the baby nation at the bottom of the globe. And there was a hint of menace in the knowledge and experience—the loss of innocence—that no longer being earth-bound entailed. The women could *throw anything else.* A new threat. Missiles from the sky. *You can take it from me,* Muriel told reporters when she returned to London that night, *that after today's experience we shall not do much on earth again.*[7]

A new ditty now did the rounds, a five-verse paean to Muriel Matters, *the pioneer of Woman's rights,* called 'In the Air'. The last verse lyrically summed up all the anxieties of the lawmakers and inventiveness of the lawbreakers, as England approached the last year of the first decade of the new century.

> What a lesson for each maid is
> To be learnt from such a case,
> Of the foolishness of ladies,
> Who would fly in Nature's face;
> Who to such mad lengths are going,
> By the winds of folly fann'd,
> That there's certainly no knowing,
> Where they'll land.[8]

27

The Envy of the World

Australia, autumn 1910

It is quite a mistake to think, as many people in this country seem to do, realised an older and wiser Vida Goldstein, *that women will immediately rush into Parliament as soon as they get the chance.*[1]

In the Australian summer of 1910 the now-seasoned political campaigner had a huge and potentially life-changing decision to make. The Commonwealth government had called a general election for 13 April: Vida had another chance to make her own dash at the national legislature. With the battle for suffrage finally won in Victoria, would she, could she, steel herself for another tilt at the Senate? No woman had stood in the 1906 federal election, and in South Australia, the only state where women were eligible to run for parliament, not a single woman had put herself forward. Did Vida have a responsibility to run? She believed with all her heart that even if she were to lose again, *every woman who stands as a candidate makes the task of the next woman candidate easier.* And she was *perfectly content to blaze the track for others.*[2]

But there was rocky ground to break on both sides of the globe, and Vida had just started to consider how she might best help her British sisters fight for the fundamental political rights they were still so far from winning. On 29 November 1909, Vida convened a public meeting at Melbourne's Athenaeum Hall. There was *an attendance of 250, of whom 230 were ladies*, according to the ARGUS.[3] The purpose of the meeting was *to tell the truth about the Suffragettes.* Vida was joined by another WPA member, Irish-born journalist Miss Agnes

Murphy—Nellie Melba's private secretary—who gave an eye-witness account of the way that *a new chivalry* had been instituted in England: *it was now women for women*.[4] Murphy had been involved in WSPU activism and testified at the trial of Mrs Pankhurst, when she, Christabel and Flora Drummond were gaoled. It was the biased reports of an antagonistic press that had poisoned the mind of the world against the suffragettes, argued Murphy, something it was difficult to understand in Australia where journalistic practice was characterised by *honesty, reasonableness and humanity*. (Nellie Martel might have begged to differ.) At the conclusion of the meeting, Vida called for a resolution of sympathy with the suffragettes and congratulated them on *their sublime courage in putting principle before party*. But where would Vida now put her principles? She was all for women, but which women? Her enfranchised but still unrepresented sisters at home, or her unenfranchised sisters abroad?

Under the glare of the January sun, there were already audible *whispers in the air* about the likelihood that she would contest the upcoming federal election. Rumours too that there would be another female candidate, Mrs D'Ebro, the vice-president of the conservative Australian Women's National League. If true, this would add an element with which Vida had not previously had to contend: not just male combatants on both sides of politics, but another woman too. While she agreed with many of the progressive policies of Deakin's incumbent government and of the opposition Labor Party, she could not stomach the anti-socialist, pro-military rhetoric of the AWNL.

Mrs D'Ebro, daughter of a Melbourne establishment family and wife of a prominent architect, was known for her *remarkable assertiveness* and other *abilities which distinguish her as a likely bidder for a position which no woman has yet achieved*. Fortunately—if bizarrely, after the bitter years of campaigning for the vote in Victoria—Vida had maintained her reputation as *the most non-political woman existing in our midst, at least as regards her personality*. This was code, of course, for the fact that she had kept her ladylike dignity in the face of torment, vilification, disappointment and setback upon setback. Unlike those crazy English suffragettes, Vida displayed *a wide and vast supply [of] all the most pleasing attributes belonging to women, a soft voice, soothing manner, pleasing ways and often merry touches of happy humour.*[5]

Yes, it was always worth having a laugh—with your enemies as well as your friends—but did she really have the energy and commitment to *rush into Parliament?* At forty-one, Vida could focus on her new journal, the WOMAN VOTER, and enjoy the company of her family, with whom she lived, and the fellowship of their Christian Science community. She could join her friend Cecilia Johns and raise poultry on one of the new women's farms springing up, or go to England and join Muriel Matters and Mrs Montefiore—surely the movement there needed a new Australian friend now that Nellie Martel had left the fold—or...

But who was she kidding? Wild horses couldn't keep her away from this campaign. As if she would let Mrs D'Ebro be the first to accomplish what no woman had yet achieved!

On 14 February 1910, Valentine's Day, Vida Goldstein opened her campaign. Not in her home town of Portland as she had in 1903 (she knew that *it is said 'Portland votes for Miss Goldstein'*) but under the wide blue skies of nearby Casterton, home of the kelpie.[6] It would be a long road—eight weeks of speeches and meetings the length and breadth of the state—to pick up one of the three Victorian Senate seats on offer. Both the Liberal and Labor parties were putting up three candidates each for the three seats; so far, there was no sign of Mrs D'Ebro.

Vida was pleased to see that the crowds were coming out to greet her again. *She had not expected,* she told a packed hall in Hamilton, *to have such a bumper house as she had on the former occasion when a number of people attended out of curiosity to see the wild woman of the woods who sought to enter Parliament.* She stood, Vida told the largely female audience, *because she wanted to represent the interests of women, children and the home.* If they had attended meetings in the legislature, as she had done for two decades now, they would see that *every subject of legislation in which women were interested was mutilated because they could not see the question from the women's point of view.*

Could they imagine watching a bill for infant life protection be introduced, only to witness nearly every member of the assembly walk out when it came to be debated? It was with the utmost difficulty that she had persuaded enough members to vote for a bill that would prevent a child being sent to prison at the age of seven. The bill passed by only three votes.

How often had she written to Prime Minister Deakin asking him to introduce a marriage and divorce bill into parliament? The Commonwealth constitution assumed these powers from the states, but still there was no federal legislation. She wanted mothers and fathers to have joint rights over their offspring—for at present women had no legal control over their children, the very reason Dora Montefiore had gone into politics almost twenty years ago—and equal grounds for divorce. Why should a man be able to obtain a divorce by proving one act of infidelity when a woman must also prove habitual drunkenness, cruelty or desertion?

She stood for equal pay for equal work.

As a genuinely patriotic Australia, she stood against the ticket system of voting, a system which was *rotten to the core.* She had seen the workings of machine politics on her tour of America—the way the men put on the tickets were controlled by business monopolies and trusts—and hoped it would never be foisted upon Australia.[7] When voting for a party's ticket, *people did not vote according to their principles, but according to the decision of the majority.* Vote for the women's candidate on 13 April, and you could still vote for two other members of your preferred party. Vote for the ticket, and vote for the devil of party government with all *its corruption and jobbery.*[8]

Thus would Vida address audiences in every part of the

state. She gave one speech and one speech only, *so as not to be more misrepresented than she could help.* If she gave twenty speeches, the press would find a way *to misrepresent every one of them.* She would keep her message clear and simple, answering questions from the floor so long as they were civil.

It was in this context that she would canvass her views on other critical election issues such as states' rights, the financial agreement with the Commonwealth (she opposed it) and the transcontinental railway (in 1903, she had been opposed to it; now that she'd travelled to Western Australia to visit her brother Selwyn, she could see the need for it).

As in 1903, she charged an admission price to her meetings: a silver coin donation—unlike other candidates, she had neither independent means nor party backing. And she introduced a novel element into her campaign: having studied the way that all the English suffrage societies now adopted their own *colours,* she wore the colours of the Women's Political Association. Lavender—*signifying the fragrance of everything good in the past.* Green—for *growth and development.* And purple—*indicating loyalty to justice and equal sovereignty of men and women.*

But foliage and lace could only get a lady so far. The 1910 election was always going to be *one of the hardest fought in the history of Australian politics.*[9] It was the first time that the contest would not be run as a three-cornered race. Deakin's Liberal Protectionist Party had merged with the conservative Anti-Socialists Party in 1909 to become the Commonwealth Liberal Party—'the Fusion', it was called—and it had been a bruising process. Some sitting members had not joined and were now recontesting as independents. Other liberal protectionists had joined the Labor Party in the wake of Deakin's perceived treachery.

In the Victorian Senate contest, two Liberals were defending their seats and Labor was defending its one. By the end of February, it was clear that Mrs D'Ebro would not stand. Vida would only have one other independent competitor, James Ronald, a Scots Presbyterian clergyman and disgruntled federal Labor Party MP who had failed to be re-endorsed when his seat was abolished. The party system that Vida so despised had won, and this election would test just how feasible it was to be not only a female candidate, but a non-party candidate. Which of those heresies would voters find worse?

Prime Minister Deakin—referred to as Judas by Labor MP Billy Hughes—would fight the election largely on the strength of his past record and his vision for defence (an Australian navy), *the peopling of North Australia* (based on mining) and a harmonious federation, with Australians united by their commitment to the national good, the Commonwealth.[10] Deakin had every expectation of *a sweeping victory* and looked forward to representing Australia at the upcoming Imperial Conference in London in 1911.[11] But he had a formidable opponent in his Labor rival for the top job: Andrew Fisher.

Fisher was a Scot—a former coalminer and a unionist—who had come up through the Queensland Labor Party, getting his political blooding during an era of drought, depression and industrial strife. He became known for his quiet, conciliatory approach to improving workers' living standards: arbitration and legislative mechanisms over lockouts and class warfare. He was a keen federalist, and secured the Labor Party's endorsement to represent Wide Bay in the Commonwealth Parliament, a contest he won with a convincing majority. In May 1901, along with other Labor parliamentarians, he formed the Commonwealth Labor Party.

It was a big year for the Ayrshire pit boy. On New Year's Eve 1901, forty-year-old Fisher married twenty-seven-year-old Margaret Irvine, the eldest daughter of his landlady in Gympie. He had been in close contact with her for a decade, watching her grow from a schoolgirl with more formal education than he'd ever received to a tall, strong woman. It was a measure of the man that he was not concerned by the discrepancy in their height: at six foot three, Margaret towered over her husband's five feet and nine inches. Even before their marriage, Fisher had been eager for Margaret to be at his side on public occasions. It had been Fisher's pleasure to take Margaret and her mother to Melbourne for the opening of the Federal Parliament in May 1901. He affectionately addressed his letters to her as *Dear Maggie*, but signed them formally as *Andrew Fisher*. Their first child, Robert, was born in September 1902, a honeymoon baby. By the time of the 1910 election, there were three more Fisher children, born at neat two-year intervals (Peggy, Henry, Andrew) and one more on the way (John, born in June). Margaret was *child built*, as her daughter Peggy tenderly noted.[12]

At the time of the 1910 election Fisher, at forty-eight, *was the sort of man who people turned to look at again*, in the words of one contemporary.[13] He had warm, dark eyes, a slightly cleft chin and a thick head of greying hair. He was clean-shaven except for a signature handlebar moustache. His personality was as becoming as his appearance. *He was slow to anger and very tolerant if he were angry*, according to Peggy, *and took such interest and care of little things like the taking of a bee very gently out of the window or the explaining of things to a little child*.[14] The Fishers kept a happy, Presbyterian, teetotal household in Melbourne, which included Margaret's mother and sisters. Fisher never swore and *disliked with great intensity the expression 'shut up'*.[15]

Fisher was a staunch supporter of women's suffrage, a position he had long held. At the 1908 Labor Party conference, he welcomed female delegates, acknowledging that their presence was an indication that women in Australia were taking an active part in the economic and political questions of the day. *As a Labor Party*, he noted, *we can be congratulated on giving [them] every facility and encouragement to do so*.[16]

And it was true. Labor had early recognised the organisational and electoral importance of mobilising women's support. Women had been attending the inter-colonial Labor congresses as early as 1884, when two of the fifty delegates were female.[17] Adult suffrage had been part of the South Australian Labor platform since 1892—a situation Mary Lee had worked hard to orchestrate, and which led directly to the historic South Australian suffrage win in 1893—and Tasmanian Labor's platform since 1896. Federal Labor put *one adult one vote* as the first item on its first platform in 1900, followed by the *total exclusion of colored and other undesirable races*.[18] Equal pay for equal work became part of the Victorian Labor Party Platform in 1908.

Labor Party stalwarts like William Spence, a New South Wales federal MP, tied sex equality back to a unionist appreciation of the fortitude and devotion of women. In his 1909 history of the labour movement in Australia, AUSTRALIA'S AWAKENING, Spence praised *the unemblazoned courage of the wives of trade unionists locked out or on strike...the grit of men, women and children to go hungry to bed every night*.[19] To Spence, the history of the labour movement was *one of self-sacrifice, heroism and suffering far greater than has ever been shown on any battlefield*.[20] This was a tradition of heroism quite distinct from the militarist norms of the day: in it, Australian women could take their place in the pantheon of martyrs.

Though ideologically and sentimentally tied to an international socialist movement for the elevation of the world's workers, the Australian Labor Party's philosophy was explicitly nationalist. Its federal platform of 1908 stated the ALP's primary objective as: *The cultivation of an Australian sentiment based upon the maintenance of racial purity, and the development in Australia of an enlightened and self-reliant community*.[21]

As enlightened racists, Australians would not only be capable of achieving colonial independence, but also of providing a beacon of hope to the imperial and international community. *Give Labor a chance—give it reasonable time*, promised William Spence in 1909, *and it will start such an era of growing prosperity in Australia as will make it the envy of the world.* Spence took pride in what the Labor Party had already achieved in Australia—claiming the social legislation for which it had become famous as a Labor victory—and offered it as a motivation for writing his history. *If the Socialist Movement of the world is helped, encouraged and stimulated by this record of our success in Australia*, he wrote, *I shall have ample reward.*

Just as the world was paying attention to what women's suffrage had achieved in the antipodes, so it was mindful of the strong performance of the Australian Labor Party as a parliamentary and legislative force. In the 1906 federal election the Labor Party, under the leadership of Chris Watson, had won a five per cent swing, picking up three seats to bring its total to twenty-six. This was the same number as George Reid's Conservative Party (running as the Anti-Socialists), forcing them into coalition with Alfred Deakin's Protectionist Party (which suffered a thirteen per cent swing against it and managed only twenty-one seats). Labor held thirty-six per cent of seats in the House of Representatives.

By comparison: in the UK general election of 1906 that saw the Liberals sweep to power, Keir Hardie's Labour Representative Committee (forerunner to the British Labour Party) took less than five per cent of seats. At the New Zealand general election of 1908, David McLaren's Independent Labour League won three per cent of seats. Canada didn't even have a federal labour party until 1917.

When it came to Labour's electoral strength, Australia was in a league of its own.

ⵙ

Vida Goldstein doubted that Labor's position on women's rights owed much to anything other than party political machinations. William Spence had said that the labour movement stood for *true self-government*, meaning *the government of Self—the preservation of Self from trespassing on the rights of others.*[22] To Spence, this was purely a class issue. Landlords and employers could not, in a nation enjoying true self-government, rule over tenants and workers. He expressed no vision of what his labour politics might mean for female citizens—whose rights were trespassed upon by men—let alone for Indigenous Australians, who were so far from self-governing that they weren't even counted as citizens.

It was this sort of ideological blind spot that made Vida wary of aligning her own political fortunes with the Labor Party. When Spence wrote: *Labor takes the home as the unit for the nation*, he meant the patriarchal home. In the same way, H. B. Higgins' Harvester Judgment—groundbreaking as it was—based its 'living wage' on what a husband must earn to support a wife and children. When he said: *Labor undertakes to change the whole tenor of the world's ideas*, Spence was talking about matters like the state control of industries such as sugar, tobacco and coal mines.[23] He didn't envision that women would take control of their own needs and represent their own interests. What of the women who were family breadwinners? What of the women who were not wives? Where Vida was a feminist with socialist leanings, Spence was a socialist, end of story. He claimed that it was *the advent of Labor in politics which brought womanhood suffrage.* But who doesn't like to walk into a clean house and take the credit for owning the mop?

The rhetoric of the home as bastion of morality and source of power—whether national or feminine—was proving sticky for Vida, too. On the 1910 election campaign trail she was criticised for having a bob each way. The Sydney STAR pointed out the hypocrisy of the *advanced woman...a glib-tongued political lady of the twentieth century* claiming that *her own pre-eminent right* to represent a portion of her country was based on the empire of the Home.

> That a woman who is so smart at repartee and so intelligent as Miss Goldstein should have to drag the feeble

old stalking horse 'Vote for the Home' out of his political stable, is one of the strongest arguments against the
presence of women on the political platform.[24]

Other newspapers eschewed Vida's *claptrap* on the age-old
grounds that she was not sufficiently womanly. The Melbourne
ADVOCATE, quoting her assertions that *I have often written the speeches
for members* and that she was thus *practically in the House now; the only
difference is that I am outside the barriers*, decried Vida's lack of *shrink-
ing modesty*, the virtue that defined women. (The ADVOCATE did
admit that this very feature might indeed qualify her as a *typical politician*.[25]) Another news outlet argued that *Nature decided the question
herself when she endowed the weaker vessel with a smaller brain pan*.[26]

Vida knew that, even on her second election campaign, she
would not be judged on the strength of her policies but on the very fact
of her presence. When she criticised Deakin on policy grounds[27] she
was accused of splitting the conservative Fusion ticket. The danger,
said the AUSTRALASIAN, came from female citizens *who are new to
the exercise of political rights, and are not so versed as men are in the duty
of regarding a vote as a public trust, to be used as reason dictates rather
than as emotions or mere sentiment may prompt*.[28] It was a measure of
just how worried the anti-Labor forces had become that Melbourne
PUNCH, claiming that Vida was *a Labour Socialist in all her politics, she
might as well be a Labour woman*, resorted to anti-Semitism to scare
conservative voters further.

> I often think that if Miss Goldstein were not of Jewish
> extraction she would be wheeling about the perambula-
> tor she talks of so much, and leaving women to settle
> their own wrongs in their own ways. But she has all the
> pushfulness of that race in her, and feels that she has a
> mission to free women.[29]

The question of Vida's racially ingrained aggression, so repellent it had prevented her from winning a husband, was raised in
the dying days of the campaign. How to respond? Perhaps she lay

back and thought of England—where women had now given up on following the rules of etiquette. Forswearing diplomatic reassurance that the women's vote would not split the ticket, she now beseeched women to do just that: *I ask electors to split the ticket*, she implored provocatively at the Town Hall in genteel Hawthorn, *as an emphatic protest against the tyranny of the ticket system*.[30] It was the closest to disobedience that the headstrong but ultimately well-mannered private schoolgirl had ever come.

Labor too may have feared that Vida would coax votes away from its candidates with her support for workers over employers and her positive stance on the New Protection.[31] But many Labor members, like Dr William Maloney in Victoria and Josiah Thomas in New South Wales, were her friends and long-time political companions. When they couldn't convince her to stand as a Labor candidate, they left her alone. Ultimately, Vida *asked to be judged by what she had said, by her manifesto*, reported the MOUNT ALEXANDER MAIL as election day neared, *and what she had done in the interests of women and children in the past*.[32] Deakin expected to be assessed on his record, and so did Vida.

And just as Deakin was campaigning on a 'put Australia first' platform, so Vida had a nationalist agenda. She told the voters of Kerang that a vote for her was a vote for a proud, self-assertive, risk-taking Commonwealth—a vote they should cast *If they desired to see Australia lead the way as the first nation to do justice to women by placing a woman in its National Parliament*.[33]

Vida, of course, knew full well that Finland had already elected nineteen women to its national parliament. By this moment of wilful blindness she made a final play for the patriotic sentiments of voters. In one of her last appearances of the campaign, three thousand women filled the Melbourne Town Hall to capacity, with three hundred more *clamouring for admission* outside the locked door. *This is probably the largest political meeting of women ever held in Australia*, the EVENING TELEGRAPH in the remote Queensland town of Charters

Towers reported, demonstrating just how far the sparks from Vida's experiment had flown.[34]

⚓

On the morning of election day, 13 April 1910, Vida awoke to a telegram from Emmeline Pankhurst: *Women's Social and Political Union wishes you success.*[35] And in fact, the result was spectacular.

Labor won 49.97 per cent of the primary vote, a stunning increase on the eighteen per cent it mustered in 1901 and thirty-six per cent in 1906. It swept all Senate seats and the majority of the seventy-five House of Representatives seats.

The victory was historic in the true sense: the first time that an openly socialist government had been elected to govern in its own right anywhere in the world. It had campaigned on three discreet virtues: moderation, respectability and competence. In other words, classic liberal territory—a fact not lost on the many liberal voters who, no longer able to support Deakin since he sided with the conservatives in 1909, now had nowhere to turn but Labor.[36]

The victory made headlines around the world, and, given that Australia was the primary proving ground for the experiment in universal adult suffrage, curiosity turned to the influence of women voters. In July, the WSPU's organ, Votes for Women, published a report from Cyrus Mason, the electoral returning officer in Melbourne, attesting to the *order, good humour and perfect sobriety* of all voters on polling day. He dismissed the usual Antis' argument that women would *rush to the polls in an excited state* by testifying that he personally saw *mothers with babies in go-carts, smiling girls with their young men* and *old ladies helped and guided courteously.*

> I can say with confidence that as soon as the Mother of Parliaments adopts the whole of the Australian manner of conducting parliamentary elections the better for Great Britain.[37]

Another correspondent, an Englishman who had recently returned from Australia and watched the elections, similarly reported that voting in the southern colonies was a pleasant family affair, like a tri-annual picnic. *Women's part in politics is taken as quite natural*, the man wrote. And, crucially: *They do not neglect their husbands' meals nor are they in any way unwomanly in appearance.*[38]

In June, the journal of the American Woman Suffrage Association, PROGRESS, reported that two local women had recently returned from Australia where they had been very taken by Vida Goldstein's campaign. She was *a young and beautiful woman*, reported Miss Mavin Fenwich and Miss Brackinridge. But that was not the most surprising thing about the elections. *The women in Australia have had the franchise for so many years*, noted the pair of travellers, *it is no longer an experiment and the results of their political efforts are attract-ing the attention of the civilised world.*[39] A reporter published in the BOSTON WOMAN'S JOURNAL commented on the decorum displayed at the Milson's Point polling station in Sydney, compared to *the hustling, the barracking and the brawling* that characterised American election days.[40]

But for Vida, no Senate berth. She received 54,000 votes, an impressive twenty-five per cent share, but it was not enough. Nonetheless she maintained the optimistic aspect she had presented in 1903. *I was not at all disappointed by the result*, she told journalists, *as some people expected me to be.*[41] She had done the job of making it easier for the next female candidate, and the next.[42] Vida regarded her 54,000 votes as *a magnificent tribute* from the people of Victoria for supporting the cause she represented: *they put justice to women before the triumph of party.* But Vida had achieved more than sweep-ing a scythe through the political wilderness. She'd taken a wrecking ball to the Liberal ascendancy in Victoria. *Woman's influence in poli-tics has been remarkably illustrated in Victoria*, assessed Queensland's GYMPIE TIMES, *where Miss Vida Goldstein's candidature has probably resulted in the defeat of three Liberal Senatorial candidates.*[43] Much to

Labor's delight, Vida had indeed split the Liberal ticket—a nil sum political game that she herself hated. Vida claimed that perhaps her greatest victory was coming out of the campaign with her principles unscathed: *in a straight-out party fight conducted on the most rigid machine 'ticket' system that has been known here, it was marvellous that the one non-party candidate, and that a woman, was not mutilated beyond recognition.*[44] Ever the optimist.

It was not only the fact that she had been taken as a serious candidate that pleased Vida. It was also that in Victoria, female voters had outnumbered male voters by eleven thousand. The fact that she had not won on the strength of this remarkable voter turnout showed that women themselves had put party over sex. To Vida, this meant that women required more education and support to know *how to be just to women*: it was still too easy for them to be swayed by arguments that *votes given to her are virtually thrown away* or that they could never trust a *spinster* or a *Bachelor Woman*.

But to other political commentators, the remarkable female participation rate pointed to a different reality. Writing anonymously for the London MORNING POST, Alfred Deakin himself conceded that the Labor leagues had worked hard at enrolling all who were eligible to vote, leading to a fifty per cent increase in turnout. And it was mostly women who worked as the recruiters. *Their women pass from house to house*, reported Deakin, *enlisting those of their own sex.*[45] The real test of Labor, Deakin wrote under the cover of journalistic inscrutability, was whether the incoming government could satisfy *the mass of our everyday citizens, male and female...stimulated by visionary aims of a new social Paradise to be conjured out of the ballot boxes.* Of one thing Deakin was sure:

> No transformation in our politics so complete or so unexpected by the general public has ever been witnessed on this side of the world...[it is] a new era in politics without precedent for its methods.[46]

Its methods involved the active participation of female citizens in delineating the national political narrative. The Labor leagues had enlisted *an army of unpaid volunteers, discipline, unity…and the complete efficiency of its machine.* Women were oiling that machine.

In her 1906 pamphlet for the WSPU, THE WOMEN's VOTE IN AUSTRALIA, Nellie Martel had argued that female citizens were the *best asset any country could wish for* because they had raised *the moral, social and spiritual tone.*[47] The 1910 election demonstrated that it was their long-range vision and organisational capacity, not their innate sex superiority, that might make women superior citizens. Not enough women had chosen Vida Goldstein to be their political representative in the Federal Parliament. But substantial numbers had worked tirelessly to ensure that their vote helped put the first Labour government in the world into office.

28

Homecoming Queen

Australia, winter 1910

In the year since Muriel Matters had showered London with WFL pamphlets from heaven, Prime Minister Asquith had dug his heels in deeper than an Irish bog—and the Votes for Women campaign had stepped up a notch.

Hundreds of suffrage meetings were held in homes, halls and public squares around the United Kingdom every week. Fundraising drives were incessant and profitable, and the funds continued to pour into the WSPU coffers, overseen by Emmeline Pethick-Lawrence. Meanwhile, the WFL (who had themselves raised over £60,000) staged a four-month rolling picket line of Westminster, hoping to doorstop Asquith. Delegations marched on Downing Street, stones were thrown, windows broken and suffragettes chained themselves to a variety of stationary objects. Scores of protesters continued to opt for prison terms rather than pay their court-ordered fines. By 1910, a total of 450 women had been gaoled. One WSPU prisoner, Miss Marion Wallace Dunlop, went on a 91-hour hunger strike in Holloway after she was gaoled for wilful damage. (This was a spontaneous act of self-denial rather than a co-ordinated campaign—unlike Muriel's stunts, which had been plotted from above.[1]) Both organisations continued touring the UK, fishing for new suffragette souls. *The storm centre of the warfare waged from East to West, from Lapland to Italy, from Canada to South Africa, was England*, wrote one chronicler of the times, *in the throes of the revolutionary suffragette movement.*[2]

In late 1909 and early 1910, Muriel and fellow WSPU member Violet Tillard travelled through Wales and Ireland, where they addressed the newly formed Irish Women's Franchise League, being pelted with potatoes and sods when they weren't being showered with affection and support. *She is an Australian*, wrote the Swansea CAMBRIAN after one of Muriel's anti-Asquith speeches to a crowd of over a thousand cheering enthusiasts, *clear-minded mistress of happy phrase, physical attractions, enthusiasm, courage and a sense of humour. The Women's Freedom League made no mistake in importing her.*[3]

The balance of trade might have been weighted in Australia's favour (wool and outspoken women cornering the market) but there was no evidence that its example would persuade the government to change its mind on the franchise. Throughout 1909, Asquith steadfastly refused to speak to suffrage delegations or introduce a womanhood suffrage bill. But by 1910, his government was in trouble. At the general election in January, the Liberals lost 123 seats: in just over two years, the Liberal landslide had caved in around Asquith's tone-deaf ears. With a slender two-seat majority over Balfour's Tories, the embattled Liberals could only form government with the support of the Irish National Party and the Independent Labour Party. In February, Asquith hinted that his government would introduce a Conciliation Bill, a legislative measure that could lead to women's suffrage on equal terms with men. Though he wouldn't be seen to *yield to coercion*, it was the first time that Asquith had appeared to temper his animosity towards the suffrage movement in any way.[4] The WSPU and the WFL agreed to call a truce to militancy while they waited to see the Conciliation Bill materialise.

It was against this backdrop of political limbo that Muriel made a decision. By 4 May 1910, just three weeks after the Australian Labor Party had clinched its world-historic victory, she was sailing towards the Western Australian coastline with her friend Violet Tillard by her side, returning to the sunburnt country she had not seen for five years. *I realised, with a tremendous rush of feeling*, reflected

Muriel as she steamed through Albany Heads, *what my own land meant to me, as never before.* As she gazed at the approaching shore, she remembered the *factors that made Australia what they are...colour everywhere*:

> In the depth of the sea, the delphinium blue of the sky, the ruddy hillside tracks ascending from rocks a combination of purple and brown. On every side the eucalypt showed its individual form; beneath its shade tangled masses of wild violet, scarlet runner and yellow wattle gorse ran wild...Land of the sun it truly is.[5]

The Heroine of the Grille had come home. Not to stay; not yet. But for now. And for a very special purpose.

⚓

The idea for a lecture tour had first been sparked in the summer of 1909 when former Adelaide journalist Beaumont Smith was scouting the London dance halls and theatres for new acts to bring to Australia. He and his boss, wealthy impresario William Anderson, were mostly signing up pantomime actors, comics and circus performers, but they were interested in anyone who could pull a crowd—and the crowds were swarming in London, Cardiff and Dublin, to see Muriel Matters. So why wouldn't Australian audiences queue to hear a first-hand account of *those unsexed hyenas in petticoats*, as the UK's attorney-general had recently called the suffragette agitators?[6] Smith had witnessed the shocking scenes of violence and struggle himself: at one rally he'd seen a policeman on horseback slap a woman in the face in broad daylight, while another woman was assaulted by a protester in full view of an indifferent officer. Why not have the drama recounted by a woman who had not only observed history being made, but also was herself playing a leading part in making it? One Victorian cynic scoffed *that bringing a suffragette to suffragists is worse than carting coal to Newcastle,*[7] but

Anderson thought he was backing a winner. Muriel accepted his invitation to mount an Australian lecture tour as soon as her English suffrage work allowed.

For Muriel, this was a (fully paid) opportunity to accomplish what Nellie Martel had been trying to do before her sudden departure from the WSPU: appeal to the women of Australia to help British women win the vote. *The women of free Finland have sent their greetings and offered to come over and help their English sisters*, Nellie had coaxed in a letter widely published in Australian papers in December 1906. *I know Australia will be ready and willing to help… English women are looking to their Australian and New Zealand sisters to stand up for them in this critical juncture of their great battle.*[8] Now that the militants' truce had been declared, Muriel had the chance to set her *dear, free sisters of Australia* straight about exactly what was happening to *the less fortunate women of England*. She need not embroider the facts with fancy work. She could tell her own story of assault and imprisonment, effrontery and fortitude, to bring home the staggering lengths to which British women must go to win their freedom.

From Albany, it was sixteen hours by rail to Perth, where all of Muriel's immediate family now lived and where Leonard Matters was waiting to greet his sister. The long train trip gave Violet the chance to gaze out on a landscape so different from any she had seen in her thirty-six years as a devout Quaker—*no English green is seen but tones of mystic blue and grey*. Muriel had no fear that her friend from the WFL caravanning days would be thrown by the unfamiliar landscape, for Tillie was *shot through with an almost daredevil gaiety when faced with situations requiring nerve and set purpose*. She might be *tall, slender* and *delicate*, with a touch of English *reticence* to her nature, but they had been in Holloway together, and Muriel knew Tillie possessed *the grimmest kind of determination and will*. When others were *edgy* or had grown *weepy with strain*, she was *ever cheerful and calm*.[9]

The train journey also gave Muriel time to reflect. As she listened to *the liquid lament of the native magpie* and watched the sunrise *quicker and fuller* than in other lands, *flooding the world in flame,* she realised that it is *useless to expect English friends aboard the train to see or feel as we do.* They could admire the stars, *cut out of the heavens, so near, so brilliant,* but they (Tillie?) couldn't be touched to the core by *the Cross of the Southern Land stretch[ed] athwart the sky.*[10]

After that, there was no rest for Muriel, *the Western Australian girl who has become world-famous,* as the local press announced her.[11] First she attended a Women's Suffrage Guild reception *to welcome her as a representative of the British movement.*[12] For the women's rights campaigners of the west, it was exciting to have such a VIP in their midst. They had not been so honoured since Vida Goldstein came to Perth on a speaking tour in 1906. They wasted no time in getting Muriel to address four meetings, at which resolutions of admiration and sympathy for the English suffragettes were passed.

There were many reasons for the general public to fete the woman who had departed from this, *her adopted state,* so many years ago.[13] Not only had Muriel's impending lecture tour been widely hyped, with papers extolling *her enthusiasm, her eloquence, her wonderful, magical* voice, but the *airship craze* had recently reached Western Australia, and inhabitants had seen *mysterious lights in the heavens and heard whizzing noise of machinery high over their heads.*[14] Here was the chance to find out what it was like to fly an airship—and over Big Ben no less!

Rarely, wrote the WEST AUSTRALIAN, *is the opportunity given to an Australian woman to become famous as has been given to Miss Matters.*[15] The Perth DAILY NEWS pointed out that Muriel was as unique as any sideshow performer, having been *associated prominently with the militant suffragists in the old country...[she] has had a series of remarkable experiences which few women have gone through.*[16] The WESTERN MAIL got a little carried away, claiming that Muriel had addressed over two million people in her *gipsy van*. But all the papers pointed out that Muriel's lectures would fill an important gap in knowledge about the British suffrage movement, which *is comparatively little known or understood by Australians* who had had to rely on *bare cable news*, or the often distorted or misrepresented gossip of visitors 'home'.[17] And those who had already caught a glimpse of Muriel knew that *the charming, young, piquante, mistress of satire* was about as far away from the old idea of *suffrage cranks* and *vinegar visaged dames with baggy, ill-fitting clothes and ugly knobs of hair* as you could get.[18] Brains, beauty, stories to tell and pictures to show: no wonder Beaumont Smith had signed her up.

Whereas in England the crowds came to see what a real enfranchised woman looked like, the people of Perth thronged to see a genuine suffragette in the flesh. Muriel's first public lecture, at the Perth Literary Institute on 19 May on the topic of 'The Women's War', was a runaway success, with eager crowds and positive press reports. Her lecture set the tone for the rest of her Australian tour, becoming a set piece on which she could improvise to suit the city or audience. Over two hours of unscripted oratory, *she held her hearers' close attention*.[19] Muriel expressed pleasure to be home. She spoke of her initial astonishment when arriving in London to see the *undignified and vulgar spirit* of some English women, about whom she'd been *priggish* enough to say: *Why do they behave in this way? In Australia we got the vote without these antics.* It was only later she realised that *justice was not to be had for the asking.* The press was against the suffrage campaigners at every turn, she pointed out, and the women of England had been *wandering forty years in the wilderness.* To whom was the vote denied? Criminals, lunatics, aliens, paupers, children—and women. *So long as women are outlaws,* Muriel told her rapt audiences, *they would be rebels.*

She briefly relayed details of the grille incident that had made her famous (*for five minutes I told the members what we thought of them*), but preferred to dwell on the ten thousand hours that WFL members had stood on the picket line, and the twenty thousand suffrage meetings convened by all societies over the past five years.[20] She demolished the standard arguments of the Antis with gusto, eliciting much laughter in lampooning the reactionary old dinosaurs of England. But she made serious and salient points too. To the argument that women should remain disenfranchised because they were not capable of bearing arms, she raised the recent spectre of the war in South Africa.

> During the Boer war, 25,000 men fell on the battle-field in the service of their country. In the same period, 25,000 women at home fell and died in giving birth to the future generation. The men marched out with the plaudits of the nation; the women fell without even praise—and with this further difference, that, whereas the men died, the women in dying gave birth to life.[21]

It was a grim reminder of the reality that faced all women, whether propertied or paupers, at a time when maternal mortality was still the number one killer of women.[22] To lighten the mood, she finished the lecture with her display of magic lantern photographs of leading suffragettes, their male supporters and political opponents, the ascent of her airship and *other interesting scenes*.[23]

Though Muriel's lectures—the second one in the series was on 'The Torch of Feminism' followed by a third on 'Inside Holloway Prison'—were generally well received, not everyone was convinced. One journalist pointed out the sheer futility of trying to convince an Englishman that he is wrong: *he has the strongest objection to be humiliated, and, when he has attained to any position of dignity, to be ridiculed*. Certainly, *a system of attempted terrorisation* where *ministers were henpecked in deadly earnest* was bound to fail. He was especially critical of Muriel's suggestion that for women to cease to be *treated as doormats* they must engage in a general strike, quoting her most inflammatory line: *We won't be wives, we won't be mothers, we won't look after the home. We will just sit and wait till we get what we are entitled to.*

If she continued to counsel such tactics, Miss Matters could be rightfully accused *of injuring unintentionally a cause* to which she had pledged herself in good faith.[24]

The 'women's strike' idea caught the attention of the Perth correspondent to the BUNBURY HERALD, too.

> This Miss Matters made some remarks that read very much like a threat that the feminine ganders would go on strike, and refuse to wash their lord and master's dirty shirts and socks, or cook his meals and, worse still, would refuse to canoodle or be canoodled.[25]

Muriel replied with a letter to the editor clarifying that she was speaking of women making a *political doormat* of themselves by aligning themselves with one political party or another.[26] *No*, she said firmly, *the days of petitioning and processing are over.* Active resistance, not toadying, was the only means to a result.[27]

After two weeks of acclimatising and agenda-setting in Perth, Muriel and Tillie left for Adelaide. They made the five-day journey by mail boat—the transcontinental railway was still being kicked around as a political football—and arrived on 4 June, to a warm hometown welcome from the suffrage societies that had been *lying in wait to prove to her that her native city has not forgotten her.*[28] Everywhere she went, Muriel was presented with bouquets of *autumn leaves and flowers* in the WFL colours of yellow, green and white. Prospective Adelaide audiences for Muriel's lectures had been treated to reports from the Western Australian press of the woman who *dares to be free with her whole heart—free from all preconceived ideas as to how women should work for their cause.*[29]

One journalist who interviewed Muriel couldn't help but be moved by her *love for humanity* and her *burning desire to help it on towards the attainment of a wider and broader ideal of life in which the two halves of humanity shall strive together for a grander national freedom.*[30] It was a relief to observers to realise that women such as Muriel, who belonged to the militant wing of the suffrage movement, were neither *unwomanly or hysterical.* Rather, *they had the stuff heroes and martyrs are made of*:

> they are prepared to sacrifice everything—money, position, friends, reputation—so that they may do something to push forward that which has flashed as a great white ideal across their hearts and lives.

Adelaide residents could not wait to see their very own racially pure Joan of Arc, the woman who had gone to the *front rank of the movement and been entrusted with all the most important work.*[31] But, although each of her three Perth lecturers had been attended better than the last, Beaumont Smith decided Muriel would have only two dates in Adelaide: 11 and 13 June. He took out large ads in the papers, touting her as *The Lady of the Grille* and *That Daring Australian Girl.*[32]

The ad in the Critic was sandwiched between competing events including a special production at the Lyceum of pictures taken at the funeral of King Edward VII, who had died on 6 May, two days after Muriel arrived in Albany. Like his mother, Victoria, Edward had been a trenchant opponent of women's suffrage. The pictorial commemoration of his passing, juxtaposed with Muriel's lecture, was a fitting montage of the changing times. An accompanying editorial spelled out the position Muriel had assumed in world historic events.

> Miss Matters has risen practically to a leadership, and had been entrusted with all the big organising movement. When one thinks that the various women's leagues, all fighting for the same cause, have a total membership of no less than three millions, one realises the honour conferred upon the Australian girl, and the high esteem in which her power as an orator is held.[33]

Three million suffragists who mourned the passing of

their king, yet looked to his son, George V, as the hope for their aspirations.

A strikingly beautiful photograph accompanied the article: a staged studio shot, with Muriel looking away from the camera towards the light, her open hand held out in a gesture of supple resolve, her lips slightly parted as if about to speak. A huge hat is tied to her head with a broad white scarf. She looks active yet contained, entreating yet endearing.

The publicity worked a treat. A third show was quickly added and the dates for her Melbourne appearances were announced for the end of June. By now, she had a string of adjectives trailing her movements: *fluent, expressive, masterful, comprehensive, lucid, racy.*[34]

In her Adelaide shows she warmed up and cut loose, perhaps remembering that she was preaching to the converted in Australia, not fishing for souls. What was the problem of *men-made law?* she asked the audience. *Women don't count. The speaker repeated that to make sure the audience heard it.* Women don't count. She gave more details of the grille incident, keeping people in stitches with a description of her arrest on the charge of obstruction: *One policeman was 6ft 2 in height; the other 6ft 'And I'—she pointed proudly at herself— 'I was the obstruction'.*[35]

The male portion of the audience particularly enjoyed her *flashes of quick humour* and *her sharp thrusts at men…who chuckled audibly at times at some of her daring hits.* A bantering relationship— for, like Vida Goldstein, Muriel never flirted with sex antagonism. Both women had tenuous relationships with their fathers but close and loving alliances with their brothers. And Muriel was also quick to point out that Australian women had got the vote, not because they'd *behaved nicely*, but because *our men had evolved sufficiently to appreciate the work of the pioneer women, who shoulder to shoulder battled with them.*

This sentiment did not go down well with at least one (female) journalist, who was old enough to remember that it was primarily due to *the untiring energy and womanly work of our grand old lady, the late Miss Spence*, that the women of South Australia had been enfranchised—*Yet she obtained our privilege without any of the violent tactics resorted to by our sisters of Great Britain.*[36] Although she was evidently piqued by Miss Matters' youthful hubris, the journalist agreed that *if the suffragists can help our less fortunate sisters then God be with them and aid them in their endeavours.*

Muriel's first two lectures were vivid. But she saved her most theatrical turns for number three: 'Life in Holloway Gaol'.

Grim descriptions of the privations suffered by the imprisoned rebel women—largely respectable, middle-class women who were supposed to reform prisons, not inhabit them—were a feature of reporting in the suffrage and mainstream press in England. Teresa Billington-Greig recognised that the success of militancy hinged on *the modern lust for excitement in the masses...the public loves a drama with lust and blood in it.*[37] Militancy, argued Billington-Greig, had an advantage over *murders and accidents* because you could inform the press beforehand when to show up. The same was true in reverse. After the fact of riots, arrests and imprisonments, women were alive to tell their shocking stories of *mad bravery*.

Muriel now found that her Australian audiences were as enchanted by her account of her time in gaol as any British reading public would be—and she milked it. After recalling the night of her arrest for obstruction, she would step offstage, only to reappear dressed in full prison garb. (*I am presuming it is a copy*, wrote one reporter, *for I suppose even political prisoners are not allowed to carry their uniforms away with them.*[38]) Dressed in her drab sack skirt and *ugly green blouse*, the broad arrow painted in dull yellow, rough blue and white check apron and dirty white cap, Muriel described in fine detail the tiny, foul-smelling cell with its wooden shelf and sleeping mat, its small ventilator *clogged with dust*. With a dramatic sweep of her skirts, Muriel revealed her *harsh and uncomfortable* undergarments and showed her stiff woollen stockings. (*Red–and–blue ones like those footballers wear.*[39]) She pointed out that her shoes were made for a woman ten inches taller.

She described the prison routine: rising at 5 a.m., shirt-making, sheet-making, only a bible for company. A male doctor to examine all prisoners. (*Miss Matters complained of this especially.*) And eventually *naked on a stone floor*, a wardress asking her religion. *Did they ever hear such cant, such hypocrisy, such humbug before?* the Wesleyan-raised Muriel regaled her audience. Even the most pious prisoners *felt half-inclined to answer—'No religious convictions'.*[40] Muriel noted that her prison term was in November, the *dreary, foggy November of England*. Was it any wonder that *her depression and sorrow were pretty real things*, as one reporter observed.[41] And yet she had not suffered the worst of it.

Muriel told a story. To prove that working-class prisoners were treated more cruelly than their genteel suffragette sisters, Lady Constance Bulwer-Lytton had disguised her identity, got herself arrested at a protest rally and subsequently been gaoled. Lady Lytton had been to prison once before, using her title, so she had a point of comparison when she was incarcerated as the *ugly seamstress* Jane Warton. None of the same courtesies were shown to her as she had previously experienced. When she refused to eat her stale bread ration, she was held down by warders and a doctor thrust a four-foot tube down her throat. (Other women attested that tubes were inserted through their rectums and vaginas.) 'Jane Warton' vomited all over her hair, clothes and the walls of her cell, and still she was force-fed liquid through the tube until her stomach was full. As the doctor left, he gave the prisoner *a slap on the cheek, not violently, but, as it were, to express his contemptuous disapproval.*[42] The whole process was repeated seven more times before her true identity was discovered and Constance Lytton was released. As Muriel commented, if the tactics of the militants were *vulgar, well, vulgarity seems to be the only way now.*[43]

Muriel concluded her hair-raising description of her incarceration with the revelation that she had come out of gaol *a wiser woman*. The ordeal had steeled her like no other experience before or since. She kept *her eyes and ears open*, vigilant for danger but also *revitalized for social reform*.

If Muriel Matters was ever lukewarm in her commitment to helping British women win the vote, prison had *set her on fire*.

⚑

With the Adelaide leg of the tour successfully squared away, Muriel and Tillie travelled to Melbourne—still the seat of Federal Parliament—which offered a very different opportunity.

Muriel's intention had never been to simply entertain audiences with her alarming anecdotes and pithy one-liners. (*Men are not able to mother a nation as well as father it*, was one of her favourites.[44]) Beaumont Smith may have wanted to put bums on seats, but Muriel wanted to change the course of history by enlisting the sympathies of enfranchised women to help their British sisters. She had told a journalist on her arrival in Perth that people in Australia had little idea of what good *a little sympathy from the colonies* could do. The mother country, while much loved by her colonial offspring, was arrogant and complacent. *It was often a very good thing for England*, Muriel noted, *when the child turned round and scolded the parent*.[45]

Lectures were not enough: something concrete must be done; some tangible outcome must occur. Melbourne was Muriel's chance to make that something happen, and not only because it was the federal capital. More importantly, her visit was to be chaperoned by one of Melbourne's most influential politicians: Vida Goldstein.

For Vida, her entire life devoted to the cause of international feminism, meeting Muriel was the closest she had yet come to standing shoulder to shoulder with a leading suffragette. For Muriel, the impeccably well-connected and respected Vida was the key that would unlock the halls of power. She would not have to chain herself to any railings to get a hearing in the big house. After all the picketing and deputations and rallies and rushing and interrupting required to get close to a politician in England, the openness and proximity of Australia's MPs was a revelation to Muriel. *The ease with which the Australian woman can approach the politician and have their wants attended to*, she reflected, *is conclusive proof of the power of the woman voter.*[46] Perhaps not every female voter with an axe to grind could wield it in the face of her parliamentary representatives, but Vida could certainly command an audience. After all, she had been writing many of the members' speeches and questions for years.

Vida welcomed Muriel and Tillie on the platform at Spencer Street on the morning of 16 June. It was very early, and a dense fog had settled around Melbourne. Muriel was tired from her *tedious over-night journey from Adelaide.*[47] Muriel stepped off the train and watched in amusement as *a slight figure of a woman, aglow with energy and enthusiasm, sped towards us with outstretched hands as a breath of spring*. It was a *great joy* for Muriel to finally meet the woman she had read and heard so much about, *the Political Grace Darling* who had done more than anyone to steer the women's movement through *rocks of party prejudice on either side*. It was *almost unimaginable*, thought Muriel, that this woman had polled over fifty thousand votes in the last Senate elections, when she had just come from *a country where women are not even allowed to vote*. Muriel felt light-headed. *One breathes more freely as a woman for a visit to this country of Australia*, she reflected, *where women stand equally with men*.

On the surface, the two women now bustling out of the station had little in common. Vida: tall and dark, forty-one, private school educated, daughter of the squattocracy and fixture of the Melbourne establishment, who had shared the platform with prime ministers and counted judges, authors and clergymen among her closest friends and allies. Muriel: small and fair, thirty-three, cabinet-maker's daughter, raised in the bush and public schooled, an aspiring actress turned political street fighter. Vida had used nothing but constitutional means to push forward the case for women's political equality. Muriel had gone to astonishing lengths to break rules. But, unlike Nellie Martel and Dora Montefiore, they were both native-born Australians, instinctively independent, and both were unmarried. Both were described by the press as having the *saving grace of humour* and a *brain of masculine strength*.[48] They got along like two peas in a politically charged pod.

Muriel had three lectures scheduled for the Princess Theatre, her most prestigious venue yet. But first, on the evening of Thursday 18 June, she was treated to a welcome reception by the Women's Political Association, with Vida making the introductions. The venue was Sargent's Café, which had opened in December 1909 to great excitement and had quickly become a popular dining and musical venue—an alternative to the men-only Savage Club and the alcohol-soaked city hotels. It was the de facto HQ of the thoroughly modern Women's Political Association.

On the evening of the eighteenth, Sargent's was decked out in the colours of both the WPA (lavender, purple and green) and the WFL, whose yellow, white and green tricolour was reproduced with golden wattle, chrysanthemums and ferns. Muriel was presented with bouquets and given a rousing welcome. Vida had invited important guests to Muriel's reception, including the Commonwealth Postmaster-General, the Hon. Josiah Thomas, and the Hon. Charles McDonald, speaker of the Federal House of Representatives. Thomas was a unionist and a Labor member (also a Methodist lay preacher and a teetotaller) who had long argued that the chief reforms for which the Labor Party was duty bound to fight were compulsory arbitration and adult suffrage. Of the two measures, he told a meeting of miners in 1901, *the franchise matter was fundamentally of greatest importance*.[49]

Now Thomas listened to the *sympathetic speeches* delivered by his friend Vida Goldstein and the *young Australienne grill-chainer* Muriel

Matters. A motion was put, to which Thomas spoke in support.

> If it was thought that a resolution passed by the
> Commonwealth Parliament advocating that the women
> of England should be given the vote would be likely to
> help the cause, he would be glad to act in the matter.[50]

Charles McDonald also spoke in fellow feeling with the cause, and Muriel was chuffed to realise that in these two esteemed gentleman she had discovered *keen militants*.

Who first came up with the idea for a parliamentary 'resolution'? Who introduced the motion that Josiah Thomas seconded that night?

On 25 June, a week later, an interview was published in the Melbourne WEEKLY TIMES in which Muriel said: *Australia could help the suffrage movement in England greatly by getting her politicians to pass resolutions of sympathy with the demand of the women of Great Britain for enfranchisement.*[51]

It was the first time that Muriel had spoken of 'resolutions' from politicians: the first practical expression of her desire to see the sensible colonial child slap the petulant imperial parent. Most likely, it was Vida who put the idea to Muriel in the two days between meeting her at the station and feting her at Sargent's; they may then have sounded out Josiah Thomas before the reception. At any rate, the idea was not a new one.

Vida had used the tactic of soliciting parliamentary support for the British cause once before. In 1907 she collected testimonials from high-ranking Australian officials, including the prime minister and other MPs, and forwarded them to England as evidence that the wide blue Australian sky had not fallen when the Commonwealth enfranchised her women.

The idea of a formal resolution—an ambitious and potentially quite insolent amplification of the previous testimonials—was an idea she had been fostering since before she befriended Muriel.

On Christmas Eve 1908, Vida wrote in her diary that Sylvia

Pankhurst had requested a petition of Australian women to put to the British government. External pressure, Sylvia thought, might help to budge a belligerent Asquith. Five days later Vida wrote to her friend and ally Dr William Maloney, asking for his assistance.[52] Instead of a petition of women, Maloney asked, why not a resolution of the Australian House of Representatives?

The idea gained no traction. Perhaps Prime Minister Deakin was too timid to act; or unwilling to prioritise the struggles of English women over more pressing matters closer to home; or unable to get support from his conservative coalition partners—if indeed the proposition was ever put to him. But after Andrew Fisher was elected—and Muriel Matters came to town—the time was ripe.

⚕

For some reason—a winter cold? exhaustion?—Muriel didn't complete her scheduled Melbourne lectures. Instead, she and Tillie travelled to Sydney where, almost a month after the luncheon at Sargent's, she played to packed houses at King's Hall in Phillip Street. Again, her appearances were heavily publicised, with journalists never failing to lead their articles with the revelation that Muriel did not fit the image of *a loud declamatory fighting suffragette*.[53] Or as one outlet put it: *she does not wear white stockings and elastic side boots or even short hair and a bowler hat*.[54] (Another noted that, despite Miss Matters' many charms and ingenuity, she had not managed to *get within cooee* of Prime Minister Asquith.[55])

As in the other major cities she had visited, Muriel attracted large and diverse crowds. She gave one special address to the Sydney Labor Council (facilitated by Annie Golding, who had knifed Nellie Martel on the witness stand at the Watchman trial). In introducing Muriel, the president of the council was at pains to talk up the SLC's record on rights for women, particularly where wages were concerned. *When women in the Old Country had the same opportunities as women in Australia*, he told the assembled members, *they might be relied upon to return a Labour majority in the House of Commons... For that reason alone, apart from its interest in human rights, Labor in Australia must wish the women of Great Britain speedy success.*[56] It was only three months since Andrew Fisher's government took office in Australia, and the labour movement was still bullish.

Sensitive to her audience's perspective, Muriel assured them that the suffragettes were confining their demands to the property vote because of *the extraordinary conservatism of the average British man.* Adult suffrage had been on the table from the outset in the Commonwealth because *the Australians were not so backwards...not so obstinate and pig-headed as the men of Great Britain.*[57] She pointed out that even before women won the vote in Australia, it would not have been necessary to stage a grille-like protest, for women in Australia wishing to attend parliamentary sittings had always been *as free to do so as men...[not] shut up in a monkey cage.*[58] When the limited franchise had been secured, she reassured the audience, then the British women would *go forward and claim equal rights with the men.* In thanking her hosts, Muriel promised to convey *the expression of Australian Labor sentiment to the Labour Party in the Old Country.*

In the last week in July, Muriel arrived back in Melbourne, greeted by *unpromising, wintry weather.*[59] She now completed the public lectures that she'd previously cancelled, adding several drawing-room addresses in Toorak and Brighton accompanied by Vida, who stuck to her new buddy's side like a thistle. To her familiar trio of lectures, Muriel added new material, including addresses on 'Prison Reform and Individual Responsibility for Corporate Sin' and 'Women as Wives, Mothers and Workers'. In her lecture on 'The Torch of Feminism', she mined history to demonstrate that women had always *rebelled against their state of subordination*, pitting their wits against men's physical force.[60]

But it was not the speaking gigs and salons that would make Muriel's long and wearying journey home ultimately worthwhile. It was what happened at Parliament House on Friday 22 July.

It was easy enough to get the three of them, Vida, Muriel and Tillie, a seat in the public gallery of the House of Representatives that day. Vida practically had a name plaque on the seat closest to Dr William Maloney, with whom she'd forged a working relationship going back more than twenty years. Maloney, born in the Eureka year of 1854, was known for his bohemian style of dress—white silk suit, bright yellow tie, waxed moustache and panama hat—which he'd adopted while travelling in Europe with the artist Tom Roberts. He'd entered the Victorian Parliament in 1889 as the Labor member for West Melbourne, on a platform of socialism, republicanism and women's enfranchisement. That year he introduced into the Victorian Parliament the first women's suffrage bill in the British Empire. Now, as the federal member for Melbourne, Vida's eccentric but loyal ally was about to go into bat for women's rights again. In the dying minutes of Friday's session, he used an adjournment sitting to propose that the word 'illegitimate' be struck from the census forms.

> I, as an Australian, object to future innocent citizens of the Commonwealth being stamped with a brand of infamy which they do not deserve in connexion with the approaching census enumeration. I wish to ask the Minister of Home Affairs if he will take steps to have the word 'illegitimate' removed from the census paper.
>
> Mrs. Williams, of Brisbane, a lady whom the Prime Minister, as a representative of Queensland, would be proud to know, has declared that a child born out of wedlock should be described, not as illegitimate, but as the legitimate child of illegitimate parents...I thank her for coining so excellent a phrase, and I ask the Minister of Home Affairs to take steps to see that the census enumeration does not stamp infamy upon hundreds of our Australian units.[61]

It was a special moment for Muriel, who was not used to sitting ringside as a woman's perspective was voiced in Parliament—but she was more excited by what had occurred prior to the adjournment. There was a *luncheon party* at Parliament House that day, to which Vida and Muriel had secured an invitation. There, over lobster salad and chicken tartare, Muriel was introduced to Prime Minister Andrew Fisher.[62] She told him of her *wish to get resolutions from a number of representative political bodies*.[63] Three months into his government, Fisher was fending off accusations that his Labor government would be unable to achieve any of its precious socialist reforms. But on this day, Fisher gave Muriel Matters his word. A motion would be introduced into the Federal Parliament *shortly*.

I have the Prime Minister's promise to that effect, Muriel told audiences who turned out to see her in the Western Australian goldfields town of Kalgoorlie in September, on a whistlestop tour en route to Perth. *Mr Fisher was very sympathetic and he and a number of his Cabinet have been very kind to me*.[64] So kind and sympathetic, in fact, that Muriel had been asked to stand for parliament as a member of the Australian Labor Party. While flattered, she told Fisher that *she considers party government iniquitous* and *prefers to go on with her work in England*.[65] In 1910 it was not every day that an actress turned activist was invited to stand for parliament.

As Muriel and Tillie prepared to leave Perth on 12 September, spring was returning a harsh edge to the western sun and the pocket-sized pugilist reflected on a truly remarkable five-month tour. She had been toasted by miners, mayors and ministers of both the cloth and the Crown. She had given speeches to the Socialist Party and the grand dames of Toorak. She had met pioneers like Rose Scott and Annie Golding. Everywhere she went, Muriel was asked to convey sympathy and support to her colleagues in Britain. Resolutions were passed expressing the heartfelt endorsement of Australian citizens for the *Votes for Women Crusade*—no motion dearer to her than the one Vida passed at the farewell dinner of the Woman's Political Association before Muriel left Melbourne, that:

> this Association always has supported and always will support the brave women who are ready to risk their own lives in the attempt to win for all women the means of self-protection and recognition of the mother as the chief factor in moulding national characters—the only sure foundation of national greatness.[66]

But most astonishing of all, she had the word of the Prime Minister of Australia that the people's resolution would be matched by a parliamentary declaration of national support.

Her collaborators would have not only the moral mothers' endorsement of their aims and principles, but the founding fathers' too.

29

Though Disaster Was Freely Prophesied

Australia, spring 1910; London, autumn 1910

If you were an Australian living through the spring of 1910, you could have been forgiven for blinking and missing something important, as law upon law, innovation upon innovation, rolled out from the Federal Parliament like tumbleweeds down a windswept beach.

In September, the Federal Treasury was given the authority to issue its own currency. The new Australian pound was still fixed to the British pound sterling—literally, the gold standard—but it represented a new national currency with the £1 note sporting the Australian coat of arms, granted by King Edward VII in 1908. Within the next two months, control of the Northern Territory was passed from South Australia to the Commonwealth, the Royal Australian Navy was named (although Australia had possessed a naval defence force for ten years) and the passage of the Seat of Government Act paved the way for the construction of the federal capital in Canberra. There were changes to the tariff system, the postal system, the arbitration system, the welfare system.

There had never been anything like the mass of business transacted at the time, wrote observer H. G. Turner, astonished at the quantity and frequency of legislation passed in the spring session of parliament, *almost without pause, by day or night*.[1] Andrew Fisher forced his fellow parliamentarians to sit for five months straight. At one point in late November, parliament convened for two consecutive all-night sittings. Watching bleary-eyed from the gallery, Turner noted that members were slugging it out *in a state of tension, very adverse to calm deliberation.* Labor was, in Turner's view, *tired of accepting what they regarded as only palliative legislation.* The ALP believed in the power of government to cure the ills of society and, what's more, its organisational prowess at the April election *gave them the right to expect success.* Deakin, himself caught in the whirlwind of Fisher's legislative agenda, realised that *nothing outside the Caucus can prevent it from carrying all its measures, no matter how drastic, revolutionary or novel they may be!*[2] With absolute majorities in both houses, Fisher had a thumping mandate and he intended to use it.

In the throw-all-the-cards-in-the-air atmosphere of the world's first elected Labor government, a few novel ideas didn't land. One MP moved to adopt the decimal system for currency, weights and measures but, although a resolution in favour was carried, the measure didn't progress *beyond the region of talk.* Neither, unsurprisingly, did the motion of a Queensland MP to have the sale of intoxicating liquor banned within the precincts of Parliament House.[3]

Vida Goldstein had a tumbleweed of her own to roll down the beach: the resolution in support of the British suffragettes promised by the prime minister. H. G. Turner considered it yet another *crack-pot* notion, but Vida was not discouraged. She had the public support of the postmaster-general, Josiah Thomas, and Muriel Matters had Prime Minister Fisher's promise that Australia would send its message of support to the English women's suffrage movement. The question was how to nudge this extra-curricular activity into such a crowded parliamentary syllabus.

‡

Opportunity knocked on Thursday 17 November 1910, the same day American aviator Ralph Johnstone died when his wingtip folded, plunging him five hundred metres to earth. Two weeks earlier Johnstone had broken the world record for highest altitude achieved in an airplane: 9714 feet, or roughly three times as high as Muriel Matters had elevated the Votes for Women message above London.

Now Labor MP Arthur Rae stood before the Australian Senate, hoping he would not come a cropper like Johnstone. Fifty-year-old Rae had captured a New South Wales Senate seat in the landslide Labor victory of 1910, after a long career as a militant unionist and serial political campaigner. Early on, he had been persuaded by Rose Scott to consider women in his radical socialist ideas about justice and equality—under her influence, it was Rae who had ensured that women's suffrage became a plank of New South Wales Labor's platform. More recently, he'd seen Muriel Matters when she delivered her 'Inside Holloway Gaol' lecture in Sydney. *I so much enjoyed your lecture*, he later wrote to Muriel, *and was so deeply impressed by your graphic pictures of some of the inmates and the causes that brought them there.*[4]

Now Rae had the chance to implement his long-frustrated desires to effect change from the top and bring a measure of fair play to the women Muriel had so evocatively channelled.[5] At 6.30 p.m. that Thursday, Rae used his allotted place in proceedings to ask an unexpected 'question' in the form of a resolution:

> 1. That this Senate is of the opinion that the extension of the suffrage to the women of Australia for States and Commonwealth Parliaments, on the same terms as to men, has had the most beneficial results. It has led to the more orderly conduct of elections, and, at the last Federal elections, the women's vote in a majority of the States showed a greater proportionate increase than that cast by men. It has given a greater prominence to legislation particularly affecting women and children, although the women have not taken up such questions to the exclusion of others of wider significance. In matters of Defence and Imperial concern they have

proved themselves as far-seeing and discriminating as men. Because the reform has brought nothing but good, though disaster was freely prophesied, we respectfully urge that all nations enjoying representative government would be well advised in granting votes to women.

2. That a copy of the foregoing resolution be cabled to the British Prime Minister.[6]

The resolution was judiciously worded. As Senator Rae took care to explain to Muriel Matters, *the form of this resolution was finally drawn up by Miss Vida Goldstein.*[7] At first Rae had given Vida a draft for her approval, but then he changed tack. *I thought it better,* he told Muriel, *that the women's point of view should be expressed.* He therefore left the formulation of the text to Vida, only changing a single word. Rae deleted *patriotic* and substituted *far-seeing.* Vida was proud to call herself an Australian patriot, but Rae was squeamish. *The word patriotism,* he explained, *is put to so many base uses that I hate to use it.*

Rae also took the liberty of adding the second clause. It was the senator's idea to cable the resolution directly to Asquith—Vida was anxious about it. She was not worried about whether the resolution would receive support in principle. As one British suffragist had recently noted of the Australian Parliament: *There is not one Anti-Suffrage member in either chamber nowadays; most of those who were formerly opponents are now quite hurt if reminded of the fact.*[8] She did not believe that the members would quibble about the sentiment.

But she had carefully phrased the resolution to respectfully urge *all nations* enjoying representative government to follow her nation's lead. In this context, the United Kingdom could be counted as but one bad apple in a basket of deplorable governments. Rae's clause, however, brought the entire basket down on Asquith's pig head and Vida feared this impertinence would skewer the whole deal.[9]

Whether warned by Vida or sensing the potential for opposition himself, Rae opened his speech with the stickiest point first:

> Some honorable senators felt rather touchy on the
> question of doing anything which might be thought to
> be in the nature of giving advice on an internal matter
> to the British Government.

Rae had his defence to this accusation. It was one that Vida
had prepared for him.

> It would ill become any honorable senator to seriously
> urge that position, seeing that on many occasions the
> Federal Parliament has expressed its opinion on very
> much more controversial matters.

Anticipating the opposition to clause 2 of the resolution, Vida
had pointed out to Rae, who was not half the political junkie that
she was, *that the Commonwealth of Australia had 'interfered' to some
purpose in the past* with regard to British foreign policy. She dredged
up the times that the Australian Parliament had passed resolutions
on Britain's employment of Chinese workers in South African mines,
on Irish home rule and on the Dogger Bank incident of 1904 which
almost led to war between Britain and Russia.[10]

Immediately after Rae introduced the motion, the Senate
broke for dinner. When it resumed at 8 p.m. the senators were
refreshed and ready to wax loquacious. *There is a very homely proverb
about youths teaching their grandmothers to suck eggs*, grumbled Senator
Lt-Col Sir Albert Gould, one of the oldest members of the Senate
and an unreconstructed Anglophile. Gould argued that a cable
message was not *in the ordinary way of doing business* and was unlikely
to go down well with Asquith who, as everybody knew, would *dare
not play a game of golf without having two or three policemen to protect
him against the energetic assaults of these ladies*. Gould felt obliged to
ask of his colleagues:

> This motion asks the Senate to pose as a body which
> is to advise the nations of the world. In other words,
> the youngest nation is to undertake the teaching of the
> most venerable nations…Is it advisable that we should

take upon ourselves the duties of a mentor to the British
Parliament in the regulation of its own affairs?...We
who are the juniors are pointing out to them what they
should do.

Rae countered: *We are not juniors; that is a fallacy. We belong to
the same race.*

Gould insisted:

Surely honorable senators see what a ridiculous position
we shall place ourselves in...we are attempting to go to
the very root of the institutions of Great Britain...[we
should] mind our own business.

Gould was fired up, but Rae was not to be flustered. He knew
that some members would be critical of a measure which *seeks to
dictate to the Imperial Parliament upon a matter of domestic legislation.*
But this was not a matter of parochial concern, such as taxation, he
argued, *it was a matter affecting human rights in their largest and most
important aspect.* Not women's rights. Human rights.

James Stewart, Labor senator for Queensland, did not shrink
from the parochial: women's suffrage had, he argued, *been the means
of placing the Labor Party in power—surely we should be failing in
our duty if we did not carry the good tidings to the uttermost ends of the
Empire.* And, he added, this matter was very much 'our own business', for *the good government of the Empire concerns every citizen of
the Empire.* Australia having discovered that women's suffrage was
such an advantage to good government, *we are duty bound* to tell the
world.

I regard Australia as a sort of social laboratory where
social, industrial and political experiments are carried
on for the benefit of humanity. Having found that some
of our experiments have brought excellent results, surely
we should be failing in our duty if we did not communi-
cate those results to our fellow-citizens throughout the
Empire?

Warming to his topic, Stewart made a case for why the experiment in women's suffrage mattered more than the trial and testing of flight:

> Discoveries in social and political science are of greater importance than discoveries of any other kind, because upon them may depend the happiness and welfare of the human family.

Stewart expressed his gratitude to Senator Rae for introducing the resolution, and a conga line of senators now assembled to support Rae's motion. Senator David O'Keefe of Tasmania felt it was not impudence but imperial duty to give advice to the mother country and (supporting Vida's backgrounding on the matter of precedents), reminded the senators that Deakin had sent a resolution to the prime minister of Great Britain regarding the importation of *hordes of Chinese* to work in the South African mines. *We may have been a little in advance of our time then*, he argued, but the Rand decision was ultimately reversed. *In this matter, also, we may be in advance of our time; but nevertheless, we are justified in passing it.* Western Australian senator George Henderson didn't expect the resolution to make a jot of difference, *given the density of Conservatism of the Old Land*, but still he supported Australia's right to send it and *assist in getting Great Britain out of that political mist and darkness in which she is living today.* Fellow Western Australian senator Hugh de Largie agreed. Australia was vindicated in respectfully offering its advice to Westminster because *we are, in politics, the pacemakers of the world.*

Only the inscrutable veteran Senator James Walker of New South Wales, almost seventy, who supported equal pay for women and opposed the Immigration Restriction Act, gave a nod to Colonel Gould's logic. Walker said he was not opposed to women's suffrage but objected *to the downright piece of impertinence which is contained in this motion. How would we like the Imperial Parliament*, he asked his fellow senators in his rich Scots brogue, *to send us a message, asking us why we refuse to receive people into Australia unless they can pass a certain examination*? (He also reminded senators that at the federal convention of 1897, *there were forty-nine so-called Conservatives, and only one Labor representative, and yet that body adopted the principle of adult suffrage.* Old warhorses have long memories and short fuses.)

Stewart had baulked at teaching Britannia to suck eggs. Now Walker hauled out another poultry-related maxim: *What is sauce for the goose is equally sauce for the gander.* If gosling Australia was to interfere in British domestic politics, she should be prepared to have her own legislation vetted for Mother Goose's approval (a situation that was already, of course, constitutionally mandatory). Rae suggested the best metaphor to test a nation's qualification for giving advice was not hens but haulage. *The Commonwealth is the up-to-date motor car,* he argued, *setting the pace for the old-fashioned stagecoach.*

ψ

Late that night, the senators finally decided to stop rattling on about grandmothers and geese. Rae wanted his resolution to go to a vote. Gould insisted that the two clauses be voted on separately. The first paragraph—the resolution itself—was unanimously resolved in the affirmative. On the question of whether the resolution be cabled to the British prime minister, the Senate divided.

The controversial clause was passed: fifteen ayes to four noes. This latter victory was of utmost importance to Rae, who believed that it was far from impudent to bring Great Britain *in sympathy and close touch with our ideals and aspirations.* It was, he argued, self-protective. The King's veto could demolish any colonial legislation therefore *it was a matter of real live importance to us* that England understand the nature and purpose of Australian democracy. To Rae, the Senate resolution was a significant act of colonial self-assertion.

True to its word, the Senate cabled the Womanhood Suffrage Resolution to Prime Minister Asquith. On 22 November, the President of the Senate announced the receipt of a cable in reply.

> I have to thank you for your telegram conveying the
> expression of opinion of the Senate on the results of the
> enfranchisement of women in Australia.[11]

Asquith kept his response short and to the point. He offered
no argument nor made any promises. He simply acknowledged
receipt of the cable, as one might register a dry-cleaning receipt in an
accounting ledger.

Following Rae's success in the Senate, Dr Maloney moved an almost
identical resolution in the House of Representatives on 25 November.
Maloney was more circumspect about claiming Australia's right to
democratic pre-eminence, citing Finland's achievement in having
recently elected twenty-six female members to the unicameral parliament, representing over ten per cent of the House. Australia, feared
Maloney, *lagged behind*. Maloney's resolution was also resolved in the
affirmative. Both houses of the Australian Parliament had now sent
a message to the world generally, and Asquith specifically, to support
the actions of the English suffrage campaigners.

The British prime minister was the primary recipient of the
cable. But a jubilant Senator Rae also compiled an almighty cc
list. He sent a copy of the resolution and accompanying debates in
HANSARD to Muriel Matters and, at Vida Goldstein's request, copies
to Emmeline Pankhurst and Millicent Garrett Fawcett as well as
suffrage leaders in Chicago, Boston, New York, the Netherlands and
Denmark.[12] *It is impossible to exaggerate the value to the movement here*,
wrote Mrs Fawcett, *of the example of Australia and New Zealand*. She
reproduced the Senate resolution word for word in the book she was
currently drafting, WOMEN'S SUFFRAGE: A SHORT HISTORY OF A
GREAT MOVEMENT.[13]

Receiving the news in America, Carrie Chapman Catt also
recognised the leadership Australia was taking in global political
affairs. *All the world knows*, she announced to the IWSA, *that an
obstinate and recalcitrant government alone* stood between the women

of Great Britain and the vote. That government was now under attack not only from its own frustrated and aggrieved people, but from what Nellie Martel called *outside forces*. Thanks to the vigorous suffrage grapevine, and Vida's very deliberate publicity campaign, the news of the audacious resolution was everywhere. *The parliament of Australia has cabled its endorsement to the British Parliament*, Catt told her networks, *and now Australian and New Zealand women are organising to aid their English sisters*. But Catt made a brasher prediction, based on Australia's track record for bold thinking and courageous action. Asia had once been the *cradle of civilisation*, argued Catt, but in time, Europe had become *the teacher and guide*.

> As Europe supplanted Asia, so it is not only possible, but quite probable, that Australia with its new democracy, its equality of rights, its youthful virility, its willingness to experiment, may yet supplant Europe as the leader of civilisation.[14]

Jessie Ackermann, who was undertaking a twenty-two-month tour of *the Southlands* and Scandinavia—places where *women enjoy citizenship*—was not quite so convinced that Australia was the next Jerusalem. Ackermann was in Australia to gather facts *first hand at short range*. She still saw Australia as *a citadel of masculine power and monopoly*.

But there was no doubt that, in 1910, Australia produced so many innovations that commentators speculated that *in this far-away queer country...all things are possible*.[15]

⚓

While the Australian legislature was preening its democratic feathers, the British Parliament was facing a constitutional crisis.

At the 1910 general election, Asquith had pledged to abolish the veto powers of the House of Lords, which had voted down Lloyd George's so-called People's Budget—legislation that the chancellor of the exchequer said *would remove the national degradation of slums and widespread poverty and destitution in a land glittering with wealth*—and which included a reform of land taxes that would hit the gentry where it hurt.

By the unwritten rules of the British constitution, the Lords could frustrate but not openly defy the will of the people. Moreover, there was a convention that the Lords would not obstruct a bill on financial matters if it passed the Commons. In the case of the People's Budget, however, the landowners had gone rogue, trashing centuries-old political niceties in an effort to cling to social and fiscal advantage.

But the Liberals' fingernail hold on power made reform of the second chamber almost impossible. In April, Asquith introduced a Parliament Bill, threatening to go directly to Edward VII to ask for the creation of hundreds of new Liberal peers if the existing Lords clung to their hereditary privilege. When Edward died unexpectedly in May, there was, in Emmeline Pankhurst's words, *a temporary softening of animosities* and *a general disposition to compromise on all troubled issues*: a truce which held equally for suffrage militancy and parliamentary conflict. Reluctant to throw the new king in hot water so early in his reign, the government convened a constitutional conference in June to broker cooperation between the warring political parties.

The struggle over the Lords' veto power would continue to be thrashed out over the coming months, but one immediate outcome of the conference was the Conciliation Bill introduced into the House of Commons on 14 June 1910. If passed, the bill would extend the right to vote to over a million British women: those over the age of thirty who owned sufficient assets to qualify for the limited property franchise. Asquith promised to give facilities for the bill to be debated and voted upon before the end of the year. The bill did not satisfy Dora Montefiore and her fellow whole-loafers in the Adult Suffrage Society, but the WFL, the NUWSS and the WSPU all agreed to support it.

The mood of cooperation and collegiality was infectious. The WCTU staged an open-air demonstration in celebration of the Conciliation Bill: *a national, indeed an inter-national affair, in which all the suffrage groups took part*, purred Emmeline Pankhurst in her new role as peacemaker.[16] Thousands of women paraded through London's streets to the Albert Hall, all dressed in summery, conciliatory white. At the head of the march were 617 women *white clad and holding long staves tipped with the broad arrow*, representing the 617 women who had been imprisoned in the struggle for their rights. Lord Lytton, whose sister Constance had been force-fed when incarcerated as Jane Warton, addressed the packed auditorium, assuring the white-clad warriors that success was at hand.

The Conciliation Bill made it to a second reading. By November, however, it was apparent that the constitutional conference had failed to reach an agreement on the issue of the Lords veto. Lloyd George explained the problem.

> Having in vain used every endeavour through conciliatory methods to win equal rights for all Britons, we are now driven to fight for fair play in our native land. We repudiate the claim put forward by 600 Tory Peers that they were born to control the destinies of 45,000,000 of their fellow-citizens, and to trample upon their wishes for the good government of their country.[17]

The chancellor made this statement on 12 November. What happened next revealed that *equal rights for all Britons* was a phrase with a very limited meaning.

Parliament reconvened for the year's final session on Friday 18 November (the day after the Australian Senate voted unanimously to send its Womanhood Suffrage Resolution to the embattled Asquith). It would be the last chance for the prime minister to make good his promise to put the Conciliation Bill to a vote. But when Asquith appeared in the House that day, it was to announce that he had advised the King to dissolve parliament. There would be another general election on 10 December to put the matter of the People's Budget and the Lords veto back in the hands of the people. It was not yet a year since Asquith had last gone to the polls and nearly lost government.

In the final days before the dissolution, only government business would be attended to. He made no mention of the Conciliation Bill, but the suffragists knew his silence meant one thing: there would not be enough time in the remaining parliamentary session to put the bill to a third and final reading. Results of the second reading indicated that the House was divided 299 to 190 in support of the Conciliation Bill. It was the largest majority on any measure yet put to that parliament. But without further facilities, there would be no vote on whether women too would be admitted to the franchise. Asquith had killed the bill. The destinies of British women would continue to be out of their own control, just as Lloyd George was accusing the Lords of making mischief with the will of 'the people'.

Emmeline Pankhurst immediately gathered the troops and called an end to the truce. Without delay, she led a deputation of over three hundred women to the Commons, marching in battalions of twelve. Emmeline's contingent, which included many elder stateswomen of the suffrage campaign including Elizabeth Garrett Anderson and Annie Cobden-Sanderson, as well as Queen Victoria's goddaughter, Princess Sophia Duleep Singh, arrived first. They made their way to the Strangers' Entrance where crowds had started to gather on news of the dissolution of parliament. There was some jostling and shouting, a sense of confusion and anticipation. But nobody was prepared for what was about to occur. *How to describe what happened to English women at the behest of an English Government is a difficult task*, Emmeline Pankhurst would later write, *the plain facts, baldly stated, I am aware will strain credulity.*[18]

The plain facts, baldly stated.

Not long after Emmeline's dozen reached the public entrance, just after 1 p.m., Home Secretary Winston Churchill decreed that no one was to be allowed to approach Westminster. Parliament Square, the open space opposite the Houses of Parliament on the other side of St Margaret Street, was as far as the approaching legations of suffragettes could get before they were stopped by the policemen Churchill had sent to control the crowd. Churchill had told police there were to be no arrests.

Emmeline watched in horror as officers of the law took Churchill's decree as licence to assault the hundreds of female protesters who were trying to get to the steps of the House to join their leader and present their petition to Asquith. For five hours, police *hustled and beat the women.* The suffragettes were punched in the face, thrown from policeman to policeman, dragged to the ground, kicked and stomped on in a grotesque show of, in Emmeline's words, *unanimous and wholesale brutality.* Sylvia Pankhurst claimed that some were *dragged down dark streets and indecently assaulted.*[19] Victims and eyewitnesses attested that the most frequent type of abuse was *the twisting round, pinching, screwing, nipping, or wringing the breast...often done in the most public way so as to inflict the utmost humiliation.*[20] One officer was seen grabbing a militant's breasts and hissing at her *you've been wanting this for a long time, haven't you?*[21] One elderly suffragist later testified that a policeman *gripped me by my thigh.* When she demanded he release her, the bobby leered, *oh my old dear, I can grip you wherever I like today.*[22]

With her sister Mary among the women being mauled by police, Emmeline—after two hours of standing helplessly by as wave after wave of militants crashed on the wall of violence—asked to see the prime minister. News of what was happening outside had filtered into the House, and Keir Hardie, along with *some of the saner and more justice-loving members*, called on Asquith to meet with the deputation. He refused, instead defaulting to his characteristic stalling tactics. He promised facilities for the Conciliation Bill in the next parliament, should his government retain office. Lord Castlereagh moved that facilities be granted immediately to resolve the bill at the present sitting. But *all save fifty-two [members] put their party loyalty before their manhood*, wept Emmeline.[23]

As Big Ben chimed seven, the mop-up began of what became known as Black Friday.

Almost one hundred and twenty arrests were made, including four men who tried to defend the brutalised suffragettes. Churchill, realising that the events of the day were already shaping up as a public relations disaster, dropped all charges. *Wild Scenes Outside the House*, read the headlines, though most early reports downplayed the violence and suggested only that the police *had been too strong for the women*.[24] No disciplinary action was taken over the officers who had left hundreds of women of all ages bruised, battered, traumatised and in some cases seriously injured.

On the night of 18 December, the WSPU resumed its stone-throwing campaign, smashing the windows of MPs including Churchill. Mary Clarke, Emmeline's favourite sister, was among the women imprisoned in the days of property destruction and violent skirmishes that followed. When it became clear that Asquith had no intention of reviving the Conciliation Bill this session, Christabel explained to a meeting of delegates at the WSPU's London head-quarters, Caxton Hall:

> The promise for next parliament is an absurd mockery of a pledge.
> They have been talking of declarations of war.
> We also declare war from this moment.[25]

On Christmas Day Mary Clarke died of a brain haemorrhage from the injuries sustained on, and exacerbated in the aftermath of, Black Friday.

She is the first to die, lamented a devastated Emmeline. *How many must follow…?*[26]

PART 3

HOPE

My very dear Comrade,

You daughters of freedom, you go back to the Newer World,
the world of the future, bearing with you the love of your
sisters in the old country…Rich is the fellowship that our
human movement stands for—our world movement.

Ever my dear Colleague, Yours affectionately.

EMMELINE PETHICK-LAWRENCE
TO VIDA GOLDSTEIN,
17 DECEMBER 1911

30

The Wonder Year

London, January 1911

The year 1911 has come, wrote Emmeline Pankhurst in her New Year Manifesto, *and with it there rises in the heart and mind of thousands of women an eager longing that this may be 'the wonder year'*.

For the leader of the militant wing of the British suffrage movement, after almost a decade of campaigning for franchise rights, 1911 was the year *that shall witness the peaceful settlement of the long and weary struggle for the political freedom of womanhood*.[1] The revolution had required ceaseless toil and occasional outbursts of insurrection, and had withstood imprisonment, vilification and brutality. But the end was in sight. Liberation was at hand. It was a noble and optimistic message of hope, penned from the comfortable confines of the WSPU's headquarters at Caxton Hall.

But the view from Stepney didn't look so promising. In the heart of London's East End, soldiers from the Scots Guards lay prone, rifles in hand, stretched out on wooden pallets to keep their starched uniforms off the muddy cobblestones. It was the 3rd of January: the Siege of Sidney Street was underway. And unlike the Siege of Hammersmith five years earlier—Dora Montefiore holed up in her commodious house by the Thames, with supportive sisters throwing jam and buns over the fence—the residents of 100 Sidney Street had reason to fear for their lives.

The police had cordoned off the neighbourhood and evacuated the residents just after midnight; now two hundred policemen surrounded the area along with the troops. Winston Churchill, conspicuous in a silk top hat, made the unusual move of arriving on the scene to witness the rapidly escalating incident. Despite the bitter winter weather, crowds had gathered—some to hiss at the home secretary, some to gawk at the spectacle of the armed soldiers lying on their stomachs in the street. Groups of children darted in and out of the crowd, as if a critical incident was a Sunday picnic.

And what was happening at 100 Sidney Street to warrant such commotion? The siege was the culmination of a series of crimes that took place in December 1910, when a gang of Latvian and Russian Jews attempted to rob a jewellery store and wound up murdering three police officers. A two-month investigation led to a tip-off that two of the gang members lived in Sidney Street. Five hours, a gun battle, the Royal Horse Artillery and two thirteen-pound field cannons later, 100 Sidney had gone up in flames and the gang members lay dead in the pyre. Also among the dead: three more police officers, and a fireman killed by flaming debris falling from the burning building. It was Churchill himself who gave the order to let the house burn to the ground. Photographs from the extraordinary day—the first time the army had been called in to assist London police—look more like the oppressive regimes from which the Latvian and Russian émigrés had fled, not the heart of the British Empire under a Liberal government.

If the British public was critical of Churchill, it was for his government's perceived laxity in allowing the immigration of over a hundred thousand Jews from Tsarist Russia, the majority of whom lived in the East End. (*Oo let 'em in?* a bystander shouted at Churchill.) Some of the émigrés fleeing pogroms and religious persecution were anarchists and international socialists. The members of the Sidney Street gang were assumed to be left-wing activists using the theft of private property to bankroll radical activities, though they may simply have been incompetent, impoverished gangsters. It made little difference. The Siege of Sidney Street was a sensational reminder— caught on film, no less, for all the world to see—that in London at the beginning of 1911, homeland security was a hot-button issue. It was the mood of crisis that persuaded the harried home secretary away from Westminster and into the ghettos of the East End on a frigid winter morning.

Revolution was in the air. And the enemy was within.

⚓

As the second decade of the twentieth century dawned, the Asquith government was holding on to power by the skin of its teeth. The general election of December 1910—the one called to thwart the Lords from blocking the People's Budget—saw the Liberals returned by the slimmest of majorities and requiring a coalition with the Irish Nationalists to govern.

Surprisingly, the WSPU decided not to pour fuel on the flames of the parliamentary conflagration. It was unlike Emmeline Pankhurst, who so believed in the value of *constant obstruction*, to call a truce. But it may have been that she did not have the strength for a fight.[2] Mary Clarke had been imprisoned five days after Black Friday for throwing a stone through a window, and had endured force-feeding in gaol. Released two days before Christmas, she could not last through the family meal, forsaking the turkey for a lie-down. When Emmeline went upstairs to check on her, she found Mary unconscious, dying of a brain haemorrhage.

Emmeline spent the night in bed with daughter Sylvia; they *clung together...stunned by our sorrow.*[3] Bad luck had rained down in a bitter triad of grief. Last Christmas, Emmeline's only son had died, followed by her mother in the spring. Now her cherished sister was gone. On 27 December, the ice matriarch of the women's movement wrote to a sympathetic member of the Liberal Party, *This year has seen the breaking for me of three of my closest bonds to this world...Can you wonder that today I want beyond all other things to end this fight quickly and get rest?*[4]

Now, in this new year, the year she hoped to be *a mountain peak of a year*, Emmeline decided on a strategy of peace. Everywhere she looked, the movement appeared to be cracking under the strain. In mid-January Teresa Billington-Greig, the secretary of the WFL, resigned from the organisation she'd helped to found over the issue of strategy. Billington-Greig decried suffrage militancy generally, and specifically denounced the leadership of the WSPU for subjecting its members to a form of slavery, exploiting the earnest desires of young women for liberation and placing them at risk for the sake of *advertisement*. The WSPU was a cult. *Emotionalism, personal tyranny, fanaticism*, she said, made militancy a curse, not a cure. Billington-Greig, herself happily married now, was particularly disillusioned by the increasingly anti-male tone of the Pankhursts' rhetoric. *Pretensions of sex-superiority*, she noted, *are like bad coins; they are just as bad whichever face is turned up.*[5]

The claim of virtuous victimhood by middle-class women behaving badly was a charade, she believed: *a spectacular suffrage show* staged by a coterie of drawing-room radicals who had successfully locked out the working-class women who were most in need of deliverance. The militant tactics of interruption and annoyance had only achieved *retaliation and brutality*. The call to rebellion had given way to *shameless boasting and booming*, and the public could see through the conceit. The WSPU had made militancy *a fetish*, a *sham terrorism*, and her own WFL was but *a mere echo* of its noisier, unabashed big sister. Apart from the grille protest—the one militant action *which escaped all condemnation from within our own society*—the WFL's more democratic structure had been a recipe for mediocrity. Heads you lose; tails you lose.

Billington-Greig went public with her savage assessment of Emmeline's *trinitarian dictatorship* in a series of published articles. But for Emmeline, there were also ructions closer to home, with evidence of tensions brewing between regional and central branches of the WSPU, as well as in-fighting between the daughters. Adela, the youngest (and the least favoured by her mother), tried to express her own concerns about the policy of militancy to Christabel, Emmeline's favourite. Christabel smelled a rat in the ranks and accused Adela of plotting to start her own breakaway suffrage organisation.[6] Adela was an avowed socialist, after all, closer in ideological tone to Mrs Montefiore than to her mother. Were Adela's extra-curricular political allegiances getting in the way of her suffrage and family loyalty? Predictably, Emmeline took Christabel's side. Eldest sister Sylvia also praised Christabel for her *daring political genius* and important role as *the originator of the tactics*.[7] Adela, increasingly the black sheep, was herded away to the back paddock.

The beleaguered Emmeline was ready for some earthly tranquility. Oddly, the easiest front on which to dampen the flames was her staunchest enemy: Asquith. His new government had promised a second Conciliation Bill in the Spring session. The bill would contain an amendment conferring the parliamentary franchise on *every woman possessed of a household qualification*. It was a half-loafers' bill, with the added restriction that a husband and wife could not be registered as voters in the same parliamentary division. One household, one vote. If it passed, the legislation—so much less democratic than the Commonwealth Franchise Act that gave every white adult a say and a potential seat in their government—would be called the Representation of the People Act, 1911. Despite Asquith's past form—and the disquieting fact that there was no mention of women's suffrage in the King's Speech in this coronation year—Emmeline chose to extend goodwill towards the government. She would turn her sights to lobbying for the Conciliation Bill and shoring up the morale of local WSPU workers while she awaited the arrival of her secret weapon.

For Emmeline Pankhurst had issued a special invitation, and her guest had finally accepted.

By 1911, Dora Montefiore, Nellie Martel and Muriel Matters had all sampled the WSPU's wares. Dora had been in the house early but had found the host too hot to handle. Nellie had settled in, made her mark and become part of the furniture but had eventually been shut out in the cold. Muriel had first tasted freedom at a WSPU meeting but had located a flavour of militancy that better suited her palate at the table of the WFL.

But there was one Australian who still had faith in the WSPU's leadership and methods. Her imminent arrival might just be the tonic, the incentive and the inspiration to unite in the face of discord. A ray of light to puncture the gloom of a fractious London winter. This could be a year of hope after all; and with any luck, the year of wonders: the year when almost eight million British women would get the vote.

31

The Heart of the Action

Melbourne, February 1911

Valentine's Day fell at the height of an Australian summer, but on 14 February 1911, Vida Goldstein stood shivering in the thin early morning light on the deck of the MALAWA, the ship that would take her westward to Fremantle, then on to London. A stiff sou'-wester blew, a headwind of substantial proportions for a steamship. *Notwithstanding the inclemency of the weather*, her friends and supporters had gathered to wish her *good speed* as she went to *help the women's cause at the heart of the action.* There was plenty of love at the docks. Members of the Women's Political Association waved to their departing president, who stood at the rail of the steamer. In her hands Vida held bundles of flowers bound together with ribbons of lavender, green and purple, pressed upon her as she boarded. Vida had been lucky to get a ticket to sail. Due to the *Coronation Exodus*, steamers couldn't *supply the demand for berths*.[1] As the MALAWA swung away from the wharf, the ribbons flapped in the breeze, the long tail of a common bouquet of aspirations that bound her to sisters on the other side of the globe.

At forty-two, Vida was making only her second journey away from her native land. When she had left for America nine years ago, as an enthusiastic emissary of the newest nation on earth, Vida had shown the Land of the Free an *object lesson* in democracy. Now, as an experienced politician, road hard and riding high, she was going *to aid the universal cause in the old land.* Though the sun was only just rising, Vida knew she was not facing the dawn. She was the dawn, casting her rays of light towards a dark horizon with *dirty weather* for the movement ahead. Fortunately, Vida was a living, breathing rainbow. It was *her own ideals of cheerfulness and courage* that would comfort and propel her loyal WPA members in her absence and inspire the British suffragettes by her very presence.

But although Vida's campaigning had been fierce and constant, it was never violent. How would she fare in a campaign now characterised by assaults in the street and force-feeding in prison? Nellie Martel had been brutalised by a crowd and Muriel Matters had been locked up, so clearly there was no diplomatic immunity for the Australian interlopers. The army had recently been brought in to demonstrate the might of the state against the menace of anarchy, a show of force that proved even a Liberal British government would turn the torch on its own people. Now Vida was sailing into the chilly wind as London burned.

A lot of people will be anxiously waiting to see what sort of splash our Vida will make in the naughty Old World, wrote PUNCH on her departure, with mock concern. The conservative rag never could understand the faithful devotion of those *who worshipped at the shrine of The Goldstein*.[2]

⚓

Sargent's Café was once again the place selected to host Vida's farewell dinner, with a short program of songs for the large and cheerful audience, followed by a speech from Miss Fullerton, who would be acting president in Vida's absence. When Miss Fullerton praised the English leaders for their invitation to *the most capable woman in Australia* those gathered *heartily applauded*.

That Miss Goldstein's *work, talents and sincerity had marked her out in pre-eminence in the eyes of such women as Mrs Pankhurst and Mrs Pethick-Lawrence* was, to Miss Fullerton, an honour to their association. Two *lady visitors from America* then took to their feet to make it known that could Vida *fit in an American lecturing tour while away*, she would be greeted everywhere with interest just as keen as she would receive in England. The fawning formalities over, Vida thanked those present for their cordiality, promised to do all in her power *to justify their high appreciation of her*, and (delaying the serving of supper), read her Manifesto.

> Fellow Members—on the eve of my departure for England, to assist in the Woman Suffrage Campaign which is being conducted with a collective statesman-ship, heroism and self-sacrifice unparalleled in any previous struggle for political liberty, I wish to empha-sise some points of connection with our work for the coming year.

For, no matter how glorious the suffrage victory had been in Australia, the struggle for justice was not over. Vida outlined the areas of particular public importance: raising the age of consent to twenty-one, a federal equal marriage and divorce law and—most crucial to ending social and industrial misery—equal pay for equal work with *efficiency, not sex* as the basis for remuneration.

But there was one more issue that exercised Vida's mind and illuminated her manifesto: the upcoming referendum. Prime Minister Fisher had earmarked 26 April as the date on which the nation, including its white women, would vote to change the ten-year-old Constitution. By 1911, there had already been two successful referen-dums (on Senate elections and state debts) and one (surplus revenue) that failed by the barest margin. Now Fisher wanted to roll the dice again in the service of Labor's industrial agenda, with amendments that would see the Commonwealth extend its powers over trade and commerce, corporations, labour and employment. A second and separate amendment would give the Commonwealth the ability to nationalise a private corporation deemed to be a monopoly.

Fisher had good reason to believe his program of reform would get up: his government, voted in only a year before the referendum date, held a thumping majority. The prime minister had a strong mandate for changing the way the still-elastic young nation did business.

It was a change that Vida Goldstein supported *unreservedly*, and she took the opportunity of her departing speech to express her personal views. *I am a citizen who takes pride in the development of a truly national Australia,* she told the audience at Sargent's in her farewell speech, *and I see only the gravest danger to our country if we take a provincial view of the working out of our industrial and social destiny, which is inextricably bound up with our political destiny.* Vida believed that today's political system must be premised on the value of *human life* rather than of property, a principle endangered by divided control of industry and commerce. For this reason, she pledged her support for the upcoming referendum. She would not be there to campaign for her vision of a humane national politics, nor to see the result, but she would watch avidly from afar.

With their leader's manifesto concluded, supper was served *amid an agreeable buzz* and after the singing of 'Auld Lang Syne' and 'For She's a Jolly Good Fellow' and *a hundred handshakes*, Vida took her leave. The hour was late, and she had *an early departure on the morrow.*[3]

⚒

When Emmeline Pankhurst wrote to Vida Goldstein to invite her to England as a guest of the WSPU, the canny leader of Britain's most prominent suffrage organisation knew she was calling in the big guns. After her second Senate tilt in 1910, Vida's reputation was cemented: by now she was almost an icon. In July 1910, a private girls' school in Melbourne asked its students to name *ten of the most distinguished women in ancient and modern times.* The first four names to top the poll were Florence Nightingale, Joan of Arc, Vida Goldstein and Eve.[4]

And her status as a conquering hero was not only local. As Vida herself was wont to remind audiences, *in regard to the workings of woman's suffrage, the whole of Europe, America and other countries are looking towards Australia. In fact, Australia is the legislative experimental station of the world.*[5] Such was her status that lazy journalists were apt to give her undue credit. *Miss Goldstein has the unique distinction of being the only lady who ever contested a parliamentary election in the English speaking world*, reported one Australian newspaper in 1909 (an assertion that would have piqued Nellie Martel, in the event that she was still policing her Australian reputation[6]).

Vida Goldstein might not be a household name in Stepney or Sheffield, but Emmeline was well aware that the deep-pocketed progressives and wide-eyed young militants of the WSPU would swarm to her. The WSPU's journal, Votes for Women, had covered her Senate campaign closely and now they would have the chance to see the modern Eve in the flesh.

For many years now, Vida had believed—and publicly proclaimed—that it was incumbent upon Australian women to come to the aid of the British suffrage movement. *Here women are enfranchised*, she had told a meeting of female industrial and political activists in Melbourne in October 1909, *and it is their duty to do what they can to assist their sisters at home in the fight they are making for their rights.*[7] Now that the battle was won in Victoria, and her latest run for a Senate seat come to naught, she was finally free to leave the ground operations to her loyal and trusted deputies in the Women's Political Association and sail towards her destiny.

For Vida, the mission was not only a personal calling, but also a point of national pride. In her Senate campaign speeches, Vida had asked electors to vote for her *if you desire to see Australia lead the way as the first nation to do justice to its women by placing a woman in its National Parliament.*[8] Australia's pre-eminence in taking *the democratic progressive view on all political questions* mirrored her own motivations and values—it was impossible to say where one ambition stopped and the other started. Emmeline's invitation was an opportunity to heed her own moral and political calling, but it was also the chance to trumpet her beloved country's achievements on the world stage.

Vida was not alone in feeling a sense of superiority in her country's industrial, social and political destiny. In an editorial in the REVIEW OF REVIEWS of February 1911, William Judkins laid out the reasons for the nation's optimism, a decade after its first birthday.

> The Commonwealth is fairly launched in 1911, and its prospects are of the brightest. In no previous period of the Commonwealth's history have flocks and herds been so numerous, granaries so full and financial prosperity so assured. There is more work than there are people to do it. Prosperity is everywhere. The Labor Party has come into power at an auspicious time.[9]

This narrative of providence and bounty was typified by one of the first events of the new year: the federal takeover of the Northern Territory. Previously administered by the colony of South Australia, the nation's Top End—*a huge slice of Australia, practically unpeopled, capable of supporting millions*—was a veritable *terra incognita*, suspected to be underpinned by the sort of mineral wealth that catalysed the 1850s Victorian goldrush. Perilous assumptions buttressed such bright visions, of course—none more glaring than the notion that the Northern Territory was terra nullius: devoid of human habitation. Indeed, as Judkins himself noted, 70,000 Aborigines lived in the Territory, with no *protection* or *education*. *The reproach of our treatment of aborigines*, he conceded, *has often been thrown at us as a people. It is well deserved.* But the sometimes-acknowledged neglect and mistreatment of the country's Indigenous people was not enough to counteract the general buoyancy of the national mood. *Labour conditions in Australasia are probably superior to those in any part of the world*, trumpeted Judkins, though he was no fan of Fisher or the socialist agenda.[10]

*

It was a good time for Vida to be heading homeward. If she had gone to England under her own steam any earlier—in 1904, say, when Nellie arrived just as Emmeline Pankhurst was setting up the London branch of the WSPU; or in 1907 when Muriel and Dora Meeson Coates were getting in on the ground floor of the new Women's Freedom League—she might have been able to capture the hearts of British suffragettes. But she would not have been as well placed to spread the word to an international audience.

For 1911 was the year that two major events were casting the global spotlight on the seat of empire. The coronation of George V on 22 June would see dignitaries and punters travel thousands of miles to participate in, or even merely glimpse, the royal pageantry. Piggybacked on to the event that marked the end of the Edwardian era would be a sitting of the Imperial Conference, the first such gathering in four years. Hosted by the King and attended by prime ministers and cabinet ministers of the UK, Australia, New Zealand, Canada, Newfoundland and South Africa,[11] the conference was empowered to discuss constitutional matters pertaining to the empire, determining the balance of power between the mother country and its colonial dependents.

Britain—insecure and anxious in the face of the enormous standing armies of Germany and France, the decreased potency of the British navy, the disaster of the Boer War and the worrying spike in home-grown industrial unrest—was desperate to make a good show of empire-wide loyalty and prosperity.

The Australians, too, were itching to parade their virtues. *There is no doubt*, William Judkins declared as luminaries prepared to embark for the Imperial Conference and coronation festivities,

> that there is coming to the public men of Australasia
> a loftier conception of their duties as citizens, and of
> the place we may take in the world, not by reason of
> commercial strength, but of personal greatness.[12]

Vida, as the most recognisable public woman in Australasia, had a similarly lofty sense of her mission. *To be an exemplary citizen in the outside world*, she considered, *one must be guided by principles of morality, responsibility and self-control.* If Prime Minister Andrew Fisher was to be the spokesman for a Labor government presiding over the working man's paradise, Vida was the special envoy for the thinking woman's nirvana. Indeed, the two facets of what she believed to be the results of an *unadulterated adult suffrage* were inextricable. *All the social reform legislation for which Australia is noted*, Vida wrote in the essay that would become the basis of her platform in Britain, *has been vigorously supported by the women voters.*[13]

And if England's home ground was a sticky wicket right now—mired in conflict, exposed to the glare of international attention—the unpredictable bounce could be to Vida's advantage. In front of this large crowd, she might just be able to bowl her national team to a triumphant victory.

⚕

As Vida Goldstein was getting her sea legs, another veteran suffrage campaigner was reacquainting herself with Australian soil. Dora Montefiore had recently crossed the seas in the opposite direction—from metropolis to periphery—returning to the place where, for her, it had all begun.

Dora arrived in Sydney in December 1910, just as Britain was going to the polls to avert the *political crisis* between Commons and Lords. She was not escaping parliamentary strife. Dora had simply come back to the city she'd left almost two decades ago to visit her son. Gilbert Vita Barrow Montefiore was now twenty-four years old and working as a representative of the British Imperial Oil company, having trained as an engineer at the University of London. The Montefiore name carried considerable heft in Sydney commercial circles and Gilbert had established a large group of friends and professional acquaintances.

In her sixtieth year, Dora was grey-haired and thinner than she'd been in her youth. She was close to her married daughter, Florence, who often accompanied her on her speaking tours through Europe. Now she was keen to spend time with her only son.

Dora was always keenly aware of the effect her suffrage activities had on her children. *Few people realise*, she opined, *what the sons and daughters of some of us militants suffered because of the publicity and downright obloquy which was attached to our actions*. Public actions that led to imprisonment, yes, but perhaps private ones that led to a sex scandal too.

> Only those who knew us intimately knew we could not be capable of some of the conduct and words ascribed to us in the Press; and young people are extremely sensitive where the reputations of their parents are concerned.[14]

Unlike Florence, Gilbert hadn't visited his mother while she was in Holloway in 1906. Perhaps he had returned to the place of his birth once his studies (paid for by Dora) were completed in order to escape his mother's high-profile status as a leading London rabble-rouser.

Or, indeed, a leading international rabble-rouser. In the years following her split from the WSPU in 1907, Dora made public speaking tours of France, Germany, Italy, Hungary and Holland. She gave lectures in flawless French and *quite imperfect* German (*It is one thing to carry on a conversation in German, and quite another thing to speak one's thoughts on a most technical subject in the open air*) to crowds of up to two thousand people. She studied Swedish, Finnish and Russian history, where she learned the valuable lesson that the *psychology of those nations which have had for centuries to submit to the power of an autocrat is fundamentally and necessarily different from that of nations which have developed along democratic lines*.[15] She met Clara

Zetkin, Frederick Engels and Daniel De Leon, the leader of the
Socialist Labor Party in America. (*One of the clearest and most deeply
thinking of the contemporary Marxists*, in Dora's opinion.[16])

In 1910 Dora travelled to America on a lecturing tour, speaking in New York, Chicago, Boston and Buffalo. In Milwaukee
she was asked by a prominent rabbi to address worshippers at his
synagogue. (*I then explained that I was not a Jewess*; the rabbi wanted
her nonetheless.) One newspaper called Dora *the most militant of the
British leaders* and characterised her visit to Chicago as *the opening
of the campaign* of...*American Suffragettes*, predicting that the tactics
used at the House of Commons would soon be employed against
the Washington legislature.[17] It made a good headline, but Dora,
like Theresa Billington-Greig, had long since lost faith in WSPU-
style militancy. Apart from recoiling at Emmeline Pankhurst's own
version of autocracy, Dora could not reconcile herself *to seeing the
young girls resisting, with physical force, the police.*

> We knew they were stronger than we were, and that we
> should have in the end to allow ourselves to be arrested,
> why, therefore, this painful physical resistance, resulting
> in torn clothes, dishevelled hair, and a loss of personal
> dignity?

Dora's pet topic was adult suffrage; her mission to convince
male socialists that *women must not be left out of the next extension of
the franchise to men*, urging the claims *of all women, so that no class
should remain unprotected by the vote, which connoted citizenship*. In
the mid-nineteenth century the Chartist movement had unceremoniously jettisoned the claims of women. Dora was damned if
the socialists would similarly throw women under the bus in the
supposedly enlightened twentieth. But she was fighting that battle
from inside the tent: by the end of her tour of the United States
in October 1910, Dora had seen enough of the faux-philanthropy
of American millionaires—*with their lavish bequests to institutions
to keep present competitive conditions where they are, and prevent the*

workers demanding radical upheavals—to be convinced that it was capitalism that must be fought (in tandem with sexism) if the world's social problems were ever to be solved.

Perhaps, after almost twenty years of constant lecturing, travelling and demonstrating (including tax resisting), Dora anticipated a quiet family reunion in Sydney. But the local press had followed her movements in England and continental Europe closely, never failing to preface a report of her latest exploit with a reminder that *Mrs Montefiore inaugurated the Woman's Suffrage movement in New South Wales.*[18] The tone of such press coverage was one of veneration, however: not the opprobrium Dora was accustomed to in England. She found herself feted by admirers, particularly in labour circles. (*Naturally*, quipped one Adelaide paper, *she is a power of strength to the socialists, for she has brains, individuality, strength of character and the all-pervading and eloquent force—money.*[19])

Dora must have realised that if she had come to Australia for a relaxing family holiday she was frankly kidding herself. Her curiosity and commitment meant that no sooner had she stepped off the boat, she was looking for contacts who could help her in *getting statistical and scientific data on which to bring my knowledge of Australian affairs up to date.*[20] When she was last living in Australia, her *work was mostly of a political character, as I was working for the vote for women.* Now she realised this sojourn was a tremendous opportunity to *study the industrial question, and find out what the vote could or could not do for working men and women.*

Which is how Dora found herself at a welcome dinner at the Commonwealth Hotel in Melbourne hosted by the executive of the Victorian Socialist Party, John Curtin presiding. Guests sang 'The Red Flag' before toasting *The Social Revolution and Mrs Montefiore.* After a *rousing and sustained reception*, Dora gave a *kindly and cultured speech.* The crowd then sang the 'Marseillaise' and moved down the road to the Socialist Hall, where an even larger gathering greeted her with cheers and *a song was sung right ringingly*. Dora proceeded to give a ninety-minute lecture on *The English Movement and Internationalism* to the *rapt attention of her delighted and appreciative listeners.*

No, Dora the international socialist, was clearly not on a simple family visit. *She said she had come to Australia*, reported one audience member, *to study our schools, our social organisations, our women's work, and what the Labor Party could do and not do.*[21] Not a speaking tour but a study tour: investigating the daily workings of the first and only elected Labour government in the world. As far as Dora Montefiore was concerned, the heart of the action was now Australia.

⚓

The question was, could Dora's undeniable reputation carry her into the nucleus of power? Vida Goldstein had leveraged her impeccable political connections to orchestrate a meeting between Muriel Matters and the prime minister. But with Vida out of the country, would Dora's international standing alone be enough to get her a meeting with Fisher? He was, after all, a very busy man, preparing for both the referendum and the long sea voyage to the Imperial Conference.

But in the end, it was easy. Dora Montefiore spotted Prime Minister Andrew Fisher exiting a political meeting in central Sydney. *I rose*, she recalled, *and followed him out into the street.* She introduced herself—needlessly, it transpired. Fisher knew who she was. They *strolled across Hyde Park to the tea kiosk.* With their matching silver hair and dark, keen eyes, the pair could have been mistaken for any man of about fifty and his elegant older sister, taking shelter from the summer sun. But they weren't discussing family affairs as they sipped their tea. They were, of course, talking politics.

Dora had seen Fisher leaving the annual Congress of the New South Wales Political Labor League, a blockbuster gathering of workers, union officials, academics, politicians and other assorted progressives staged over ten days. Though not a member, Dora had managed to score a guest pass to join the six hundred delegates to debate and vote on motions of party policy. The swollen numbers could be attributed to the jubilant fact that in October of 1910, the Political Labor League swept to power in the New South Wales election, forming the state's first Labor government with a fifteen per cent swing and an absolute majority. James McGowen, the son of a Lancashire boilermaker, was now premier.

For Dora, seeing a labour party in power was *somewhat of a novelty in democratic evolution* that begged to be observed up close and personal. She could read the stated objectives of the PLL—number one of which was *the cultivation of an Australian sentiment based upon the maintenance of racial purity, and the development in Australia of an enlightened and self reliant community*—but to study the personalities of the players she needed to be in the room.[22] And so it was that she was a face in the crowd when the prime minister rose to open the congress on 26 January.

Fisher began by addressing the conference as *Ladies and Gentlemen*, a salutation novel enough for Dora to log in her notes of the proceedings, and particularly acknowledged the *women delegates* present, taking care with his language. (One of the items up for review at the conference was *that the term woman be used in all cases instead of female*.[23]) He concluded with an affirmation of internationalism, assuring all delegates that *the successes achieved in Australia were stimulating workers in other parts of the world*. Labor was, he claimed with pride, a party *whose sympathies extended beyond Australia and the Empire to the suffering people in any part of the world. (Applause)*.[24] Dora's first impression of Fisher was that he was *a spare, well-knit, white-haired man* who gave the impression of *thoughtful doggedness*.[25]

Over successive days of scrutiny, Dora watched the negotiation of various additions and amendments to the party platform, including universal health care, free secondary and university education and *a literary and artistic section, dealing with the encouragement of literature and the arts in Australia.*

She sketched pen portraits of the major players. McGowen was an *honest, if somewhat crude, personality.* Billy Hughes, the federal attorney-general, she considered *one of the most baffling personalities in Australian politics…unscrupulous…a Nietzsche man* whose *ambition and love of power* appeared to be *limitless.*

But it was Fisher that Dora dissected most closely. She concluded that *he would defend a position, I should say, better than he would attack, and his temperament is more complex than simple.* More a collie than a bulldog, though a vicious sense of humour popped up when he argued that constitutional reforms were necessary to control *the great trusts and corporations that were already getting their 'fangs' into the 'vitals' of Australia.*[26] Unlike some of the other speakers, Fisher was not prone to wafting or ranting. *He is patient and painstaking in explaining points*, noted Dora, and spoke *openly and candidly.* He had confessed, however, to *a rooted objection to interviews* that did not bode well for Dora's ambition to get a personal hearing with the leader of the nation that was, as Premier McGowen told delegates, *the hope of the civilised world.*[27]

And yet, here she was, taking tea with the man who had just slipped out from a room of six hundred of the party faithful. *Naturally*, Dora later wrote in a series of articles titled 'A Labour Party in Power', *my first question was: 'Well, Mr Fisher, what is your feeling about the division just taken?'* Naturally. The division was over a minor amendment to the wording of one plank of the New South Wales Political Labor League's platform, put forward by the Rockhoppers' Union. Could there be a more arcane ice-breaker?

But Fisher took the question, and the woman asking it, seriously. *'Personally'*, he replied, *'I consider it matters very little what the wording of the Objective is, for it is well known what are our ultimate aims, and mere forms of words are of little consequence'.*

Fisher was a big-picture guy. And Dora was a serious intellect, infinitely more worldly than the pit boy from Ayrshire who had migrated at just the right time for a lad with aspirations to change the world. They got on famously.

Did he not *feel sometimes that the movement is somewhat insular,* Dora asked, *and that it might gain in breadth by sending delegates to the triennial Socialist International Congresses?* Fisher agreed it would be good for the Australian labour movement *to be formally linked up with the movement in other countries.* That settled, the pair continued *chatting on Labour problems of the hour,* discussing everything including the price of fish. The upcoming referendum, Fisher said, was to unify industrial clout in the hands of the federal government. *Australia, new though the country is,* explained Dora for her later readers, *is already riddled with the wire worm of rings and combines. There are jam, fruit and fish rings, and serious threat of the two great meat rings being formed,* a serious issue given that meat was *the only cheap commodity of which Australia can boast.* Dora also grilled Fisher about the cost of living in Sydney *which, as a practical housekeeper, I found almost double that in England.* Fisher contended that when he and Margaret were last in England, she'd said living was dearer *at home* than *out here.*

Back and forwards they went, on topics including land nationalisation, treasury bills, *the iron law of Wages,* and a potential split in the Labor Party between industrial unionists and *those for whom political action had too many charms.* At times Fisher *laughed heartily.*

(The one subject they did not address, in *an interview* of well over an hour, was women's suffrage. At a time when the women of England were risking their freedom and physical safety to assert their citizenship rights, and even Home Secretary Winston Churchill needed *a personal body guard of two hundred police,* Dora Montefiore sat at a Sydney tea kiosk in a public park sparring affectionately about international socialism with the prime minister.[28])

Altogether, reflected a satisfied Dora, *the impression left on my mind after this long and really interesting talk with the man who represents the political democratic aspiration of the people of Australia* was positive and hopeful. But *perhaps even he did not gauge the strength of the industrial revolutionary forces*, which were *ranging themselves all over the world for the final struggle.*

Sure, Fisher was genuine in wanting to *improve* the conditions of the workers, a principle shared by Roosevelt and Lloyd George. But would he ultimately concede that which labour demanded: *THE FULL REWARD OF INDUSTRY* based on *a Socialist order of society?* Dora had her doubts. *The ideals of that new order can surely have nothing to say to those who join the Coronation festivities.*

After closing the Labor Congress just prior to Valentine's Day, Andrew Fisher's next appointment was the coronation of George V.

32

Our Vida

London, March 1911

Muriel Matters waited on the Victoria Station platform at 7.40 p.m. on Sunday 19 March feeling a little nervous. Surrounded by thousands of adoring suffragettes, she might not even be able to find Vida—far less help cut a swathe through British society for her.

VOTES FOR WOMEN had been tempting its readers since January with hints about the *Distinguished Visitor to Speak* at the Albert Hall on 23 March. Finally, the WSPU leadership announced that *We are very grateful to Miss Goldstein for promising to come all this way to address us*.[1] By the time Vida's train pulled in at Victoria, a colossal crowd, including both Emmelines—Pankhurst and Pethick-Lawrence— was waiting to greet the woman the WSPU had been billing as *a speaker of great power…under whose leadership Victoria finally won their vote.*

'Is it Royalty passing?' 'Is the King coming?' 'What are all these people waiting for?' *were among the many questions asked at the railway station,* reported one paper, *of those waiting to welcome Miss Vida Goldstein on her arrival in London.*[2] London had never seen *anything like the welcome she got,* wrote one observer. *It was a welcome that a general like Kitchener might well have been proud of.*[3] A hero's welcome.

It was not just the suffrage press—the mainstream dailies, too, covered Vida's visit. The reportage in the LEEDS MERCURY was typical, revealing under the headline *Champion Lady Candidate,* that 1) Vida had come to London *to help her unenfranchised sisters in this benighted land*; 2) she had stood twice for the Senate in the

Commonwealth Parliament (unsuccessfully); and 3) she was *a contemporary of Madame Melba* at the Presbyterian Ladies College. Only the last of these fun facts was incorrect. Nellie Mitchell (not yet Melba) had been eight years ahead of Vida, but by 1911 the diva's global fame was such that even a spurious association was a feather in Vida's cap. It was not inconceivable that Emmeline Pankhurst herself fed the line to the press. Good impresarios always puff their talent.

Muriel was no longer so close to the action that she could set the record straight. Though she had lost none of her activist spirit, Muriel's priorities had shifted. On her return to England after the sell-out Australian tour, and fast approaching her thirty-fifth birthday, Muriel had resigned from the Women's Freedom League. When she departed the organisation that had made her a household name as the Lady of the Grille, Muriel barely took a bow. She quietly replaced heat-seeking publicity stunts with the cold, hard slog of slum work.

Unlike Teresa Billington-Greig, who had always been Muriel's favourite of the leadership team, Muriel wrote neither inflammatory articles nor a tell-all memoir detailing her reasons for leaving the organised suffrage movement. Instead, she gave a long, measured interview to the BRITISH-AUSTRALASIAN, a publication serving the antipodean expats of London. The story was entitled 'Australian Women in Politics'. Asked why she had joined the suffragettes in England, Muriel replied: *I have always been a democrat, and democracy means the equality of woman as well as man.*[4] It seemed a straightforward proposition.

But to Muriel's mind, the women's suffrage movement in England had become the preserve of *the educated and middle-class woman.* Returning to the substance of what had first compelled her to hold a torch up to injustice—the plight of vulnerable and exploited actresses—Muriel had decided that *the great problems in this country, in the future, are the position of women and poverty.*

There were any number of recent examples of working-class women around the world acting in solidarity to improve their lot. Even as Muriel stood here at Victoria Station, eleven thousand workers at the Singer sewing machine factory in Glasgow—the largest manufacturing concern in Scotland, with a twenty-five per cent female workforce—were on strike. They had gone out after a dozen *girl pieceworkers* were laid off.[5] Industrial strife was rampant across Great Britain, with maritime workers, dockers and transport workers all engaged in strikes in late 1910 and early 1911.

The mood of mutiny seemed to be infecting women along with men, and authorities were eager to avert the kinds of female-led industrial protests now infamous across the Atlantic. The International Ladies Garment Workers Union had staged two mass strikes in New York. The first, in 1909, was sparked by a walkout of workers at the Triangle Shirtwaist Factory. Soon, twenty thousand shirtmakers—almost two-thirds of the largely female workforce—had downed needles in a quest for better pay and conditions. The strike lasted fourteen weeks, and was followed by another general strike, known as the 'Great Revolt', of sixty thousand cloakmakers. Many of the organisers were Jewish immigrants; supporters of the strike took a traditional Yiddish oath of solidarity: *If I turn traitor to the cause I now pledge, may this hand wither from the arm I now raise.*

Such was the global zeitgeist, the first International Women's Day was being celebrated on this very day, 19 March, with a million people demonstrating for equal rights across Europe, prompted by socialist Clara Zetkin's call for wage, employment and political justice.

Muriel was no traitor to the cause that had animated her waking life for the past six years, but she had always seen the vote as a means to an end—specifically, the end of social injustice. Now she had come to believe that the vote alone could not, would not, relieve the distress of the forty per cent of London's population who lived in dire poverty. Certainly not when the loudest of the English suffrage activists refused to campaign for universal adult suffrage. Like Dora Montefiore, Muriel determined to use her skills to fight directly for social reform.

Of course I am still working for the feminist movement before all else, she told the British-Australasian, *for without the aid and advice of women, no country can advance and improve as it should*. But she felt her duty as a fully awakened (and enfranchised) woman was in the trenches. There were many fronts on which to serve. She could have holed up dockside in Bermondsey, for example, where eighty per cent of the residents lived in grim poverty. Instead she posted herself in the slums of Lambeth, an area in central London crammed with tenements housing the working poor of the local manufacturing industries, including Royal Doulton, which made dinner sets for West End dowagers. Here Muriel would establish a women's settlement—a sanctuary of skill-based education in hygiene and mothercraft. She would teach poor women face to face, not preach to their more privileged sisters from the platform.[6]

In Australia, Muriel had admired *the great progress that women's work has made*. Labor women in particular, she noted, were *taking up their political responsibilities in a creditable manner, the result of the training of a practical Colonial life*. Just as personally witnessing the misery of women and children in the slums of Melbourne had forged a young Vida into a political being at her mother's side, Muriel felt her destiny was now conjoined with *these unfortunate women, whose condition is generally the result of the horrible conditions under which they live*. Violet Tillard—Tilly—who had accompanied Muriel to Australia and back, would be ever at her side. The photo accompanying the interview in the British-Australasian showed a more pensive Muriel, eyes downcast, less jaunty and carefree than her earlier staged portraits. Perhaps, having seen the world from an airship, she was done with the big picture: the minutiae of daily life beckoned.

There was only one complication. Muriel's erstwhile beau, Bryceson Treharne, now director of the Adelaide Conservatorium, had recently proposed to her. Muriel was well advanced into marrying age. Just as she was setting about relocating to Lambeth, she was faced with the thorny perennial clawing at the convictions of all young feminists. Work for the benefit of every mother. Or become a mother herself.

There was so much to discuss with Vida, a woman who had turned down marriage proposals like a housekeeper turns down sheets. If only she could see her friend's shining dark eyes in the sea of faces presently drowning Victoria Station.

⚓

Had the Royal Albert Hall ever looked as glorious as it did on the evening of 23 March 1911? Vida had nothing to compare it to, but Queen Victoria had famously been too overwhelmed to speak when she opened it in 1867. It had been designed to evoke an ancient amphitheatre, and the view from the stage, where Vida now sat, was certainly epic. Draped from the magnificent wood-panelled walls were suffragette banners. Spread out before her was a sea of suffragettes, dripping and soggy from *the drenching day—a perfect torrent.*[7] They were crammed into the stalls and virtually hanging from the balconies and boxes. The Albert Hall was built to accommodate five thousand concert goers, but there were reportedly ten thousand here to see her speak. Incredible, given that the *cold and damp* that evening was *enough to ruin the success of any Melbourne meeting.*[8] And even more impressive given that in the case of *a full let*—the use of private boxes—commercial advertising was prohibited. All these people had turned out *merely through individual effort.* The WSPU's surreptitious spruiking had done the trick. People all over England and Scotland, not just London, knew that Vida was here to tell *the old-world folk…of the new world and its new women.*[9]

Vida needed to put the whirlwind of the last four days behind her as she composed herself to speak. She had arrived in London

after almost a month's journey, via Perth, Colombo and Bombay—
and there had been all those women at Victoria Station, *lined up,
three or four deep, on either side of the station entrance*, and *cheer after
cheer* erupting.[10] The reunion on the platform with her ever-ebullient
friend Muriel, whose glowing face was *almost the first that flashed
upon me in the crowd.*[11] Their meeting was happy but brief—just
enough time to pledge a holiday together towards the end of Vida's
trip—then Emmeline Pankhurst whisked away her prize visitor to
her rooms at the Inns of Court Hotel, where Vida would be staying.[12]
A surge of reporters, all wanting an interview. A WSPU meeting.
A dinner with the Pethick-Lawrences. A tour of Westminster led by
none other than Keir Hardie, grand old man of the British Labour
Party.

Now Vida knew why Muriel had put herself at great personal
risk to stage her most famous militant protest. To Vida, standing
behind that iron trellis in the Ladies Gallery, the grille represented
the smallness of the English mind, a symbol of British contempt for
Woman, the mother of the race.[13] She could barely contain her own
fury at the *humiliation*, but chose instead to hold her fire.[14] She was
in London at the behest of the militants, but not yet prepared to be
thrown in gaol. She'd been bred a democrat, and a feminist one at
that. The grille was quite simply galling.

But there was nothing standing between Vida and an audience
now. No metal bars. And no trace of the hierarchy and reserve for
which the English were noted. She sat beside Mrs Pankhurst, Mrs
Pethick-Lawrence, Christabel Pankhurst, Annie Kenney and Dr
Annie Besant—titans of the militant suffrage pantheon. Thus far they
had treated her splendidly. *How often it is said English people are cold*,
Vida reflected, basking in the glow of adulation. *I certainly have experienced nothing of it. I have been simply overwhelmed with kindness.*

Before Vida had the chance to be overwhelmed with applause
a choir burst into passionate song. Another *very great attraction* billed
for the Albert Hall meeting was a rendition of the new anthem of

the cause, a rousing hymn composed by Dr Ethel Smyth, with lyrics by the actress Cicely Hamilton—Dora Meeson Coates' friend. 'The March of the Women' would be performed en masse for the first time tonight and *men and women suffragists who have strong voices* had been instructed to join the choir (with the added incentive of obtaining lower orchestra seats for a reduced price).[15] Protest songs had been a feature of the British movement, with at least four compositions in high rotation, generally set to well-known tunes such as 'Onward Christian Soldiers'. But 'The March of the Women' was special. Ethel Smyth had a doctorate in music and counted Tchaikovsky, Brahms and Schumann as her peers. She had not enjoyed critical success, however: her compositions were considered too 'masculine'. In 1910, at the age of fifty-two, Smyth took a hiatus from her career and joined the WSPU. High art's loss was the suffrage movement's gain, as Vida could now hear.

> Shout, shout, up with your song!
> Cry with the wind for the dawn is breaking.
> March, march, swing you along,
> Wide blows our banner and hope is waking.

Sylvia Pankhurst described the *swelling music* of 'The March of the Women' as *strong and martial, bold with the joy of battle and endeavour.*[16] The entire audience joined in, the Albert Hall merely a repository for what Annie Kenney called *the Soul of the Movement… the burning enthusiasm…charged with suffragette electricity.*[17]

As the anthem was sung, Vida had a chance to stare at the famous personages around her. Mrs Pankhurst, *rather short and slight, with a particularly sweet face, framed by soft, wavy, grey hair.* Mrs Pethick-Lawrence: *a tall, commanding woman, with a most attractive face.* The enigmatic Christabel, *a slip of a girl, charming and quite an unusual type.* A small woman, but *I can quite imagine her conquering a hostile crowd with her quickness and wit.* The General, Flora Drummond, was present too: *short and stout but there all the time.* And Lady Constance, the woman who had been to prison under two guises—noble and char—was *tall and fragile, loving and lovable, willing to die for the cause.* A sacrifice never required in Australia.

When Emmeline rose to speak, it was with her characteristic brio. *None of her pictures do her the slightest likeness,* remarked Bessie Rischbieth, a young Australian suffragist in London, on first seeing Emmeline in person. *Her face is so soft and full of soul. Really as I listened I felt my back-bone growing longer, as though you gained courage and freedom from her.*[18] Enthusiasm is infectious and Mrs Pankhurst was as viral as they came. As chair of the meeting, Mrs Pankhurst proposed a resolution calling for the enactment in 1911 of the Conciliation Committee's promised Women's Suffrage Bill. She further called upon women *to unite in determined militant protest against any attempt on the part of the Prime Minister* to prevent it.[19] The time for stalling, prevaricating and obfuscating was over. The resolution was passed.

Following a speech from Mrs Pethick-Lawrence, it was finally Vida's turn to take the rostrum. In the clear, confident, undeniably 'womanly' tone for which she was renowned, Vida told the spellbound audience that she brought *a message of sympathy from Australia.* She went on, part fawning guest, part arrogant envoy, one hundred per cent politician:

> I shall always be glad to think that the truly enfranchised women of Australia, women enfranchised in spirit as in fact, recognised the inner meaning of this movement from the very beginning. In 1905, when those two girls, Christabel Pankhurst and Annie Kenney, fired the shot, heard around the world by all lovers of freedom, we knew in Australia they had heralded a new age of chivalry, the chivalry of woman towards woman.[20]

Vida assured the crowd that *we in Australia are proud to think that we are of your blood and race.* The ties that bind were strengthened, not frayed, by the differences in the roads Australian and English women needed to travel to *gain the charter of our womanhood.*

In *our young country* the path had been *comparatively easy*—the road of *persistence* rather than *martyrdom*. In England, all such peaceful methods had been ineffectual. Therefore, in the name of the mothers—the spiritual leaders—*these Australian women*:

> we are on the side of you militant women, and we offer you our deepest gratitude for having demonstrated to an unbelieving world the real existence of the sisterhood of women.

Vida went on to speak of the humiliation she felt when sitting behind the grille and the pride she felt *to think that it was one of my own countrywomen, Muriel Matters, who had a hand in damaging it!* She then turned to her main take-home message: how women's role as active citizens, as voters, in Australia had had an immediate and positive effect on legislative reform. It was capitalism, invented and organised by men, not gender per se, that had worked to oppress women so effectively. *Men have relentlessly sucked women into the industrial whirlpool, they have made a devastating war on women,* Vida told a breathless crowd. *Now women with the vote in Australia are seeking to protect themselves, and men also, by establishing the principle of equal pay for equal work.* Don't be fooled, warned Vida, *it is all moonshine for people to tell you that the vote has no effect on the economic status of women!* In every session of parliament since women won their franchise, equal pay for equal work was discussed. And *everywhere you go you hear women pleading earnestly that war is a barbaric method of settling international disputes.*

Vida reminded the crowd that in just two months there was to be an Imperial Conference here in London. At that grand meeting, there would be at least a few men representing women voters. *Our Australian representatives,* advised Vida (perhaps speaking as much to the those men themselves, through the global press, as to the suffragettes in the audience), *go into that conference instructed by us as women to do certain things.* Was it not an unthinkable proposition that *England's grand-daughters* should have an equal voice with the men at the conference, when *England's own daughters* should have no voice at all?

Having orchestrated a crescendo of provocation, Vida steadied. *I believe this is a most critical year for your movement*, she predicted. *I do hope—I believe—that it will be a year of peace.* Come May 5, when the Conciliation Bill was slated to go before parliament, the women of England would see that God was on their side.

Christabel, who directly followed Vida in the order of speakers, thought some backup might be wise. Inspired by the words and the mood of the evening, *we decided to prepare the most imposing peaceful demonstration that we could imagine, a great women's procession and Pageant of Empire to proceed through London at mid-summer.*[21] Christabel announced the date—Saturday 17 June—and called on the constitutional suffragists of the NUWSS to join with the militants in a demonstration of unparalleled solidarity.

Women, exhorted Christabel, *our call to you is this: Be united. Make yourselves a great conquering army. Let us be so many, so strong, so brave, so proud that nothing outside matters.*[22] In preparation for the June march of the great conquering army of women, the WSPU would *fill the halls all Spring* with speakers, including Vida, who was always referred to as *the leading suffragist in Australia.*[23]

As Vida had not booked her return passage, she would be able to attend this blockbuster rally, the likes of which she had never before seen. She would not only be able to troop shoulder to shoulder with these heroic women, but also mobilise her own legion of foot soldiers from the multitude of Australians living in England.

At ten o'clock *the monster meeting, to attend which I had travelled so many thousand miles*, was over. Vida was exhausted and exhilarated. Without artificial amplification, Vida's message had reached into every corner. *Everyone says that I could be heard in the remotest part of the hall*, Vidas reported to the WPA members at home. *I could see the people applauding away in the balcony, where they looked like flies.* Her conviction that she'd aced the space was confirmed by a fellow

Australian who was present that night. Florence Rankin told Vida that, despite her misgivings about the notoriously testing acoustics of the Albert Hall, *you were more easily heard than anyone I have ever heard there either man or woman.*[24]

By the end of the evening, the WSPU had collected another £6000 towards the £100,000 fund-raising target set by Mrs Pethick-Lawrence, long the financial brains of the operation. Now it was no more than £10,000 short. And Vida had collected an army of new fans. *Crowds thronged round me afterwards*, she later wrote home to the WPA members, *amongst them many whose names are familiar to you.* Name-checking was superfluous in the face of such a personal and public relations triumph.

Vida's Albert Hall debut had been, by her own reckoning, *a magnificent success in every way.*

♆

If 'The March of the Women' brought the house down at the Albert Hall, a less turgid tune was taking all of London by storm. 'The Land Where the Women Wear the Trousers', written and performed by expat Australian vaudeville star Billy Williams,[25] was an instant hit with its catchy melody and graphic lyrics:

> I've been reading in the papers of a very funny land
> It's the land where the women wear the trousers
> Where woman is the boss and poor old man is second
>   hand
> In the land where the women wear the trousers…
>
> The fellows all go out on Sundays dressed in
>   petticoats
> They're not allowed in parliament
> The girls have all the votes…
> In the land where the women wear the trousers.

Williams' tongue-in-cheek tribute to the global reputation of his native land was classic topsy-turvy, cross-dressing, role-reversing fare. It provided a high street soundtrack to the political anxieties animating the high politics in Westminster: a bit of comic relief.

But not everybody was laughing. Two days after Vida's magnificent success, Florence Rankin wrote to her countrywoman. Florence declared she was *a Mrs Fawcett follower*, but was writing to Vida because she had been struck by *the high plane on to which you lifted the whole controversy.* Rankin offered her congratulations and admitted *it was a great pleasure to hear 'my' Australia acquit itself so well.*[26]

The Australian press was less enamoured of the nation's de facto ambassador of democratic freedom. *Great commotion in Women's League circles*, reported the Brisbane TRUTH, *because Vida Goldstein has asserted in London that Australian women approved of the militant methods of the suffragettes.*[27] The conservative Australian Women's National League[28] had drawn to the media's attention a statement Vida made to the British press in her first doorstop interview at Mrs Pankhurst's rooms, and later repeated in her Albert Hall speech. The article went on to claim *that sundry petticoats...have risen to say that Vida is a perverter of the truth, and that we do not believe in the policeman smacking etc.* Even *dear old* Rose Scott did not condone Vida's approving of militancy, seemingly on behalf of all Australian women (though TRUTH found a way of making fun of every woman in the story: conservative, pacifist and militant).

The fact that an Australian women's organisation had taken aim at the most prominent Australian woman on the international political stage was newsworthy. The QUEENSLANDER reported that the AWNL was furious about Vida Goldstein *arrogating to herself the right to speak for Australian women in sympathy with the militant suffragette.*[29] One aggrieved woman wrote to say: *She certainly does not represent the views of the Women's Liberal League of NSW.* Mrs Eva Hughes, blue-blood president of the AWNL, issued a statement repudiating Vida's claim that Australian women approved of the *methods adopted by the militant suffragettes.*[30] Much to the media's

delight, a cat-fighting class war had been triggered. The secretary of
the Women Workers' Union, Caroline Nicholson, was quoted in the
RIVERINE HERALD in support of Vida.

> Women are perfectly justified in taking up arms and
> becoming militant when they don't get what they desire
> by peaceful methods. They have never yet got anything
> by being peaceful and never will; they must make them-
> selves a nuisance till they get their rights.

Nicholson vouched that she agreed with Miss Goldstein *and I
speak for the great majority of Labor women.*[31]

The issue became a national barbeque stopper, refreshing the
commentariat's memory of events so recent, and yet now so taken
for granted, that they generally went unremarked. *In Australia,*
wrote the WEST AUSTRALIAN, *where women enjoy the same franchise
privileges as men, the opposition to the women's suffrage movement in
Great Britain is somewhat difficult to understand.*[32] Still, who could
agree with Miss Goldstein's apparent sympathy with the militant
policy of the suffragettes? *Storming the House of Commons by means of
a balloon, padlocking themselves to the grille and wrecking the windows of
the Prime Minister's official residence,* argued the WEST AUSTRALIAN
with seeming disregard for the fact that the first two atrocities were
committed by an Australian woman, *all contribute to the gaiety of the
nation…but such conduct cannot be adjudged as anything but deplorable
tactics.* Given that Miss Goldstein was usually such a wise head, the
paper concluded that she must have *allowed her enthusiasm to cloud her
judgement.* The WEEKLY TIMES reckoned Australians should have
seen it coming, given that when Muriel Matters, that *militant little
lady,* was in town, she was *Miss Goldstein's pet protégé.*[33] Some outlets
gave Vida the benefit of the doubt, reckoning that her line was a
white lie to appease her hosts who, after all, had paid for her passage
to England.

The Women's Political Association, scrambling to protect
their absent leader from the fallout, blamed the unreliability of the

intercontinental telegraph. Acting president Miss Fullerton was certain that Miss Goldstein must have been misunderstood. *What they all knew she must have said*, asserted Fullerton, *was not that the women of Australia were in favour of militant methods, but that the progressive women of Australia were.*[34] PUNCH was having none of the hair-splitting. Reliably, it had a field day.

> Evidently Our Vida has developed into a fierce Suffragette since she inhaled the London fog. It seems to have affected her memory also, for she told the audience at the Albert Hall last week that 'Australia sympathised with the militant policy adopted by the women seeking the suffrage in England.' Now, that is just what Australia does not do. We sympathise with the women who want the suffrage and can't get it, but think their 'militant policy' absurd and ridiculous and unnecessary, and calculated to defeat the very aim it is intended to realise.[35]

It mattered little what Vida had actually said.

What she did actually say, in an interview conducted on the day of her arrival and published in the BRITISH-AUSTRALASIAN on the day of her Albert Hall engagement, was that militant tactics were never employed in Australia, *but not because the women of Australia were not ready to employ them.* She had personal knowledge of a group of women *waiting for the word*, ready to break the windows of the Victorian Parliament should a suffrage bill not be introduced. A member of the Legislative Assembly had *promised to lead them to the attack*; there had even been a scheme to kidnap the premier. But the bill was introduced and the crisis averted. The extreme measures proved unnecessary but *there was never any doubt that the Australian women were perfectly ready to become militant to obtain the vote.*[36]

Was Vida defending the commitment of Australian women against the assumption that they had got their vote effortlessly—that they were soft? Did she think this tactic would improve her chances of getting a fair hearing in England, where Dora Montefiore, Nellie

Martel, Dora Meeson Coates and Muriel Matters had for years now earnt their militant stripes through their deeds, not words?

Whatever the motivation—hubris or self-doubt—the golden girl of Australian politics looked finally to have lost her sheen.

33

Counting for Nothing

London, April 1911

The British census of 1911, scheduled for the night of Sunday 2 April, was intended to be the most widespread ever. Civil administration was the beating heart of empire: there would be no moor so soggy, no valley so secluded, no alley so dark or slum so foetid that the intrepid census-takers would be deterred from their mission. In this most imperial of years, the census would not only provide a snapshot of the mother country's current demography, but also furnish an archive of its organisational prowess for future generations of historians.

On that Sunday evening, each of the United Kingdom's thirty-four million people would be enumerated. Heads of households would be asked how long they had been married, how many children had been born, how many had died, the age, occupation and nationality of each of their householders and whether they had any infirmities (the choices being: *Totally Deaf, Totally Blind, Deaf and Dumb, Imbecile* and *Feeble-Minded*). Every statistic was sacred.

Boycotting the census was Dora Montefiore's idea.

Before leaving London for her American speaking tour in 1910, Dora had penned an inflammatory article for JUSTICE magazine about the *so-called 'Conciliation Bill'* in which she denounced all political players for selling working women down the river. Exactly who was being conciliatory? *Liberals, Radicals and Labourites*, who had thrown *all principle to the winds*? Mrs Fawcett, with her adherence to the *reactionary axiom that the basis of the franchise in this country must and shall be property interests?* The thirty Labour MPs who had voted for the Conciliation Bill? Appeasers to a man, guilty of *flat treachery*, with a leader, Keir Hardie, who had become a *pitiable compromiser* since he was elected. The British Labour Party was not a Labour Party at all, fumed Dora. They were beggars at the master's table.

That left the supposedly radical WSPU. *We had established the London portion of that organisation on a democratic basis*, said Dora (reminding readers of her leading role in the WSPU's early days). Working women had demonstrated at her house in Hammersmith during her tax resistance campaign. Even the WSPU membership card, designed by Sylvia Pankhurst, represented working women *with bared arms lifted above their heads, or carrying babies in their shawls, demanding democratically the vote.* But when Emmeline and Christabel came to London in 1906, things changed. The East End women were *snubbed and discouraged.* Sylvia's membership card was withdrawn and replaced by *the bourgeois type.* Money was needed, and it was found among the aristocracy. *Now the colour that most offends these classes is red.* No wonder the WSPU accepted the Conciliation Bill. The measure would do nothing to enfranchise Dora—she was not a householder—just as it would leave tens of millions of British women (and men) without a vote.

There could be no conciliation, no appeasement, Dora insisted, until British workers enjoyed what their Australian counterparts took for granted: universal adult suffrage. Rejecting the bill that now had suffragettes and suffragists united in hope, Dora proposed another plan. *Next year, I believe a Census is to be taken, and I call then upon all unenfranchised women to refuse to give any details to Census officials.*

The year of George V's coronation would indeed furnish the next chance to count his loyal subjects. But Dora was not concerned with her duties as a subject: it was her own sovereign rights, and those of others, that interested her. *Women are not citizens*, her article concluded, *why, therefore, should we fulfil any obligations of citizen-ship?*[1]

⚶

The quasi-religious fervour that attended the census made it the perfect target for iconoclasts. If civil administration was so important to the British establishment, what better way to attack it than through civil disobedience?

The logic echoed Dora Montefiore's tax resistance antics of five years earlier. *If women don't count,* the reasoning went, *neither should they be counted.* Tax resistance was often criticised as ineffectual, however, because women didn't control enough capital to make an impact. Even if the Tax Resistance League had as many members as the WSPU (it didn't) there would not be sufficient loss of government income to register a blip. But the whole point of the census was its comprehensiveness—and that could be so easily disrupted.

By the spring of 1911, Dora's idea had taken hold and *No votes, no census* became the slogan of the hour. At a Women's Freedom League meeting in Hampstead in mid-February, Edith How-Martyn (who had once scooted around London in a car following Muriel's wayward airship) told her audience of the plan. Unless Asquith promised to pass the Conciliation Bill by 1 April, women should write on their census papers: *No votes for women, no census. I will fill up the paper when I am a citizen.* The *utmost penalty,* How-Martyn assured her audience, was a £5 fine.[2] Of course it was always possible to refuse to pay the fine: that would result in an automatic one-month gaol term, a tactic that suffragettes already used regularly. Annie Kenney believed this to be the real endgame of the census protest: *we hoped to fill every prison cell in the country.*[3] Not through window-smashing, rail-chaining, stump-mounting or politician-heckling, but through the artless act of saying no.

It was just the sort of orchestrated campaign that the Women's Freedom League, with its principles of non-violent resistance, preferred. Charlotte Despard encouraged all members to participate in the boycott. Furthermore, because it involved no destruction

or obstruction, the action would not breach the truce declared by
Emmeline Pankhurst at the beginning of the year, so the WSPU
was on board too.[4] Even non-militant suffragists threatened to
boycott the census. They were constitutionalists, after all, and refusing to fill out a form was like the flip side of signing a petition. We
humbly pray…not to be counted. (It was a good thing Dora was out
of the country, studying the internal workings of the Labor Party in
Sydney, that spring. The very triad whose politics she'd panned were
now using her tactic to campaign for the limited franchise Dora so
despised. Not that they were giving Dora the credit for census resistance; that went to Edith How-Martyn and the Women's Freedom
League.[5])

Unlike Muriel Matters' grille and airship protests, which turned
on the element of surprise, the census protest was an open secret.
Suffragettes Say They Will Spoil the Census, reported the DUNDEE
EVENING TELEGRAPH by early March.[6] *The members of the Women's
Social and Political Union are proposing to employ the forthcoming census as
an engine for their propaganda*, said the BIRMINGHAM MAIL.[7] The BATH
CHRONICLE noted that *Suffragettes of this City* were *bent on evading the
Census*, before helpfully advertising the fact that a large house in the
district had been rented for the purpose of accommodating *evaders* on
census night, *who were asked to bring food, a rug and a pillow*.[8]

Tax resistance had worked on the suffrage landscape like
spot fires: little outbursts of non-compliance scattered across vast
territories of income earners and property owners. Though the Tax
Resistance League offered support and guidance to its members, by
its very nature, tax resistance implicated individuals. Census resistance would be more of a flash flood, carrying along thousands of
protesters in its wake. As such, preparations needed to be made for
the mass evacuation of suffragettes from their regular places of residence of the night of 2 April. The large house in Bath was but one
life raft to ride out the deluge.

From the WSPU's London headquarter, *any number of zealous young ladies* were working at *high pressure* to send out hundreds of census-resisting forms, offering helpful tips and promises of assistance to lodgers, boarders, landlords and male and female occupiers. A reporter found Jessie Kenney *furiously addressing envelopes* and asked her about the public's response. *Thousands of men and women are promising to join us*, she told him.

> There will be anti-census dances, smoking concerts, and social parties given on the Sunday night by friends of the movement, and a number of people who are in sympathy with us are going out of town so that we can fill their houses with resisting suffragists.[9]

Kenney explained that all men and women who wanted to render the census form incomplete must neither sleep at home on the Sunday night before the official forms were sent out, nor return home until twelve o'clock the following day. Should parents or landlords fill in any particulars about a family member or tenant who was in fact absent that night, it would make them liable to a fine for giving false information. The WSPU would set up various safe houses across the city, where suffragettes would be able to spend the night. The WSPU's North West London shop at 215 High Road, Kilburn, which sold suffrage posters, books, penny postcards and other propaganda items, was able to accommodate two hundred women hoping to 'vanish for the vote'.[10]

Officially, the WSPU's strategy was to reduce the value of the government's statistics—and therefore its basis for future public policy—by refusing to submit returns. As Emmeline Pankhurst wrote in a letter to the editor of THE TIMES:

> The Census is a numbering of the people. Until women count as people for the purpose of representation in the councils of the nation as well as for the purposes of taxation, we shall refuse to be numbered.[11]

The government, trying to avert the boycott, retaliated that reliable census data was needed to plan the welfare, housing and health reforms it had promised the nation. After all, it was to implement this liberal agenda that the Liberals had been elected, and why they were fighting a constitutional battle royal with the House of Lords. One woman stated that all it would take for her to *be good* on census night was for Asquith to send them word that he would give facilities for passing the Conciliation Bill.[12]

To injure the accuracy of the census, was how one press report boiled down the public debate. It was a very dry description of what the suffragettes intended to do.[13]

All-night events were planned across England, Scotland and Wales. In London, the WSPU organised a concert at Queen's Hall and dramatic entertainment at the Scala Theatre. It hired out the Aldwych Skating Rink from 3 a.m. to 8 a.m. for rollerskating. It was anticipated that thousands of census evaders, women and men, would simply walk around the streets all night, like well-heeled hobos. Some wealthy suffragists rented abandoned mansions to host mass evasions. WSPU stalwart Jessie Stephenson rented a manor house in Manchester and promised there would be *sacred music, recitations, speeches, and (after 12 midnight) a whist drive will take place.* There would be rooms set aside for dancing and others for cards. *The day would be Sunday*, she announced in her general invitation to Manchester's suffragists, *but at midnight it would be Monday, and the revels would begin.* She called the house *Census Lodge*. Mass evasions were a generous but risky strategy. Technically, the landlord was responsible for the compliance of his or her occupants. Jessie Stephenson was informed by the Chief Constable of Manchester that she could be fined £5 or do one month in prison for each person she housed on the night, the prison terms to be served consecutively. *The sentences*, he warned her, in case of large numbers, *might mean the rest of your life in gaol.*[14]

If the queen bees of the WSPU courted substantial danger, the daily life of the worker bees was one of self-discipline and relentless service. *We lived like nuns*, explained Annie Kenney: *no concerts, no theatres, no smoking; work and sleep to prepare us for more work, was the unwritten order of the day.* Though often *at breaking point*, physically exhausted and emotionally spent, for Kenney the sacrifice was justified not only by the underlying principles of the cause, but the personal fulfilment and mateship it offered.

> We were free and alone in a great brilliant city, scores of young women scarcely out of their teens met together in a revolutionary movement, outlaws or breakers of laws, independent of everything and everybody, fearless and self-confident.[15]

Was it too much to expect that the brave young warriors—breaking taboos as well as laws—might like some fun and frivolity with their duty and devotion? The coronation year was to be *a year of rejoicing*, as Annie Kenney put it, so why not make this protest joyful? Why not make the night of 2 April a night to remember? A festival of nonconformity. An all-night party of protest.

☽

It poured rain all day. That was how actress and suffragette Kate Parry Frye recorded *Sunday, April 2nd 1911 Census Day* in her diary.[16] Kate was residing at the Swan Hotel in Maldon, Essex, laid up in bed with a rotten cold and unable to *walk about* as she'd planned. She ate rice pudding and bread and butter that her landlady fed her, and turned out the lights at 10 p.m. She couldn't wander the streets of Maldon all night, but she could bluntly refuse to fill out the form. *I did not go down in the Census*, Kate proudly wrote in her diary. In fact, despite Kate's belief that she'd evaded the enumerator, she was recorded in the Swan Hotel's census return, probably by her kindly landlady, who wanted the poor girl neither to starve through her illness nor go to gaol through her spirited nature.

Though no longer a member of the WFL, Muriel Matters

was eager to join the thousands of suffragettes evading the census. What she and Tilly did, prosaically enough, was simply stay home in their rented rooms in Lambeth. She didn't hide from the census collector. She didn't attempt to block his access to her townhouse at 91 Fentiman Road. Rather, she kindly accepted the questionnaire, which she then proceeded to deface. *No Vote, No Census*, she scribbled across the form, following the WFL's script. Then she improvised. *As I am not a person under the franchise laws, I am not a person for census purposes.*[17] As for the signed declaration that she had filled out the form 'correctly and to the best of her ability'? Muriel scratched that line out.

In Chelsea, Miss Capron of 20 Halsey Street protected two nameless evaders while filling up her form with an epistle of cheerful resistance: *Sorry that I cannot conscientiously give the information— qualified for citizenship, except for being a woman, the Authorities deny me this priviledge [sic] while not scrupling to impose tasks and burdens upon me—I am therefore logical and justified, in common with many others, in refusing the information. Should the Conciliation Bill pass the House of Commons this Session, I will with pleasure give the required information at any later date. N. M. Capron.*

Vida Goldstein was also in Chelsea on the night of Sunday 2 April. After her smashing debut at the Albert Hall on 23 March, she'd been winning over crowds in Manchester as part of a lecture tour of England's big manufacturing towns. On census night she was back in London and registered as an evader from 22 Rawlings Street. *Particulars unobtainable*, noted the enumerator, *suffragette stayed out all night*.

Nellie Martel may not have been an active member of any suffrage society since her enigmatic departure from the WSPU in early 1910, but she was still a believer in the cause. The enumerator marked her *absent when called for* from her two-room home at 8 Francis Street, London.

All over the land, the census revealed a pattern of protest, like a quilt pieced together with squares of ducking, weaving, hedging, skirting, stonewalling and avoidance, all edged in the blunt language of bureaucracy.

In Sheffield, Adela Pankhurst and Helen Archdale hosted a mass evasion in Helen's home at 45 Marlborough Road. A total of fifty-seven people sheltered in the eight-room house on 2 April, including one male and forty-eight female *visitors*.

In rural Cheshire, Miss E. Woodall's house at 13 Abbey Square, Chester, was listed as *uninhabited* with *name deleted*. Miss Woodall was a WFL member.

In Bloomsbury, Mrs Forsyth of 59 Carlisle Mansions, Carlisle Place, instructed her female caretaker to write on the census form: *The family is away and consists only of women who do not count as citizens and therefore should not be counted in the census. The House of Lords lately decided that 'Women are not Persons'.*

In northern England, Mrs Rose Hyland (*aged about 72, of private means*) noted that she was present but a *resister* at her twelve-room home, Holly Bank, in Conyngham Road. The widow Hyland harboured eighty-eight people, including seventy-four women and eleven men, registering her guests as *Suffragists here for evading Census*.

In London, Emmeline Pankhurst wrote *No Vote No Census* on her form before attending the WSPU concert at Queen's Hall. She then *walked about* with a thousand other evaders, promenading around Trafalgar Square until midnight. Later, along with Christabel, she joined 568 other suffragettes at the largest mass evasion in the country: the rollerskating organised at the Aldwych Rink proved the most popular spot to while away the evening. At least seventy of the skylarking census shirkers were men. There were 230 evaders at the Gardenia Restaurant in Covent Garden and 208 at Jessie Stephenson's rented mansion in Manchester. Whether it was the whist drive or the *rooms set aside for those wishing to sleep*, Stephenson's inducements worked a treat.

Ethel Smyth spent the evening with Emmeline Pankhurst. The pair left the skating rink before its official 8 a.m. closing in order to watch the sun rise over the Thames from Emmeline's rooms at the Inns of Court Hotel in High Holborn, the same rooms in which Vida Goldstein stayed when she first reached London. Ethel was either sleep-deprived or overcome with the immensity of the occasion. *Our foreheads pressed against the window pane, staring silently into the dawn*, she reflected, *gradually we realised that her love for down-trodden women...her hope of better things for them...my music... our friendship...that all this was part of the mystery that was holding our eyes.*[18] The local census enumerator had his sights set on the vision of the two women in the window too. On Emmeline's census form, the registrar stated that although she'd been counted at the Aldwych Skating Rink, *I find however that this lady returned to the Hotel at 5am on the morning of the 3rd April 1911. Under the circumstances I have allowed her name to stand and be counted herein.*[19]

Enumerators pieced together local tittle-tattle to surmise the whereabouts of residents. Jane Ratcliffe, 51, of Rusholme complied with the census but none of her family were present. *There are also 3 daughters at this house*, the enumerator wrote on the schedule, *avoided Census last night and I am told at Victoria Park.*

While the Salvation Army gathered hundreds of London's homeless people into various shelters *where they were enumerated*, hundreds of well-heeled, comfortably housed burghers spilled out of their residences to walk the streets.[20] It was the local constabulary, rather than census collectors, who were given the task of counting those sleeping (or walking, dancing, skating) out of doors that night, marking *the first time that the census of the homeless has been taken by the police.*[21] In Edinburgh, Bradford, Portsmouth and elsewhere, police tracked the unusual flow of people in cafes and restaurants from dusk to dawn, roughly estimating their numbers. These meandering suffrage campaigners were officially tallied as *homeless*.

Schedules flooded back to the census office defaced with

various scratchings and scrawlings: *Suffragist. Refuses Information*; *No Vote No Census*; *Flat filled with Census Resisters*; *Votes for Women*; *Particulars refused until I get a vote*. With weapons no more potent than pen and ink, the women of Britain performed a mass dereliction of civic duty.

Not all avowed suffragists were willing to play the 'battle of the census' game. Millicent Fawcett gave her occupation as *writer* and happily filled out the relevant information for her household, which included her sister Agnes (retired house decorator), unmarried daughter Philippa (42, LCC, Education Department) and three servants. Lady Frances Balfour, president of the conservative London Society for Women's Suffrage, signalled in a letter to the editor that none of her ladies would be joining the protest.[22]

Dora Meeson Coates was at home in her two-room Chelsea studio on census night. She too complied with the census, recording her occupation as *artist* and her status as *married 8 years, no children*. Perhaps it was one thing to protest injustice through her art, but another to deliberately sabotage a perfectly sane and reasonable government process. Dora's friend, mentor and fellow Artists' Suffrage League member sixty-year-old Emily Ford, also complied. Their neighbour Cecily Hamilton was an evader.

Unlike a parade, which required a visible show of solidarity, the census resistance came down to a quiet conscience vote. PUNCH enjoyed reporting that indeed not all of the country's women had *decided to take leave of their census*.[23]

The enormous organisational effort and public relations battle only momentarily frightened the bureaucratic horses. In the first weeks after census night, authorities kept a tight lid on the results, hoping to prevent any leaks that might undermine the prestige of the national head count. In the House of Commons on 5 April, John Burns, the minister responsible, asserted confidently that he *did not anticipate that the suffragette agitation against the census would have any appreciable effect upon the accuracy of the statistics to population.* According to the information that had thus far reached him *the number of individuals who had evaded being enumerated was altogether negligible (hear, hear).* When asked whether he intended to prosecute deliberate evaders, Burns told his parliamentary colleagues *No. In the hour of success mercy and magnanimity…*The reporter noted that *the remainder of the sentence was drowned in laughter.*[24] Suffragette antics always provided parliamentarians with an excuse for a good chuckle.

But in fact 5 April was too early to tell. It would be months before the government statisticians could give an accurate account of census night. For now, both sides were claiming a win. For the suffrage campaigners, the policy of widespread non-violent civil disobedience was a success: saturation media coverage and no prosecutions. For the government, the night had passed with no repeat of the Black Friday scenes and no immediate loss of government prestige.

Emmeline Pankhurst expressed the most concrete outcome of the census resistance: *The resisters had a very good time.*[25]

⚵

In a gesture of imperial symmetry, the first national Australian census was also held on 2 April 1911.

In 1901, when population statistics were still collected by the separate colonies, there were 3,773,801 people tallied, including 1,977,928 white males and 1,795,873 white females. Indigenous Australians were not counted. When Vida Goldstein predicted that *our young Australian nation is bound to achieve greatness [for] it is the first nation to make justice the foundation of its Constitution*, she did not factor racial equality in her reckoning.[26]

Ten years later, the population debate in Australia was not about whether women 'counted' as citizens—only cranks and knuckle-draggers would argue that adult suffrage had not been a boon for the nation—but about the purity of the race. Of the 4,455,005 people enumerated on 2 April (an increase of eighteen per cent since the Federation census), only 42,230 were *non-European*. 19,939 *full-blood Aboriginals* were included in a separate population table—technically in Australia, but politically and philosophically not of Australia.[27]

  The present numbers [of non-Europeans] do not constitute a danger, argued social scientist Dr Clarence Northcott, *but the proximity of the dense populations from which they sprang* constituted an ever-present threat to the social, political and economic effects of mass immigration.[28] The White Australia Policy—the ruling Labor Party's number one platform item—kept the hordes at bay. According to Northcott, the WAP and its legislative twin, the Immigration Restriction Act, are *guarding a land that offers the last opportunity for the development of the higher races and the higher civilization.*

  There were few prepared to argue with Northcott's supposition, though some might quibble about the logic used to reach his conclusion. When Vida Goldstein stopped in Colombo en route to London, she was not only confronted by the visible power imbalance between men and women (who carried heavy loads while their unencumbered husbands looked on) but also the uncomfortable experience of being driven in a rickshaw.

  As someone who had probably never met an Indigenous Australian, Vida experienced *a feeling of self-contempt* for treating *even the most degraded type of black man as an animal.* The experience solidified her deep-seated sentiments:

> I left Colombo believing more firmly than ever in the wisdom of a White Australia. At this stage of our civilisation the black and white cannot dwell together without both deteriorating…The coloured man takes all the vices of the white man, and the white man becomes dehumanised. He is so accustomed to being waited on hand and foot that he never does a thing for himself when he can get a coloured man to do it, and he is

so full of contempt for the coloured man that he sees
everything out of focus, and his tendency is to live only
for himself and in himself.

Vida's solution to the problem she identified was appropriately
black and white: racial segregation. In this way she was every bit the
proud, patriotic Australian.

⚜

Prime Minister Andrew Fisher left for London on 7 April with more
on his mind than head counts. He knew, as the REVIEW OF REVIEWS
so piquantly put it, that Australasia was *in Empire Mood*. His seat at
the table of the Imperial Conference was booked to discuss *matters
of mutual interest* to Australia and the mother country: communication treaties, mail and telegraph routes, copyright and trademarks, as
well as emigration, labour exchanges and protection of *the rights and
liberties of the coloured citizens of the Empire to travel, trade and settle
in the Dominions*. The battleground there was how to treat the 294
million Indians recorded in the 1901 census. Would these subjects of
King George be allowed to move freely around *the piebald Empire*?[29]
How confidently could Australia reserve its sovereign right to draw
the colour line around its borders? How much colonial self-assertion
would it take to press the case for protection?

And just how much authority would Prime Minister Fisher
have to speak for his nation anyway, by the time the conference
opened in May? His constitutional referendum was to be held on
25 April: Fisher would still be at sea when he was telegraphed the
results. It was a crucial test of the electorate's continued appetite for
Labor's agenda now that it governed the nation. If Australia's (white)
men and women spat the referendum back in Fisher's face, could he
still trumpet the achievements of his nation at the conference?

Like many a politician, he was getting it in the neck from both
sides. Anti-Labor mouthpieces like the REVIEW OF REVIEWS were

claiming that ninety-nine per cent of Australia's fame as the world's social laboratory was due to the work of Liberals like Deakin, not the aggressive unionism of Labor. *The fact is*, wrote editor William Judkins, *the country is thoroughly against the whole policy of Labor politically. This country is a democratic one. It is a working community. Its legislation is all liberal.*[30] Over on the other wing, socialists like Dora Montefiore were criticising the Labor Party for not being international enough in its outlook, viewing Fisher's participation in the upcoming coronation festivities as *a wasteful exhibition of colonial flunkeyism.*[31] It was a particular bind for a man who didn't like to use the words 'shut up'.

Margaret Fisher stood by her husband's side as they embarked. Andrew had attended the coronation of Edward VII in 1902 but she had been *too near Robert's birth* to attend. Nine years later, Robert would be accompanying his parents on the five-month trip abroad, but Margaret was leaving behind her other four children: Peggy, 7, Henry, 5, Andrew, 3 and John, *a babe of eight months.* She was worried about abandoning the little ones to the care of her mother, but she was the wife of the prime minister. It was expected of her to accompany him to such a major imperial event. And besides, *she sought always to help Dad in every way and not hinder him.* She would never think to cause him any *distress and embarrassment.*[32]

With so much weighing on her husband's mind, did Margaret stop to tell Andrew that there would be one more Fisher to count at the next census? Margaret, with her magnificent *child built* body, was pregnant again.

34

A Festival of Empire

London, May 1911

It had been a rough couple of years for Dora Meeson Coates.

In May 1909, both her beloved parents died. On the same day. Her father had been ailing for a few weeks, his degeneration diagnosed as the effects of bronchitis, when without warning her mother suffered a fatal heart attack. Her father died a few hours later. The dual loss was, in her words, *a shattering blow. Without my father's strong hand*—at times repressive but always steadfast—*to guide me* Dora felt like *a rudderless ship*. The Meesons were *our best friends and comrades*, wrote Dora. George provided what Dora needed most: *love and patient sympathy*. It was what *got her through*.

The anguished couple moved back into Dora's parents' Ealing home, which eased the financial burden of surviving as artists but lost them the companionship of the close Chelsea community. In the spring of 1910, *still stunned by the blow of the loss of both parents*, the couple travelled to Italy, Paris and Luxembourg: a grand tour of art galleries, where Dora was uncomfortably reminded how dissimilar their tastes in painting were. (George preferred the heavy oils of the Italian masters; she revelled in the delicate frescoes.) She recalled too their unspoken pact: *always he was the master and I the apprentice*—not to mention being his amanuensis. Dora became *a fairly efficient ghost*, working on his paintings when he was too ill or tired or downhearted. George was *a gentle force…painfully alive to the misery of the world*. But he was also the truest, most constant and most solid thing in her life. She rarely left him on his own.

When they returned to England the couple found themselves in Chelsea again, leasing a studio in a nest of artists' residences off King's Road. They had some furniture now, souvenired from her parents' home, and they bought a few pieces of antique furniture. George was particularly fond of a large Marie-Antoinette mirror *which he placed under the window facing his sitters. He found it kept them interested either to look at themselves or to watch him at work reflected in the glass.* By the spring of 1911, George was enjoying some welcome success as a portrait painter. Dora was happy and relieved for him, and always willing to step in when his vain and restless subjects could no longer be distracted like toddlers by their own reflected image. *He generally finished the hands of his sitters from mine*, she admitted, *as, although not in any way beautiful, he found they gave him better than a model the form and pose he needed.* Dora was cheap and could keep still.

The warmth and promise of spring was good for Dora. Two years had passed since her bereavement, and the artist community in Chelsea was her substitute family. There were plays put on in their studio, with up to fifty friends taking the roles of shepherds and nymphs in their *garden pastorals*. There were *dancing parties* and suffrage meetings and charades nights and boxing practice with George's *men-artist friends*. George had a surprising reputation for his boxing prowess, *so swift, sure and unexpected was his play*. And he was giving Dora boxing lessons, which she found *great fun and wonderful exercise*.

There was an uncomfortable scene in this bohemian pastoral, though. A professor from the prestigious Slade School came scouting for an exhibition. After looking through the jumble of George and Dora's works, he told her to send *a little landscape* of hers to a particular gallery. *But we don't want anything of your husband's* the professor told Dora plainly, having barely even glanced at George's portraits. Neither of them ever submitted work to the gallery.

It was a tricky balance, this business of staying afloat, pitching towards independence, tipping back into a stable place of mutual regard and reciprocal reward. When the census man came knocking on 2 April, Dora leant towards compliance. She would never say it, but that summer of 1908 when, inspired by her new artist and suffrage friends and their *huge canvasses*, she had painted a tall, bold banner to aid the cause—it was a moment when Dora had truly steered her own course. She so admired *people who did things*.

⚓

By 4 May, Vida had been in England for almost six weeks. She had attended innumerable receptions in her honour, as well as addressing crowds in public halls and private parlours in the north and south of the country. She published letters and articles in journals and newspapers. She had met with constitutionalists and Conservatives, Labourites and Liberals. There had been little rest and plenty of talk. But she was a good listener, too, and when, on 4 May, Prime Minister Asquith finally divulged that he had received a resolution from the Australian Senate via cablegram six months earlier, Vida was all ears. She waited for the reaction. What she heard was the sound of deafening silence.

The Senate resolution had been widely publicised in the suffrage press under the banner of *Australia's Advice*, but sank without a trace in the mainstream media.[1] For months now, the general press had been maintaining a boycott of any news or information related to suffrage activities. (Thus the Albert Hall meeting, attended by ten thousand people, did not rate a mention in the major London dailies—a situation described by many in the suffrage movement as a scandalous indictment of British liberty, supposedly based on freedom of the press.[2])

On 4 May, a way was found to sidestep the press boycott and force Asquith's hand in parliament. Labour MP Philip Snowden, whose wife Ethel was a prominent socialist feminist, asked the prime minister a question. Had Mr Asquith received from Australia a resolution of the Senate declaring that *the extension of the suffrage to the women of Australia for States and Commonwealth Parliament had brought nothing but good, urging all nations enjoying representative Government to grant votes to women*? And had His Majesty's Government considered this resolution *with a view of acting upon the advice given*? Asquith replied that he had indeed received a copy of the resolution but he *regretted to say the minds of the Government were still divided as to the expediency of woman suffrage.*[3] This being foreign affairs news, not suffrage news, the press duly reported the exchange. Asquith's reply did not bode well for the fate of the Conciliation Bill.

Vida had of course heard all about Asquith's famous smoke-screens, stonewalls and parliamentary obfuscations. But just as it was unexpectedly humiliating to actually sit behind the grille—the experience of it much worse than the idea of it—so it was now maddeningly irritating to witness Asquith's blithe deflection of the Senate resolution she'd worked so hard to engineer. The arrogance steeled her patriotic heart. If ever she might have felt a sense of belonging in this strange land, Vida was now achingly aware of her status as an outlander.

White women were safe in their political rights while in Australasia, but when they left the sanctuary of the antipodes, they were again vulnerable to a precipitous loss of status. Once in England, Australian women were no longer voters—as Nellie Martel, Muriel Matters and Dora Montefiore had been pointing out at every opportunity for the last five years. But there was a further dilemma.

In Australia, laws had been passed to safeguard the British subject status of Australia's married women. Customarily, a woman assumed the nationality of her husband upon marriage, just as her name, children and property became his. In 1903, urged on by campaigns run by the Women's Political Association and other female-led lobby groups, the Naturalisation Act 1903 created equal nationality laws for men and women, meaning that a woman, in Vida's words, no longer acquired on marriage *the legal status and individuality* of her husband.[4] To Vida, the Naturalisation Act was an example of the fact that *all the social reform legislation for which Australia is noted has been vigorously supported by women voters.*[5] But should an Australian woman marry a non-British national (a Frenchman, say, or an American) and live with him in England, under the British Naturalisation Act she acquired his legal identity and automatically lost her right to British subject status. It was like being transported back to the days of the *femme covert*—the 'hidden' legal status that the Married Women's Property Acts had begun to peel back in the 1870s.

Vida determined to throw her energies behind a solution to the problem with a very specific name. Just as she had set up the Women's Political Association in Melbourne to bring together like-minded female advocates for social justice, so she knew that an activist lobby group would be the way to draw together compatible campaigners from among the thousands of Australasian women presently living in London.

On the night of 4 May, Vida happened *to be entertained to dinner* by the Men's League for Women's Suffrage at Pagani's Restaurant in central London. It would be an ecumenical affair, with speeches by Mrs Fawcett, Mrs Despard and Christabel Pankhurst, representing each of the three major suffrage associations. William Pember Reeves, who had been New Zealand's agent-general in London until 1905 and was now running the London School of Economics, was slated to chair. Although Reeves had gallingly pioneered the 'one fine day' school of argument about New Zealand women's historic attainment of the vote he, along with Sir John Cockburn, had been a loud and regular mouthpiece for the virtues of women's suffrage. His wife Maude Pember Reeves, a Fabian who ran in the same circles as George Bernard Shaw and H. G. Wells, was also a force in the Australasian expat suffrage scene.

The WSPU had *hoped that a number of Colonials* would attend the MLWS dinner for Vida, and Vida now hoped so too. She knew exactly the sort of lobby group she wanted to establish in London: the Australian and New Zealand Women Voters' Committee. It would be the first time that Australia and New Zealand joined forces in an acronym representing Australasian kinship. Two sister dominions joined by the political pre-eminence of their female citizens. They would be the ANZWVC.

But on the night of the dinner, Vida kept her plans off the official agenda and restricted herself to her well-worn narrative: how Australian women had won their vote, what they were doing with it now they had it, and some of her own adventures on the campaign trail. She included the key takeaway that victory had been achieved because *our men electors have a keener sense of justice than the men in England have*—despite the mendacity of the press.

She concluded on a note of romantic optimism: *I am quite sure that this year of 1911 you will see the men of England lay at the feet of the women of England the beautiful red and white roses of chivalry and justice.*

One of the distinguished guests, Laurence Houseman, wrapped up the formal part of the evening with a bizarre parable based on Edward Lear's poem, 'The Duck and the Kangaroo'. In the present case, Houseman began, the kangaroo represented *this great wide woman's movement, so startling in its progressive leaps and bounds.* The duck was practical politics, *the Conciliation Bill, the rather small temporary expression of it.* It is the kangaroo, he chortled to the crowd, that takes the duck *into the great world.*[6]

⚚

Dora Meeson Coates was among the founding members of the ANZWC when it met for the first time on 11 May, a week after the jaunty dinner at Pagani's. Maybe she sensed an affinity with Vida.

They were both native-born Victorians, both practising Christian Scientists, both forty-two years old and childless. Maybe she was a little star-struck—Vida Goldstein was after all *the biggest thing that had happened in the women's movement for some time in England*, as Stella Miles Franklin noticed when she arrived in London in 1911.[7]

Sir John Cockburn's wife, Lady Sarah Cockburn, was the founding president. She and her husband had been active suffrage campaigners since moving to London from Adelaide in 1898, when John became agent-general of South Australia. Lady Anna Stout came forward as the heavyweight from New Zealand, the colonial counter-punch of Vida Goldstein. At this first meeting, the founding objective of the committee was formulated and affirmed.

> To watch over the interests of Australian and New Zealand women under Imperial legislation, and to promote their welfare generally from this side of the world. To help forward the Women's Movement in every part of the British Empire.

The first part of the objective was defensive: to protect their own. The second part was offensive: to leverage their unique status to assert the rights of others. The dual purposes were indissoluble. *This stigma cast by English law on Australasian women*, Vida wrote in an article for VOTES FOR WOMEN, must be removed, *and the best way to remove it is to enfranchise English women.*[8]

The committee adopted three founding principles.

1. To represent to the Imperial Conference *the disabilities of Australian and New Zealand women under the Naturalisation Act*;

2. To represent to Asquith *the loss of political status* incurred by Australian and New Zealand women who lived in Great Britain;

3. *To make arrangements for an Australian and New Zealand contingent in the Women's Procession on June 17th.*

Like Vida's WPA in Victoria, the ANZWVC would be *educational and political*. Implicitly, the work of the committee would also be constitutional. Neither Australia nor New Zealand had won its

pre-eminent status as *pacemakers of the world* through militant means.
There was no reason to start now. For Vida, whose reputation at
home took a savage blow when she was seen to endorse the tactics
of the WSPU on behalf of all Australian women, it was particularly
important to toe the legal line. It was also important to demonstrate
her national allegiance over suffrage party politics, something she'd
been careful about previously. When a reporter asked her before she
left Australia how long she was likely to remain in England, she said
that while there would be *plenty to do* in *the old land…I'm afraid I'm a
woman and will long for home—Australia.*[9]

The ANZWVC's avowed function was to lobby the heads of
government at the forthcoming Imperial Conference—their own
governments as well as Britain's. But the committee's first order of
business was more immediate. In late February the colonial secretary,
Mr Lewis Harcourt, had made an appearance at an anti-suffrage
demonstration at the Albert Hall. Now the ANZWVC executive
sent a letter to Harcourt expressing its deep regret at his actions
*holding as they do that his public opposition to the enfranchisement of
women is a slight upon those two Dominions in which equal suffrage is
an integral part of the Constitution.*[10] When Harcourt didn't reply,
the ANZWVC passed on a copy of his reactionary speech to the
prime ministers of Australia and New Zealand, Andrew Fisher and
Sir Joseph Ward. The committee asked to be informed whether *the
public condemnation of any Constitutional principle accepted in any of
the self-governing Dominions is compatible with the tenure of office of
Colonial Secretary.* In other words, could Harcourt get away with
trashing the founding political and philosophical tenets of two cherished members of the imperial family?

The colonial secretary was on notice that Australian and
New Zealand women would not stand idly by and watch their
national ideals be so diminished. Vida had long maintained that
women's enfranchisement was necessary not only for *the protection of women and children* and for *industrial well-being,* but also for

national righteousness.[11] Embracing (white) women as equal citizens was critical to a country's fundamental rectitude, its honesty and decency. The ANZWVC action was also, therefore, a reminder to the respective prime ministers that women's suffrage was not window-dressing for self-government, something to be dusted down and shown off when useful for display. It was a structural beam in the edifice of Australasian democracy. In Australia's case, women voters had contributed to the federation that was the bedrock of the Commonwealth. To undermine the centrality of their civic role, as the colonial secretary was now doing, was an insult to the nation. Would Fisher accede to the slur or stand up for the integrity of his citizens? Was he sovereign man or sycophantic mouse?

The ANZWVC had fired its first rhetorical salvo. The next challenge was to persuade Fisher to add the iniquitous British Naturalisation Act to the agenda for the Imperial Conference. Oh, and also to rally the thousands of Australian women who lived in London, drawn to the centre of the imperial action, to join the Women's Procession on 17 June, only six weeks away.

Nellie Melba's accompanist, Agnes Murphy, had signed up. So had the pioneer educators Harriet Newcomb and Margaret Hodge, English women who had opened a school in Sydney that fielded one of the first female cricket teams.[12] They had returned 'home' in 1908 due to Hodge's ill health; now Newcomb urged London's antipodean women to join the ANZWVCs. These fortunate souls, beseeched Miss Newcomb, *must not forget their duty towards their sisters of the Motherland who are struggling to obtain the powers and privileges which the women of the South already possess and which they regard as a sacred trust.*[13]

Could Nellie Martel also be drawn out of the woodwork? Would Muriel Matters be brought back into the fold? For now, Dora Meeson Coates had been coaxed out of her grief and into a new family outside the Chelsea bubble, one that anchored her to where she came from, and gave her a fresh sense of purpose. She was an

ANZWVC. And Vida Goldstein had an empire-wide league of
her own.

⽶

Margaret and Andrew Fisher arrived in London on 14 May to the
biggest brouhaha the city had seen in years. It was nothing like the
deadly Siege of Sidney Street, thankfully, although authorities were
working hard to suppress industrial unrest in the East End, and the
government, still unable to deliver on its promised social reforms,
feared a summer epidemic of 'strike fever'.[14]

No, the commotion into which the Fishers arrived was not a
calamity but a carnival. The Festival of Empire opened at the Crystal
Palace on 12 May, touted as the civic centrepiece of coronation celebrations. Each of the five countries of the British Empire—Canada,
South Africa, New Zealand, Australia and Newfoundland[15]—put
on a display of their chief products and hence chief purpose to the
empire. The items were displayed in models of each country's parliamentary buildings, built to a three-quarter scale. The All Red Route,
a miniature train with rail cars carrying eighty passengers each, took
more than sixty thousand people a day (10 a.m. to 11 p.m.) around
a twenty-minute circuit where they would feast the eye on *a living
picture of the more salient characteristics of the British Empire*.[16]

Newfoundland where *split codfish are drying on the flakes*;
Jamaican *darkies at work amid the sugar cane*; the mystery of an Indian
jungle complete with *Mr Stripes, the tiger*. Next stop Australia:
Sydney, *the most beautiful harbour in the world* and a lofty Blue
Mountains waterfall *down which real water is falling* at a rate of sixty
million gallons (230 million litres) per day; a sheep run *and sheep-
shearing in actual operation. (Not live sheep, but dummies.)* Then on to
New Zealand: frozen mutton *loaded for the home market* and Rotorua
geysers *in action*; South African *natives at work and play*, goldfields,
diamond mines. It's a small empire after all.

The King himself opened the festival of his empire before a huge crowd. *We hope every success will crown the labours of those who, promoting this Festival of Empire, have striven to serve the cause of Imperial unity, and to awaken interest on the historic part of our great mother city.*[17]

If Dora Montefiore had been present, she would have dismissed the King's speech as so much sentimental claptrap. This *three months' orgie of pageantry*, she lamented from the land of real sheep-shearing, *this one-sided and vulgarly blatant interpretation of the evolution, culmination and responsibility of Empire.* The fifteen thousand people who would be performing daily at the festival, all those codfish splitters and cane cutters, were labouring at their own expense. This—this exploitation and corruption—was the only truly accurate representation of empire, *a record of deeds of filibustering and of crime.* Dora exhorted the socialists of London to hold a pageant of their own, a nightly vigil on the Thames Embankment,

> In which the actors should be the unemployed men and women of this city, the underfed children, the homeless wanderers, whom the stress of competition and the daily increasing pressure of industrialisation have thrust outside the pale of society.

This—this is the heart of the great and boastful Empire! she thundered. The sound of empire was not trumpets and waterfalls but *the weak cry of the hungry babe drawing the empty breast.* This was what *Americans and Japanese and Continental Europeans should come and study and take to heart.*[18] Couldn't they see that the world was burning to the ground? The future was not the rise of nation-states and the coming together of imperial networks of trade and political economy. It was a new world order, based on peace and justice, of international bonds of collective strength. Not global hierarchies of domination and subservience.

They didn't see, though. Dora's was a voice in the wilderness, much like the Australian republican ranting from his soapbox in the Domain: *some wild-tongued Anarchist haranguing a crowd—to its amusement—decrying the Monarchy.*[19] Nothing, claimed the REVIEW OF REVIEWS in full festival mode, *is more characteristic of the people of Australia than their passionate loyalty to the British Empire.*

> We may consider our life freer than that of the people of Great Britain. We may wonder why they put up with certain anachronisms in political and social life. That, however, is their business, and the son loves the father none the less for these hoary antiquities in his make-up.

It remained to be seen whether the daughters of empire were as forgiving of the mother.

⚓

Andrew and Margaret Fisher were in Egypt, enjoying a stopover at the Pyramids, when news came that the referendum had been lost. It was a bitter blow. Fisher had staked much of his prime ministerial authority on his plan to reduce the power of monopolies and give the federal government more control over industrial relations. It had always been a risk to leave the ambitious little Welshman, Billy Hughes, in charge of the government (and hence the government's Yes campaign) while Fisher attended the Imperial Conference. Some in the press had referred to the London trip as *a little junketing.*[20] PUNCH had decided *it is the wives of politicians who are driving them off to London*, the none-too-subtle implication being that women like Mrs Fisher and Mrs McGowen, the wife of the New South Wales premier, were *packing all their clothes and belongings* to parade their colonial finery in front of royalty.[21] It now looked like the coronation might have cost Fisher not just his manly reign over a frivolous wife, but also control of the government's agenda.

Those analysing the results of the election didn't consider Fisher's absence from the last three weeks of the Yes campaign a major factor. Rather, pundits acknowledged that just as Fisher's government had swept into power at the last federal election due to the superior organising skills of Labor women, so the No vote was largely mobilised by female voters. *It was the women's vote that turned the scale*, argued Miss Rose-Soley in an article republished in REVIEW OF REVIEWS. *The fact is universally acknowledged. For once, while men hesitated, women rushed off to the polling booth with their minds made up.* Women constituted the majority of voters on the rolls, in some districts surpassing male electors by more than four thousand. *The female vote is quite sufficient to turn the scale when it pleases*, surmised Miss Rose-Soley. And it wasn't the Labor women turning on Fisher.

> It was the Liberal, otherwise the anti-Labor, vote that won because the Liberal woman had suddenly become ashamed of herself. She had it dinned into her ears to satiety that her supineness lost the last elections.

Liberal women had been called *lazy, indifferent voters* (Vida Goldstein had certainly said this) while Labor women were *nothing of the sort*. It wouldn't have mattered whether Fisher was standing on a soapbox in the Domain or climbing the Pyramids of Giza. *The Liberal woman pulled herself together and exercised her privilege.*[22]

Whether Fisher had come undone courtesy of a newly energised groundswell of conservative women, or a conniving deputy or an electorate for which too much progressive change had come too quickly, one thing was certain. His prestige was shaken by the referendum results. It was not the white horse of success upon which he would have liked to charge into London, rising to his advance reputation as the first elected Labour head of government in the world.

Dora Montefiore had little sympathy. She had *nothing to say to those who join in Coronation festivities*. And in particular, she had nothing good to say to Vida Goldstein.

35

An Inconvenient Period of Domestic Cleaning

London, June 1911

The English summer of 1911 was the hottest on record.[1]

Stifling, sleepless nights and humid days tested the famed British civility. All over the country, weary workers adjusted their routines to accommodate the heat. In Lancashire, quarrymen began to rise at dawn and knock off by midday to avoid the most searing hours. Scorched pastures forced dairy farmers to raise the price of milk; asphalt melted on newly macadamised roads; food spoilt and sewage spewed out of foetid drains. THE TIMES began running a *Deaths by Heat* column—a change from endless reports about preparations for the coronation on 22 June, but not a pleasant one.

England felt different—torpid, dreamy, like a nation dragging its feet—and it looked different too. One journalist noted that *the crannies and rifts in walled Sussex hedgerows where one looks for rare ferns and other treasures hold only handfuls of dry dust.*[2] And then there were outbreaks of unexpected joy. City boys, blissfully unaware of the desiccated state of the Sussex hedgerows, swam naked in Regents Canal and Hyde Park Lake. Women lucky enough to escape to the seaside were reminded that *bathing dresses must extend from the neck to the knees.* Newspapers ran ads for lotions and creams that would prevent inadvertent suntans.

*

If Margaret Fisher peered out the window of her suite at the Hotel Cecil, she could watch the couples promenading along the Thames Embankment, trying to catch a hint of breeze. It was all a bit of a fuss about nothing, this constant moaning about the heat. On the sultriest days the temperature peaked at thirty-three degrees Celsius; most days it hovered around twenty-seven. For a girl from Gympie, this heatwave was a storm in a pretty bone-china teacup. It had hardly put a knot in the long string of engagements and amusements she and Andrew had managed to pack in. And at the Cecil, Europe's biggest hotel, the Fishers' rosewood suite with its sitting room overlooking the river and Westminster made a fine headquarters in which to greet the cavalcade of visitors Andrew received daily.

Margaret knew the British press called her *the yes no lady*: she was considered a difficult person to interview. It wasn't that she was trying to be evasive. Her prevarication *was simply because she could in no way discuss political news that had not already been made public unless Dad suggested to her to do so.*[3] It's true that the typical Australian woman was characterised by *her fearlessness, her grit and her entire absence of artificiality and diffidence*, as the social commentators liked to remark,[4] but there were certain things a prime minister's wife couldn't say or do, Australian or not.

She certainly couldn't be a public figure in her own right, like Catherine Helen Spence or Vida Goldstein.[5] She needed to be gracious and charming at all the gigantic luncheon parties and welcome dinners and to all the visitors who popped by to get Andrew's ear. No wonder Alfred Deakin's delicate wife Pattie had noted after her 1907 trip to London, *it is one long whirl of dressing, motoring, dining and talking and I am weary and homesick.* Pattie would *drop into bed in tears overtired and feeling it quite impossible to do the list of the next day's engagements.* She had been surprised to find herself a person of great prominence, hailed and feted. She hadn't anticipated meeting such *a number of Sir and Lady this and that besides a few lords and their much diamonded wives.*[6]

Fortunately, Margaret Fisher was made of sturdy stuff, for in this coronation year, with the heads of empire gathered for the Imperial Conference, there was no end to the sirs and ladies. And at least, pregnant as she was, this baby would be her sixth: she knew what to expect and she knew absolutely that there was no rest to be expected.

Not that all the functions were a bore. The British Labour Party banquet at the Holborn Restaurant on 25 May had been a vortex of admiration and adulation. As the REVIEW OF REVIEWS noted, Fisher was *the spokesman of the first Democracy that has arrived, not only in Power, but in office.*[7] It was a great responsibility, as well as a mark of honour. Both the party and the unions were looking to Australia to determine whether, as one union official put it, *the working classes were able to govern.*[8] Tonight's dinner was chaired by Ramsay McDonald, leader of the parliamentary Labour Party, and also attended by Mr McGowen, the Premier of New South Wales. And Andrew, not given to despondency, had gone onto the front foot after the referendum result, eager to reassert his authority. Don't dwell on the nation's setbacks; focus on its triumphs!

His speech that night was designed to flatter his own government while diplomatically pointing out his hosts' flaws. *The Australian democracy is not a one-sided affair,* Fisher reminded his audience, *for it includes the women. (Cheers). We in Australia, include the women not merely in our industrial movement but also in our democracy (hear, hear).* Margaret's husband had always espoused the virtues of women's suffrage. Not all of his colleagues could say the same, but even so,

> I am happy to be able to say that not a single representa-
> tive of any political party in Australia would dare to
> suggest that giving the franchise to women has been
> anything but good for the Commonwealth. They have
> helped us in many ways and they will help you in many
> ways when they have the vote in your country.[9]

Vida Goldstein was also a guest that night. It was only a pity

One of a series of stereograph images of the Women's Coronation Procession. Nellie Martel is uncharacteristically almost out of frame on the far right. London, 17 June 1911.

Mrs McGowen stands between a pregnant Margaret Fisher and a proud Vida Goldstein, who managed to muster a large Australian contingent to the Women's Coronation Procession. They wear the empire colours as a right, and not as a privilege.

Above: Dora Meeson Coates in 1933, aged sixty-four. The photograph is in the British National Portrait Gallery collection.

Above: Dora Montefiore reproduced this portrait, taken in Sydney in 1923, in her memoir *From a Victorian to a Modern* (1927). The same image was used in a 1932 profile of Dora in *The Vote* under the heading 'Mrs Dora Montefiore: Suffragist, Democrat, Internationalist'.

Right: The prime ministerial Fisher family after Labor's historic 1910 election victory. From left, Robert, Andrew Jr, Henry, Margaret Jr (Peggy) and the lap baby, John.

Photographer Christina Broom in pole position to capture the historical pageant in the Women's Coronation Procession, 17 June 1911.

A 1928 reunion of prominent suffragettes, held to mark the tenth anniversary of (some) British women getting the vote. Muriel Matters is in the back row, second from the right. Teresa Billington-Greig stands on the right. Emmeline Pethick-Lawrence is in the front row, second from the left, with Sylvia Pankhurst third from the left.

Vida Goldstein at the Eagle Farm home of the Blathwayt family in Bath, England in 1911. The Blathwayts gave refuge to over sixty suffragettes from 1909–12, to rest and convalesce after their release from prison. Vida planted a tree in the Blathwayts' suffrage arboretum as a symbol of hope for her British sisters' political equality.

that Muriel Matters could not be there to join them in the mother country, less than a year after they'd conspired to send an audacious message to her by way of the Senate resolution.

Muriel was still lying low in Lambeth. Perhaps her new fiancé, Mr Treharne, did not want her associating with her old suffrage cronies—the new director of the Adelaide Conservatorium had never been a fan of the votes for women caper. When the Adelaide press announced the engagement of the city's esteemed maestro and its infamous daughter, they were clear that Muriel's brilliant career was over. *The spinster days of little suffragette, Miss Muriel Matters, are numbered*, reported the KALGOORLIE SUN, *as her betrothal to Mr Bryceson Treharne…is announced. Mr Treharne…is of a very unassuming and retiring nature, and the women's vote will interest him but little.*[10]

At any rate, she was not at the Labour Party dinner, nor was she among the delegations that soon began to arrive at the Cecil.

The first was the NUWSS, whose deputation of sixteen upstanding members was headed by none other than Mrs Fawcett herself. The purpose of their visit on 3 June (*a fine, warm day*) was to obtain information about the *workings of woman suffrage in the Commonwealth*.[11] Mrs Fawcett couldn't help but notice that since his arrival in England, Mr Fisher had been speaking *constantly* about his *entire satisfaction with the results of woman suffrage* and she was eager to hear the good news directly from the source.[12] Mrs Fawcett *desired cordially to welcome Mr Fisher to England as the official representative not only of the men, but of the women of Australia*, but her next line was surely for the benefit of the journalists in the room: *What our Prime Minister only talked about*, she intoned, *Australia had done.*[13]

A good politician knows his audience, and Fisher quickly confirmed to the constitutionalists that he did not intend *to come violently into conflict with the people who managed this country.*[14] The deputation assured him that their methods of agitation were quite sound. Mrs Fawcett then asked whether he could confirm the rumours of naysayers that in Australia the extension of the franchise had led to domestic unhappiness and had *deteriorated women in general*. Fisher chuckled. *Of course he could not speak for all women, but speaking for the one he knew best, he thought it had slightly improved Mrs Fisher. (Laughter)*. After dismissing a number of other false reports, Fisher answered Mrs Fawcett's final question. What was it like for Australian women to come to the mother country? *He had no doubt*, was the reply, *that they would feel degraded at losing their citizen rights, and most of them, if they were true Australians, would make a few remarks about it. (Laughter)*.

Fisher's sentiment was light-hearted, but not frivolous. Indeed, within a few days, Margaret was welcoming a deputation of her countrywomen into their lively Hotel Cecil suites. The ANZWVCs were here. Shortly after forming the committee, a subcommittee, which included Vida and Anna Stout, had drafted a letter to Asquith. It asked the prime minister to receive a small deputation of Australian and New Zealand women so they *could lay before you our point of view* concerning *our loss of political status on coming to live in England*. The letter was polite—even deferential, with an acknowledgment *that your time is very fully occupied*—but the request was either ignored or denied, which now led the ANZWVCs to Fisher's door.

Anna Stout represented New Zealand; Vida, Lady Cockburn and Miss Murphy did the honours for Australia. Vida did the talking. She knew that Fisher's Labor ministry had lobbied him to make woman suffrage an agenda item at the Imperial Conference. He had declined.[15] Vida was not impressed by his logic: *Australians, he says, would resent an impeachment at the Imperial Conference of the White Australia Policy.*

She drew Fisher's attention to *the loss of political status when a woman came from the Antipodes to this unenlightened country*. A draft Naturalisation Bill was to be discussed at the Imperial Conference: could this bill not be *brought into harmony* with the Australian and New Zealand Acts? Australian men coming to England were able to vote, but Australian women could not. Could the prime minster do anything about this iniquitous anomaly?

The straight Scot equivocated. Various details in the Australasian and UK acts did not presently align. He was sure that eventually the incongruities would be amended. For the men, perhaps, countered Vida; *but will it be applied to women?*

Fisher had only two hobbies: chess and taking photographs on his box brownie. Now was not the time for happy snaps.

> Mr Fisher: We shall see when it comes. The statute is not yet passed.
>
> Miss Goldstein: Well, so long as it is raised.
>
> Mr Fisher: It has been raised.
>
> Miss Goldstein: Does that refer to women as well as men?
>
> Mr Fisher: We hope so, at all events.

Vida continued to press. Fisher continued to avoid the question. The fundamental principle of *legislative independence* was at stake, he argued. Australia could no more tell the mother parliament how to write its laws than the other way around. Indeed, they would not have got woman suffrage in Australia in the first place if not for legislative independence. *It was only because of free self-government that the Australian Government and other Dominion Governments had been able to make progress*, argued Fisher. Vida would not be argued down. *We only want our own rights which we have possessed in Australia and New Zealand safeguarded here.*

She'd asked Asquith for an audience and he'd refused. She'd asked Fisher for an undertaking to make Australian women's rights an agenda item at the Imperial Conference, and he'd refused. The only win Vida managed was to get the last word. She didn't want the minor ANZWVC victory to end on a sour note, a dissension in the national ranks that would no doubt be reported in the press.

Miss Goldstein asked if he'd ever got through a deputation of men in 15 minutes, reported VOTES FOR WOMEN, *and Mr Fisher agreed he never had.*[16]

⚕

All over London, observed the MORNING POST, the *finishing touches* were being given alike to *the most elaborate as to the most humble manifestations of loyalty*. Flags and bunting were being sewn in scarlet, purple and gold, ready to drape over buildings, statues and the triumphal arches that were emerging to span London's streets like ligneous rainbows. *Not in the memory of the modern Londoner*, noted one correspondent, *has there been such an array of outdoor entertainment*: concerts, exhibitions, pageants—the peerless weather aiding the conspicuous display of fealty to the Crown.[17]

As the papers liked to remind readers, the monarch ruled over the entire United Kingdom of Great Britain and Ireland as well as dominions and dependencies that covered *a quarter of the habitable globe* and embraced nearly *one third of the human race*.[18] The very purpose of the coronation was to seal the compact between sovereign and nation. The impending coronation certainly had people in a holiday mood, *gay and festive*. According to the press, which did its best to conceal the stench of poverty and the whiff of dissent with its honeyed descriptions of civic pride and royal fidelity, nothing could dent the *universal public rejoicing*.[19] Not even the recent memory of Black Friday and Sidney Street, or the rolling strikes and the looming constitutional crisis.

If there was a fair amount of denial, the Imperial Conference was having another interesting psychological effect on the nation. The MORNING POST likened the arrival of the parliamentarians from overseas to a reunion between parents and their adult children. This month of June was like *the steamy upset of washing day*,

> when the lady of the house is visibly embarrassed at their coming, and is divided between the pleasure of seeing them and the painful thought that they might come at a time when she was better prepared to do justice both to herself and to them.

Britain had been going through *an inconvenient period of domestic cleaning.* The industrial strife throughout the nation, the xenophobic tensions in the East End, the neverending woman problem, the standoff with the Lords. The mother country had hoped all this mess would be cleaned up before *our children from the Dominions were paying us their visit.* Still, although the stove might not be quite as thoroughly blacked as *the Mother of Parliaments* could have hoped, she offered *a warm, though soap-suddy hand.* With other European nations putting their political and military houses in frighteningly good order, the promise of *a Federated Empire* was more important than ever. [20]

The question was, would Britannia's colonial daughters accept the sudsy maternal embrace? Or would they use this moment of vulnerability to tug at the apron strings?

At the Imperial Conference, there was some indication that Daughter Australia was in a bolshy mood. It was a delicate balance. There were important governance issues to negotiate, issues of mutual trade and mutual defence being top of the agenda. Asquith's main aim appeared to be to get the unqualified support of the dominions in the event of a war against Germany. [21] Fisher was hoping to secure a greater say in British foreign policy and, in particular, a role in international arbitration to prevent war.

How then to demonstrate loyalty to the matriarch, yet express enough independence and autonomy to retain a healthy self-regard and a prudent self-interest? How to bow, but not scrape, to the sense of superiority that Britain's parliamentarians often exuded? Men like the former Viceroy of India, Lord Curzon, who liked to *sneer at these great self-governing colonies as lacking in political sagacity.* On the question of women's suffrage, for example, Curzon had held the line that *the mother country, as a Sovereign Imperial State, is totally different from the colonies whose politics, as being merely parochial, can afford no guidance to us.* To Curzon, the resolutions of the Australian Parliament had been so much gasbagging. No precedent existed, argued Curzon, for giving women a share *in government of a great country or Empire.*[22]

The dominions were clear on one point: they wanted closer consultation in matters of defence. Fisher was adamant:

> Hitherto the dominions have not, as far as my knowledge goes, been consulted prior to negotiations being entered into by the Mother Country with other countries…I hold strongly to the view—with great deference to the opinions of His Majesty's ministers in the United Kingdom—that that is a weak link in the chain of our common interests.[23]

Fisher did not necessarily expect his viewpoint to be heeded. Australia had already sent a message, loud and clear, last November with its advice to enfranchise Britain's women in the common interest of imperial democracy. The missive had seemingly gone in one of Asquith's tin ears and out the other.

Fisher's fellow delegate William Lyne[24] was now eager to remind his hosts that the parent might have something to learn from the child.

> In the Dominion Parliaments it is possible to make experiments in legislation which are not open to the Parliament of the UK, but I hope the Mother of Parliaments will be able to derive some advantage from the experiments in legislation made by the Overseas Dominions and perhaps find guidance in them in some respects. (Hear, hear).

It was only in *such intimate intermingling* of the representatives of empire, argued Lyne, that ideas could be *adequately expressed* which were *so pregnant with good for the whole*. And just in case these metaphors were too subtle, he made himself perfectly clear. It was well and good to discuss mutual needs and concerns, but *the Dominions must be allowed to manage their own affairs in their own way.*[25]

There were a host of functions that operated as satellite

events to the central conference, pressing wider concerns outside the restrictive atmosphere of Westminster. Andrew Fisher used the occasion of a luncheon at the National Liberal Club to defend his nation's record of pushing the boundaries, invoking the Harvester Judgment as evidence that Australia was on the right track:

> We have not in Australia travelled on a road that led to the destruction of liberty or to the prevention of true progress. Our social legislation is calculated to prevent the degradation of labour, to enable men and women to live in a standard of comfort which human beings ought to live, and to give to everyone the right to sell his labour at a price that would enable him to keep his wife and family in a reasonable state of comfort. (Cheers.)[26]

There was not an Australian who came to London who did not write home about the shocking prevalence of poverty. Fisher told anyone who would listen that Australia's social legislation was contributing to *the peace of the world and the protection of the down trodden.*[27]

Fisher's speeches were widely reported in the London papers, but it was left to an American correspondent to analyse the net effect of his remarks. Australia's prime minister, noted the NEW-YORK TRIBUNE, *has been shocking the English by his outspokenness.*[28]

It was not only what Fisher said that overturned propriety, but also what he did. An unostentatious man, he recoiled when his private secretary informed him he would have to wear court dress at the coronation or not attend at all. Fisher eventually consented to a fitting but *swore positively that he would not wear the lace,* and tore off the trimmings.[29] He declined the various honorary titles and degrees he was offered—he simply did not appear at Oxford and Cambridge with the prime ministers of other dominions for the conferral ceremonies—with the reasoning that *having no education to speak of, it would not be a compliment to the university.* Fisher tried to cloak his principled decisions in self-deprecation, but everyone knew it was a snub.

Mrs Fisher's demeanour was more ambiguous. She soon tired of the endless round of luncheons and 'at homes' (there were at least half a dozen per day) and withdrew from social events, preferring to go sightseeing and shopping with other touring-party wives. *She does not like dressing up and being on her best behaviour every day at all sorts of places*, reported PUNCH. *Besides, she was always being watched and criticised and sized up as though she came from a cannibal island.*[30] Margaret was certainly no winsome English rose; more like a towering cactus. Good in the heat, but spiky. She was also, of course, eight weeks pregnant.

If Margaret had her own reason to withdraw from *the giddy whirl*, Andrew Fisher's rejection of English pretensions was a case of leading by example, manifesting the democratic temper that he consciously and consistently claimed for his nation. *The time has come*, he told the guests at a function for the British Association for Labour Legislation, *when a better distribution of wealth must take place*. It was incumbent on the *Mother of Parliaments* to become the frontrunner. Indeed *we in the self-governing colonies would be proud if she did so, but we claim the right to step out in our own way.*[31] By the choices he himself was making in London, by his very conduct and bearing, Fisher proved the point. It did not go unnoticed. The LIVERPOOL COURIER remarked that Mr and Mrs Fisher:

> are two handsome people as one could desire to see, and have the atmosphere of the colonies about them…It lies, I think in the greater ease, the more democratic life, the greater freedom between men and men and women and women.[32]

At every turn, the Fishers ran their own race.

Fisher also used the public stage to talk up the benefits of emigration to Australia. It was his way of demonstrating that, despite Labor's affection for immigration restriction policies, the party was not opposed to emigration per se as political rivals were wont to claim. In London, Fisher spruiked the future life of British children *in a country where the standard of living and comfort was very high*—but it was not only material comfort that distinguished the advantages of his nation. Australia was also a place *where men and women had the franchise equally.* This was a strong selling point. *In Australia,* argued Fisher, *there was democracy of the purest kind*: Australians did British liberty better than the Brits.

It was a feature that William Lyne was also keen to publicise when he spoke at a NUWSS 'at home'. *Australian women had used their vote to purify Parliament,* he told the gathering, *now their Parliament was one of the model Parliaments in the world.*[33] He added that Commonwealth MPs only *spent on an average 4d per week in the refreshment bar,* presumably far less than their British counterparts without the watchful eye of female voters to curtail their boozing. THE TIMES broke its suffrage-coverage boycott to report the meeting and Lyne's speech was widely covered in the Australian press under the banner *Australia's Model Parliament.*[34]

Fisher's publicising of Australia's democratic charms was ably assisted by the suffrage press, who were delighted to finally have a progressive prime minister in their midst. The same week that the Imperial Conference opened, the WSPU used a provocative illustration by Alfred Pearse (signing his work as A. Patriot) as the front cover for its popular publication, VOTES FOR WOMEN.[35] A woman sits on the floor, slumped over a chair, face down, her head in her arms. At her feet is a baby, swaddled in sheets, its little mouth open, having just taken its last breath. 'For These We Fight' was the title of the sketch. The caption read:

> In South Australia in 1893 the number of babies who died under 12 months old was 1,245. In 1894 women got the vote; new laws and regulations were brought in, and in 1908 the number of babies who died under 12 months old was 616, less than half what it was before.

Politicians would huff and puff, but statistics didn't lie.

*

But not everybody was buying Fisher's smug boosterism. Refusing to kiss imperial arse was one thing, but promoting a fantasy of Australia's unsurpassed merits was another. In the Australian edition of the REVIEW OF REVIEWS, editor William Judkins poked fun at the bumptiousness of Fisher's claims that Australia had *set the Empire—nay, the whole world—an object lesson for which it had long awaited.*[36] The universal love of his own people, Judkins pointed out, had eluded Fisher. The referendum results represented a swing away from the Labor Party, which the people had found *arrogant, boastful and unbearable in its manners.*

Labor's overweening immodesty was particularly distasteful given that it had done nothing to stop one of *the foulest blots on the annals of the English-speaking race*: the treatment of Aborigines. The *blood runs cold*, castigated Judkins, at recent reports from the Northern Territory of *wholesale murder, systematic slavery and the worst crimes against women and children...the young female children are regularly bartered and sold.* That the Labor government had taken over the administration of the Northern Territory from South Australia was a step in the right direction. *Let us hope*, warned Judkins, *now that Mr Fisher has taken the matter in hand, that something may be done to wipe this stain from the escutcheon of Australia.*[37]

Judkins' choice of language was topical. Fisher had in fact proposed a new 'escutcheon'—the shield that forms the focal point of a coat of arms—to the colonial office for approval in 1911. The new arms also dropped the word Advance (which Fisher despised since, he insisted, Australia already was advanced) from before Australia, offered a less cartoonish portrayal of the kangaroo and emu and substituted wattle for the green grassy knoll on which they stood.

As far as Asquith was concerned, neither cosmetic nor policy changes to Australia's image mattered a jot when it came to the main sticking point of the Imperial Conference. The dominions would not be consulted when it came to matters of British foreign policy. While the mother country bore the defence burden, she would have supremacy in all imperial relationships. Asquith was cracking the age-old parental whip: she who pays must be obeyed.

⚓

Saturday, June 17, 1911 will be a historic date in the annals of England, predicted the Adelaide REGISTER, *the procession of women…will be the greatest ever witnessed in the history of the world.*[38]

It was a big call. But there was no doubt, less than a week out from the (predicted) historic date, that enthusiasm for the Women's Coronation Procession appeared to match the mania for the main event itself.

Remarkably, Emmeline Pankhurst's truce had held. The second reading of the Second Conciliation Bill had passed on 5 May with a huge majority, after eighty-six city, town and district councils passed resolutions in favour of the measure that would finally give votes to women on the same terms as men.[39] (Vida was at Westminster that day. *Only woman suffrage* could have persuaded her to sit behind the grille for the five-hour reading.[40]) But facilities for the bill still had to be granted: that was the procedural step that the government had used consistently thus far to trip up the suffrage campaign. By the last week of May, it was clear that Asquith had no intention of finding time to debate the bill in the current session of parliament—but he promised a full week would be set aside for another second reading of the bill in 1912.

Emmeline chose to take Asquith at his word. Perhaps it was the glorious sunshine infusing her with optimism. Or perhaps it was a disciplined desire not to do anything that might ruin the prospects of the women's procession making its historic mark. Though the WSPU was principally sponsoring the event on 17 June, twenty-eight other suffrage groups had agreed to take part—including the NUWSS and the WFL, responding to the call that as women were not included in the royal processions, they must stage their own salute to King,

Country and Empire. A sudden outbreak of militancy—smashing windows at the Crystal Palace, say, or derailing the All Red Route or harassing MPs in front of their overseas guests—would threaten the participation of the peace-loving suffragists as well as alienating the devoutly royalist public.

Instead of sabotaging the welcome-home party for the children of empire, Emmeline took the opportunity to point out that Australian women had been enfranchised in the year of Edward VII's coronation. *The year 1911 is a significant one*, Votes for Women proclaimed. *It is a Coronation Year, and it is fitting, therefore, that it should witness the crowning of womanhood by an act of justice long overdue.* But there was a more salient point to be made. *It is also the year of a great Imperial Conference, when statesmen representing enfranchised women from the daughter countries will, among others, throng the Capital of the Empire.*

Why not make use of the daughter countries and their enlightened leaders? The march would be not only *National*, but *Imperial*. *Every part of the Empire will be represented.* The daughters would all be present to witness the event that would see the *crowning of the womanhood of the United Kingdom as a Sovereign half of a Sovereign people*. Emmeline announced that Australia would be represented in the procession by Vida Goldstein and Lady Cockburn, while New Zealand would be led in the procession by Anna Stout. *And in the ranks*, she guaranteed, *will be many women who already exercise the franchise in their own country*.[41] What was needed was thousands of women to join them, to make the march a *March of Victory*!

The WSPU was clear-sighted about the difficulty of getting the people out into the streets. *London is a great city*, Votes for Women warned, *its population will be nearly doubled during the month of June. How are those millions to know? How is their interest to be aroused?*[42] With all the competing events this summer, the task was to ensure people knew where to be, and when. As Vida herself soon realised, *wherever Royalty is present in this country no one thinks of anybody or anything else*[43]—so the effort required would be even greater than usual. And with the continuing press boycott ruling out mainstream media coverage, grass-roots PR was the only option.

To this end, a large army of canvassers was sought to distribute handbills in the street and to convince traders to put up window posters, and householders to put posters in their gardens. Another, more striking, tactic was to drape banners from upper windows and balconies along prominent streets. *Cheap banners, roughly made,* could be obtained from WSPU headquarters, *but when they can be made with care and finish at home they are more effective.*[44] There were *countless other ways* of advertising the procession, Votes for Women assured its readers: drawing-room meetings, market-square and street meetings, stand-up-on-a-chair-in-a-crowd meetings. (It was the sort of work that Nellie Martel had loved and been so good at. How hard it must have been for *the Australian lady* to hide in the shadows when she could now have been in her element.)

At least the stars of the various suffrage associations were in alignment. The Women's Freedom League was as diligent in promoting the event as the WSPU. Its journal, The Vote, proclaimed on 13 May that *in a few weeks it will be given to the people in London to witness the greatest procession ever known in the world's history.*[45] On 3 June, as the great day approached, the WFL made a rabid pitch for participation from its members. *Put every atom of energy, enthusiasm and ingenuity that you possess into the Freedom League section of the great procession,* said The Vote, *the procession that will set London's great streets and squares aglitter with the most beautiful display of colour, grace and movement that has ever been seen in their midst.*[46] A column in the international section of The Vote made a plea: *Will all Americans and suffragists and sympathisers of other nationalities willing to walk in this procession send their names as soon as possible?*[47] If all went to plan, women from across the globe would soon marshal at the Embankment to demonstrate an esprit de corps in which *distinction of class, creed, party, race will be forgotten.*[48] Nations outside the empire were sending their dignitaries to fete King George at his coronation, and so too the Women's Coronation Procession would receive its share of international supplicants. *Every civilized country of the world is sending its delegates to take part in it,* reported the REGISTER. It was hoped that Indian women, wrapped in their saris, would form a particularly picturesque part of the empire float.

If the organisers' prophecies were fulfilled, the procession would be four miles long and would stretch from the Houses of Parliament to the Albert Hall, where a monster rally would later take place. Tens of thousands of women united in their demand for a boon that the British Parliament consistently failed to grant them would gather in a show of determination and strength. Tens of thousands of women *walking five abreast, with pennants flying, banners held aloft, colours of every hue and shade and gradation blazing in the sun.* Tens of thousands of women *with faces to the dawn.*[49] Crowds would line London's streets, drawn by the sheer spectacle of it all, to watch the women march shoulder to shoulder. They had come in 1908 when the spectacle was a national curiosity. Surely they would come now, when it was billed as a major tourist attraction.

There will be groups of working women, sweated women, factory workers, wrote the GEELONG ADVERTISER, reporting the build-up from the other side of the planet, *as well as contingents of nurses, typists, teachers, sanitary inspectors, gardeners and gymnastics teachers; there will be mothers of families, and those engaged in domestic occupations.*

Should the months of advertising, recruiting and mobilising pay off, there would be university educated women parading in their academic regalia. There would be artists carrying banners bearing immaculately stitched slogans: Votes for Women; Deeds Not Words; Who would be free themselves must strike the blow; Liberty or Death. Names of banner-bearers were urgently required by organisers. It was not the most glamorous job; *scarred hands and aching backs* were the price for flying the flag of freedom.[50]

Women were encouraged to spare no expense—or spend not

a penny, depending on their circumstances. The WSPU had almost £100,000 in its fighting fund. Women were encouraged to wear white dresses—or, if not white, then *green or golden brown*—though they were assured *that it is much more important that they should come than that they should wear dresses of a certain shade.* As for hats, this was up to individual preference too. It was becoming fashionable to forgo headwear, a trend that *has much to recommend it, for hats take up a lot of space these days.* But for those who felt *unfinished* without a hat, a lace or silk scarf would be fit for purpose.[51]

There would be contingents of Welsh suffragettes, Irish suffragettes and male suffragettes, supporting their sisters, daughters, wives and mothers. Catholic women. Jewish women. *The best known and most popular actresses of the day* would march beside equally famous singers and musicians and *a large and influential contingent of women writers.* There would be a historical pageant of women representing *notable characters from the dawn of history:* Florence Nightingale, Jenny Lind, Mrs Carlyle, Grace Darling. There would also be a special pageant consisting of seven hundred women clothed in white and wearing plain prison caps, to represent the number of imprisonments suffered by women since the beginning of the militant suffrage movement six years ago.

All over London there were women preparing for the day. *Rooms full of volunteer artists,* reported suffragette Elizabeth Robins, *bent over historical designs…women cutting fabrics, women sewing, women stencilling banners, gilding emblems…women who have never worked hard before have been working for the pageant these hot June days, from eight in the a.m. till 10 at night.*[52] Dripping in their drawing rooms, these volunteer gentlewomen may have entertained a thought (perhaps for the first time) *about the sweated women who have no choice.* Young women, flouting their parents' wishes, signed up as needlewomen, machinists, and *cutters-out of pictures.* Girls who were usually too occupied with study to lend a hand to the cause were asked to put aside their books and volunteer. Youth was desired as both a practical and figurative commodity. As one poet in the NUWSS publication COMMON CAUSE declaimed, it was at this procession that *the world shall grow younger and fairer.*[53]

And the ANZWVCs were there to remind all and sundry what a young and fair nation—in both the moral and racial senses of the world—could accomplish. Through Vida, they'd already reminded the Australian delegates to the Imperial Conference that women had *helped to elect the men* who would be representing their country at the conference.[54] She and Anna Stout had also brought the question of iniquitous naturalisation laws *before the notice of every member of the Conference.*[55] It was the standard hard-slog lobbying work that Vida had spent her whole adult life doing. But there was one trick she hoped she could pull off for which there was no precedent. At the initial meeting of the ANZWVC in May, it was agreed to ask Margaret Fisher to head the Australian contingent in the Women's Coronation Procession.

Vida not only had a longstanding association with the Fishers, she was also *the woman of the moment in Suffragette circles*, as even the Sydney TRUTH had to admit. If anyone could twist an arm, it was Vida. So it wasn't impossible that the prime minister's wife would break with tradition and make her own stand on the most pressing political issue of the day.

But she'd been very happy to withdraw from the London circus—would she consent to head back into the fray? Could a woman of such stature be seen to swim with what one US congressman characterised as *a great world-tide* rising *steadily and irresistibly?*[56] Would Margaret lead the wave of ANZWVCs going over the top, or would she stay in her bunker at the Cecil and watch the gathering troops on the Embankment from her window?

Regardless of Mrs Fisher, Australia's brigade would have to make a good showing or lose significant face. Australia would march at the top of the procession, along with New Zealand, in recognition of Australasia's world-leading status as democratic exemplar.

The Contingent from the Commonwealth of Australia promises to be influential and large, Vida wrote in VOTES FOR WOMEN in mid-May.[57] She called upon all Australians currently travelling or residing in London to make contact with her, *to discuss the means by which they, as women voters, could help their British sisters in the struggle for the vote.*[58] On Saturday 17 June, wrote Vida,

> every Australasian woman, who is enfranchised in spirit, as well as in the letter of the law, will consider it her solemn duty to show her sympathy with the women of this country, who have laboured for over 50 years for the franchise.

It was a stern invocation. Vida's reputation as the leader of the Australian suffrage movement was on the line. Did she really have the pulling power? *Miss Vida Goldstein is anxious to get into direct communication with her countrywomen,* revealed an advertisement in VOTES FOR WOMEN, *and all letters addressed to 4 Clements Inn, W.C., will reach her without delay.*[59]

But Vida herself had an agonising decision to make. The International Women's Suffrage Alliance was holding its biennial congress in Stockholm in 1911. Carrie Chapman Catt, the IWSA president, had been pleading with Vida—representing *our best beloved suffrage achievement, Australia*[60]—to attend one of these special events since the inaugural meeting in Washington nine years ago. And Vida had yearned to go; but the expense of the journey and the time away from her Victorian suffrage work had always made it impossible. Now she was finally in the right hemisphere at the right time—and the blasted conference dates clashed with the Women's Coronation Procession! As talented and as determined a woman as Vida had proved herself, she could not be in two places at once.

Across the globe, from Cape Town to Calcutta, from Melbourne to Munich, the international press waited to see what the British suffragettes would do next. *It may be that victory is close at hand,* wrote the Dover Express on 2 June, *and this may prove to be the last great effort which women will have to make in order to obtain the vote.*[61] But would a peaceful, picturesque show of numbers be sufficient? Perhaps the procession would end in a riot. Would there be more arrests, more violence? More blows taken for the cause?

On 16 June, Elizabeth Robins predicted in the Westminster Gazette that after the world witnessed *four miles of women marching towards one goal,* British MPs would no longer be able to claim *that enough women are not enough in earnest about the idea.*[62] You would have had to be living in a cave these past five years to doubt the dead seriousness of the suffragettes. *To those who are still in ignorance of the great force of public opinion behind the demand for women's enfranchise-ment,* wagered the Adelaide Register, the procession would be *a revelation of the solidarity of women.*

It could be, as Vida Goldstein prophesied, *the greatest procession known in history.*[63] But first the people must turn up. It was, after all, so frightfully hot.

36

The Greatest Procession Known in History

London, 17 June 1911

It was no surprise to anyone when the soft pink dawn of Saturday 17 June ripened into a spectacular golden day. The Women's Coronation Procession threatened to become the *Melting March*, as one wag put it.[1]

There was certainly no chance of it being a repeat of the Mud March of 1907, when women had first taken to the streets en masse to protest their political exclusion and advocate their citizenship rights. In the intervening four years the world had watched the British suffrage movement transform from a staid, bluestocking affair to a youthful riot of colour and exuberance.[2] During this period—*The Four Years War*, Emmeline Pethick-Lawrence called it—the world had also seen a handful of powerful men impose on the British polity, through their mulish arrogance, a regime of vengeful persecution and the tacit indulgence of police brutality. In the process, the British public morphed from apathetic bystanders to fervent spectators, hungry for the next episode in the serial melodrama of the suffragettes.

The transformation in the women's movement from sleeping giant to seething termagant had been aided, and in many ways prompted, by what Emmeline Pankhurst had termed *outside forces*. Nellie Martel leading the first outdoor protest meeting at Westminster on 12 May 1905; Dora Montefiore's headline-grabbing Siege of Hammersmith in June 1906 adding passive resistance to the arsenal of civil disobe-dience; Muriel Matters performing the most spectacular deeds of daring rectitude, in the House and in the heavens. All claiming the status of enfranchised Australian women as both motivation and authority for their brazen actions. All gaoled for their transgressions.

And Vida Goldstein, playing the game of political brinkmanship from abroad; negotiating—indeed drafting—a resolution from the Australian Parliament to the British government, a statesman in everything but title and salary. Now the canny diplomat was here, in the metropole, the centre of the action, still marshalling the forces of moral and patriotic coercion. Raising a corps of ground troops—the ANZWVCs—organised to keep up the pressure and influence decision-making in London in a more rigorous and sustainable way than show-stopping political fireworks.

As a newly minted foundational ANZWVC, Dora Meeson Coates had to make a choice: follow her high-profile countrywoman into the front line or continue to skirt the flanks of the movement. She too had brought skill and dedication—and the heady sense of entitlement mixed with grievance that characterised other Australian activists in Britain—to the suffrage campaign. Through her artistic contributions to NUWSS and WFL propaganda and her flirtation with mild militancy—postering and parading, but not census-resisting or window-breaking—Dora had defied her conformist upbringing and her cautious husband. She had identified with the cause; contributed to it. But she had not led by example. Today, Dora had the opportunity to march in the front line of history. Literally.

For Australia and New Zealand—in honour of those countries' pre-eminent, path-breaking achievements in the global campaign for women's enfranchisement—had been given pole position in the Women's Coronation Procession, forming up behind the leadership of the WSPU. *The significance of the procession will be world-wide*, reported the London correspondent for the Adelaide REGISTER, *for the procession will not only be national in its character, but also Imperial and international.*[3] Noting that Australian women had been enfranchised in the coronation year of Edward VII, the journalist predicted that *the crowning glory of the Coronation year of King George V will be the emancipation of the women at the heart and centre of the Empire.* The gift of historical coincidence made the imminent success of the British suffrage movement appear inevitable.

⚓

If Vida was concerned that people would not turn up to witness the great event, she needn't have worried. You couldn't hold them back. *It was Suffrage Day!* exclaimed Christabel Pankhurst. *The climax of all peaceful effort! In this direction there was nothing left to do.*[4] For the spectators, nothing to do but watch the passing parade. For the peaceful protesters, nothing to do but walk together, heads held high. Selectively, the women marshalled in their suffrage societies and professional or geographical groupings. Collectively, they embodied the full spectrum of British womanhood.

An elated Christabel Pankhurst described the mass of women who came together that day:

> Toilers from factory workshop, field and garret; wave after wave, rank after rank...Endless it seemed— Science, Art, Medicine, Culture, Ethics, Music, Drama, Poverty, Slumdom, Youth, Age, Sorrow, Labour, Motherhood—all there represented.[5]

Mother, Christabel wrote later, *walked at the head.*[6]

All of the publicising, pushing and puffing had paid off. Suffragists and suffragettes alike had been asked to form up at the Embankment at 5.30 p.m., organised into contingents. And there they were: forty thousand women. Several thousand *man sympathisers.* One thousand banners. One hundred female marching bands. Twenty-eight societies. Horses. Floats. Costumes. And the colours. Everywhere, the colours.

The streets were thronged with cheering crowds, noted Christabel.[7] From the Thames to Trafalgar Square, past Pall Mall and Piccadilly, a surge of onlookers craned to get a glimpse of the extravagant display wending its way past London's most iconic landmarks. People stood six or eight deep on either side of the streets. Taxis and buses lined the streets, with people poking their heads out from inside or standing on top. People scrambled to fill the seats in the stands that had been erected for the royal pageantry of the following week. They leaned out of the upper windows of clubs and private residences, watching *the advance of that great army marching five abreast.*[8] To the Antis, remarked the REVIEW OF REVIEWS, *who looked down from the club windows in Pall Mall,* the procession *must have seemed like a deadly boa constrictor stretching its coil around its fascinated victim.*[9]

The best vantage point for the snaking line of dissenters was from outside Green Park near Piccadilly, where *one obtained a splendid view of the cortege as it came down the slope of the hill with the gorgeous, changing, scintillating, iridescent colours of the banners flashing in the sun.*[10] Photographer Christina Broom set up her camera and tripod in the middle of the Embankment, where she could capture the fine-grain detail of the women as, in the words of one participant, *they walked in the dust of the summer's day*: broad hats to keep off the late afternoon sun, flat shoes peeping out below full summer frocks and skirts that fell to the ground, gloved hands gripping banner poles, flags and hand-crafted emblems (shamrocks for the Irish, elephants for the Indians, lattice gates for the prisoners). Some objects in motion became a blur on Broom's glass plates; other images show the sharp-edged defiance of young women staring straight into the camera.[11]

This was no jumble of humanity: the order of the march was strictly sorted and tightly choreographed. A printed program of the event, sold for a penny by the WSPU, made it clear that nothing had been left to chance. Should the police choose to strike that day, holding back the tide with batons and fists as they had on Black Friday, the assailants would encounter not a rabble but a fully realised formation. Taking the lead was General Drummond—on horseback, naturally, and clad in a green habit. At a mare's breadth walked Miss Charlotte Marsh, the colour bearer, a young woman with *a crown of gold hair*, who had been force-fed in Holloway. Behind her rode Joan of Arc on a white steed of her own, played by silver-helmeted, flag-bearing Miss Marjorie Annan Bryce, the daughter of a Scottish businessman and Liberal politician. Then came the WSPU committee officials— the Emmelines, with Christabel and Mabel Tuke—walking tall, all resplendent in white. Christabel wearing her academic regalia; her mother, steely blue gaze fixed ahead, mouth set, a step ahead of the pack.

Next came the prisoners' pageant, the cohort that Emmeline Pethick-Lawrence considered to be the most *significant and beautiful*, with the seven hundred women marching to represent the seven hundred who had to date been incarcerated in the struggle for the vote. They too wore white frocks and wide-brimmed hats, some trimmed with daisies, and each carried a simple white flag. Rising from their midst was a large banner depicting, in Emmeline's words, *a symbolic woman with a broken chain in her hands and the inscription: From Prison to Citizenship.*[12]

Following the prisoners' pageant was the historical pageant, *illustrating*, according to the official program, *the great political power held by women in the past history of these Isles, the last vestige of which was lost with the vote in 1832 when the Reform Bill was passed.* In order to look forward to a new dawn, the suffragettes consistently looked back to prior female heroines whose deeds provided historical inspiration for the modern movement.

Thus here, costumed in gorgeous fabrics with exquisite stitching (that £100,000 war chest the WSPU had amassed was being put to extravagant use) were the Abbess Hilda with her attendant nuns. Peeresses summoned to parliament in the reign of Edward III. Women governors, custodians of castles, high sheriffs of counties and justices of the peace. Burgesses on the parliamentary register in the reign of Elizabeth. Freewomen of various companies and corporations: mercers, stationers, drapers, grocers and fishmongers. Women who were voteless after the Reform Bill, in their early Victorian costume: Charlotte Bronte, Grace Darling, Harriet Martineau, Florence Nightingale. And behind them, the women trailing at the end of a glorious but fractured history, came the women who had started a new era in female sovereignty.

For here came the *Representatives of Countries where women have the vote*: New Zealand, Australia, Norway and Finland, plus American women representing the enfranchised states of Utah, Colorado, Wyoming, Idaho and Washington.

Following this scene-setting, breathtaking beginning, the procession stretched for a further four miles.

The empire pageant, a stunning horse-drawn float of white canvas, linen and lace, rising like a triumphal wedding cake, decorated with upright nymphs holding the emblems of the colonies and dependencies: the maple leaf, the Indian elephant, the springbok and the New Zealand tree-fern; gilded harps and shamrocks, the red dragon of Wales, Scotland's *rampant lion*, and the kangaroo. The West Indian, Mediterranean, African and Pacific colonies were technically represented by white-robed brides of empire who *sat at the feet* of the King, but they were denied a motif, the charm bracelet of empire missing a few symbolic links.[13]

Now came the International Contingent, as many women from as many lands as could be scooped up from London's immigrant population and bulging tourist quarters: Sweden, Switzerland, Portugal, Italy, Russia, Romania, Germany, Spain. Nation-states with armies and churches and factories and universities—but no enfranchised women.

And now the hoi-polloi of suffrage societies: from the Actresses' Franchise League through the Gymnastic Teachers' Suffrage Society and the Jewish Women's Suffrage Society to the Women's Freedom League, along with the endless regional and municipal branches of the WSPU and NUWSS. At the head of the NUWSS section was Mrs Fawcett, leading ten thousand members of the oldest established constitutional organisation. Being drawn along in a bath chair: Mrs Saul Solomon of South Africa, who had been rendered an invalid in the Black Friday attack. She represented all the women whose bodies, but not spirits, had been crushed that day. Mrs Solomon carried a banner with the subtly insubordinate message: *Join the next Deputation*.[14]

Finally, bringing up the rear, waiting patiently at the Embankment for three hours as the other cabs left the ranks, were the men's groups: the Men's Political Union for Women's Enfranchisement, the Men's League for Women's Suffrage, the Men's Committee for Justice to Women, and assorted *Friends and Sympathisers*. By the time these contingents reached the Albert Hall, the sell-out meeting hosted by Emmeline Pankhurst that marked the end of the procession had well and truly finished. *The tail of that great army*, enthused one participant, *had not even started when the leaders reached their destination*.[15] The men—the procession's appendage— arrived in darkness.

The women have had triumphal processions before, said THE TIMES, *but this was beyond them all in numbers and effect!*[16]

Of the most imposing and inspiring character, admitted the DAILY NEWS.

Never before has such pageantry passed through the streets of London, judged the DAILY CHRONICLE.

A red letter day in the history of the movement for the emancipation of women, reported the REVIEW OF REVIEWS for distant Australasian readers who were also *in Empire mood*.[17]

An astonishing demonstration, said the MANCHESTER GUARDIAN, the only daily newspaper to have consistently eschewed the press boycott,

> but more astonishing the acceptance, the enthusiasm in the streets. The police have so much confidence in the women that they left them to their huge task unaided. For a men's procession half the size there would have been barricades.

And that was the truth. The Women's Coronation Procession had passed off non-violently: a diplomatic demonstration of the aspirations and achievements of forty thousand women. *Forty thousand women with faces to the dawn*, as THE VOTE summed up the mood of optimism and unity.[18] If the coronation was intended to be *an object-lesson in the power and dignity of Imperial manhood*, as suffragette Elizabeth Robins wrote, then the Women's Coronation Procession had demonstrated just what *a splendidly barbaric Pageant of militarism* his crowning would be. By contrast, the event *projected, guided, marshalled by British women* was *an homage to a peaceful Ruler.*[19] Despite the military metaphors they themselves used, the women's methods had remained pacific and conciliatory.

And the British public returned the favour. Those forty thousand brave faces were neither spat in nor smacked down nor scorned. From press and punters alike, *words of encouragement and salutation were generously thrown out, in a diversity of tongues, from such a cosmopolitan crowd as London has seldom seen before.* No one hurled *the old time-worn requests to 'go home and do the washing' or 'mend father's socks'.* Kate Parry Frye, who had come up on the train from Buckinghamshire for the day to volunteer as a group captain, was surprised to find that *the crowd was so quiet—hardly a rude remark and constant applause all the way for us.*[20] No one threw rocks at their heads or dragged them from their homemade horse-drawn conveyances.

Is it any wonder that militants, constitutionalists and commentators agreed that, after such a show of *loyal comradeship*, of sisterly solidarity and popular adulation, *the days of contempt, of ridicule and*

of real antagonism to the cause of woman suffrage had gone for ever?[21]
The Women's Coronation Procession was a stunning public relations
coup.

The question remaining was how Asquith would respond to
the shift in public opinion.

♆

The George Rose Stereograph Company of Melbourne captured
three images of *the Great Suffragette Demonstration of London*, as the
stereoscope photographs are labelled. The first, taken from a slightly
elevated position at the back of a crowd (Rose appears not to have
enjoyed the same access to the front line as Christina Broom) is of
the empire car. Emerging from a sea of straw boaters and trimmed
bonnets is the horse-drawn wedding cake passing through Trafalgar
Square. The stereoscope, with its 3D effect, shows the lily white float
hovering, as it seems, before the sepia brown buildings of central
London. An apparition of imperial loveliness.

The second image shows *The Australian Section forming up
on the Thames Embankment*, according to the printed caption.[22] In
this picture, a dozen or so women wearing simple white dresses and
unpretentious hats mill about beneath a modest banner, waiting for
their turn to set off from Blackfriars Bridge towards the Albert Hall.
They have gilt kangaroos on sticks—the sort that an enterprising
souvenir vendor might sell at a fair—and the banner depicts the
Australian coat of arms: the official one, with the cock-legged emu,
the cartoon kangaroo and the Advance Australia logo that Andrew
Fisher so deplored and had tried to have expunged. It's impossible
to tell whether the design is stitched or printed onto the white fabric
backing, but it is unmistakably hokey, a cheap graphic ill-befitting
the nation that had *pioneered [women] into citizenship*.[23]

There is another noteworthy detail, so peripheral as to be easily
missed. On the far right, almost out of shot, is the unmistakable

face of Nellie Martel. She is, uncharacteristically, half-hidden and peeking out from behind two other figures. Though she is not mentioned in any of the accounts of the day, neither personal testimonies nor newspaper reports, Nellie had quite evidently been unable to stay away from the action. Like a moth to the flame, she had gravitated back to the Australian contingent, to the nation with which she always associated most strongly, at least in terms of her political identity. *Our Australian friend*, as Christabel Pankhurst had called her in more congenial times, had come out to support her adopted countrywomen. True to form, she was wearing a most flamboyant hat, cut from a dark cloth, and trimmed with a ring of large white flowers—chrysanthemums or carnations. Her smiling face is almost dwarfed by its enormous brim. On the fringe, then, but hardly inconspicuous. And there's the familiar twinkle in her eye, the same one that peered over Emmeline Pankhurst and Charlotte Despard around a conference table in the early days at Caxton Hall. A twinkle that reassures the observer that you cannot keep a stellar woman down.

The third image in the Rose stereograph set captures five upright women (ten, if you're looking at the photograph as intended, through the stereographic viewer), standing in a row, stiff as boards, in front of the Advance Australia banner. They stare into the camera. Each wears a spray of tri-coloured ribbons pinned to the left lapel. Both the Australian and New Zealand contingents chose red, white and blue for their 'colours' on the day, *as being the only women*, explained one of the marchers, *who are entitled to wear the 'Empire' colours as a right, and not as a privilege.*[24] Unlike the spontaneous image that captured Nellie in the background, this is a posed shot. A staged moment in history. The caption names three of the women: Mrs Fisher, Mrs McGowen and Miss Vida Goldstein.[25]

Of course Vida hadn't gone to the Stockholm Congress. *I would not have missed that march for anything on earth*, she later told a reporter.[26] Mrs Catt was disappointed in her decision but *no other was possible.* Vida had previously admitted in a letter home to the WPA that she was being run off her feet in England, with so many speaking engagements that sleep was barely an option. But she loved *every minute of my work and the splendid women I am working with.*[27] She could no sooner abandon these women than forsake her God. *Since…women in the United Kingdom gaining the vote means so much to women in all parts of the world*, she reasoned, *we who have it must do all we can to help those who are deprived of it, and Australians must make a brave show in the procession as peacemakers.* It was in that last week before the procession, the very time she'd need to be en route to Stockholm, *when I shall be most needed, and could not think of leaving those who brought me here just at such a critical moment.*

Perhaps it is the exhaustion, or the brave show, or the mild regret that tells on Vida's face in the stereograph.[28] She looks pinched and careworn, the strain of duty overwhelming the triumph of raising a contingent of over 170 Australian and New Zealand women. Or perhaps it is simply quiet Edwardian pride: what one Australian woman in London who marched that day noted as *an air of serious dignity* among her compatriots.[29]

Margaret Fisher, in the middle of the group, towers above them all, her height, bulk and naturally thick waist disguising the early stages of her pregnancy. She wears a plain, unassuming skirt and jacket, in keeping with her aversion to *dressing up*, and signalling that her presence rather than her attire is what is noteworthy about her astonishing addition to the Australian contingent. Atop her natural six feet and three inches, however, Margaret has added a voluminous purple hat, trimmed with the ostrich feathers that Andrew had acquired in Cairo.[30]

Vida (whose own hat adds at least six inches to her tall, slender elegance) later revealed that she was able to extract Margaret's promise to *walk in our procession* at the dinner given by the British Labour Party. The presence of the prime minister's wife was *a tremendous help* in encouraging other Australian women to take part in the procession[31] and it was not by any stretch an undertaking that could be taken for granted. Vida acknowledged that Mrs Fisher had been *a warm sympathiser in the great economic and ethical movement in which women in every part of the world are engaged.*[32] But sympathy was one thing; partaking was a horse of a different colour. Her participation was a political act, a statement of defiance. It meant either that her husband, the Prime Minister of Australia, also supported the public demonstrations of the militant suffrage campaigners, or that she was acting in violation of her husband's wishes. Either scenario was a reflection on the man at least as much as his wife. Given that Vida had copped so much flak for claiming that Australian women sanctioned the tactics of the suffragettes, the fact that Andrew Fisher's wife was marching at the head of a contingent of Australian women—behind the official Coat of Arms of Australia, in a WSPU-sponsored rally—was an incontrovertible no-confidence motion in the British government.

The significance of Mrs Fisher's presence was not lost on the press. It was noted in the extensive Australian and British media coverage of the event. The MANCHESTER GUARDIAN was typical in remarking that Australia had *the wife of the Prime Minister of Australia,* among its contingent.[33] Melbourne PUNCH, in its routinely disparaging way, managed to remind readers that a peaceful procession was the happy outcome of the day, but far from guaranteed.

> Let us hope Mrs Prime Minister and Mrs Premier made express stipulation that, in the event of a row, they were not expected to kick, bite, slap or otherwise maim or maltreat a policeman. In Australia the sex secured the suffrage without finding it necessary to tear policemen's hair or kick in the shins of Ministers of the Crown, and both the Australian ladies mentioned, being unused to the game, would probably make a mess of it if they attempted to operate among the militant propagandists of the London movement.[34]

The real issue was not whether Margaret Fisher or Mrs McGowen might be disposed to bite and kick like tantruming toddlers, but whether, in the event of a Black Friday-style attack, they would have been subject to the same police and mob brutality— including assault, battery and sexual violation—as the suffragettes had been in the past. In 1911 not even a prime minister's wife travelled with a bodyguard.

But if there was safety in numbers, then Margaret would be sheltered in the company of at least 170 other Australian and New Zealand women. In the front row of the contingent, marching behind Margaret, were Mrs McGowen, Mrs Batchelor, Mrs Bowman (wife of the leader of the opposition in Queensland), Lady Cockburn—and Vida Goldstein, the only woman whose ambassadorial status was won by merit, not marriage. Some of the women who brought up the rear were well known to English and Australian audiences: actors Inez Bensusan and Madge Titherage, singer Carrie Haase, writers Constance Clyde and Alice Grant Rosman. According to Vida, Margaret Fisher had the support of the onlookers, too, *her tall figure instantly recognised and cheered by the crowd.*[35] Bystanders applauded all the groups that passed, *but gave a particularly hearty welcome to the Australians.* (Given that it took three hours for the procession to pass by any given point, the Australians may have benefitted from their early spot in the draw.)

Vida's interpretation of the demonstrative clamour was that the sightseers recognised the gilt kangaroos carried by the marchers as *representing Australia 'where women vote'* and congratulated the contingent accordingly. But *best of all* the praise were the 'coo-ees'— *real unmistakable Australian coo-ees*—that rang out from the crowd *surprisingly often.* Like Muriel, who'd enjoyed the fellow-feeling of countrymen on her vanning tours around England, expressed by the inimitable bush call, Vida was buoyed by the affinity of the gesture. *Everytime we heard them we straightened ourselves up and stepped out more briskly,* she admitted, *to do extra credit to Australia. Those coo-ees*

put new life into us, and made us feel as if we could walk miles further.
The sense of being a nation on show was palpable.

And if the comradeship and applause were not support
enough, Margaret Fisher was flanked by not one but three sizable
material expressions of national association and self-belief. For the
crude cloth bearing the humorously exaggerated figures of a kangaroo and emu was not the only banner that the Australian brigade
raised that day.[36] There was also a large scarlet silk flag *with the stars*
of the Southern Cross flung across it, carried by Vida's sister-in-law, Mrs
Selwyn Goldstein, a native of Perth.[37] Vida described its shimmering effect:

> [it] floated gaily in the breeze, as if boasting of the proud
> position held by Australia in being the first country in
> the world to grant to women the national franchise and
> the right to hold Parliamentary office.

But the third banner, carried at the rear of the Australian
contingent, was the largest and by far the most beautiful and skil-
fully wrought. It bore neither distinctive flora and fauna nor orienting
constellation. Its message was figurative but not obtuse. Literary, and
literal.

Trust the Women Mother As I Have Done.

ψ

Three summers earlier, Dora Meeson Coates had, as she phrased it,
designed and painted a very large banner for the Commonwealth—the
same banner she now carried, along with Miss Alice Trechmann and
Miss Madden, in front of an international audience of well-wishers.
Dora was pleased to be o*ne of the four bearers who staggered under its*
weight when we passed a windy corner. George walked *devotedly along-*
side all the way, begging in vain to be allowed to help us.[38] A friendly
policeman even nudged him and said *Give the poor girl a hand!*

Fashionably classical in imagery but electrifyingly eccentric in intent the banner remained. Mother Britannia, draped in white, holding her sceptre and staring into the middle distance; Daughter Minerva, bearing the heraldry of the Australian Commonwealth, reaching out, entreating, offering advice. All who lined Whitehall Place and stood on Waterloo Bridge to watch the procession slither past would have understood the meaning of Dora's banner, just as the onlookers on Suffrage Saturday in 1908 had appreciated the artistry and innovation of the work. But the meaning had changed.

In 1908, the statement was bold, but its political context had as much to do with domestic affairs as international relations. In 1908, the suffrage movement was castigating a hypocritical Liberal government that had won office on the promise that it would 'trust the people'. Dora's banner had a double-meaning. Trust the people, half of whom are women, as Dora's native country had done without ill-consequence.

But three years is an eternity in politics. In the context of all that had occurred in the past few months, let alone years, the meaning had now changed. Asquith's government was no longer merely insincere; it was downright treacherous. And Australia was no longer a distant homeland of an expat artist, a far-flung light-house casting its beam on the shoals and reefs of illiberal policies. It was now a nation that had reverse-colonised the landscape of ideas: the ideas of freedom, representation and democracy that were the cornerstones of the new twentieth-century democratic state. It had sent its ambassadors and missives across the seas, from periphery to metropole, conquering the high ground of ideological innovation.

Just last November, the Australian Parliament had cabled a resolution to the British Parliament, piercing its flag of ownership in the heart of British liberty. Worrywarts in the Senate had been concerned that the resolution would be viewed as impertinent. They were more distressed to learn it had been ignored. Then Australia's most senior ex-officio minister for enfranchisement, Vida Goldstein, had come in person to drive the message home, which she had done tirelessly for three months now, in public and private forums, through speeches, articles, letters and personal lobbying.

Following on Vida's heels came the Prime Minister of Australia himself, Andrew Fisher, *our Andy*, as some of the papers called him, not always with affection. Fisher didn't go as far as the ANZWVCs were pushing him. Concerned at the potential blowback for some of Australia's own democratically dubious laws and attitudes, he'd declined to make women's suffrage an agenda item at the Imperial Conference. But he had been an outspoken advocate for his nation's innovative approach to gender relations. He consistently affirmed that universal suffrage had been beneficial for both women and men, raising the tone of politics and national life generally, while not for a second threatening the sanctity of the home or the hallmarks of femininity. Furthermore, he had high-handedly pushed the barrow of colonial self-assertion—if not independence—claiming a greater stake in matters of imperial defence. The Prime Minister of Australia was asking his British counterparts not only to trust the women, but to trust the dominions. *No more striking method could have been devised for bringing Australasia into prominence*, the BRITISH-AUSTRALASIAN wrote of Dora's *big banner*.[39]

In 1908, Dora's banner represented the ambitions of female Australians in London—a message from the enfranchised women within. Now, it represented Australia itself—a message from the demonstrably confident and democratically superior nation without. The new wave of Australasian progressivism had come crashing on to the old world's crumbling shores.

The beauty and effect of Dora's banner was almost invariably commented upon by observers and correspondents: the message thoroughly absorbed, even if the words were sometimes jumbled: *Trust Your Women, Mother. We Have Done So.*[40] *Mother, trust your daughters as I have done.*[41] As in 1908, Dora's masterwork was singled out among the thousand-odd banners carried on the day as one of the crowd favourites.

One English writer commented on the effect of the Australian intervention into British politics:

> Australian women who value their privilege will be glad to know that the testimony of Australians with regard to the working of womanhood suffrage in Australia has had something to do with the set of the tide here in favour of womanhood suffrage.[42]

Whether or not Australians, individually or collectively, had built up enough moral and political momentum to turn the tide of British affairs, the effort had at the very least confirmed the young nation's belief in its own power and efficacy. One Australian woman studying at the London School of Domestic Economy regarded *the fact of our having proved to the world our political fitness a fine object lesson.*[43]

Remarkably, Melbourne PUNCH—never one to blow the trumpet of suffragists—agreed. *There has never been a time when Australia wanted to bulk larger in the eyes of the world*, it wrote in advance of Fisher's departure for London. *All the partners of the Empire are to be in London, and Australia should take her place as the most advanced, the most important, the ablest of them all.*[44]

Dora's artistically accomplished and politically persuasive banner played an intrinsic part in helping Australia to *bulk large*.

⚜

But not all of the Australian women who had played a part in the struggle were there to march in lock step.

The same current affairs column in the ALBURY BANNER AND WODONGA EXPRESS that reported the Women's Coronation Procession—*five miles of misguided women*, according to the disgruntled columnist—also noted *the marriage of a celebrated suffragette...a young lady who achieved considerable fame by her strenuous exertions in the cause of woman suffrage.*[45] The woman who had recently been joined in *matrimonial felicity* with a musician was Muriel Matters. It was a tongue in cheek report, full of the cheap sexist shots that women's enfranchisement tended to flush out. It was also wrong. Muriel Matters did not marry Bryceson Treharne.[46] But nor did she join Vida and her fellow Australians in the Women's Coronation Procession. Instead, she and Tilly had returned to vanning, undertaking a caravan tour of Buckinghamshire for the Tax Resistance League, where she continued to deliver her characteristic *verbal thunderbolts.*[47]

Not all Australians were consumed with pride at their bulking, crowing nation, fortified by numbers and legitimated by the de facto approval of the federal government. The criticism of Australia's role in the procession came not from the conservative press—who, like PUNCH, were content to parody rather than censure—but from Socialist commentators. *Mrs Fisher and Mrs McGowen, wives of Australian Labor Ministers,* wrote a disgusted Dora Montefiore in the WORKER, *walked in the procession, and thereby gave their countenance and support to an undemocratic measure, intended to act as a bulwark against the increasing demand for adult suffrage.*[48]

This supposed rise of the whole-loafers wasn't really reflected in feeling on the ground in England. The Adult Suffrage League was a minority voice in the chorus of the women's movement. But it was certainly a cause that Dora Montefiore remained committed to and she tried valiantly to raise it, from the distance of her Sydney base, amidst the imperial sound and light show that the suffragettes had bought into so wholeheartedly.

As her long and fiery WORKER article pointed out, the history of franchise reform in England was *a staggering example of the triumphant rule of the classes over the masses.* She wanted to set the record straight (again): *the militant suffragists, when we first organised in London, had with us the working women of the East End...working women came twice a week to demonstrate in front of my house, when I was besieged for six weeks by bailiffs.* But when Dora's ever-reviled

Pankhursts came to town, they soon discovered that *the singing of revolutionary songs* didn't sit well with the rich society ladies whose silken pockets they wanted to plunder. Drawing room meetings replaced factory floor meetings. The political rights of property and privilege replaced the democratic rights of all women. It was iniquitous—and left-wing ladies like Vida and Mrs Fisher should have known better. If they had really desired to help forward the political emancipation of the men and women of their class, they should have publicly endorsed the adult suffrage demand and *damped the ardour of the propertied ladies.*

Vida took Dora's rebuke personally, as she was intended to. She acknowledged the plight of the working class: in England she'd seen *more evidence of animality and poverty than I've seen anywhere else.*[49] The women especially distressed her: *they looked regular viragoes, half-sodden with drink.* But the fact of the matter was that the demand for universal adult suffrage in Britain was weak. *We are all adult suffragists in our country*, Vida wrote home to the WPA, *but in England there is absolutely no demand for [it].* Even the labour organisations weren't putting up a fight. So given that in England the issue was a dead letter, she saw little reason to agitate for the whole loaf while she was visiting. Better to help her sisters get the sustenance they were asking for than lecture them on the benefits of a better diet.

And Vida had not lost her political toughness swanning around at those English tea parties. *We are sorry*, she wrote, *that Mrs Montefiore, who must know so well what it costs a woman to come out boldly and agitate for reform, should impute these motives to women whose moral courage is universally acknowledged.* She had certainly not met anyone *capable of the treachery* with which Dora charged the leaders of the British suffrage movement. In deflecting the criticism of her WSPU allies, Vida was also defending herself against Dora's public reproach.

*

But if there was some bad blood within the Australian sisterhood, it wasn't enough to mar the glory and the optimism of forty thousand women marching to the cheers, not the jeers, of a sympathetic crowd. The British prime minster had promised facilities for the Conciliation Bill at the next session. A new king was about to be crowned. The sun was shining on London, the metropolis of a nation and empire drunk on its own giddy good fortune.

Today, announced Vida Goldstein on 17 June 1911 from the eye of the storm, *the general feeling is that victory is at hand.*

When she boarded the ship to return to Australia six months later, Vida carried with her an exquisite gift from Emmeline Pethick-Lawrence: a rose topaz set with pearls *to wear for friendship's sake.* Even more precious were the words that accompanied it:

> My very dear Comrade,
>
> We shall never lose the sense of touch with you and the strength of that unity with our sisters overseas which you have made so real.
>
> You daughters of freedom, you go back to the Newer World, the world of the future, bearing with you the love of your sisters in the old country.
>
> Rich is the fellowship, that our human movement stands for—our world movement.
>
> Ever my dear Colleague, Yours affectionately.
> Emmeline[50]

CONCLUSION

History in the Making

After a while, if you repress the origins, it will be as though
the founding revolution simply never happened.

TERRY EAGLETON
Ibsen and the Nightmare of History, 2008

1911 proved to be a false dawn for English women.

In November Asquith announced a Manhood Suffrage Bill, to
be presented in the next parliamentary session. This measure paved
the way for an extended franchise for men. It would allow for a female
franchise only if the Commons saw fit to introduce an amendment—
which, in the absence of government support, would never get up.
The Conciliation Bill had been scuttled and the suffrage campaigners sunk in a clean strike.

Emmeline Pankhurst—so confident of a peaceful resolution to
the Four Years War that she'd agreed to undertake a speaking tour of
America in the second half of 1911—now wrote to Christabel from
Minneapolis: *Protest imperative!* The truce was over.

Truth be told, the writing was on the wall well before that.
The summer of 1911 continued in a national pantomime of over-
the-top pageantry and under-the-surface tension with the King and

his court centre stage. But the audience should have been shouting, 'Over there! Look over there!'

Over there…to Bermondsey, a densely populated working-class borough two miles from the City where, in August, the factories emptied as fifteen thousand female workers went on strike. The Bermondsey Women's Uprising, as it became known worldwide, was attributed to the combination of the usual appalling pay and conditions and the effects of the long, hot summer. Spoiled food; rising infant mortality; a general air of irritability and fed-upness. And a mood of female defiance. These women—who weren't unionised—took to the streets, marching together with banners and a sense of industrial solidarity that had previously been the exclusive domain of their fathers, brothers and sons. The streets were now their streets. They expected more and better. Prominent among the organisers who came in to lend moral and organisational support was Muriel Matters.[1]

Over there…to Ireland where, while George V was being crowned in London, a Sinn Fein meeting in Dublin was condemning all Irish participation in the coronation festivities. Where anti-imperial sentiment received a boost in August, when the constitutional deadlock between the House of Commons and the House of Lords was broken though legislation restricting the Lords' veto. The same legislation, the Parliament Act, also made Irish home rule a possibility in the future. The threat of self-government was sufficient to see seventy thousand Unionists and Orangemen (staunch opponents of home rule) march in protest the following month.

And further over there—to Germany. In 1911, Kaiser Wilhelm was squabbling with France and Spain over territory in Morocco. In August, Germany sent a warship to make its intentions clear. Britain backed France. A new arms race between the great industrial powers of Europe was underway. The lines between aggression and defence became blurred. The hawks circled—and swooped.

The glorious late summer of Edwardian England was about to shatter like a cheap vase.

Writing her memoir three years later, in 1914, Emmeline Pankhurst could see through the clear lens of hindsight what was not so readily apparent at the time. *A mountain peak of a year was 1911,* she wrote, *and that June the world's happiest month for long to come.*

⚓

For the WSPU, Asquith's intransigence made protest not only imperative but also incendiary. The period of suffragette militancy with which we are now most familiar started with Asquith's act of personal and parliamentary belligerence in November 1911. The window-smashing. The letterbox fires. The torching of hedges and golf courses. The slashing of famous works of art. Wholesale destruction of property, public and private, was now an official campaign strategy rather than an occasional publicity stunt. The stone—not the banner, the meeting or the demonstration—was the new weapon of choice.

The Cat and Mouse Act was the government's response: a revolving door of gaolings, hunger strikes and force-feedings: release from prison when near death, rearrest when recovered. *You will go down in history as the man who tortured innocent women,* one MP barked at Asquith on the floor of the Commons.[2] But still, throughout the next year, and the next, Asquith and his ministers refused to budge. The full-scale arson, bombing and stone-throwing campaign was as divisive within the suffrage movement as it was offensive to the government and obnoxious to the general public. The Pethick-Lawrences and two of the Pankhurst daughters, Sylvia and Adela, became estranged from Emmeline as Mother's hold on the leadership became a full nelson.

Yet there were still plenty of true believers, Christabel included—and none more ardent than Emily Wilding Davison. Davison, a university-educated activist who was arrested nine times, went on seven hunger strikes and was force-fed almost fifty times, wrote herself into the history books by throwing herself in front of the King's horse at Epsom on 4 June 1913, while news cameras filmed the race. Her death made her the suffrage movement's first bona fide martyr. Her funeral procession of five thousand mourners was held on 14 June, almost two years to the day from the Women's Coronation Procession in which women had worn white to symbolise the moral purity of their struggle. It has been described as 'the last of the great suffragette spectacles'.[3] Emmeline Pankhurst was not able to join the black-clad masses channelling their bereavement through London's streets, having been rearrested that morning under the Cat and Mouse Act. 'Hated and loved, praised and blamed,' writes her biographer, Emmeline was nothing if not *the most talked of person in the world today.*[4]

In Australia, which had enjoyed its status as the most talked-about country in the world—*the van of nations*—political women looked on in horror and awe.[5] On 10 June 1913, Vida Goldstein's WOMAN VOTER opened its regular column on *the Civil War now being waged in England* with a reflection: *History in the making is no different from history that is already made.*[6] The suffragettes had resorted to extreme tactics, but the principles for which they fought held true for all women who had struggled against oppression throughout the ages. Emily Wilding Davison's *self-immolation*, her *death petition*, as Vida called it, was a sacrifice for all women wronged by political, moral (i.e. sexual) and industrial *slavery.*[7]

Meanwhile, Vida was locked in her own domestic battle: another attempt at a parliamentary seat, this time in the House of Representatives in the ultra-conservative electorate of Kooyong. Again, she stood as an independent. Again, she lost. Vida's open endorsement of and assistance to the suffragettes undoubtedly cost her votes, but some commentators believed that had she stood as a member of the Victorian Labor Party in a working-class seat, she would have triumphed. *We struck another blow for Freedom, Justice, Truth, Principle*, Vida declared to her supporters on 17 June 1913, after her trouncing. *What a glorious campaign it was!* [8] Some thought her stance as self-sabotaging and ultimately futile as having your head trampled by a royal racehorse.

Nor was Andrew Fisher riding high by the southern winter of 1913. At the federal election, Fisher's government lost office to the Liberal Party by a single seat, though the ALP retained its majority in the Senate. Moreover, of the six referendum questions put to voters at that election, not one was successful. Fisher had been fighting an uphill battle since his return from London after the Imperial Conference, the trouble starting before he even boarded the ship. He'd granted a meeting with journalist William Stead, *the prince of interviewers*, for the English edition of REVIEW OF REVIEWS. In it, Fisher praised *the ties of sympathy between our Dominion and the American Republic* while appearing to condone various measures for loosening the apron strings of empire. *We are independent, self-governing communities*, Fisher was quoted as saying of the five dominions...*free to take our own course, in our own interests, without anyone preventing us. There is no necessity for us to say we will or we will not take part in England's wars.* [9]

It was a bold addendum to the various acts of colonial self-assertion Fisher had made during his stay in London. Stead characterised him as *a responsible man...not afraid of ideas*—which included, according to Stead's interpretation, 'cutting the painter': the contemporary idiom for establishing constitutional independence from Britain and making the Commonwealth of Australia a completely self-governing republic. Stead was all right with that: if Fisher was in favour of *dissolving the ancient Empire of Britain*, it was to make way for a higher ideal of a *great World State in which brother nations associate in peace and mutual service.* [10]

But by the time Fisher stepped off the boat in Melbourne, there was hell to pay. He had to do some fancy footwork to disavow what appeared to be an almost treasonous sentiment. Fisher made the time-honoured politician's protest that he'd been taken out of context, the Labor Party blamed the *Australian capitalistic press* for whipping up a frenzy and eventually the furore died down.

Fisher's government had continued to implement important measures of social legislation, such as the Maternity Allowance of 1912, carrying on the pioneering innovations of the social laboratory down under.[11] Australia continued to be seen as *a paradise for Women...the cynosure of all eyes*.[12] But by mid-1913 Fisher's grip was slipping. It was Dora Montefiore who analysed the root cause of popular disaffection with the world's first elected socialist government. *The Labor Party is no longer a working-class party*, she wrote in an article called 'The Rebellion Down Under' for the London DAILY HERALD in August 1913, *it is the party of the rising Australian manufacturers...This party cannot, and will not, free the workers; the workers must free themselves.* The convergent and sometimes conflicting forces of nationalism, imperialism, socialism, federalism and feminism created a distinctive political culture in Australia in its first decade and a half of nationhood—a culture that produced bedfellows not only strange but sometimes unfaithful.

Vida Goldstein and her Women's Political Party remained loyal to the WSPU, but for the most part Australian suffragists had concluded that British women must fight their own battle for freedom. And even Vida pulled back. Throughout 1912 and 1913 she continued to petition the British Parliament through the ground troops of the ANZWVC, but her predominant claims were for reform of the iniquitous naturalisation laws that discriminated against Australian women. It was for *National reasons* that she continued to meddle in British politics.

But Vida's English adventures had not been in vain. For one thing, she now found herself returning the hospitality of the Pankhurst family. When Emmeline decided that her increasingly refractory daughter, Adela, must leave the nest, it was towards Vida that she pushed her. Adela was crushed. The paltry £20 of loose change that was Emmeline's parting gift was less insulting than her mother's rejection. Whereas Vida had arrived in London to a cheering throng, twenty-nine-year-old Adela disembarked in Melbourne a lonely, if stoic, figure. *I felt that in another country*, she wrote, *I should find my feet and, happiness, perhaps.*[13]

Adela embarked for Australia on 2 February 1914. How was she to know she was sailing away from a continent that was lurching towards war?

⚉

The historian Paul Ham subtitled his book *1914* 'The Year the World Ended'. 'The democratic ideals of a more humane and tolerant world, expressed in art and literature', Ham argues, 'were to be throttled, ignored or postponed.' With the onset of World War I, the forces of conservatism fought back against a generation of radicalism, idealism and experimentation. The 'party was over'.[14]

Certainly, the Edwardian suffrage era was over. Emily Wilding Davison would be the suffragettes' first and last martyr. With the announcement on 4 August 1914 that Britain was at war with Germany, Emmeline Pankhurst called the WSPU's final truce. She suspended all militant activity. The government responded by unconditionally releasing all suffrage prisoners. The sacrifices required for the deliverance of God, King and Country trumped the sacrifices of women for the cause of their own freedom.

Emmeline had utter faith that, in exchange for their war work, British women would be duly granted their citizenship rights. Millicent Garrett Fawcett had a different interpretation of Asquith's motivations: the war gave him *a ladder down which he could climb in renunciation of his former errors.*[15]

And climb down he did. It was the service of women in World War I, not suffrage activism, that was the official rationale for passage of the Representation of the People Act 1918, which granted

British women over the age of thirty the right to vote, enfranchising 8.5 million of them.[16]

For Australia, the cataclysmic event that ostensibly marked the end of British women's political bondage precipitated the birth of a nation. Or at least a new national narrative. It was, we are told, Australia's participation in World War I—and specifically, the Gallipoli campaign—that proved our worth in the eyes of the world. Australia's confidence as a nation can be attributed, it is said, to its performance in the Great War. This narrative has established the tendency to equate patriotism with military service, rather than with national traditions associated with progressive reform and democratic rights.[17]

In 1982, historian Bill Gammage proposed that 'in the twentieth century, no Australian, for or against Anzac, has ever discerned or proposed a stronger national tradition'.[18] Coming so soon after Federation, his argument goes, the Gallipoli campaign provided a 'blood sacrifice' in which nationhood, grit and grief were inextricably intertwined. As Gammage explained, here was the moment in which anxiety about whether Australians 'could help Britain in war as much as they expected Britain to help them' was finally cast aside: for Australia had excelled 'on the stage of the world'.[19]

John Hirst has nominated this blood-soaked event as 'the occasion when by common consent Australians threw off their colonial self-doubt and believed themselves to be a nation'.[20]

Gammage's remark exemplifies a trend in historical scholarship to explain *why* Australians were (and are) so powerfully drawn to the Anzac legend as a primary foundation story. But Hirst sought to justify why it should *naturally* be so. 'People,' he asserted, 'are stirred into hero worship by daring, recklessness, self-sacrifice, grace, a master player or a master spirit.' And just in case we were unsure quite whom Hirst might have had in mind as risk-taking nation-builders, he adds: 'For obvious reasons it has been mostly men who have been able to achieve heroic status.'[21]

But as we have seen, five years before Gallipoli the Commonwealth of Australia asserted that it was 'bound to achieve greatness' because of its democratic agility and proficiency, its socio-political courage and grace. By 1914, Australia was riding a wave of optimism, confidence and hearty self-belief to which the events of 1910–11, both at home and abroad, had greatly contributed. As early as 1908, an English observer noted that *Australians feel themselves a chosen people, different and superior from any other race.*[22] And not long before the outbreak of World War I, sociologist Clarence Northcott's study of the Australian character depicted a people marked by courage and initiative, with much in their *thought and outlook...that is spirited and idealistic even if their philosophy of life is a reckless optimism.*[23]

Northcott was mostly describing a people whose mettle had been tested not by war, but in peace. Until 1914, the Australians had known war only at Britain's side against the Boers in South Africa. (Also, of course, on the contested territories in their own country against Indigenous owners and occupants whose sovereignty had never been ceded. But at the turn of the twentieth century, these brutal killing fields of the Australian frontier were not discussed in martial terms.) In 1908, the Argus reported the Reverend Doctor Bevan's confidence that the *Australian Ideal* was rooted in *the practical activities of common life and in the critical moments of national life.* His example? *The striving of women for effectiveness in making the franchise a reality.*[24]

Before 1914, before Gallipoli, young Australia had burst onto the global stage not only promising hope for a better future, but also delivering evidence of how that future might be gained. In the social laboratory of the antipodes, Australian women and men had together come up with an experimental formula for robust democracy and had tested its results. Trial had not produced error. The sky had not fallen. The proof of concept was there for the world to see and to emulate.

Up till February 1914, the WSPU's Votes for Women was

still running a regular column called *In Australia, Where Women Vote*, giving updates of measures improving conditions for women and children, equal pay cases, opening of the public service employment to women and the Maternity Allowance: a payment from general revenue direct to all mothers, married or not, as remuneration for and *recognition of the rights of citizen-mothers*. The Maternity Allowance was described by one politician at the time as *a grave and great departure from the existing order of things*. Andew Fisher justified it on patriotic grounds: *Maternity is more dangerous than going to war.*[25]

Fisher may have had in mind the words of a particular American journalist. In 1906 the Boston Woman's Journal recognised that Federation in Australia was the moment that *democracy won such an historical triumph as still echoes around the world.*[26] The men who had worked so arduously to enshrine women's suffrage as a cornerstone of the Federation ideal have *served their country more efficiently in peace than the soldier does in war.* But *they could [not] have achieved much if it had not been for the women.*

Andrew Fisher is remembered now for saying that Australia would follow Britain into war until *the last man and the last shilling.* Who recalls that he also told a captive London audience that *a true democracy can only be maintained honestly and fairly by including women as well as men in the electorate of the country?*[27]

Or that two weeks later, Fisher's wife marched at the head of a contingent of proud Australians, sheltered in the lee of a huge banner that proclaimed to the world that Australia, not Mother, knew best.

Seen in this context, Gallipoli—with its militarist narrative of youthful sacrifice, not youthful optimism—was not the birth of the nation. It was the death of the nation we were well on the way to becoming.[28]

⚶

So how did Dora Meeson Coates' banner go from being the artistic and political jewel in the crown of the Women's Coronation Procession (not to mention Australian patriotism) to being tucked away in a dimly lit corridor of Parliament House?

Well, not all British suffragettes or suffragists laid down their swords when their nation went to war. They continued to hold processions and outdoor meetings, where banners were carried, including by Australian women living in London. After Vida's return, Margaret Hodge and Harriet Newcomb kept the ANZWVC alive, organising contingents of expat marchers with their native banners.

Another who continued to agitate for women's rights was Sylvia Pankhurst. On 11 April 1916, she organised a demonstration of East End women in Trafalgar Square. They carried banners, including one that read: *Coercion is not Government*. Thousands came out to watch the procession of the Workers' Suffrage Federation, who were protesting against the restriction of popular liberties in England (much as Vida Goldstein and other Australian suffragists, unionists and religious groups were leading anti-militarist campaigns against the Wartime Restrictions Act in Melbourne and Sydney). The crowd that day, suspicious that the event was motivated by the peace movement, *rushed the procession the moment it entered the square*. The angry mob *seized and tore up the banners and flags*, snapping poles while processionists were jostled and speakers were showered with bags of flour. The suffrage demonstrators retreated and the crowd, *led by some Australian soldiers*, sang the national anthem.[29] Australian newspapers reported the affray, where *Australian and New Zealand soldiers broke up a 'human suffrage' meeting* dousing women with red and yellow ochre.[30] An eleven-year-old girl was pelted. Particularly unruly Anzacs were arrested.

Dora's banner had been on show once again in Hyde Park in 1912, but that was its last reported airing. Perhaps the increase in militancy after *the wonder year* dissuaded Dora (or George) from high-profile engagement in suffrage activities. Perhaps, once the truce was called in 1914, Dora found alternative avenues for the expression of her morality and worldview. Perhaps the destructive behaviour of Anzacs in London made her fear for the integrity of both her artwork and her country's reputation.

Whatever the cause, Dora Meeson Coates' magnificent banner slipped from view for the best part of a century.

Then, in the mid-1980s, the Fawcett Library, a British collection relating to women's history, including a large collection of suffrage memorabilia, was clearing out its storerooms for renovations. *On the top of the library shelving—a pragmatic rather than ideal situation*[31]—they found an uncatalogued banner folded up, gathering dust, and sent it to be restored. They had no idea of the banner's provenance, but the object was distinctive. Banners made for the great pre-war suffragette processions were generally embroidered, whereas this one was painted, oil on hessian. Perhaps for that reason the conservators botched the restoration, rendering *the canvas banner solid.*[32] It could no longer be folded or rolled up, and the library had space neither to store nor exhibit it. Across the top of the banner was written *Commonwealth of Australia.* They alerted Dale Spender, an Australian feminist scholar living in London.

Spender wrote to the Commonwealth government, making a case for the banner's 'return' to Australia. The timing was good. Australia would be celebrating its bicentenary the following year and, as Susan Ryan, then minister assisting the prime minister for the status of women, noted: *there are very few items available for display which record women's part in the early political process of this country. The Banner would, I believe, go some way towards filling this obvious gap.*[33] It was not just 'herstory' that suffered for lack of concrete memorials. The banner represented no less than the material heritage of Australian democracy itself. This was the bigger picture.

It was *rare (unheard of!) for the library to part with such material,* Spender wrote,[34] but eventually a deal was struck. The Women's Suffrage Banner, as it was now referred to, was purchased from the

Fawcett Library by the National Women's Consultative Committee, with funds from the Australian Bicentennial Authority, brokered and managed by the Office for the Status of Women, as a bicentennial gift to the *women of Australia*.[35]

James Mollison, Director of the National Gallery of Australia, was excited. *It had been thought until now in artistic circles that the banner had been lost or destroyed*, Mollison wrote.[36] (Meeson's talent as an oil painter and portraitist was well established, but no one in the art world had viewed her most ambitious work.) The ACTU requested to borrow it for its 'Art and Shared Belief' exhibition at the Royal Exhibition Building, to be displayed next to Judy Chicago's *The Dinner Party*.[37]

Interestingly, many feminists were less thrilled—mainly on the grounds that the bicentennial celebrations themselves were indefensible. *Dear Sisters*, wrote Di Lucas of the ACT to the NWCC, *collusion with the ABA is collusion with invasion and genocide. I support the sovereignty of the Aboriginal people and regard the 1988 'celebrations' as an exercise in crass commercialisation and nationalism, colonialism and racism*.[38] Sue Hird, writing for the Women Against Racism Collective, highlighted *the fact that by celebrating 200 years of white invasion of Australia you fail to acknowledge the aboriginal people*.[39]

NWCC convenor Edith Hall replied that the banner handback activities would not be *celebratory*. *We are emphasising the need for 'eternal vigilance' to protect those gains achieved*, she assured Di Lucas, *and for renewed vigour and involvement of all women in political action, with the aim of equality for all*.[40]

The issue was the appropriateness of using bicentennial blood money to buy the banner. None of the sisterhood pointed out that it was only white Australian women whose victories the banner celebrated. Nationalism, colonialism and racism were as integral to the banner's history as to the history of the Commonwealth itself.

*

The banner arrived in Canberra on 12 February 1988, eighty years after it had been created in a light-filled Chelsea studio. On 8 March 1988, International Women's Day, Prime Minister Bob Hawke officiated at a *historic handover* ceremony at the Lodge. In front of a crowd that included politicians (mostly female, if the photographs are anything to go by), journalists and members of Dora Meeson Coates' family, Hawke unveiled the banner, which hung from the rafters of a portico in the garden. The sun beat down. Senator Margaret Reynolds, who had done more than anyone to broker the handover, was draped in white linen, beaming. In his speech, Hawke referred to Australian women's role *in the forefront of the achievement of franchise rights.*[41]

The official rationale for the twenty-five-thousand-dollar public spend was broad: the banner would *remind and inform women of their political and social history and the need for continued and renewed involvement in the political process.* Margaret Reynolds' interest was more historically specific, though just as politically pointed. The banner, she said in an OSW press release, *represents the efforts of Australian women to assist in achieving female suffrage in Britain. Australian women led the way at the turn of the century and are still at the forefront of international progress in raising the status of women.*[42]

While women at the garden party lined up to have their photographs taken next to the banner, protestors rallied outside the Lodge, proclaiming that the banner's purchase by the ABA had sullied the work. *Take the Taint Off Dora's Paint*, demanded one of the protestors' banners. Mrs Tanya McConvell was quoted: the banner *should not be associated with white supremacy in Australia.*[43] She was clearly unaware that the history of women's suffrage was intimately bound to the history of white imperialism.

After the fuss of the handover on 8 March 1988, the banner was whisked off for conservation—the National Gallery of Australia expected the work to take two weeks. Over a year later Margaret Reynolds began to make enquiries as to its whereabouts. In October

1989 it was located in a storage unit. No conservation work had yet been carried out. But eventually the National Museum of Australia agreed to conserve the banner, and the architects for the new Parliament House proposed it be permanently exhibited in the foyer to the main committee room, *where it would have a close conceptual relationship with the historical period of the Opening of Parliament paintings located there.*[44] Later advice recommended it be placed next to Tom Roberts' painting. The final say went to the textile conservators who recommended that, even housed in a humidity-controlled display case, the banner would need to avoid strong spot-lighting. They proposed the left-hand wall of the *public pause space* leading to the committee room foyer. The banner had finally found its home.[45]

In 1988, Dale Spender was commissioned by the Office of the Status of Women to prepare a banner educational kit for schools. Her brief was to *explain the connections between the British and Australian [suffrage] campaigns* taking care that *the Australian campaign is presented as a direct response by the Australian women to their own circumstances and not simply as derivative upon the British movement.* Stress was to be placed *upon non-violent tactics* and all means taken to explain *the context for militant strategies.* In other words, the message was to be nationalist and moderate.

Spender fulfilled her commission. The banner, she explained, *depicts a female figure of 'Australia' urging the figure of 'Britannia' to trust the women—as Australia, where women already had the vote, had done.* Nothing to startle the horses here. But she went further in arguing the banner's importance in Australian and indeed world history.

> The Commonwealth of Australia Banner depicts women's pride in their responsibility and commitment. Its presence on the British suffrage scene points to their international awareness and participation. The Banner is a symbol of women's success, for to have convinced

men that they should give away their exclusive power and grant votes to women was one of the greatest political victories there has been.[46]

Perhaps Spender's interpretation, emphasising the global over the local, was not patriotic enough. Perhaps it was too in-your-face feminist, pitching the message in terms of historic sex antagonism, rather than as a benign history tutorial. There is no evidence that the kit Spender was contracted to write was ever printed or distributed. The story of Australian women's leadership in an international movement of radical political consequence was left to rest in a yellowing folder in the archives: abandoned like the banner itself.

ψ

In 1988, Bob Hawke presented Dora Meeson's banner as *a gift to the women of Australia*. The official rationale for purchasing it was to *remind and inform women of their political and social history*. But the story that the banner tells is not just Australian women's story. It is Australia's story.

Of course, an object's meaning is not static, frozen in time. What the banner meant in 1908 when it was made is different from what it meant in 1911 when the wife of the prime minister rallied beneath it. What it meant in a fading Edwardian England or a freshly minted Australia is not necessarily what it means now. How it was used then is not how it is used now. It was once a dynamic object, made for a purpose, to be paraded, carried aloft, raised inspirationally above a crowd. It is now a static object, rigid, behind glass, never to touch the wind. But perhaps in both instances—in its active and passive state—the banner can function as a means to mobilise, to prod, to hector; even to lecture.

Dora Meeson Coates' extraordinary gift is the ceaseless material reminder that nation-building is not the exclusive prerogative of men (or indeed any other faction of society). Nor is the story of the suffrage movement relevant only to a few academic purveyors of 'women's history'. In creating the banner, Dora unwittingly created a founding document, telling us as much about the aspirations and identity of the young nation as the still-wet constitution itself.

The banner represents a particular historical moment but asks a timeless question: what does it mean to count? Or, indeed, to count for nothing? To stand up and be counted, as citizens and as individuals?

Is there a legacy, 'an object lesson', for our present lives? As a new form of Australian citizenship led to the creation of the welfare state, can women—who historically have understood the challenges of being treated equally—continue to advocate for a world where justice is prized?

At a moment when the Anzac legend threatens to subsume Australia's collective identity and purpose, and when democratic and human rights the world over remain persistently under attack, Dora Meeson Coates' beautiful banner is a reminder that before the Sons of Empire died on the beach at Gallipoli and rebirthed a nation, we were the Daughters of Freedom: and this was the story of us.

EPILOGUE

Vida Goldstein became a staunch campaigner for the peace movement in Australia during World War I. With Adela Pankhurst, she founded the Women's Peace Army. Vida became a regular speaker at Yarra Bank mass meetings, where tens of thousands would come to hear her united message of pacifism, socialism and feminism; she also led huge anti-conscription rallies. As a result of these activities she came to be considered an enemy of the state and subject to security surveillance. (Taking a leaf out of the suffragettes' playbook for insubordination, when THE WOMAN VOTER was censored, Vida simply published the redacted articles with blank spaces where words had been deleted.)

Vida stood for election to the Federal Parliament three more times, in 1913, 1914 and 1917. In each case she stood as an independent and in each case, she lost.

In 1919, she travelled to Europe where she wrote extensively—essays and political pamphlets about 'the Australian experiment' and her experience of the suffrage campaigns. She became increasingly internationalist in her outlook, attending the International Women's Peace Congress in Zurich. Returning to Australia in 1922, Vida was disappointed by what she saw as the political apathy and materialism of young women, who knew little of the sacrifices that had been made for their freedom.

Vida retired from public life after that, although she continued to be interested and engaged in political affairs. She lived quietly at home with her sisters and various female friends, sustained by the Christian Science church, where she practised as a faith healer. When the first women were elected to the Australian Parliament in 1943 (Dorothy Tangney in the Senate and Enid Lyons in the House of Representatives), Vida was dismayed that neither woman called herself a feminist.

Edith How-Martyn encouraged Vida to write her memoirs, but she never did. *My present work takes all my time*, she said. *It means very late hours—but what does that matter when one is helping others to live?*

She died in relative obscurity on 15 August 1949, aged eighty. The following year, the League of Women Voters inaugurated an essay prize in her honour. In 1984 the federal electorate of Goldstein was created in her name: a blue-ribbon Liberal seat. She is one of only two Australians included among the 999 women commemorated in American artist Judy Chicago's famous *Dinner Party*.

In 2008—the centenary of the female franchise in Victoria—a memorial park bench was installed in Vida's honour in her home town of Portland. Journalists quipped that Vida Goldstein had finally won a seat.

Dora Montefiore returned to England after her 1911 study tour of Australia but, true to her word, she did not rejoin the suffragette militancy. She continued to support the Tax Resistance League, but was increasingly drawn to international socialism as her liberation movement of choice. In 1913, Dora was once again in hot water when she organised to have the starving children of striking Irish workers billeted in the homes of British comrades. She opened the *Dublin Kiddies' Fund* and soon found homes in England and Scotland for 350 Irish children, with their parents' consent. An incensed Catholic Archbishop of Dublin blocked the plan and Dora found her photo splashed across the papers: leaving the police courts, charged with kidnapping. The scheme was abandoned.

Though a pacifist, Dora did her war work in France, assisting in the kitchens of the French army base in Calais. When she discovered that her son had volunteered to fight in the Australian army in 1916, she returned to England *to make a home for him whenever he was on leave*. Dora continued to write and publish articles on socialism, Bolshevism, adult suffrage, democracy and *the crimes of imperialism* and to speak at conferences across Europe. In 1919, she stood as the Labour candidate for Hammersmith in the London City Council elections.

When Dora applied for a visa to return to Australia in 1923, to visit her now-widowed daughter-in-law and grandchild, an extensive security briefing clocked her *as a well-known communist...dangerous and undesirable...an advocate of world-wide revolution and anarchy*. She was eventually permitted entry into Australia on the undertaking that she *refrained from propaganda of a seditious nature*. (She didn't.)

In 1930, Dora organised a reunion dinner of twenty former suffragettes at the Minerva Club, *old colleagues and fellow workers in the great struggle*, including Annie Kenney, Teresa Billington-Greig, Sylvia Pankhurst and an eighty-six-year-old Charlotte Despard. Dora's motivation? She wanted *to feel their handshakes and to be re-assured that all was not forgotten...remembrance is the essence of comradeship*.

In 1924 Dora served as Australia's delegate to the Moscow International Communist Congress. Pulling together the strands of her globe-trotting, trend-setting life, Dora published her memoir, *From a Victorian to a Modern*, in 1925. She retired from public life in 1929 when she lost the sight in one eye. When Dora Montefiore died in Hastings, England, on 21 December 1933, aged eighty-two, she was remembered by the DAILY HERALD as *a pioneer of social democracy*. One of her last actions was to dictate a letter to a friend *denouncing the reactionary view of women adopted by Mussolini and Hitler*.

Dora left a sizable estate to her grandchildren. In accordance with the wishes expressed in her will, she was cremated and her ashes were buried in the grave of her husband, George Montefiore, in the cemetery at Albany, Western Australia.

It's unclear how **Nellie Martel** spent the war years, but by 1918 she had resurfaced after a long hiatus from the public glare. At the 1918 UK general election she went back on the hustings, prominently advocating for Ralph Milbanke Hudson, a British shipowner who, partly due to Nellie's spruiking, became the Conservative MP for Sunderland from 1918–22. She argued that the electorate needed *men of business capacity* and that the newly enfranchised women needed to vote for Hudson. In December 1918, Nellie, once famed for her generous hospitality among Sydney circles, hosted Christmas festivities for Australian soldiers stationed in London.

Nellie continued to speak at the occasional women's meeting, reminding listeners of the votes she had garnered in her Australian Senate campaign. She attended the reunion dinner organised by Dora Montefiore in 1930, telling the gathered friends that *it was now many years ago since she had known her in Australia as a worker for Votes for Women*. Nellie and Charles lived in Kensington from 1918; when Charles died in 1935, Nellie moved to Notting Hill, where she lived as a widow for five years, before joining her husband in the salon in the sky. She was eighty-five years old.

Probate on Nellie Martel's estate reveals that she continued to own property, and a sizable share portfolio, in Australia. But she does not appear to have returned to the country that both cemented and savaged her reputation as a political force of nature.

In 1912 **Dora Meeson Coates** became the first Australian woman elected to the Royal Institute of Oil Painters, a rare honour for any woman. *Water in movement* remained her favourite subject to paint, particularly the Thames. She became a popular *market artist*, selling small works as tourist souvenirs. In 1913, Dora sailed to Australia for an exhibition at the Athenaeum in Melbourne, where one of her sisters was once again living. George's works were also on show, but he did not accompany her on the trip. He was beset by a nervous breakdown that involved insomnia, depression and an addiction to sleeping narcotics. Dora's work sold well at the exhibition but only one of George's paintings was purchased. Dora rationalised the discrepancy: her work was cheaper. She returned to England, determined that she would never leave George alone again.

During the war, Dora joined a WFL-initiated women's police auxiliary, working in a munitions factory and sheltering refugees in the Chelsea studio. George was appointed by the AIF as an official war artist, painting generals in London rather than soldiers at the front. They both despised the work of the Cubists and Futurists who Dora believed were only *out to secure a certain notoriety*. In 1921, no longer struggling financially, Dora and George spent a year living in Australia, enjoying the open spaces and the light, but abhorring that Australians were *so wrapped up in the material side of existence, such as their sports*. George died in 1930; four years later, Dora sent works to Melbourne for their final joint show.

Dora Meeson Coates died in Chelsea in 1955, aged eighty-six. Her sister's descendants were in Canberra to witness the handover of the Women's Suffrage Banner in 1988.

Though she didn't attempt to export any Irish orphans, **Muriel Matters** was also involved in the Dublin industrial strife and worker lockouts of 1913. But campaigning for workers' and women's rights had to share centre stage with a new element in Muriel's life: marriage. It was international news when Muriel accepted the proposal of Dr William Porter, a recently divorced American dentist living in London. Porter was tall, dark and handsome, but it took three proposals before thirty-six-year-old Muriel said yes. They were married in October 1914 in a quiet ceremony at the Kensington Registry Office. Insisting on retaining her name, she became known as Muriel Matters-Porter.

She was still active in suffrage activities, though she had now rejected the militantism of both the WSPU and the WFL, preferring to lend her organising and speaking services to the NUWSS. Porter had no wish to curtail his wife's activism, which increasingly focused on the needs of impoverished and undereducated children, whether in Dublin or Lambeth.

In 1915 she went to the Hague as the delegate of the Union of Democratic Control to the International Congress of Women. She was a pacifist and spoke out against what she considered the perversion of Christian principles to justify war. She wanted to build *a new order, to rebuild life on higher levels* and believed it was women's duty to begin construction. In 1916, Muriel began training in the Montessori method—a progressive form of early childhood education—in Barcelona and was soon working as the resident teacher at the Mother's Arms School in East London, run by Sylvia Pankhurst.

In 1922, Muriel set off for her second lecture tour of Australia. This time, rather than raising awareness of the British suffragette campaigns, she was spruiking the virtues of the Montessori method. Two years later, she stood as the Labour candidate for Hastings, where she and Dr Porter had established their home base. Her infamy as the Heroine of the Grille attracted attention but did not always work in her favour. Muriel had to distance herself from the later acts of suffragette violence that had come to characterise the whole militant movement. In any case, Hastings was a safe Tory seat that would not be won by Labour until 1997.

William Porter died in 1949 and Muriel continued to live a quiet life by the sea, nourishing her feminist, Christian Scientist and socialist leanings through reading and reflection, occasionally entertaining journalists with tales of her former derring-do. Muriel Matters died in November 1969—six months after my birth—aged ninety-two.

ACKNOWLEDGMENTS

I like big books and I cannot lie. My first thanks is to you, Michael Heyward, for letting me write them. To have such a generous publisher is a gift, if not a miracle. Heartfelt thanks also to the stupendously talented crew at Text, who work so hard on design, publicity and marketing, especially Kirsty Wilson, Alice Lewinsky, Jane Watkins, Stef Italia and Imogen Stubbs. Thank you, Chong, for the incredible cover; making suffrage sexy again. I am blessed to be part of the Text family.

I need a whole separate paragraph to tell you how great my editor is. Mandy Brett, thank you for your skill, dedication, intellect and vision. You saw the narrative thread in the muddy morass of first-draft brain dump, and you pulled tight. (You even got rid of all my horrible mixed metaphors.) You made this a better book, and I am deeply grateful. Every author needs a Mandy. Only a few of us are lucky enough to have her. Also you need to know that Mandy is really funny. Laughing with your editor is a good thing.

My agent, Jacinta Dimase, leapt on my cockamamie idea for a trilogy based on the material heritage of Australian democracy, and sold it to Text before I had time to blink. Thank you, Jacinta, for being my defender, champion and chief hand-holder.

Big books require patient readers, particularly when in ugly duckling draft form. Anna Clark and John Goldlust read the whole manuscript in its earliest stages and offered vital structural advice and equally significant encouragement. Frank Bongiorno,

Kim Rubenstein and Judith Brett picked up factual inaccuracies in the final stages. Ruth Leonards was, as always, my first and most enthusiastic reader. Thank you all. Any remaining faults are on me.

My La Trobe University History family rivals my Text family for comfort and joy. Thank you especially to Katie Holmes, Liz Conor, Tim Jones, Anne Rees, Holly Wilson, Liam Flood and the whole Tuesday morning tea mob for your support, interest and friendship. We miss you Tracey Banivanua-Mar. You scared me into believing this book was possible and maybe even necessary.

Several accomplished people gave their valuable time to do my shitty legwork. Thank you Kate Laing, Lillian Pearce and Nikita Vanderbyl in Australia, Violeta Gilbert in New Zealand and Lisa Plotkin in England for your research assistance. Your tedium was my treasure.

Collegiality can never be taken for granted. Thank you, Robert Wainwright, Eileen Luscombe and James Keating, for sharing the fruits of your suffrage journeys with me. Thanks also to Libby Stewart at the Museum of Australian Democracy at Old Parliament House and Frances Bedford and her team at the Muriel Matters Society Archives. Frances, you are some kind of wonderful. Joe Connor, Lucy McLaren and Alex West at Renegade Films fuelled the first round of my suffrage fire when we made *Utopia Girls* in 2011. Thanks for allowing me to borrow from our research notes and script.

Many thanks to Simon Hearder and the estate of Dora Meeson Coates for granting permission to reproduce his ancestor's glorious banner.

Hannah Kent offered me big-hearted and wise words when I needed them most. *Just try to make it about the story that needs to be told, and find the wonder in it,* she emailed on a day of extreme doubt. Thank you, Hannah. I reckon I found it.

Finally, to my actual family. Thanks to all of you, but particularly to Bernard and Noah Wright for the burly hugs and for never letting me take myself too seriously. *What's for dinner?* is a very grounding question. Thank you, Esther Wright, for telling me to keep at it even when we both knew you'd prefer that I was there to tuck you in. And for all the late-night emoji kissy faces. You guys are the best.

My love and gratitude to Damien Wright. Big books mean long, solitary hours and Damien became accustomed to excusing my absence at parties. *She's in 1911,* he'd explain to the hosts, *she'll be back.* Thank you, darling. I'm back.

ILLUSTRATIONS

Plate section one: *Purity*

1   Program for the inauguration of the Australian Commonwealth [PRG 280/1/4/534]. Collection of the State Library of South Australia.

2   *Portrait Dora B. M. Montefiore*. Hamon, Augustin Frédéric Adolphe (photographer Devereux, F.O.). Retrieved from International Institute of Social History.

3   *Ellen Alma Martel*, 3 April 1902. Creelman & Co. (Sydney, NSW). Collection of the National Library of Australia.

4   *Quiz,* 4 April 1901. Courtesy of the Muriel Matters Society Inc.

5   *Portrait of Dora Meeson Coates*, 21 December 1895. *Australian Town and Country Journal* (Sydney, NSW : 1870–1907), p. 39. Collection of the State Library of South Australia.

6   *An invitation to meet their Royal Highnesses the Duke and Duchess of Cornwall and York in celebration of the opening of the first Parliament of the Commonwealth of Australia*, 1901. Ashton, Julian; Ashton, Howard; & Von Drehnen, Otto. Collection of the National Library of Australia.

7   *Portrait of Vida Goldstein*, 1903. Collection of the National Library of Australia.

Plate section two: *Courage*

1   Dora Meeson (1869–1955) The Women's Suffrage Banner: Trust the women... (1908). Reproduced by permission of Lt-Col Simon Hearder on behalf of the heirs in copyright. Gifts Collection, Parliament House Art Collection, Canberra, ACT.

2   *Special meeting in Emmeline Pethick-Lawrence's apartment to consider the future of the suffragettes*, 1906. Pankhurst, Estelle Sylvia; collector Barratt (London). Retrieved from International Institute of Social History.

3   *Muriel's airship*. Trinity Mirror / Mirrorpix / Alamy Stock Photo.

4   *Photographs of suffrage demonstrations and campaigning activities*. Collection of the National Library of Australia.

5 *Dora Montefiore at Clare Lodge during the Siege of Hammersmith*, 2 June 1906. *Sphere* (London, UK : 1900–64). Collection of State Library of Victoria.

6 *Woman Officially Placed within the House of Commons*, 7 November 1908. Drawn by S. Begg. *Illustrated London News* (London, UK: 1842–2003). Courtesy of the Eileen Luscombe Collection.

Plate section three: *Hope*

1 & 2 *Stereograph of the Women's Coronation Process*. 'The Rose Stereographs, Melbourne, Sydney, Wellington & London': photographer George Rose, 1911. Courtesy of the Eileen Luscombe Collection.

3 *Frontispiece of Dora Montefiore. From a Victorian to a Modern* [London?] : E. Archer, 1927.

4 *Dora Meeson Coates by Lafayette*, 28 November 1933. © National Portrait Gallery, London.

5 *Andrew Fisher family (Mr Fisher and wife, 3 boys, 1 girl and baby)*. NAA: M1406, 2.

6 *Voteless women gathered at the Women's Coronation Procession*, 17 June 1911. Photograph by Christina Broom. © Museum of London.

7 *Reunion of suffragettes*, 8 February 1928. *Illustrated London News* (London, UK : 1842–2003). Courtesy of the Muriel Matters Society Inc.

8 *Vida Goldstein*, 1911. © Bath In Time.

Endpaper

Women's Social and Political Union. © Museum of London.

Notes

INTRODUCTION

1   http://www.aph.gov.au/Visit_Parliament/Art/Top_5_Treasures/Great_Hall_Tapestry

2   http://www.aph.gov.au/Visit_Parliament/Art/Top_5_Treasures/Great_Hall_Embroidery

3   Only John Gorton bucks the trend: he is in cocky mode, with a red cravat, tan jacket and blue slacks. His portrait is also the only one painted by a female artist, June Mendoza.

4   https://www.foundingdocs.gov.au/item-did-104.html

5   Jenny Hocking, 'The palace treats Australia as the colonial child not to be trusted with knowledge of its own history', *Guardian*, 6 September 2017.

6   Myra Scott, 'How Australia Led the Way: Dora Meeson Coates and British Suffrage.' Canberra: Parliament of Australia, 2003, 46, 53.

7   *The Vote*, 13 May 1911, 27.

8   Jessie Ackermann, *Australia From a Woman's Point of View*. London, Cassell, 1913, vii.

9   'Women's Banner is Coming Home', *National Times*, 11 October 1987, NAA A463 1987/3770

10 Email correspondence with Samantha Pollock, Acting Assistant Director, Art Collection & Exhibitions, Parliament House, 3 July 2017, and Lachlan Murray, Collection Management Officer, Art Collection & Exhibitions, Parliament House, 10 July 2017.

11 See for example Barbara Caine, 'Australian Feminism and the British Militant Suffragettes.' In *Department of the Senate Occasional Lecture Series*. Canberra: Parliament of Australia, 2003; Susan Magarey, *Passions of the First Wave Feminists*, Sydney: UNSW Press, 2001, 188; Ann Nugent, 'Nellie Alma Martel and the Women's Social and Political Union, 1905–09.' *Hecate* 31, no. 1 (2005); Angela Woollacott, 'Australian Women's Metropolitan Activism: From Suffrage to Imperial Vanguard to Commonwealth Feminism.' In *Women's Suffrage in the British Empire: Citizenship, Nation, Race*, edited by

Ian Fletcher. Oxon: Routledge, 2012; James Keating, '"The Defection of the Women": The New Zealand Contagious Diseases Act Repeal Campaign and Transnational Feminist Dialogue in the Late Nineteenth Century.' *Women's History Review* 25, no. 2 (2016): 187–206; James Keating, '"An Utter Absence of National Feeling": Australian Women and the International Suffrage Movement 1900–1914.' *Australian Historical Studies* 47, no. 3 (2016): 462–81; Kate Laing, '"The White Australia Nettle": Women's Internationalism, Peace and the White Australia Policy in the Interwar Years.' *History Australia* 14, no. 2 (2017): 218–36.

12   Brougham Villiers. 'Introduction.' In *The Case for Women's Suffrage*, edited by Brougham Villiers, 1–21. London: T.H. Unwin, 1907, 10

13   https://lowyinstitutepoll.lowyinstitute.org/democracy/

14   http://www.abc.net.au/radionational/programs/breakfast/broken-democracy/5996650

15   http://www.thedailybell.com/news-analysis/9-in-10-americans-are-disillusioned-with-democracy/

16   Dora Montefiore, 'Why Women Need Woman Suffrage; and Why We Need It Now.' *Shafts*, December (1896).

17   To better understand the mindset, see for example Marilyn Lake, 'Personality, Individuality, Nationality: Feminist Conceptions of Citizenship, 1902–1940.' *Australian Feminist Studies* 9, no. 19 (1994): 25–38; Marilyn Lake, 'State Socialism for Australian Mothers: Andrew Fisher's Radical Maternalism in International and Local Contexts.' *Labour History* 102, no. May (2012): 55–70; Judith Smart, 'Modernity and Mother-Heartedness: Spirituality and Religious Meaning in Australian Women's Suffrage and Citizenship Movements.' In *Women's Suffrage in the British Empire: Citizenship, Nation and Race*, edited by Ian Christopher et al. Oxon: Routledge, 2012.

18   A.G. Gardiner, *Pillars of Society*. London: James Nisbet, 1913, 273.

19   Gardiner, 274.

20   Ackermann, *Woman's Point of View*, 3.

21   Ackermann, *Woman's Point of View*, 262.

22   Bernard Keane, 'Australia Bids for Global Village Idiot Status once more', *Crikey*, 27 June 2017.

23   Senator Thomas Glassey, Commonwealth Franchise Bill, Second Reading, 10 April 1902.

CHAPTER 1: THE RISING SUN

1   'The Dawn of Federation', *Queenslander*, 19 January 1901, 124.

2   'The Australian Commonwealth, The Dawn of a Nation', *Launceston Examiner*, 1 January 1901, 6

3   'Our Nation's Natal Day', *Adelaide Observer*, 5 January 1901, 13.

4   'The Dawn of Federation', *Sydney Morning Herald*, 25 December 1900 3. O'Sullivan promoted an audacious scheme to immortalise the foundation of the

Australian Commonwealth with a Statue of Liberty style monument, appealing to England for funds to build *a great national memorial infinitely superior to
that of 'Liberty' in New York Harbor, or 'Germania' on the Rhine*. The statue would
be situated on a little island in Sydney Harbour, *upon which is an obsolete fortifi-
cation called Fort Denison*. This way, the passengers and crew of every ship that
sailed through Sydney Harbour would see it: thousands of Australians would
contemplate with pride…the great event which it commemorates, and millions of
international visitors would salute an event fraught with *momentous consequences
to mankind*. The statue would be called 'Australia Facing the Dawn'. Despite,
or perhaps because of, the extravagant claims of his pitch, O'Sullivan failed to
attract either Australian or English supporters to the scheme he considered *the
keystone of the democratic arch. Mudgee Guardian*, 1 May 1902, 15.

5 'The New Nation', *National Advocate*, 1 January 1901, 2.

6 'Australia: A Nation's Birth', Adelaide *Advertiser*, 1 January 1901, 7.

7 'A New Century, A New Nation', *Adelaide Observer*, 5 January 1901, 29.

8 'Our Nation's Natal Day', *Adelaide Observer*, 5 January 1901, 13.

9 'The New Nation and the New Century', *Table Talk*, 3 January 1901, 21.

10 'The New-Born Nation', *Barrier Miner*, 16 February 1901, 5.

11 *Adelaide Chronicle*, 25 May 1901, 37.

12 'The Australian Commonwealth and the Dawn of Australian Unity', *Ovens
    and Murray Advertiser*, 5 January 1901, 8.

13 Margaret, Anderson, *When Australia Was a Woman: Images of a Nation*. Perth:
    Western Australian Museum, 1998, 6.

14 Anderson, 9.

15 Anderson, 12.

16 quoted in Gavin Souter, *Lion and Kangaroo: The Initiation of Australia*.
    Melbourne: Text, 1976, 48.

17 Rudyard Kipling, 'The Young Queen'. Kipling later added a subtitle to the
    poem to remind readers of the original context: 'The Commonwealth of
    Australia, inaugurated New Year's Day 1901', http://www.kiplingsociety.
    co.uk/rg_youngqueen1.htm

18 Souter, 51.

19 Souter, 23.

20 Ada Cambridge, *Thirty Years in Australia*, quoted in Florence Gay, *In Praise of
    Australia: An Anthology in Prose and Verse*. London: Constable, 1912, 59.

21 Alice Zimmern, *Women's Suffrage in Many Lands*. London: The Athenaeum
    Press, 1909, foreword.

22 Irene, Cockroft, *New Dawn Women: Women in the Arts and Crafts and Suffrage
    Movement at the Dawn of the Twentieth Century*. Compton: Watts Gallery,
    2005, 5.

23 *The Dawn*, 1 May 1899, 7.

24 John Docker, *The Nervous Nineties: Australian Cultural Life in the 1890s*.
    Melbourne: Oxford University Press, 1991, 49.

25 Docker, 49.

26 Marilyn Lake, 'The Inviolable Woman: Feminist Conceptions of Citizenship in Australia, 1900–1945.' *Gender and History* 8, no. 2 (1996), 202.

27 Cockroft, *New Dawn Women*, 5.

28 Cockroft, 33.

29 Jessie Ackermann, *What Women Have Done with the Vote*. New York: WM Feakins, 1913, 34.

CHAPTER 2: A CONDITION AKIN TO STUPOR

1 *Ovens and Murray Advertiser*, 10 March 1900, 9.

2 *Ovens and Murray Advertiser*, 10 March 1900, 9.

3 *Sydney Morning Herald*, 22 February 1900.

4 Adelaide *Advertiser* 22 February 1900.

5 quoted in Janet McCalman, *Sex and Suffering: Women's Health and a Women's Hospital*, Carlton: Melbourne University Press, 1998.

6 McCalman, 133.

CHAPTER 3: THE SHRIEKING SISTERHOOD

1 https://www.thoughtco.com/susan-b-anthony-quotes-3525404

2 Vida was named after her maternal uncle, David Hawkins. *Bessie Rischbieth Papers*, National Library of Australia, MS MS2004. 2004/4/42a. She was keen that her then unusual name be pronounced correctly: *Vida with an 'eye'*. Goldstein was similarly pronounced 'stine', not 'steen'. Henderson, Leslie. Vida Goldstein 1869–1949: Biographical notes by her niece, Leslie M. Henderson, 1966 January, State Library of Victoria, MS 7930.

3 Bomford, Janette M. *That Dangerous and Persuasive Woman: Vida Goldstein*. Carlton: Melbourne University Press, 1993, 1.

4 Tregenza, John. *Professor of Democracy: The Life of Charles Henry Pearson, 1830–1894, Oxford Don and Australian Radical*. Melbourne: Melbourne University Publishing, 1968, 78.

5 Vida Goldstein papers.

6 This theory of Dugdale's motivation is proposed by her biographer, Susan Priestley, *Henrietta August Dudgale: An Activist 1827–1918*. Melbourne: Melbourne Books, 2011.

7 *Argus*, 13 April 1869, 7.

8 For further details on the goldrush origins of women's suffrage see Clare Wright, *The Forgotten Rebels of Eureka*. Melbourne: Text Publishing, 2013, 450–453; Clare Wright, 'Golden Opportunities: The Early Origins of Women's Suffrage in Victoria', *Victorian Historical Journal*, Women's Suffrage Centenary Issue, vol. 79, no. 2, 2008, 210–24.

9 *Ballarat Times*, 12 September 1856.

10 *Woman's Sphere*, Issue 1, September 1900, 4.

11 '*Homo sum, humani nihil a me alienum puto*', or 'I am human, and I think that nothing of that which is human is alien to me.'

12 *Table Talk*, 27 October 1899, 5.

13 'News of the Day', *Age*, 15 August 1899, 4.

14 *The Woman's Sphere*, September 1900, 2.

15 *The Rural Australian*, 1894.

16 *Age*, 3 March 1900, 9.

17 *Truth*, 4 March 1900, 6.

18 *The Woman's Sphere*, December 1900, 34.

19 *Tocsin*, 16 January 1902, 7.

20 *The Woman's Sphere*, June 1901, 81.

CHAPTER 4: THEY DID WHAT THEY COULD

1 Darling Point is what is now known as Edgecliff in Sydney's eastern suburbs. The Octagon forms one of the four-hectare complex of buildings of Ascham School, an elite private school for girls.

2 Dora Montefiore, *From a Victorian to a Modern*. London: E. Archer, 1927, 30.

3 On 17 July 1889, George died at sea on his return from a business trip to London. He was on board the SS *Britannia*, near Albany in Western Australia, when he suffered a strangulated hernia. He was thirty-eight years old.

4 Dora Montefiore, *From a Victorian*, 30.

5 Dora Montefiore, *From a Victorian*, 6.

6 https://www.constitutionalcentre.wa.gov.au/ExhibitionsOnline/ ANationAtLast/Pages/The1891NationalAustraliaAustraliasian Convention. aspx

7 Dora Montefiore, *From a Victorian*, 32.

8 *Northern Star*, 4 March 1891, 5.

9 *Sydney Morning Herald*, 22 April 1891, 4.

10 Dora Montefiore, *From a Victorian*, 39.

11 *Australian Star*, 14 May 1891, 2.

12 *Express and Telegraph*, 14 May 1891, 2.

13 Dora Montefiore, *From a Victorian*, 6.

14 *National Advocate*, 10 June 1891, 1.

15 Lady Windeyer, quoted in the *Sydney Morning Herald*, 10 June 1891, 4.

16 Dora Montefiore, *From a Victorian*, 7.

17 *Daily Telegraph*, 16 May 1891, 1.

CHAPTER 5: SETTING THE TORRENS ON FIRE

1 John Cockburn, *The Working of Woman Suffrage in New Zealand and South Australia*. This speech, delivered by Cockburn in London in 1897, was

published as a pamphlet by the National Union of Women's Suffrage Societies. The Women's Library, London School of Economics, PC/06/396-11/35.

2   *South Australian Register*, 14 April 1890, 5.

3   *Adelaide Observer*, 15 August 1891, 8.

4   Catherine Helen Spence, *Catherine Helen Spence: An Autobiography*. Adelaide: WK Thomas, 1910, 164.

5   Vida Goldstein, *Review of Reviews*, 20 June 1904.

6   Spence, *Autobiography*, 24.

7   Spence, *Autobiography*, 37.

8   *South Australian Register*, 14 April 1890, 5.

9   Until the early twentieth century, 'conservatives' and 'liberals' were loose groupings of individuals with mutual vested interests rather than formal political parties. Conservatives generally represented property and pastoral concerns, and dominated the upper houses of colonial parliaments where only those who met property qualifications were eligible for election. John Hirst, *The Strange Birth of Colonial Democracy*, Sydney: Allen and Unwin, 1988, 2.

10 Audrey Oldfield, *Woman Suffrage in Australia: A Gift or a Struggle?* Cambridge: Cambridge University Press, 1992, 25.

11 *South Australian Chronicle*, 5 December 1891, 3.

12 Differences in the spelling of Labour/Labor abound in this early period of formalised political parties. The Australian Labor Party, founded as a federal party after the first sitting of the Australian Parliament in 1901, used *Labour* until 1912 when it switched to *Labor*. To avoid confusion, this book uses the modern spelling throughout.

13 Margaret Glass, *Charles Cameron Kingston: Federation Father*. Melbourne: Melbourne University Press, 1997, 91.

14 This is Glass's theory.

15 Alfred Deakin, *The Federal Story*. Melbourne: Robertson, 1944, 35.

16 quoted in Glass, *Charles Cameron Kingston*, 103.

17 Spence, *Autobiography*, 77.

18 *South Australian Register*, 18 December 1884, 4.

19 *South Australian Chronicle*, 22 December 1894, 30.

20 *Adelaide Observer*, 22 December 1894, 27.

21 *Adelaide Observer*, 22 December 1894, 27.

22 W. Sidney Smith, *Outlines of the Women's Franchise Movement in New Zealand*. Dunedin: Whitcombe and Tomes, 1902, 3.

23 Smith, *Women's Franchise Movement*, 31.

24 Lady Anna Stout, *Adult Suffrage in New Zealand*, The Women's Library, LSE. PC/06/396–11/35, leaflet no. 21.

25 https://nzhistory.govt.nz/politics/womens-suffrage/about-the-petition

26 W. Sidney Smith, *Women's Franchise Movement*, 84.

27 Rt Hon Richard Seddon, Speech to Deputation, Hotel Cecil, London, 7 August 1902, published as a penny pamphlet. The Women's Library, LSE. PC/06/396–11/35.

28 quoted in James Keating, 'The Defection of the Women', 191.

29 William Pember Reeves, *State Experiments in Australia and New Zealand*. London: Grant Richards, 1902, 112.

30 WP Reeves, *State Experiments*, 103.

31 quoted in Helen Irving, *To Constitute a Nation: A Cultural History of Australia's Constitution*. Melbourne: Cambridge University Press, 1999, 174.

CHAPTER 6: A SERIES OF MIRACLES

1 *Bunyip*, 9 April 1897, 2.

2 *The Vote*, 19 February 1910.

3 Perth *Daily News*, 1 April 1910.

4 Deakin, *The Federal Story*, 166.

5 Irving, *To Constitute a Nation*, x.

6 quoted in Irving, *To Constitute a Nation*, 8.

7 Spence, *Autobiography*, 81.

8 Spence, *Autobiography*, 93.

CHAPTER 7: NATIONAL HOUSEKEEPING

1 Nellie's brother was David Morley Charleston, who won a seat in the South Australian Parliament on the United Labor Party ticket in 1891. After his victory, the South Australian *Register* noted his pro-suffrage sentiments: *Recognising the success achieved at the polling booth was largely due to the women of South Australia he said he hoped the time was not far distant when they would be able to exercise their influence in a more direct manner.* In 1891, David Charleston, along with Mary Lee and Catherine Helen Spence, made a deputation to the staunch anti-suffrage premier, Thomas Playford, arguing for the justice of the female franchise.

2 *Daily Telegraph*, 22 February 1896, 2.

3 Nellie Martel, *The Women's Vote in Australia*. London: The Women's Press, 1907, 1–2.

4 *Barrier Miner*, 1 April 1897, 3.

5 Adelaide, Petition No 2. In favour of equal voting rights for both sexes in elections for Federal Parliaments. From Women's Suffrage League of New South Wales. National Archives of Australia, R216, 2.

6 Pember Reeves, *State Experiments*, 127.

7 *Sunday Times*, 4 April 1897, 11.

8 *Launceston Examiner*, 9 April 1897, 3.

9 Deakin, *The Federal Story*, 73, 59.

10 Pember Reeves, *State Experiments*, 127.

11 Deakin, *The Federal Story*, 73.

12 *Barrier Miner*, 1 April 1897, 3.

13 *Maitland Mercury*, 17 April 1897, 2.

14 The saying was a common jibe at hot-winded politicians and other bores. See for example *The Catholic Press*, 4 July 1912, 14; *The World's News*, 19 April 1924, 48.

15 *Daily Telegraph*, 16 April 1867, 6.

16 Ackermann, *What Women Have Done*, 24.

17 Irving, *To Constitute*, 179.

18 Oldfield, *Gift or Struggle*, 51.

19 *Argus*, 26 April 1900, 7.

20 Marilyn Lake, '"In the Interests of the Home": Rose Scott's Feminist Opposition to Federation.' In *Makers of Miracles: The Cast in the Federation Story*, edited by David Williams and John Headon, Melbourne: Melbourne University Publishing, 2000, 125.

21 quoted in Lake, *Interests*, 125.

22 quoted in Irving, *To Constitute*, 184.

23 quoted in Irving, *To Constitute*, 186.

24 Helen Irving, *Gender and the Constitution: Equity and Agency in Comparative Constitutional Design*. Melbourne: Cambridge University Press, 2008, 14.

CHAPTER 8: THE GREAT DAY

1 Alexandra Hasluck (ed), *Audrey Tennyson's Vice-Regal Days: The Australian Letters of Audrey Lady Tennyson*. Canberra: National Library of Australia, 1978, 156–157.

2 *Brisbane Worker*, 26 January 1901, 3. The full quote is interesting, and runs counter to the mass outpouring of imperial grief. *A good woman, a good wife and mother has passed away. But, happily, the world still contains many more such. She was of the same flesh as all other women, and subject to the same natural law... For the adversity or the prosperity of the British nation during her reign, therefore, the dead Queen is not to be regarded as responsible. As a ruler she had to do as she was instructed by her ministers. As a woman it is that Her Majesty is to be judged. And in this respect, when all is said and done, she was no better or no worse than most women.* The *Sydney Truth* borrowed the same sentiment two years later, in order to kick suffragists who were attempting to rise above their station. *Queen Victoria was a good woman, a good wife, and mother; but she was not the only good woman the world has ever known, though she is one of the few who never had any temptation to be otherwise. Sydney Truth*, 8 February 1903, 8.

3 The future George V was created Duke of York in 1892 and was usually referred to by that title until he ascended the throne in 1910. On Queen Victoria's death he inherited the title of Duke of Cornwall and was briefly known as the Duke of Cornwall and York.

4   'Cutting the painter' was the Federation-era idiom for loosening constitutional ties with England with a view to Australia becoming a republic. See for example, *Sydney Morning Herald*, 5 February 1902, 8. The expression refers to the seafaring term meaning 'to set adrift' when cutting a ship loose from its moorings.

5   Elections for the seventy-five seats in the inaugural Parliament of Australia were held on 29 and 30 March 1901. Voting was voluntary and the franchise was determined by each state's laws; accordingly, South Australian and Western Australian women could exercise their right to determine the new nation's lawmakers. Indigenous South Australians were also eligible to vote, and some probably did.

6   Margaret Anderson makes the point that although the new nation was invariably described in the feminine, there was 'a profound disjunction between allegorical women and actual women's social and political boundaries' in the Victorian/Edwardian era. Anderson, *When Australia Was a Woman*, 14.

CHAPTER 9: MAY 1901

1   *Evening News*, 26 February 1897, 7.

2   *Sydney Morning Herald*, 9 June 1898, 7.

3   *Worker*, 22 October 1898, 7. The public spat was between Rose Scott and Henry Willis. Nellie appears to have been caught in the middle.

4   *Sydney Morning Herald*, 23 April 1898, 1.

5   *Evening News*, 16 June 1899, 3.

6   *Mountaineer*, 16 June 1899, 2.

7   *Sydney Morning Herald*, 17 June 1899, 10.

8   quoted in Judith Allen, *Rose Scott: Vision and Revision in Feminism*. Melbourne: Oxford University Publishing, 1994, 199.

9   *Truth*, 2 December 1900, 6.

10   Scott's biographer, Judith Allen, describes the fallout more delicately: 'hasty motions of censure, half-hearted apologies and eventual stand-offs resulted'.

11   quoted in Allen, *Rose Scott*, 166.

12   *Australian Star*, 28 Sept 1901, 3.

13   *Sydney Morning Herald*, 1 October 1901, 9.

14   *Worker*, 12 October 1901, 8.

15   Robert Wainwright, *Miss Muriel Matters*. Sydney: Harper Collins, 2017, 37.

16   Wainwright, 38.

17   *Southern Sphere*, 1 July 1910, 12.

18   *Sydney Morning Herald*, 15 October 1898, 10.

19   Docker, *Nervous Nineties*, xxvii.

20   *Quiz*, 6 December 1900, 19.

21   quoted in Helen M. Van Der Poorten, 'Rignall, George Richard (1839–1912)', Australian Dictionary of Biography, National Centre of Biography, Australian

National University, http://adb.anu.edu.au/biography/rignall-george-richard-4478/text7311, published first in hardcopy 1976, accessed online 1 November 2017.

22 *Quiz*, 30 May 1901, 8.

23 Jo Sweatman, 'When Australian Art was in its sturdy youth', *Argus*, 5 April 1941, 4.

24 Dora Meeson Coates, *George Coates: His Life and Work*. London: Temple Press, 1937, 1.

25 Scott, Myra. 'The Art of George James Coates (1869–1930) and Dora Meeson Coates (1869–1955).' MA thesis, University of Melbourne, 1992, 40.

26 Scott, *The Art of*, 23. John Meeson's controlling nature was presumably not helped by the death of the youngest of his four girls, Gertie, in 1890.

27 Meeson Coates, *George Coates*, 8.

28 *Sydney Morning Herald*, 5 September 1895, 4.

29 *Sydney Morning Herald*, 21 December 1895, 9; *Sunbury News*, 15 February 1896, 1.

30 *Table Talk*, 11 October 1895, 6.

31 *Argus*, 19 December 1895, 3

32 *Australian Town and Country Journal*, 21 December 1895, 39.

33 *Table Talk*, 25 December 1896, 16.

34 Meeson Coates, *George Coates*, 8.

35 Dora Montefiore, 'L'Inspiratrice', *Le Journal Des Femmes*, November 1892.

36 Dora Montefiore, *From a Victorian*, 5.

37 Emmeline Pankhurst, *My Own Story*. London: Everleigh Nash, 1914, 12.

38 Millicent Garrett Fawcett, *What I Remember*. London: Fisher Unwin, 1924, 192.

39 Dora Montefiore, *From a Victorian*, 40.

40 Brake, Laurel; Demoor, Marysa, eds. (2009), 'Shafts (1892–1899)', *Dictionary of Nineteenth-Century Journalism*, Academia Press, 568.

41 Dora Montefiore, *Shafts*, vol. 4, issue 1, 1896, 6.

42 Dora Montefiore, *From a Victorian*, 7.

43 Elizabeth Cady Stanton, Susan B. Anthony, and Matilda Joslyn Gage. *History of Woman Suffrage*. Rochester, NY: Charles Mann, 1887, 15.

44 Dora Montefiore, 'Shall Women Refuse Their Taxes?', *The Woman's Signal*, 17 June 1897, 383.

45 Dora Montefiore, *From a Victorian*, 39.

46 Britain's military endeavours were supported by its Imperial allies: the Australian colonies, Canada, India and New Zealand. Historian Henry Reynolds argues that the Boer War was 'as much a watershed for the Australian colonies as Federation'. The war, coming as it did in 1899, while the Australian people were still determining what a federal constitution would look like, raised

several pertinent questions: 'How independent were the five colonies that had their own parliaments? Did they have any capacity to develop relations with foreign powers?…Was there an obligation to provide assistance to the mother country?' Federation, argues Reynolds, would not change the situation: 'The new Commonwealth had no greater autonomy than the individual colonies had been able to exercise…it remained shackled to the Colonial Office'. Henry Reynolds, *Unnecessary Wars*, Sydney: NewSouth, 2016, 38–9.

47 Fawcett, *A Short History*, 58. Certainly, the Boer War stimulated imperial loyalties: 16,000 men from the Australian colonies signed up. Henry Reynolds suggests that the Boer War may even have been a British strategy for shoring up imperial unity given various signs of dissent in the late nineteenth century, including demands for self-government in South Africa, and increased nationalism in Australia and New Zealand. He calls it 'martial grooming'. Reynolds, *Unnecessary Wars*, 197.

48 'Catalogue of Blunders', *Review of Reviews*, 20 October 1903.

CHAPTER 10: A SPLENDID OBJECT LESSON

1 International Women's Conference, *Age*, 11 December 1901, 8.

2 *Sydney Mail and NSW Advertiser*, 11 January 1902, 99.

3 *Tocsin*, 17 July 1902, 4.

4 Vida Goldstein, *Papers*.

5 Vida Goldstein Fawcett Library AJCP 2309.

6 For Roosevelt 'gripping my hand in a vice' see Vida Goldstein *Papers*. The emphasis is Goldstein's.

7 *Boston Woman's Journal*, 15 February, 1902.

8 *Woman's Sphere*, 10 April 1902, 164.

9 *Woman's Sphere*, 10 April 1902, 164.

10 Select Committee on Woman Suffrage, US Senate, 18 February 1902.

11 See, for example, *Washington Post*, 16 February 1902; *New York Times*, 2 March 1902.

12 Vida Goldstein, 'The Australian Woman in Politics', *Review of Reviews*, 20 January 1904, 47–50.

13 Vida Goldstein, 'Woman Suffrage in Australia' (1912), *Papers*.

14 New Zealand won the right to vote in national elections in 1893, but not eligibility to sit in parliament. Finland was the second country to legislate for both women's suffrage and eligibility, in 1906.

15 Vida Goldstein, 'Should Women Enter Parliament?' in *Review of Reviews*, 20 August 1908, 135–136, quotation on 136.

16 Vida Goldstein, 'The Australian Woman in Politics', 47. *Review of Reviews* was an international conduit for reform issues, with editions published in London, America and Melbourne.

17 *Review of Reviews*, 1 March 1902.

18   *Commercial Tribune*, 20 June 1902.

19   Vida Goldstein, *Papers*.

20   Vida Goldstein, *Papers*.

21   Vida Goldstein, *Papers*.

22   Vida Goldstein, *Papers*.

23   Women's Political Association, 'The Life and Work of Miss Vida Goldstein'(n.d), State Library of Victoria, Australian Manuscripts Collection, MS 9594.

24   Vida Goldstein, *Papers*. Vida was known for her wit and good-natured ribbing of opponents, what was referred to as 'taking her followers out of winding'. Leslie Henderson, biographical notes, State Library Of Victoria Australian Manuscripts Collection, MS 7930, Box 332/4.

25   *Queenslander*, 12 July 1902, 78.

26   *Daily Telegraph*, 20 August 1902, 9.

27   *Table Talk*, 28 August 1902, 3.

28   *Table Talk*, 30 October 1902, 6.

29   *Bendigo Adverstiser*, 1 September 1902, 5.

30   Vida Goldstein, *Papers*

31   Vida Goldstein, *Papers*.

32   *Age*, 29 July 1902, 8.

33   *Woman's Sphere*, 10 October 1902, 218.

34   Stanton et al, *History of Woman Suffrage*. Inscriptions appear in volumes 1, 2 and 3. State Library of Victoria Rare Books Collection.

CHAPTER 11: THE QUESTION OF HOW WHITE

1   *Daily Telegraph*, 20 August 1902, 9.

2   *The Dawn*, 1 September 1901, 7.

3   All quotes from National Archives of Australia A6/1901/354.

4   *Western Mail*, 19 April 1902, 44.

5   William Guthrie Spence, *Australia's Awakening: Thirty Years in the Life of an Australian Agitator*. Melbourne: The Workers' Trustees, 1909, 376.

6   *Review of Reviews*, September 1911, xiii.

7   Gwenda Tavan, *The Long Slow Death of White Australia*. Melbourne: Scribe, 2005, 9.

8   Florence Gay, *In Praise of Australia: An Anthology in Prose and Verse*. London: Constable, 1912, 167.

9   Deakin, *Federated Australia*, 24 September 1901, 77. Alfred Deakin was, in fact, the anonymous Australian correspondent for the *London Morning Post*, even during his prime ministership.

10   Judith Brett, *The Enigmatic Mr Deakin*. Melbourne: Text, 2017, 290.

11 Judith Brett, *The Enigmatic Mr Deakin*, 342, 360.

12 Spence, *Australia's Awakening*, 381.

13 There was no mention of Australian 'citizenship' in the Commonwealth consti-
    tution. Australians were all technically designated as 'British subjects' until 26
    January 1949. I am therefore using the term in its current colloquial (rather than
    strictly legalistic) sense. For a discussion of the emergence of modern citizen-
    ship and women's relationship to it, see Helen Irving, *Citizenship, Alienage and
    the Modern Constitutional State: A Gendered History*. Cambridge: Cambridge
    University Press, 2016. For a discussion of women, the constitution and repre-
    sentative democracy see Deborah Cass and Kim Rubenstein, 'Representation/s
    of Women in the Australian Constitutional System', *Adelaide Law Review*,
    vol. 17, 1995, 3–48.

14 Deakin, *Federated Australia*, 24 September 1901, 77.

15 *Western Mail*, 19 April 1902, 44.

16 *Kalgoorlie Miner*, 8 May 1902, 4.

17 Historian Judith Smart has contextualised this contest within the moderni-
    sation process of the late nineteenth-century, a response to forces including
    industrialisation, urbanisation and the disintegration of traditional communi-
    ties. Increased mobility, coupled with a disruption in family and community
    identities, required the search for a new basis of unity and order, new means of
    belonging and affect. 'The preoccupation with defining appropriate criteria for
    citizenship', Smart argues, was a key component in both the women's suffrage
    movement and federation-era nation-building. Judith Smart, 'Modernity and
    Mother-Heartedness', 51.

18 The Franchise Act was one of the few pieces of major legislation to be intro-
    duced into the Senate before the House of Representatives.

19 NAA A2863/1902/8.

20 NAA A1559/1902/8. Section 44 of the constitution stipulated a range of other
    exclusions for who could be elected to Parliament: those with *an allegiance to a
    foreign power* (dual nationals) or insolvents. Such people were not ineligible to
    vote.

21 NAA A2863/1902/8. The inclusion of Maoris was intended to act as an
    incentive to New Zealand to join the Commonwealth, as had been mooted
    since 1891. As O'Connor stated in debate, *we hope that the day will come when
    New Zealand will be a member of the Federation.* Any New Zealand govern-
    ment would want Maoris *on an equal footing.* The provision was granted on
    the assumption that, as Senator Styles put it, *There is no fear of Maoris coming to
    Australia in any number, but if the Asians should get a foothold here they would soon
    swamp us. Hansard*, Senate, 29 May 1902, 13009.

22 *Hansard*, Senate, 10 April 1902.

23 Deakin, *Federated Australia*, 8 October 1901, 28.

24 *Hansard*, Senate, 10 April 1902.

25 *Hansard*, Senate, 29 May 1902.

26 *Hansard*, Senate, 29 May 1902.

27 *Hansard*, Senate, 10 April 1902.

28 *Hansard*, House of Representatives, 24 April 1902.

29 *Hansard*, Senate, 29 May 1902.

30 *Kalgoorlie Miner*, 8 May 1902, 4.

31 For a discussion of the effects of this historical turning point, see Pat Stretton and Christine Finnimore, 'Black Fellow Citizens: Aborigines and the Commonwealth Franchise', *Australian Historical Studies*, 25:101, 1993, 521–35; Murray Goot, 'The Aboriginal Franchise and Its Consequences', *Australian Journal of Politics and History*, 52:4, 2006, 517–61.

CHAPTER 12: THE WORLD FAIRLY STOOD AGHAST

1 H.G. Turner, *The First Decade of the Australian Commonwealth: A Chronicle of Contemporary Politics, 1901–1910*. Melbourne: Mason, Firth and McCutcheon, 1911, 24.

2 Pember Reeves, *State Experiments*, 103.

3 'The Working of Women's Suffrage in New Zealand and South Australia', Speeches by Hon WP Reeves and Hon JA Cockburn, 1897, The Women's Library, PC/06/396–11/35

4 Edith Palliser, 'The International Movement for Women's Suffrage.' In *The Case for Women's Suffrage*, edited by Brougham Villiers, London: T.F. Unwin, 1907, 138.

5 *Woman's Journal*, 3 May 1902, 138.

6 Bluegrass Blade, from the *Commercial Tribune*, 20 June 1902.

7 Stanton, *History of Woman Suffrage*, vol. 6, 29.

8 Clarence H. Northcott, *Australian Social Development*. New York: Columbia University Press, 1918, 32.

9 Northcott, *Australian Social Development*, 204.

10 Zimmern, *Women's Suffrage*, 160.

11 Zimmern, *Australian Social Development*, 170.

12 *Review of Reviews*, 20 October 1903.

13 Ackermann, *What Women Did*, 21.

14 *Review of Reviews*, 20 July 1903.

15 Percy Rowland, 'The Beginnings of an Australian National Character.' *Nineteenth Century* 52, no. 307 (1902), 403.

16 Rowland, 'The Beginnings', 401.

17 Rowlands, 'The Beginnings', 411.

18 Goldstein, *The Political Woman in Australia*, 105.

CHAPTER 13: THE MODERN EVE

1 quoted in Judith Allen, *Rose Scott*, 118.

2 Bomford, *That Dangerous*, 29.

3   *Woman's Sphere*, 10 November 1903, 367.

4   *Brisbane Week*, 27 November 1903, 24; *Great Southern Advocate*, 26 November 1903, 5; *North Western Advocate and the Emu Bay Times*, 14 October 1903, 2. There were hundreds of reports of Vida's election speeches published nationally. This vignette is an amalgam of the three references here cited. Vida spoke in so many venues she was known to repeat her speeches.

5   Vida Goldstein, 'The Australian Woman in Politics', *Review of Reviews*, 20 January 1904.

6   Vida Goldstein, 'The Australian Woman'.

7   Vida Goldstein, 'Should Women Enter Parliament?' *Review of Reviews*, 20 August 1903.

8   *Woman's Sphere*, 10 August 1903, 334.

9   Compulsory voting was introduced in Australia in 1924.

10 Adelaide *Register*, 23 September 1903, 4.

11 *Great Southern Advocate*, 8 October, 1903, 3.

12 C.J. Martin, 'What Women are Doing in Australia', *Womanhood: the magazine of woman's progress and interests, political, legal, social, and intellectual, and of health and beauty culture*, vol. 10 no. 58, 1903, 259.

13 Richard Seddon, 7 August 1902, The Women's Library, PC/06/396–11/35

14 Cockburn, 'The Working of Woman Suffrage'.

15 *Woman's Sphere*, 10 August 1903, 334.

16 Vida Goldstein, 'The Political Woman in Australia.' *Nineteenth Century* 56, no. 329 (1904), 106.

17 Jessie Ackermann, *What Women Have Done*, 8.

18 *Woman's Sphere*, 10 August 1903, 334.

19 *Argus*, 8 August 1903, 9.

20 Goldstein, *The Political Woman in Australia*, 105.

21 Some of those in Vida's own camp feared for her personal wellbeing. Author Stella Miles Franklin, a close friend of Vida's, wrote to Rose Scott fretting that she knew a man who had met Vida and confided that '*she was absolutely repellent—metallic and repulsive'. I do wish she would melt more, don't you?*, Franklin asked Scott. Nonsense, Scott countered. *There is nothing to melt. There is no reserve force of love or self-sacrifice as one sees in some people.* Quoted in Allen, *Rose Scott*, 200.

22 quoted in *Woman's Sphere*, 10 September 1903, 344. The *Woman's Sphere* compiled 'various views' of Vida's candidacy from news outlets around the country.

23 quoted in *Woman's Sphere*, 10 September 1903, 344.

24 'Petticoats in Parliament', *Review of Reviews*, 20 August 1903.

25 *Argus*, 14 October 1903, 6.

26 *Argus*, 14 October 1903, 6; *Young Chronicle*, 21 November 1903; Brisbane *Telegraph*, 31 October 1903, 13.

27   *Telegraph*, 31 October 1903, 13

28   Kate Laing, *White Australia Nettle*, 225.

29   *Great Southern Advocate*, 26 November 1903, 5.

30   *Great Southern Advocate*, 8 October 1903, 3.

31   For further reading on this topic see for example, Marilyn Lake, 'Women and Whiteness.' *Australian Historical Studies* 32, no. 117 (2001): 228–342.

32   *Ovens and Murray Advertiser*, 5 December 1903, 7. This article, like many, described Vida's appearance at her election rallies. Unlike others, it noted the gendered hypocrisy, remarking that *no one thinks of a male politician's dress…but a lady politician is a very different person.*

33   *Young Chronicle*, 21 November 1903.

34   *Benalla Standard*, 1 December, 1903, 2.

CHAPTER 14: SHE LOVED POLITICS

1   The studio was in Margaret Street in Sydney's CBD, nestled beside the Scots Church, opposite Wynyard Park. The position couldn't be more prominent or central.

2   *The Dawn*, 1 October 1903, 28.

3   *Daily Telegraph*, 20 August 1902, 5.

4   Martel, *The Woman's Vote*, 2.

5   Nellie Martel, 'Women's Votes in New Zealand and Australia.' In *The Case for Women's Suffrage*, edited by Brougham Villiers, London: T.H. Unwin, 1907, 146.

6   These exact words belong to Josephine Butler, in a plea to NZ women to use their votes to stop the reintroduction of the Contagious Diseases Act which were *an insult to womanhood*. State Library of Victoria, AJCP, M2308.

7   *The Dawn*, 1 August 1903, 6.

8   *Truth*, 22 November 1903, 8.

9   *Boulder Evening Star*, 2 October 1903, 3.

10   *Daily Telegraph*, 31 October 1903, 11.

11   *Newsletter: an Australian Paper for Australian People*, 21 November 1903, 9.

12   Macleay, *Argus*, 12 December 1903, 12.

13   *Watchman*, 12 December 1903, 4.

14   *Watchman*, 12 December 1903, 4.

15   *Watchman*, 21 November 1903, 5.

16   *Daily Telegraph*, 21 November 1903, 10.

17   *Truth*, 22 November 1903, 2.

18   *Balmain Observer*, 21 November 1903, 3.

19   *Sydney Morning Herald*, 2 September 1903, 12.

20   *Newcastle Morning Herald*, 28 November 1903, 5.

21   *The Dawn*, 1 December 1903, 28.

22   *Truth* 29 November 1903, 6.

CHAPTER 15: THE GREATEST DAY THAT EVER DAWNED

1   *The Dawn*, 1 January 1904, 5.

2   Goldstein, 'The Australian Woman'.

3   *Review of Reviews*, 20 June 1903.

4   Lake, 'State Socialism', 64.

5   Cockburn, 'The Working of Woman Suffrage'.

6   quoted in Brett, *Enigmatic Mr Deakin*, 290.

7   Lady Julia Holder. 'Equal Suffrage in Australia.' In *Congressional Publications on Woman Suffrage*: National American Woman Suffrage Association, 1904.

8   quoted in Lake, 'State Socialism', 63.

9   Tom Mann, 'The Political and Industrial Situation in Australia.' *Nineteenth Century* 56, no. 331 (September 1904), 479.

10   Tom Mann, 'Political and Industrial', 491.

11   Dora Montefiore, 'Women Voters in Australia.' *New Age*, 22 September 1904, 827.

12   Montefiore, 'Women Voters', 602.

13   Brougham Villiers, *The Case for Women's Suffrage*, 9.

14   Brougham Villiers, *The Case for Women's Suffrage*, 21.

15   *The Dawn*, 1 January 1904, 5.

16   Goldstein, 'The Political Woman', 110.

CHAPTER 16: THE FATEFUL 12TH MAY

1   *Daily Telegraph*, 13 May 1905, 10. There were 670 seats in the House of Commons at this time.

2   Montefiore, *From a Victorian*, 43.

3   Pankhurst, *My Own Story*, 42.

4   Broughton Villiers, 21.

5   Elizabeth Crawford, *The Women's Suffrage Movement: A Reference Guide 1866–1928*, London: UCL Press, 1999, 198.

6   *Illustrated London News*, 20 May 1905, 724.

7   *Daily News*, 13 May 1905, 8.

8   *Daily News*, 13 May 1905, 8.

9   *Daily News*, 17 May 1905, 5.

10   *Standard*, 13 May 1905, 7.

11   *Daily News*, 13 May 1905, 8.

12   *Daily News*, 13 May 1905, 6.

13 *Daily News*, 13 May 1905, 8.

14 *The Dawn*, 1 July 1905, 7. For the text of *the remarkable declaration of no confi-dence*, which Keir Hardie tabled in the House of Commons on 19 May, see *London Evening Standard*, 20 May 1905, 4. See also the *Morning Post*, 20 May 1905, 5, which noted the *considerable merriment* that was created by the wording of the petition. The petition is the only aspect of the women's actions on *the fateful 12th* that was reported.

15 *Truth*, 20 March 1904, 5.

16 *Truth*, 20 March 1904, 5.

17 *Freeman's Journal*, 3 June 1905, 29.

18 *Truth*, 21 August 1904, 6.

19 *Evening News*, 7 October 1904, 4.

20 *Evening News*, 7 October 1904, 4.

21 *Richmond River Herald*, 14 October 1904, 5.

22 *Newsletter: an Australian Paper for Australian People*, 15 October 1904, 9.

23 in Zimmern, *Women's Suffrage*, 158.

24 Crawford, *The Women's Suffrage Movement*, 727.

25 Sylvia Pankhurst, *The Suffragette Movement: An Intimate Account*. London: Longmans, 1931, 62.

26 *Sunday Sun*, 16 April 1905, 4.

27 Martel, *The Women's Vote*, 3, 7.

28 *Daily News*, 3 April 1905, 8.

29 Christabel Pankhurst, *Unshackled: The Story of How We Won the Vote*. London: Hutchinson, 1959, 47.

30 E. Pankhurst, *My Story*, 42.

31 S. Pankhurst, *The Suffragette*, 14.

32 S. Pankhurst, *The Suffragette*, 183.

33 quoted in Elizabth Crawford, *The Women's Suffrage Movement*, 198.

34 Sylvia Pankhurst, *The Life of Emmeline Pankhurst: The Suffragette Struggle for Women's Citizenship*. London: T. Werner Laurie Ltd, 1935. 51.

35 *The Dawn*, 1 June 1905, 5.

36 C. Pankhurst, *Unshackled*, 62.

37 Ann Nugent, *Nellie Alma Martel*, 144.

38 E. Pankhurst, *My Story*, 56.

39 *Daily News*, 15 May 1905, 5.

CHAPTER 17: NO MORE PEACE

1 *Northam Adverstiser*, 22 July 1905, 1.

2 *Critic*, 6 July 1904, 13.

3 Wainwright, *Miss Muriel Matters*, 62.

4   *The Vote*, 19 February 1910, 196.

5   Angela Woollacott, *To Try Her Fortune in London: Australian Women, Colonialism, and Modernity*. Oxford: Oxford University Press, 2001, 157.

6   *My Brilliant Career*, the story of Sybylla Melvyn, a headstrong bush girl determined to forge an unconventional female path, was published in 1901.

7   Perth *Daily News*, 9 November 1905, 10.

8   Wainwright puts Muriel's good fortune down to a combination of these three factors. Wainwright, *Miss Muriel Matters*, 69.

9   *Boulder Evening Star*, 8 November 1906, 3.

10 Louise Mack, *The Romance of a Woman at Thirty*. London: Alston Rivers, 1911, 132.

11 *Advertiser*, 23 January 1906, 6.

12 *Critic*, 24 January 1906, 20.

13 Muriel Matters, 'My Impressions as an Agitator', in Mrs Leonard Matters, *Australasians Who Count in London and Who Counts in Western Australia*. London: Jas. Truscott, 1913, 161–2.

14 Muriel Matters, interview in *The Southern Sphere*, 1 July 1910, 12.

15 *Weekly Times*, 25 June 1910, 10.

16 *Weekly Times*, 25 June 1910, 10.

17 Matters, *My Impressions*, 161–2.

18 *Weekly Times*, 25 June 1910, 10.

19 Emmeline Pethick-Lawrence, *My Part in a Changing World*. London: Victor Gollancz, 1938, 253.

20 E. Pankhurst, *My Own Story*, 45.

21 *Manchester Guardian*, 16 October 1905, 10.

22 *Manchester Guardian*, 16 October 1905, 10.

23 E. Pankhurst, *My Own Story*, 50.

24 Montefiore, *Victorian to Modern*, Marxists Internet Archive, transcription by Ted Crawford, np.

25 C. Pankhurst, *Unshackled*, 47.

26 Frederick Pethick-Lawrence, *Women's Fight for the Vote*. London: The Women's Press, 1910, 13. Fred was born Frederick Lawrence. When he married socialist feminist Emmeline Pethick in 1901, the couple took the combined surname Pethick-Lawrence, becoming the Brangelinas of the Edwardian era.

27 The woman was Minnie Baldock. Dora Montefiore accused Sylvia Pankhurst of misrepresenting history by writing in *The Suffragette* that Annie Kenney lived with her when she first came to London. Dora insisted that Kenney arrived on Dora's step, and Dora sent her to live with Baldock. Crawford, *Women's Suffrage Movement*, 25.

28 Dora Montefiore, *New Age*, 24 December 1903, 827.

29 Dora Montefiore, *New Age*, 22 September 1904, 602.

30 Ackermann, *What Women Have Done*, 30.

31 F. Pethick-Lawrence, *Women's Fight*, 70–84.

32 Martel, *Women's Votes in New Zealand and Australia*, 153.

33 *The Era*, 24 March 1906, 15.

CHAPTER 18: THE SIEGE OF FORT MONTEFIORE

1 Jill Liddington, *The Life and Times of a Respectable Rebel: Selina Cooper 1864–1946*. London: Virago, 1984, 170.

2 Montefiore, *Victorian to Modern*, Marxists Internet Archive, np.

3 *Washington Post*, 25 May 1906, 6. The *New York Times* also covered the story under the headline 'Calls Asquith Assassin: Suffragist Wants Windows Stoned', 25 May 1906, 8.

4 Adelaide *Register*, 27 June 1906, 6.

5 Adelaide *Register*, 27 June 1906, 6.

6 *New Age*, quoted in *WA Record*, 8 October 1904, 5. Dora also argued that *Australia needs population to develop its wealth and resources. Womanhood*, vol. XII, no. 72, 1904, pvii.

7 Gawler *Bunyip*, 15 July 1904, 4.

8 *Brisbane Telegraph*, 18 July 1904, 5.

9 Gawler *Bunyip*, 15 July 1904, 4.

10 quoted in Christine Collette, 'Socialism and Scandal: the sexual politics of the early Labour Movement', *History Workshop Journal*, vol. 23, no. 1, 1 March 1987, 103.

11 Collette, 'Socialism and Scandal', 102. Nymphomania is the female equivalent.

12 Dora's fear was not without foundation. George's bid for the seat of Hammersmith at the general election was rejected by the ILP, and Dora was forced to resign as acting recording secretary of the International Women's Congress of the SDF. Collette, 'Socialism and Scandal', 106. Furthermore, when Elizabeth Wolstenholme became pregnant, aged 40, to her lover, Ben Elmy, it was her feminist friends who urged the couple to marry 'in order that the honour of the women's movement not be besmirched'. Crawford, *Women's Suffrage Movement*, 191.

13 quoted in Karen Hunt, 'Journeying through Suffrage: The Politics of Dora Montefiore.' In *The Suffrage Reader: Charting Direction In British Suffrage History*, edited by Clare Eustance, Ryan, Joan and Ugolini, Laura. Leicester: Leicester University Press, 2000, 172.

14 Dora Montefiore, 'Taxation without Representation Is Tyranny.' *New Age*, 22 June 1905, 394.

15 *West London Observer*, 22 December 1905, 8.

16 *Observer*, 27 May 1906, 6.

17 Montefiore, *Victorian to Modern*, 81.

18 Montefiore, *Victorian to Modern*, 78.

19 *Manchester Guardian*, 28 May 1906, 8.

20 Adelaide *Advertiser*, 26 June 1906, 4.

21 Adelaide *Advertiser*, 26 June 1906, 4.

22 *Gippsland Gazette*, 31 July 1906, 3.

23 Montefiore, *Victorian to Modern*, 75.

24 *Gippsland Gazette*, 31 July 1906, 3.

25 *Scrutineer and Berrima District Press*, 5 September 1906, 5.

26 S. Pankhurst, *The Life of Emmeline Pankhurst*, 184.

27 *Observer*, 1 July 1906 5.

28 Montefiore, *Victorian to Modern*, 77.

29 Fawcett, *What I Remember*, 181.

30 Diane Atkinson, *The Suffragettes in Pictures*. London: Museum of London, 1996, 36.

31 Adelaide *Register*, 25 October 1906, 5.

32 Montefiore, *Victorian to Modern*, 92.

33 *Brisbane Telegraph*, 25 October 1906, 4.

34 Montefiore, *Victorian to Modern*, 92.

35 Adelaide *Register*, 26 October 1906, 5.

36 *Evening Star*, 25 October 1906, 3; Adelaide *Register*, 26 October 1906, 5.

37 Teresa Billington-Greig, *The Militant Suffrage Movement: Emancipation in a Hurry*. London: Frank Palmer, 1911, 68.

38 *Darling Downs Gazette*, 26 October 1906, 5.

39 Adelaide *Register* 2 November 1906, 5.

40 Adelaide *Register*, 26 October 1906, 5. Many Australian papers reported that it was Edith How-Martyn who, on being arrested, claimed to be an enfranchised Australian woman who had once polled 20,000 votes. It was clearly Nellie Martel.

41 Montefiore, *Victorian to Modern*, 95.

42 June Purvis, *Emmeline Pankhurst: A Biography*. London: Routledge, 2002, 88.

43 S. Pankhurst, *Suffragette*, 1931, 237.

44 quoted in Purves, *Emmeline Pankhurst*, 88.

45 *Brisbane Telegraph*, 3 November 1906, 4.

46 *Truth*, 4 November 1906, 9.

47 *Clarence and Richmond Examiner*, 22 September 1906, 5.

48 *Hobart Mercury*, 6 December 1906, 6.

49 Billington-Greig, *Militant Suffrage*, 68.

50 Billington-Greig, *Militant Suffrage*, 72.

CHAPTER 19: ELECTRIFY THE HOUSE

1   Dora Meeson Coates, *George Coates*, 59–62.

2   Dora Meeson Coates, *George Coates*, 11–17.

3   Scott, *The Art of*, 22.

4   Dora Meeson Coates, *George Coates*, 26.

5   Scott, *The Art of*, 25.

6   Dora Meeson Coates, *George Coates*, 62.

7   Scott, *The Art of*, 36.

8   Scott, *The Art of*, 24.

9   Scott, *The Art of*, 25.

10 Carol Mills, 'Expatriate Australian Black and White Artists: Ruby and Will Dyson and Their Circle in London.' In *Working papers in Australian Studies*. London: Menzies Centre for Australian Studies, 1988, 6.

11 Dora Meeson Coates, *George Coates*, 43.

12 Crawford, *Women's Suffrage Movement*, 257.

13 Crawford, *Women's Suffrage Movement*, 358.

14 Scott, *The Art of*, 28.

15 Lisa Tickner, *The Spectacle of Women: Imagery of the Suffrage Campaign 1907–14*. London: Chatto and Windus, 1987, 16.

16 Tickner, *Spectacle of Women*, 16.

17 Diane Atkinson, *Purple, White and Green*, 41.

18 Villiers, 11.

19 Kenney, vii.

20 Scott, *The Art of*, 27.

21 Martel, 'Women's Vote in Australia', 10.

22 *Adelaide Observer*, 23 March 1907, 45.

23 Another Australian rank and file member of the WSPU, Miss Constance Clyde, a journalist, was imprisoned after the Opening of Parliament demonstration. *Molong Argus*, 5 April 1907, 1.

24 Tickner, *Spectacle of Women*, 74.

25 quoted in Tickner, *Spectacle of Women*, 78.

26 *The Graphic*, Supplement, 16 February 1907, 3, reproduced in Tickner, *Spectacle of Women*, 77.

27 *Adelaide Observer*, 23 March 1907, 45.

CHAPTER 20: THE SOCIAL LABORATORY

1   *Ex parte H.V. McKay (1907)* is commonly known as the Harvester Judgment.

2   Deakin, *Federated Australia*, 216.

3   Vida may also have drawn on the work of Maud Pember Reeves, wife of William Pember Reeves. She had been active in the New Zealand suffrage

movement. The couple moved from New Zealand to London when William was appointed agent-general in 1896. Maud was a Fabian and a feminist, credited with having persuaded the London Fabians (including Bertrand Russell and H.G. Wells) to support women's suffrage. Maud had studied the effects of poverty on households and infant mortality rates. Her findings would be published in an influential pamphlet, *Round About a Pound a Week*, in 1913. Maud maintained that, coming from New Zealand, socialism was *just glorified common sense*. H.G. Wells maintained that Maud's absorption in the suffrage movement was *a form of sublimation* due to her sexual frustration in her marriage. Ruth Fry, *Maud and Amber: A New Zealand Mother and Daughter and the Women's Cause, 1865–1981*. Canterbury: Canterbury University Press, 1992, 74, 39.

4   'The Women's Franchise in Australia', *The New Witness*, n.d, University of Manchester archives, IWSA 3/2.

5   Ackermann, *Australia From a Woman's Point of View*, 1913, 2.

6   Martel, *Woman's Vote*, 3.

7   Zimmern, *Women's Suffrage*, 168.

8   Pember Reeves, *Effect of Woman Suffrage*, 4.

9   People's Suffrage Federation leaflet no. 21, n.d. The Women's Library, LSE, PC/06/396–11/35.

10 Ackermann in fact held that Australia was the *least* likely place where women could remedy the centuries-old maladies of law and custom, given the tone of politics and the calibre of politicians. In Australia, she wrote, *party spirit is so fierce and bitter and that any man was welcome to a seat if he is glib of tongue and tinged with the microbe of words or the germ of speech.* Ackermann, *Australia From a Woman's Point of View*, 30.

11 quoted in Keating, *An Utter Absence*, 467.

12 *Argus*, 30 May 1908, 20.

13 *Melbourne Leader*, 11 January 1908, 46.

14 *Melbourne Leader*, 11 January 1908, 46.

15 Zimmern, *Women's Suffrage*, 168.

16 Vida Goldstein, 'Woman Suffrage'.

17 *Argus*, 26 October 1907, 20.

18 Zimmern, *Women's Suffrage*, 168.

19 Goldstein, 'Woman Suffrage', np.

20 Goldstein, 'Woman Suffrage', np.

21 Teresa Billington married Frederick Greig in February 1907.

22 Billington-Greig, *Militant Suffrage*, 1.

23 Billington-Greig, *Militant Suffrage*, 6–27.

24 Brougham Villiers, *The Case for*, 12.

CHAPTER 21: TRUST THE WOMEN

1   Tickner, *Spectacle of Women*, xii.

2   Tickner makes the important point that the art of the suffrage movement was 'not a footnote or an illustration to the 'real' political history going on elsewhere, but an integral part of the fabric of social conflict with its own contradictions and ironies and its own power to shape thought, focus debates and stimulate action.' Tickner, *Spectacle of Women*, ix.

3   Tickner, *Spectacle of Women*, 52.

4   Ethel Snowden, *The Feminist Movement*. London: Collins, 1913, 13.

5   Smart, 'Modernity and mother-heartedness', 54–6.

6   Bramwell Booth, Mrs. *Mothers of the Empire and Other Addresses*. London: Salvation Army Book Department, 1914, 1.

7   For more on the missionary work of organisations like the WCTU, the Salvation Army, see Smart, 'Modernity and mother-heartedness', 52.

8   Oliver Banks. *Becoming a Feminist: The Social Origins of First Wave Feminism*. London: Wheatsheaf Books, 1986, 26. The exception was where feminist daughters had feminist mothers, as in the example of the Pankhursts. First wave feminists were also more likely to have close and warm relationships with fathers who encouraged their daughters to be unconventional or break the mould, taking particular interest in their education and treating them equally with sons. Elizabeth Garrett Anderson's mother, for example, *begged her with tears and entreaties* not to train as a doctor. Banks, 28.

9   Cicely Hamilton; with sketches by M. Lowndes, D. Meeson Coates, C. Hedley Charlton, *Beware! A Warning to Suffragists*. London: Artists Suffrage League, 1909.

10 Meeson Coates, *George Coates*, 40.

11 Meeson Coates, *George Coates*, 43.

12 Doughty, Lady Eugenia. *The Cheerful Way*. London: Adam and Charles Black, 1912.

13 *Votes for Women*, 16 April 1908, cxc.

14 Anon, 'Not prophecy but history', 1908?

15 *Justice*, 23 July 1901, 7.

16 Tickner, *Spectacle of Women*, 58.

17 This lovely sentiment belongs to Tickner, *Spectacle of Women*, 60.

18 quoted in Tickner, *Spectacle of Women*, 60.

19 quoted in Tickner, *Spectacle of Women*, 62.

20 Tickner, *Spectacle of Women*, 63.

21 *Faringdon Advertiser*, Saturday 20 June, 1908, 2.

22 Fawcett, *What I Remember*, 191.

23 *Woman Worker*, 19 June 1908, 66.

24 *Morning Post*, 15 June 1908, 7.

25　source unidentified June 14 1908, clipping files, TWL 10/01.

26　*Lancashire Daily*, 15 June 1908, 3.

27　see for example *Salisbury Times*, 19 June 1908, 3.

28　source unidentified, clipping files, TWL 10/01.

29　*Telegraph*, nd, clipping files, TWL 10/01.

30　clipping files, TWL 10/01.

31　John Playford, 'Cockburn, Sir John Alexander (1850–1929)', Australian Dictionary of Biography, National Centre of Biography, Australian National University, http://adb.anu.edu.au/biography/cockburn-sir-john-alexander-5701/text9637, published first in hardcopy 1981, accessed online 1 December 2017.

32　*Woman Worker*, 19 June 1908, 66.

33　*Women's Franchise*, vol. II no. 8, 1908, 82.

CHAPTER 22: FORCE MAJEURE

1　E. Pankhurst, *My Own Story*, 111.

2　*Shrewsbury Chronicle*, 19 June 1908, 9.

3　*The Times*, 20 June 1908, 5.

4　*The Times*, 20 June 1908, 5.

5　S. Pankhurst, *The Life of*, 241.

6　Snowden, *Woman Socialist*, 258.

7　E. Pankhurst, *My Own Story*, 58.

8　Purvis, *Emmeline Pankhurst*, 99.

9　E. Pankhurst, *My Own Story*, 58.

10　Annie Kenney, *Memories of a Militant*. London: Edward Arnold, 1924, 138.

11　E. Pankhurst, *My Own Story*, 52.

12　E. Pankhurst, *My Own Story*, 66.

13　S. Pankhurst, *The Life of*, 72.

14　*Kalgoorlie Miner*, 21 January 1908, 5.

15　S. Pankhurst, *The Life of*, 185–187.

16　TWL PC/08.

17　TWL PC/08.

18　letter from Nellie Martel to Mary Ann Rawle, 1909, TWL 7/MAR/04/09.

19　Frederick Pethick-Lawrence, cited in E. Pankhurst, *My Own Story*, 111.

20　S. Pankhurst, *The Suffragette*, 245; unidentified clipping files, TWL 10/01.

21　E. Pankhurst, *My Own Story*, 111.

22　S. Pankhurst, *The Suffragette*, 246.

23　'Half a million in Hyde Park', unidentified clipping files, TWL 10/01.

24　The phrase is Nellie's. *Votes for Women*, no. 14, 1908, 236.

25 No evidence exists of the contents of Nellie Martel's speech at the Hyde Park demonstration. These words are taken from reports of a speech she delivered at an open air meeting in Leicester in September 1907. *Women's Franchise*, 19 September 1907, 132 and in a report published in *Women's Franchise* summing up the Colne Valley by-election campaign. *Women's Franchise*, no. 5, 1907, 65 and her address to north-west Manchester in April 1908, reported in full in the *Manchester Guardian* and reprinted in *Votes for Women*, 16 April 1908, cxc; 'Women's Suffrage in Australia', *Manchester Guardian*, 3 September 1908, 12.

26 'Votes for Women', *Daily Mirror*, nd, clipping files, TWL 10/01. The statement is in relation to Mrs Pankhurst's platform but the circumstance was general.

27 'Half a Million in Hyde Park', source unidentified, nd, clipping files, TWL 10/01.

28 *Daily Mail*, quoted in *Votes for Women*, 25 June 1908, 261.

29 'Votes for Women', *Daily Mirror*, nd, clipping files, TWL 10/01.

30 *Daily Mail*, quoted in *Votes for Women*, 25 June 1908, 261.

31 'Votes for Women', *Daily Mirror*, nd, clippings files, TWL 10/01.

CHAPTER 23: A GENEROUS FEELING OF SOLIDARITY

1   E. Pankhurst, *My Own Story*, 115.

2   S. Pankhurst, *The Suffragette*, 249–54.

3   quoted in Purvis, *Emmeline Pankhurst*, 104.

4   Wainwright, *Miss Muriel Matters*, 104.

5   quoted in Wainwright, *Miss Muriel Matters*, 93.

6   Mrs Leonard Matters, *Australians Who Count*, 76.

7   Mrs Leonard Matters, *Australians Who Count*, 76.

8   *Rischbieth Papers* 2004/1/6.

9   Matters, 'My Impressions', 162.

10 Mrs Leonard Matters, *Australians Who Count*, 76.

11 Marion Holmes, Concerning MM, *The Vote* 19/2/1910.

12 Later that month the Liberal Party found another seat for Churchill to contest in a by-election. Despite WFL and WSPU interference, he won the seat and returned to cabinet.

13 quoted in Wainwright, *Miss Muriel Matters*, 102.

14 Marion Holmes, 'Concerning Muriel Matters', *The Vote*, 19 February 1910, 196.

15 Wainwright, *Miss Muriel Matters*, 112.

16 Matters, 'My Impressions', 163.

17 *Women's Franchise*, vol. II, no. 5, 1908, 56.

18 Marion Holmes, 'Concerning Muriel Matters', *The Vote*, 19 February 1910, 196.

19 *Surrey Mirror*, 19 May 1908, 4.

20 'Australian Women In Politics: An Interview with Miss Muriel Matters', *British–Australasian*, 9 February 1911, 9.

21 *Women's Franchise,* 4 September 1908, 583.

22 *Women's Franchise,* 4 September 1908, 583.

23 quoted in Crawford, *Women's Suffrage Movement*, 421.

24 Montefiore, *Victorian to Modern*, Marxist Archive Online, np.

25 http://mentalfloss.com/article/57988/11-unbelievable-moments-cocaines-early-medical-history

26 Crawford, *Women's Suffrage Movement*, 422.

27 Dora Montefiore, 'A Bundle of Fallacies.' *The Social Democrat* 5, no. 2 (15 February 1901), 48–9.

28 Montefiore, *Victorian to Modern*, Marxist Archive Online, np.

29 quoted in Hunt, 'Journeying', 171.

30 There is some evidence that Dora went as a delegate of the WFL, but no evidence that she was ever a member of the WFL. It was not uncommon for women to be members of multiple suffrage associations. Crawford, *Women's Suffrage Movement*, 421.

31 Following the political unrest in Russia in 1905, and an associated Finnish general strike in 1906, Finland demanded democratic reform of its own parliament and constitution. As women had been on the front lines of the general strike, their claim to universal suffrage was considered valid and approved by the Tsar. Finland became the first European nation to grant women the right to vote in 1906, also mandating the eligibility to stand for the unicameral parliament. Though this breakthrough was a triumph for the international women's movement, it was not perceived to be a precedent for the non-European world. Under the arbitrary control of Russia, Finland's success was seen as an inspiring yet ultimately unreliable example for democracies like Great Britain and America. *Finland is old enough and has a creditable history*, explained Carrie Chapman Catt, *but its people are in a state of revolution; what the Czar has given, he may take away.* Zimmern, *Women's Suffrage*, 158.

32 They didn't. The union of South Africa occurred on 31 May 1901, but white South African women didn't get the vote until 1930. South Africa's first all-race elections were held in 1994. Regine Deutsch, *The International Woman Suffrage Alliance: Its History from 1904 to 1929*. Vida Goldstein Memorial Collection Commemorating Women's Achievements in National Development. London 1929, 119.

33 Deutsch, *International Woman Suffrage*, 60–72.

34 Deutsch, *International Woman Suffrage*, 83.

CHAPTER 24: CHAIN GANG

1 'Heat Wave Continues', *Yorkshire Evening Post*, 30 September 1908, 6.

2 *Coventry Evening Telegraph*, 30 September 1908, 2.

3   E. Pankhurst, *My Own Story*, 118.

4   E. Pankhurst, *My Own Story*, 118.

5   quoted in Purvis, *Emmeline Pankhurst*, 113.

6   E. Pankhurst, *My Own Story*, 126.

7   E. Pankhurst, *My Own Story*, 133.

8   *Willesden Chronicle*, 30 October 1908, 7.

9   quoted in Purvis, *Emmeline Pankhurst*, 115.

10 S. Pankhurst, *The Suffragette*, 1911, 328.

11 quoted in Wainwright, *Miss Muriel Matters*, 155.

12 quoted in Crawford, *Women's Suffrage Movement*, 392.

13 *British–Australasian*, 9 February 1911, 9.

14 quoted in Wainwright, *Miss Muriel Matters*, 157.

15 *Rischbieth Papers* 2004/3/392.

16 *Hampshire Telegraph*, 31 October 1908, 4.

17 *Nottingham Evening Post*, 29 October 1908, 3.

18 *Grantham Journal*, 31 October, 1908, 7.

19 S. Pankhurst, *Life of*, 294.

20 Billington-Greig, *Militant Suffrage*, 28.

CHAPTER 25: ROWDY AND REPELLENT

1   According to the unpublished research of Eileen Luscombe, the WFL minutes of 1958 note that Muriel later believed that Helen Fox was a police stooge. Luscombe believes, however, that Fox was the lover of a man who was wealthy and well connected in Fabian circles and she was therefore pulled from further suffragette activities in order to supress her name for fear of scandal to the family. Email correspondence with Eileen Luscombe 12 May 2018.

2   *Sheffield Evening Telegraph*, 29 October 1908, 6.

3   *Gadfly*, 28 October 1908, 15.

4   *Western Mail*, 7 November 1908, 39.

5   *Age*, 12 November 1908, 6.

6   *Advocate*, 5 December 1908, 13.

7   *Age*, 16 December 1908, 12.

8   *Truth*, 23 January 1909, 5.

9   *Molong Argus*, 5 April 1907, 1.

10 *Observer*, 25 January 1908, 24.

11 *Table Talk*, 23 January 1908, 10.

12 *Table Talk*, 30 January 1908, 26.

13 *Register*, 30 October 1908, 4.

14 *Truth*, 10 January 1909, 6. Perle blanc is face powder, made from ground pearls.

15 *Votes for Women*, September 1908, 447.

16 Ann Nugent, 'Sister Suffragettes', *National Library of Australia News*, February 2003, 7.

17 *Manchester Guardian*, 7 November 1908, 11.

18 Nugent, 'Nellie Alma Martel', 156.

19 Nugent, 'Nellie Alma Martel', 156.

20 Purvis, *Emmeline Pankhurst*, 81. Purves' biography of Pankhurst is not concerned with Nellie Martel. She uses this exchange between Robins and Pankhurst as evidence that Emmeline could be caring and thoughtful and not always the narcissist she is often portrayed as.

21 quoted in Nugent, 'Nellie Alma Martel', 156.

22 TWL 7/MAR/04/09.

23 Ethel Hill and Olga Shafer, *Great Suffragists and Why: Modern Makers of History*. London: H.J. Drane, 1909, 172.

24 For an account of Deakin's strategy regarding the Great White Fleet, see Brett, *Enigmatic Mr Deakin*, 365–70.

25 International Woman Suffrage Alliance, *Report of the Fourth Conference of the International Woman Suffrage Alliance, Amsterdam, 1908*. Amsterdam: F. Van Rossen, 1908, 84.

26 Bomford, *That Dangerous*, 88.

27 International Woman Suffrage Alliance, *Report of the Fourth Conference*, 84.

28 *Women's Franchise*, vol. II 28, 1909, 330.

29 *Women's Franchise*, vol. II 28, 1909, 330.

30 'Miss Goldstein Joyful', *Progress*, January 1909, 4.

CHAPTER 26: FIGHT AND FLIGHT

1 *Weekly Times*, 25 June 1901, quoted in Wainwright, *Miss Muriel Matters*, 196.

2 *Colac Herald*, 26 February 1909, 6.

3 *Queensland Figaro*, 11 February 1909, 15.

4 *Northern Daily Telegraph*, 17 February 1909, 2.

5 quoted in Wainwright, *Miss Muriel Matters*, 198.

6 *The Times*, 17 February 1909, 10.

7 *Hull Daily Mail*, 17 February 1909, 3.

8 *The Observer*, 21 February 1909, 6.

CHAPTER 27: THE ENVY OF THE WORLD

1 *British–Australasian*, 23 March 1911, 22.

2 *British–Australasian*, 23 March 1911, 22.

3 *Argus*, 30 November 1909, 8.

4 *Riverine Herald*, 6 December 1909, 3.

5   *Brisbane Telegraph*, 15 January 1910, 11.

6   *Worker*, 10 February 1910, 7.

7   Goldstein, 'The Political Woman in Australia', 108.

8   *Hamilton Spectator*, 16 February 1910, 3.

9   *The British-Australasian*, 23 March 1911, 22.

10 Deakin, *Federated Australia*, 19 April 1910, 284.

11 Brett, *Enigmatic Mr Deakin*, 393.

12 Fisher papers NLA MS 2919, 9c, Box 5, folder 26.

13 David Day, *Andrew Fisher: Prime Minister of Australia*. Sydney: Fourth Estate, 2008, 192.

14 Fisher papers, MS 2919, 9c, Box 5, folder 25.

15 Fisher papers, MS 2919, 9c, Box 5, folder 25.

16 quoted in Day, *Andrew Fisher*, 190.

17 Spence, *Australia's Awakening*, 496.

18 Spence, *Australia's Awakening*, 625.

19 Spence, *Australia's Awakening*, 16.

20 Spence, *Australia's Awakening*, 16.

21 Spence, *Australia's Awakening*, 625. Its secondary objective was *The securing of the full results of their industry to all producers by the collective ownership of monopolies.*

22 Spence, *Australia's Awakening*, 582.

23 Spence, *Australia's Awakening*, 595.

24 *Star*, 4 March, 1910, 4.

25 *Melbourne Advocate*, 5 March 1910, 24.

26 *South Eastern Times*, 6 May 1910, 3.

27 Vida disagreed with Deakin's position on the Financial Agreement and laid out her reasoning against the constitutional change that would be required to administer it (there was also a referendum question on the issue to be posed at the ballot box on election day).

28 *Australasian*, 12 March 1910, 38.

29 *Punch*, 13 April 1910, 22.

30 *Argus* 13 April 1910, 4.

31 *Age*, 5 April 1910, 8.

32 *Mt Alexander Mail*, 24 March 1910, 2.

33 *Kerang New Times*, 25 March 1910, 5.

34 *Evening Telegraph*, 8 April 1910, 5.

35 *Truth*, 28 May 1910, 6.

36 David Day, *Andrew Fisher*, 191.

37 *Votes for Women*, 29 July 1910, 734.

38   *Votes for Women* 13 May 1910, 531.

39   *Progress*, June 1910, 3.

40   *Woman's Journal*, 8 April 1911, 107.

41   *The British-Australasian*, 23 March 1911, 22.

42   Australia's first female prime minister, Julia Gillard, would claim this same achievement after she was rolled from office by an internal party revolt in June 2013. *Australian*, 29 June 2013, online.

43   *Gympie Times and Mary River Mining Gazette*, 16 April 1910, 2.

44   *Numurkah Leader*, 27 May 1910, 4.

45   Deakin, 8 March 1910, *Federated Australia*, 280.

46   Deakin, 19 April 1910, *Federated Australia*, 284.

47   Martel, *Women's Vote*, 10.

CHAPTER 28: HOMECOMING QUEEN

1   Crawford, *Women's Suffrage Movement*, 179.

2   Deutsch, *International Woman Suffrage*, 15.

3   quoted in Wainwright, *Miss Muriel Matters*, 214.

4   E. Pankhurst, *My Own Story*, 166.

5   Matters, 'Our Australian Tour', *The Vote*, 1 October 1910, 267.

6   quoted in Wainwright , *Miss Muriel Matters*, 210.

7   *Bendigo Independent*, 26 August 1909, 7.

8   *Newcastle Morning Herald*, 6 December 1906, 3.

9   Matters, unpublished obituary of Violet Tillard, MMS.

10   Matters, 'Our Australian Tour', *The Vote*, 1 October 1910, 267.

11   *Truth*, 14 May 1910, 11.

12   Matters, 'Our Australian Tour', *The Vote*, 1 October 1910, 267.

13   *West Australian*, 11 May 1910, 9.

14   Perth *Daily News*, 1 April 1910, 10; *Bendigo Independent*, 26 Aug 1909, 7.

15   *West Australian*, 11 May 1910, 9.

16   *Daily News*, 14 May 1910, 5.

17   *Daily News*, 14 May 1910, 5.

18   *Truth*, 28 May 1910, 6.

19   *Advertiser*, 13 June 1910, 8.

20   *Melbourne Leader*, 11 June 1910, 45.

21   *Advertiser*, 13 June 1910, 8.

22   Maternal mortality rates worldwide did not begin to decrease until the 1930s. Sixty years later, in developed countries, the rates were one-fiftieth of what they had been earlier in the century. http://ajcn.nutrition.org/content/72/1/241s. full

23 *Daily News,* 20 May 1910, 5.

24 *West Australian*, 20 May 1910, 4.

25 *Bunbury Herald*, 24 May 1910, 3.

26 *West Australian*, 24 May 1910, 2.

27 Matters, 'Our Australian Tour', *The Vote*, 1 October 1910, 267.

28 *Daily Herald*, 4 June 1910, 5.

29 *Western Mail,* 28 May 1910, 40.

30 *Western Mail*, 28 May 1910, 40.

31 Adelaide *Advertiser,* 1 June 1910, 8.

32 *Critic*, 1 June 1910, 15.

33 *Critic*, 1 June 1910 ,14.

34 *Evening Journal*, 14 June 1910, 2; *Chronicle*, 18 June 1910, 54.

35 *Evening Journal*, 14 June 1910, 2.

36 *Chronicle*, 18 June 1910, 54. Catherine Helen Spence died on 3 April 1910, aged 85.

37 Billington-Greig, *Militant Suffrage*, 140.

38 *Chronicle*, 18 June 1910, 54.

39 *Evening Journal,* 14 June 1910, 2.

40 *Evening Journal*, 14 June 1910, 2.

41 *Benalla Standard*, 4 July 1910, 3.

42 The quote is Lady Lytton's. June Purvis, Force feeding of Hunger Striking Suffragettes, https://www.timeshighereducation.com/news/force-feeding-of-hunger-striking-suffragettes/93438.article

43 *Benalla Standard*, 4 July 1910, 3.

44 *Age*, 20 June 1910, 7.

45 *Hobart Mercury*, 5 September 1910, 3.

46 Matters, 'Our Australian Tour,' *The Vote*, 1 October 1910, 267.

47 Matters, *The Christian Commonwealth*, 21 December 1910.

48 *Gippsland Times*, 23 January 1911 2; *Table Talk*, 23 June 1919, 10.

49 *Barrier Miner*, 10 April 1901, 2.

50 *West Australian*, 20 June 1910, 5.

51 *Weekly Times*, 25 June 1910, 10.

52 Goldstein, Diary, 1908.

53 *Benalla Standard*, 5 July 1910, 3.

54 *West Gippsland Gazette*, 12 July 1910, 2.

55 *Clarence and Richmond Examiner*, 5 July 1910, 5.

56 *Bathurst Times*, 15 July 1910, 2; *Worker*, 21 July 1910, 3.

57 *Worker*, 21 July 1910, 3.

58 *Worker*, 21 July 1910, 3.

59 *Argus*, 23 July 1910, 16.

60 *Argus*, 26 July 1910, 8.

61 *Hansard*, House of Representatives, 22 July 1910, 683.

62 *The Vote*, 8 October 1910, 287. Muriel mentions the luncheon party in the published report of her Australian tour, but not the menu. This detail I have fabricated from other luncheon menus of a similar social ilk during this era.

63 *Evening Star*, 2 September 1910, 3.

64 *Evening Star*, 2 September 1910, 3.

65 *Evening Star*, 2 September 1910, 3.

66 Matters, 'Our Australian Tour,' *The Vote*, 1 October 1910, 267.

CHAPTER 29: THOUGH DISASTER WAS FREELY PROPHESIED

1   Turner, *The First Decade*, 308.

2   Deakin, *Federated Australia*, 284

3   Turner, *The First Decade*, 308.

4   *The Vote*, 21 January 1911, 157.

5   A. Frank Farrell, 'Rae, Arthur Edward (1860–1943)', *Australian Dictionary of Biography*, National Centre of Biography, Australian National University, http://adb.anu.edu.au/biography/rae-arthur-edward-8148/text14237, published first in hardcopy 1988, accessed online 21 December 2017.

6   *Hansard*, Senate, 17 November 1910, 6300–14.

7   *The Vote*, 21 January 1911, 157.

8   *Common Cause*, 10 February 1910, republished in People's Suffrage Federation leaflet no. 25, TWL @ LSE PC/06/396–11/35

9   Matters, *Christian Commonwealth*, 21 December 1910.

10 Matters, *Christian Commonwealth*, 21 December 1910.

11 *Hansard*, 22 November 1910.

12 Matters, *Christian Commonwealth*, 21 December 1910.

13 Millicent Garrett Fawcett, *Women's Suffrage: A Short History of a Great Movement*. London: TC and EC Jack, 1912, 43.

14 IWSA, *Report of Sixth Congress*, President's Address.

15 *Sydney Morning Herald*, 9 August 1911, 5.

16 E. Pankhurst, *My Own Story*, 166.

17 *Yorkshire Observer*, 12 November 1910. Derby *Daily Telegraph*, 12 November 1910, 2.

18 E. Pankhurst, *My Own Story*, 179.

19 S. Pankhurst, *Life of*, 97.

20 The description is taken from a published report about the violence on 18 November compiled from witness and victim statements. Quoted in Purvis, *Emmeline Pankhurst*, 150.

21 Linklater, Andro. *An Unhusbanded Life: Charlotte Despard, Suffragette, Socialist and Sinn Feiner.* London: Hutchinson, 1980, 140.

22 Linklater, *An Unhusbanded Life*, 140.

23 quoted in Purvis, *Emmeline Pankhurst*, 151.

24 *Coventry Evening Telegraph*, 18 November 1910, 3.

25 quoted in Purvis, *Emmeline Pankhurst*, 151.

26 Purvis, *Emmeline Pankhurst*, 154; Crawford, *Women's Suffrage Movement*, 154. Mary Clarke, imprisoned for throwing a stone through a window, was released two days before Christmas. She could not last out the family meal, forsaking turkey for a lie down. When Emmeline went upstairs to check on her ailing sister, she found Mary unconscious, dying of a brain haemorrhage. Emmeline spent the night in bed with daughter Sylvia, *clung together...stunned by our sorrow.* Emmeline had lost her son, her mother and her sister within a year.

CHAPTER 30: THE WONDER YEAR

1 C. Pankhurst, *Unshackled*, 172.

2 E. Pankhurst, *My Own Story*, 18.

3 S. Pankhurst, *The Suffragette*, 98.

4 Purvis, *Emmeline Pankhurst*, 154.

5 Billington-Greig wrote this in the book she would publish later in 1911, *The Militant Suffrage Movement*, sub-titled, 'Emancipation in a Hurry'.

6 Purvis, *Emmeline Pankhurst*, 155.

7 S. Pankhurst, *The Suffragette*, np.

CHAPTER 31: THE HEART OF THE ACTION

1 *Review of Reviews*, February 1911, xxxi.

2 *Punch*, 16 February 1911, 22.

3 All quotes in this section from *Woman Voter*, 6 March 1911, 1.

4 *Melbourne Advocate*, 9 July 1910, 26.

5 *Box Hill Reporter*, 14 May 1909, 7.

6 *Box Hill Reporter*, 14 May 1909, 7.

7 *Argus*, 21 October 1909, 8.

8 *Votes for Women*, vol. 3, no. 108, 1910, 426.

9 *Review of Reviews*, February 1911.

10 *Review of Reviews*, May 1911. Judkins was anti-suffrage, too, at least where British women were concerned.

11 Newfoundland had not yet joined the federation of Canadian provinces. New Zealand had by now determined that it would never join the Australian federation, though the possibility was still contemplated, at least by Australian politicians, until at least 1902.

12 *Review of Reviews*, July 1911.

13 Vida Goldstein, *Woman Suffrage in Australia*, 1911, VG Papers, TWL.

14 Montefiore, *Victorian to Modern*, Marxist Archive Online, np.

15 Montefiore, *Victorian to Modern*, Marxist Archive Online, np.

16 Montefiore, *Victorian to Modern*, Marxist Archive Online, np.

17 Syndicated to *Clarence and Richmond Examiner*, 24 May 1910, 5.

18 *Bega Gazette*, 15 July 1899, 2.

19 *Critic*, 25 January 1911, 18.

20 Montefiore, *Victorian to Modern*, Marxist Archive Online, np.

21 'Our Comrade Dora B. Montefiore in Melbourne', *Justice*, 21 January 1911, 2.

22 Montefiore, 'A Labour Party in Power I', *Justice*, 15 April 1911, 15.

23 Montefiore, 'A Labour Party in Power I', *Justice*, 15 April 1911, 15.

24 *Crookwell Gazette*, 31 January 1911, 2.

25 Montefiore, 'A Labour Party in Power II', *Justice*, 22 April 1911, 15.

26 *Singleton Argus*, 31 January 1911, 4.

27 *Goulburn Evening Penny Post*, 28 January 1911, 6.

28 Letter of Muriel Matters to Bessie Rischbieth, 2 December 1910, *Rischbieth Papers*, MS 2004/3/1.

CHAPTER 32: OUR VIDA

1 *Woman Voter*, 6 March 1911, 11.

2 *Worker*, 11 May 1911, 7.

3 *Goldstein Papers*, SLV, MS 7865.

4 *British-Australasian*, 9 February 1911, 9.

5 *Portsmouth Evening News*, 23 March 1911, 8.

6 In this quest, Muriel would be guided by the teachings of Mary Baker Eddy, the founder of the Christian Scientists, who had died aged eighty-nine on 3 December 1910. Eddy's spiritual leadership was contained in her landmark book, *Science and Health with a Key to the Scriptures*, the work that had influenced Vida Goldstein in her conversion to Christian Science. Vida, it appears, had laid more than one path for Muriel during her recent trip to Australia.

7 Crawford, Elizabeth, ed. *Campaigning for the Vote: Kate Parry Frye's Suffrage Diary*. London: Francis Boutle, 2013, 39.

8 Vida's own report of the meeting, *Woman Voter*, 1 June 1911, 1.

9 *Woman Voter*, 1 May 1911, 3. *The Woman Voter*, edited by Vida's sister Aileen in Vida's absence, reported the UK tour in detail.

10 *Worker*, 11 May 1911, 7.

11 *Woman Voter*, 1 May 1911, 3.

12 Bomford, *That Dangerous and Persuasive*, 105.

13 *Rischbieth Papers*, 2004/4/232.

14 *Woman Voter*, 11 October 1917, 2.

15 *Votes for Women*, vol. 4, no. 155, 1911, 339.

16 S. Pankhurst, *The Suffragette Movement*, 394.

17 Kenney, *Memories*, 139.

18 *Rischbieth Papers*, 2004/1/12. Bessie was in London for four months in 1913. This remark is contained in letter to her niece written on 18 July 1913.

19 *Manchester Guardian*, 25 March 1911, 6.

20 *Votes for Women*, 31 March 1911, no. 160, 419.

21 C. Pankhurst, *Unshackled*, 172.

22 June Purvis, *Christabel Pankhurst: A Biography*. London and New York: Routledge, 2018, 242.

23 E. Pethick-Lawrence, *My Part*, 254.

24 *Rischbieth Papers*, MS 2004/4/1–44, Florence Rankin to Vida Goldstein, 25 March, 1911.

25 At only thirty-two years of age, Williams had already recorded hundreds of commercially popular ditties and music hall songs with titles like *When Father Papered the Parlour* and *Little Willie's Woodbines*. Williams had first gone to London in 1899, where he made his name as Australia's first pop recording star. He returned to tour Australia in 1910 where, like Muriel, touring her homeland in the same year, he was greeted as a prodigal son. It was during that tour that Williams penned *The Land Where the Women Wear the Trousers*. www.move.com.au/disc/australias-billy-williams

26 *Rischbieth Papers*, MS 2004/4/1–44, Florence Rankin to Vida Goldstein, 25 March 1911.

27 Brisbane *Truth*, 2 April 1911, 6.

28 The Australian Women's National League was established in 1904 to safeguard monarchy and empire while combating socialism and protecting the interests of women and the home. By 1908 it had 10,000 members in Victoria alone, by far the largest women's organisation. The AWNL campaigned for suffrage in Victoria, helping to convince conservative politicians that not all female voters would be of a socialist persuasion like Vida Goldstein and the Women's Political Association. The AWNL played a pivotal role in the formation of the Australian Liberal Party. For a discussion of the influence and impact of the AWNL on Australian democracy see Marian Quartly, 'The Australian Women's National League and Democracy, 1904–1921', *Women's History Review*, vol. 15, 2001, 35–50.

29 *Queenslander*, 13 May 1911, 5.

30 *Perth Western Mail*, 25 March 1911, 20.

31 *Riverine Herald*, 24 March 1911, 2.

32 *West Australian*, 29 March 1911, 6.

33 Melbourne *Weekly Times*, 29 April 1911, 9.

34 *Age*, 28 March 1911, 6.

35 Melbourne *Punch*, 30 March 1911, 32.

36 *British-Australasian*, 23 March 1911, 22.

CHAPTER 33: COUNTING FOR NOTHING

1   Montefiore, 'The "Conciliation" Bill', *Justice*, 23 July 1910, 7.

2   *Brisbane Telegraph*, 4 April 1911, 2.

3   Kenney, *Memories*, 168.

4   Christabel Pankhurst predicted that the census would be used as ammunition for increased interference in women's lives, particularly working-class women. C. Pankhurst, *Unshackled*, 143.

5   Jill Liddington attributes the first mention of the census protest to a WFL National Executive Committee meeting in June 1910. Dora's article was first published on 23 July but was likely written earlier as Dora was in America from April to October 1910. Dora Montefiore and Edith How-Martyn were in prison together and may well have continued a friendship or correspondence.

6   *Dundee Evening Telegraph*, 9 March 1911, 2.

7   *Birmingham Mail*, 27 March 1911, 2.

8   *Bath Chronicle and Weekly Gazette*, 30 March 1911, 8.

9   *Dundee Evening Telegraph*, 9 March 1911, 2.

10 Diane Atkinson, *The Suffragettes in Pictures*. London: Museum of London, 1996, 98.

11 E. Pankhurst, *My Own Story*, 191.

12 *Hampstead and Highgate Express*, 25 March 1911, 5.

13 *World News Sydney*, 1 April 1911, 14.

14 Jill Liddington, *Vanishing for the Vote: Suffrage, Citizenship and the Battle for the Census*. Manchester: Manchester University Press, 2014, 173.

15 Kenney, *Memories*, 110.

16 Crawford, *Campaigning*, 42. Unless otherwise cited, all details of census night evasion from Liddington, *Vanishing*.

17 quoted in Wainwright, *Miss Muriel Matters*, 252. Tilly wrote a version of the same sentiment: *No Vote No Census. Should women become persons in the eyes of the law this session—full information will be forwarded.* Margaret Jewson was also registered as present at 91 Fentiman Road that night.

18 Purvis, *Emmeline Pankhurst*, 159.

19 Liddington, *Vanishing*, 248.

20 *West Australian*, 4 April 1911, 7.

21 *Globe*, 29 March 1911, 4.

22 *Gloucestershire Echo*, 24 March 1911, 3.

23 *Gloucestershire Echo*, 24 March 1911, 3.

24 *Gloucestershire Echo*, 5 April 1911, 4.

25 E. Pankhurst, *My Own Story*, 193.

26 Goldstein, 'Woman Suffrage in Australia'.

27 A 1907 Commonwealth report concluded that *an enumeration of them has never been seriously undertaken in connection with any state census.*

28 Northcott, *Australian Social Development*, 158.

29 *Review of Reviews*, May 1911.

30 *Review of Reviews*, May 1911, June 1911.

31 Dora Montefiore, 'Australian Workers Condemn the Coronation', *Justice*, 6 May 1911, 1.

32 Reminiscences of Peggy Fisher, *Fisher Papers*, NLA, MS 2919 Box 5, folder 26.

CHAPTER 34: A FESTIVAL OF EMPIRE

1 Scott, 'How Australia Led the Way', 22.

2 'The Press Boycott', *Votes for Women*, 28 April, 1911, vol. 4, no. 164, 490. Emmeline Pankhurst published articles about the Resolution, reproducing it in full, on 6 January and 13 January 1911 in *Votes for Women*. 'Australia's Advice'—a report of the debate of the Australian Senate on the Votes for Women resolution on 17 November 1910, was published by the Woman's Press as a penny pamphlet.

3 *Dublin Daily Express*, 5 May 1911, 10.

4 Goldstein, 'How the Vote Was Won in Australia', 10.

5 Goldstein, 'How the Vote Was Won in Australia', 9.

6 *Votes for Women*, 'In Honour of Miss Goldstein', vol. 4, no. 166, 1911, 532.

7 Stella Miles Franklin in *Goldstein Papers*.

8 *Votes for Women*, 26 May 1911, 558.

9 *Kalgoorlie Sun*, 26 February 1911, 8.

10 A.J.R, *The Suffrage Annual*, 1913.

11 Goldstein, 'How Australia Gave Women Votes,' *Votes for Women*, vol. 4, no. 165, 1911, 513.

12 Margaret Bettison, 'Newcomb, Harriet Christina (1854–1942)', *Australian Dictionary of Biography*, National Centre of Biography, Australian National University, http://adb.anu.edu.au/biography/newcomb-harriet-christina-13270/text23471, published first in hardcopy 2005, accessed online 14 March 2018.

13 quoted in Woollacott, *Metropolitan Activism*, 209.

14 To the British government's relief, there had been no local repercussions after the tragic Shirtwaist factory fire in New York City on 25 March, the deadliest industrial catastrophe in the city's history, in which 146 garment workers were killed—123 of them women, mostly Jewish and Italian immigrants aged sixteen to twenty-three. Those who didn't die in the blaze were killed when they jumped from the upper floors of the burning building, where workers were locked in to prevent them taking breaks. The fire led to a steep rise in union membership, an idea exercising the minds of the 11,000 Singer Manufacturing strikers in Scotland who had only recently gone back to work. Four hundred of

the 'ringleaders' of the strike were sacked, precipitating further unionisation of the manufacturing sector.

15 India, Malaya and other Crown colonies were classified differently: as dependencies, not British Dominions—of which there was a sixth, the Irish Free State.

16 *Review of Reviews*, July 1911.

17 *Northern Whig*, 13 May 1911, 7.

18 Dora Montefiore, 'Pageants', *Justice*, 16 April 1910, 5.

19 *Review of Reviews*, September 1911.

20 *Punch*, 16 February 1911, 22.

21 *Punch*, 16 February 1911, 22.

22 *Review of Reviews*, December 1911.

CHAPTER 35: AN INCONVENIENT PERIOD OF DOMESTIC CLEANING

1 The record for the hottest July day was set in 1911 and not broken until 2006.

2 *The Times*, 28 July 1911. Quoted in http://www.independent.co.uk/environment/long-hot-summer-the-great-british-heatwave-of-1911-5329910.html

3 *Fisher papers*, NLA MS 2919 Box 5, folder 26.

4 Northcott, *Australian Social Development*, 20.

5 Diane Langmore, 'Prime Ministers' Wives: Women in the Background.' In *Makers of Miracles: The Cast of the Federation Story*, edited by David Williams and John Headon. Melbourne: Melbourne University Publishing, 2000, 120.

6 Diane Langmore, *Prime Minister's Wives: The Public and Private Lives of Ten Australian Women*. Melbourne: McPhee Gribble, 1992, 27.

7 *Review of Reviews*, July 1911, 450.

8 Thos. McKernall of Miners' Union, Kilmarnock, quoted in Day, *Andrew Fisher*, 226.

9 *Votes for Women*, vol. 4, no. 169, 1911, 577.

10 *Kalgoorlie Sun*, 30 April 1911, 13. Muriel's engagement was reported widely in Australia.

11 *The Times*, 3 June 1911, 7. The visit of the NUWSS deputation was also reported by the *Morning Post*, the *Daily Telegraph*, the *Morning Leader* and other papers, in a clear indication that the press boycott was suspended at least while the Australian PM was in town.

12 Fawcett, *Women's Suffrage*, 42.

13 *The Common Cause*, vol. 3, no. 113, 154.

14 *The Times*, 3 June 1911, 7.

15 The Women's Library, LSE, 7VDG

16 *Votes for Women*, vol. 4, no. 172, 1911, 633.

17 *The New York Clipper*, 3 June 1911, 12.

18 *Mid Sussex Times*, 22 June 1911, 6.

19 *Pall Mall Gazette*, 24 June 1911.

20 *Morning Post*, 20 June 1911. Reprinted in *Sheffield Daily Telegraph*, 20 June 1911, 7.

21 Day, *Andrew Fisher*, 228.

22 Mitchell, J. Malcolm. *Colonial Statesmen and Votes for Women: Lord Curzon Answered.* London: Women's Freedom League, 1912.

23 quoted in Souter, *Lion and Kangaroo*, 197.

24 William Lyne was a veteran political player who was, at that stage, a pro-Labor independent in the Federal Parliament.

25 *Daily Telegraph*, 20 June 1911.

26 *Morning Post*, 21 June 1911.

27 *Daily Chronicle*, 30 June 1911.

28 *New-York Tribune*, 26 June 1911.

29 *Shepherd diary*, NAA, A1632, 1, part 2, 32.

30 *Shepherd diary*, NAA, A1632, 1, part 2, 32.

31 *The Times*, 30 June 1911.

32 *Liverpool Courier*, 5 July 1911.

33 *The Times*, 1 August 1911, 13.

34 *Hobart Mercury* 2 August 1911, 5.

35 A. Patriot was the pseudonym of artist and illustrator Alfred Pearse. Pearse was a weekly contributor to *Votes for Women* and also designed posters for the suffrage campaign. With Laurence Houseman, he set up the Suffrage Atelier in 1909, a collective of male and female artists dedicated to votes for women.

36 *Review of Reviews*, July 1911.

37 *Review of Reviews*, June 1911.

38 Adelaide *Register*, 12 June 1911, 7.

39 Purvis, *Emmeline Pankhurst*, 162.

40 *Woman Voter*, 1 July 1911, 5.

41 *Votes for Women*, vol. iv, no. 164, 1911, 489.

42 *Votes for Women*, 12 May 1911, 523.

43 *Woman Voter*, 1 July 1911, 5.

44 *Votes for Women*, vol. 4, no. 166, 1911, 523.

45 *The Vote*, 13 May 1911, 27.

46 *The Vote*, 3 June 1911, 66.

47 *The Vote*, 20 May 1911, 42.

48 *The Vote*, 10 June 1911, 83.

49 *The Vote*, 24 June 1911, 110.

50 *The Vote*, 10 June 1911, 83.

51 *The Vote*, 10 June 1911, 83.

52 Robins, Elizabeth. *Way Stations*. London: Hodder and Soughton, 1913, 248.

53 *Common Cause*, 22 June 1911, 214.

54 *Woman Voter*, 1 July 1911, 1.

55 *Woman Voter*, 10 September 1912, 2.

56 Mr Stephens, California, US House of Representatives, 12 January 1915, National American Woman Suffrage, 1915.

57 *Votes for Women*, 19 May 1911, 549.

58 *Votes for Women*, 12 May 1911, 533.

59 *Votes for Women*, 19 May 1911, 549.

60 IWSA, *Report of 6th Congress*.

61 *The Dover Express and East Kent News*, 2 June 1911. 5.

62 Robins, *Way Stations*, 252.

63 *Votes for Women*, 9 June 1911, 595.

CHAPTER 36: THE GREATEST PROCESSION KNOWN IN HISTORY

1 Beatrice Harraden to Vida Goldstein, *Rischbieth Papers*, MS 2004/4/1–44.

2 E. Pethick-Lawrence, *My Part in a Changing World*, 84.

3 Adelaide *Register*, 12 June 1911, 7.

4 C. Pankhurst, *Unshackled*, 185. Vida evidently worked herself to the bone to make the procession a success. George Bernard Shaw wrote to her two days before the march, *Dear Miss Goldstein, No matter how much you may be occupied with the Procession, you must eat, unless you wish it to be your funeral procession. Why not eat here? Will you lunch with us tomorrow (Friday) at 1.30pm?* Goldstein papers, SLV, MS 8648.

5 quoted in Tickner, *Spectacle of Women*, 66.

6 C. Pankhurst, *Unshackled*, 184.

7 C. Pankhurst, *Unshackled*, 184.

8 E. Pethick-Lawrence, *My Part in a Changing World*, 254.

9 *Review of Reviews*, September 1911.

10 *The Vote*, 24 June 1911, 111.

11 *Melbourne Weekly Times*, 29 July 1911, 13.

12 E. Pethick-Lawrence, *My Part in a Changing World*, 254.

13 Robins, *Come and See*, 250.

14 *Age*, 26 July 1911, 12.

15 Miss E.M. Doberer, *Clarence and Richmond Examiner*, 10 August 1911, 7.

16 quoted in *A Changing World*, 253. Same for other quotes in the following paragraphs.

17 *Review of Reviews*, September 1911.

18 *The Vote*, 24 June 1911, 110.

19 Robins, *Come and See*, 246.

20 Crawford, *Campaigning*, 54.

21 *The Vote*, 24 June 1911, 110.

22 This is a rare find. Many thanks to Eileen Luscombe for sharing her copy with me.

23 Jessie Ackermann, *Australia*, vii. Miss Majorie Birks and Miss Moore are holding the banner.

24 *Age*, 26 July 1911, 12.

25 It is probable that the other two are Lady Cockburn and Lady Macmillan, the next most politically and socially prominent women to march in the Australian contingent.

26 *British-Australasian*, 22 June 1911, 19.

27 *Woman Voter*, 1 July 1911, 5.

28 By 1911 developments in photographic technology meant that subjects did not have to stand still for long periods of time to take a clear image. A prolonged exposure cannot account for the tension in the women's faces and postures. With thanks to Jane Lydon for advice on the history of photography.

29 *Weekly Times*, 29 July 1911, 13.

30 *Fisher papers*, MS 2919 Box 5, folder 26. Margaret Fisher's hat is on display at the Museum of Democracy at Old Parliament House.

31 *Woman Voter*, 1 July 1911, 5.

32 *Woman Voter*, October 1911. 1.

33 *Manchester Guardian*, 12 June 1911, 8.

34 *Punch*, 22 June 1911, 11.

35 *British-Australasian*, 22 June 1911, 19. See also *Age* 26 July 1911, 12.

36 *Western Mail*, 29 July 1911, 40.

37 *Melbourne Weekly Times*, 29 July 1911, 13.

38 In the spring of 1911, London's artists were asked for advice about how to decorate the city for the Coronation. The *Standard* published a long interview with George Coates regarding his views on the part Australia should play in the embellishment of the royal procession route. His ideas included *a triumphal golden arch surmounted by a gigantic figure of a stock rider* as well as distinctive animals, flowers and fruit. But, according to Dora, his suggestions were overlooked. In the end, *the only part we both took in the coronation festivities was to walk in the women's procession*. Alice Trechmann and Miss Madden are named as the standard bearers of Dora's banner in other reports of the procession. Dora's reminiscences say there were four people carrying the banner, including herself but not George. The identity of a possible fourth bearer remains a mystery.

39 *British-Australasian*, 22 June 1911, 19.

40 *Western Mail*, 29 July 1911, 40.

41 *Launceston Examiner*, 5 August 1911, 2.

42 *Launceston Examiner*, 5 August 1911, 2.

43 *Woman Voter*, 6 April 1911, 8.

44 *Punch*, 27 April 1911, 4. *Punch* always needed a butt for its retrograde humour, and in this case it was not the suffragists, but Fisher himself, whom *Punch* regarded as *a joke...a primeval, practical joke played at the expense of the whole nation.*

45 *Albury Banner and Wodonga Express*, 23 June 1911, 26.

46 Wainwright, *Miss Muriel Matters*, 251–3. How adequately Muriel conveyed her intention to turn down his proposal is unclear, as Treharne did resign from his job at the Conservatorium to sail to London to settle there with his bride.

47 *Bexhill-on-Sea Observer*, 3 June 1911, 4.

48 *Wagga Worker*, 3 August 1911, 23.

49 Letter to *Woman Voter*, 20 July 1911, 1.

50 Letter, Emmeline Pethick-Lawrence to Vida Goldstein, 17 December 1911, TWL, 9/20/063.

CONCLUSION: HISTORY IN THE MAKING

1 Muriel was joined by Dr Marion Phillips, a thirty-year-old Jewish Australian woman who had earned a PhD in political history at the London School of Economics. Phillips became the first Australian woman to be elected to a national parliament when she won a seat in the UK House of Commons in 1929. She was fifty-one years old.

2 quoted in Purvis, *Emmeline Pankhurst*, 189.

3 June Purvis, 'Remembering Emily Wilding Davison (1872–1913)'. *Women's History Review*, 22 (3): 353–62, 358.

4 Purvis, *Emmeline Pankhurst*, 237.

5 *Standard*, 22 April 1911, 3.

6 *Woman Voter*, 10 June 1913, 3.

7 *Woman Voter*, 17 June 1913, 3.

8 *Woman Voter*, 17 June 1913, 1.

9 *Review of Reviews*, September 191, 25.

10 *Review of Reviews*, September 1911. Stead perished on the maiden voyage of the *Titanic* when it sank in April 1912.

11 The Maternity Allowance was paid from general revenue direct to all mothers. (There were, of course, racial exclusions.) The payment was the equivalent of five weeks of a working woman's wages. It was not seen as a dole, but a right, irrespective of whether the mother was 'deserving', 'respectable', rich or poor, married or unmarried. The payment was intended as an entitlement of citizen-mothers as recognition of the costs of bearing children. Marilyn Lake shows that the Maternity Allowance was both popular and well-utilised among

women. See Lake, 'State Socialism', 55–61.

12 *Sydney Sun*, 27 April 1913, 19.

13 Adela Pankhurst Walsh cited in Purvis, *Emmeline Pankhurst*, 249.

14 Ham, Paul. *1914: The Year the World Ended*. North Sydney: Heinemann, 2013, 9. Ham argues that the bourgeois, bohemian 'party' went from 1870 until 1914.

15 Fawcett, *What I Remember*, 236. According to Fawcett, it was not only Asquith who needed a legitimate escape route. Unlike Australian politicians such as Edmund Barton, who had performed abrupt about-faces in their support for the female franchise, all British MPs needed to find *ropes and routes down [to] make their descent safely and with dignity.*

16 Age was not the only qualification (the voting age for men was twenty-one, and the property qualification was abolished for men with this same Act, enfranchising 5.6 million working-class men over twenty-one). To be eligible to vote, women also needed to be either married to a member of the Local Government Register, a property owner or a graduate voting in a university constituency. Unlike Australia, where all natural-born or naturalised women could vote so long as they were not Indigenous, only forty per cent of British women got the franchise in 1918. Women like Annie Kenney were denied the rights that Christabel Pankhurst now had, though they had fought shoulder to shoulder. It would not be until 1928 that British women won electoral equality with men.

17 Historian Sean Scalmer has called on today's historians to resist the temptation to frame the national story 'in martial terms' instead displacing 'the white-citizen soldier' from the centre of the story when there is not sufficient evidence to support such centrality. Sean Scalmer, 'Peace, Patriotism and the Australian Commonwealth: historiographical observations on nations and movements', *History Australia*, 14:2, 2017, 287–8.

18 Bill Gammage, 'Anzac', in John Carroll (ed), *Intruders in the Bush: The Australian Quest for Identity* (Melbourne: Oxford University Press, 1982), 115.

19 Gammage, *'Anzac'*, 115.

20 John Hirst, *Sense and Nonsense in Australian History*, 47. Hirst's essay is a direct response to the publication of Patricia Grimshaw et al's *Creating a Nation*, in which the authors delineate the myriad ways in which Australian women contributed to nation-building.

21 Hirst, *Sense and Nonsense*, 48.

22 *Ovens and Murray Advertiser*, 5 September 1908, 2.

23 Northcott, *Australian Social Development*, 9.

24 *Argus*, 21 August 1908, 7.

25 Lake, 'State Socialism', 55–7.

26 *Boston Woman's Journal*, 6 October 1906, np.

27 Speech to Labor Banquet, published widely, but here *Votes for Women*, vol. 4, no. 169, 1911, 577.

28 One Australian journalist recognised the shift as early as 1916. *The war is*

making us see many things in a new light, he wrote, *A certain youthful tendency to brag that has been characteristic of us, a certain provincial narrowness and superiority, and a consequent rudeness to other peoples are no longer befitting a nation that is entitled to inscribe 'Anzac' on its banners. Sun*, 10 December, 1916. For a longer discussion of this argument, see Clare Wright, '"A Splendid Object Lesson": A Transnational Perspective on the Birth of the Australian Nation'. *Journal of Women's History*, 26(4), 2014, 12–36; Lake, Marilyn. '1914: Death of a Nation.' *History Australia* 12, no. 1 (2015): 7–24.

29　*Kalgoorlie Miner*, 11 April 1916, 5.

30　*Truth*, 11 June 1916, 7.

31　Maureen Castens to Ms G. Hart, 12 January 1988 NAA: A463 1987/2824.

32　'Women's Banner is Coming Home', *National Times*, 11 October 1987 NAA A463 1987/3770.

33　Susan Ryan, 24 December 1987, NAA: A463 1987/2824.

34　Dale Spender to Gillian Bonham, 30 June 1987 Women's Suffrage Banner Historical Research Report, NAA A463 1987/3770.

35　The NWCC was an umbrella organisation representing sixteen women's associations, *more traditional women's organisations and feminists alike.* Briefing to the Prime Minister by Sue Brooks, January 1988. NAA A463 1987/3770.

36　James Mollison to Edith Hall, Appendix, Women's Suffrage Banner Historical Research Report NAA A463 1987/3770.

37　The ACTU's request was denied.

38　Di Lucas to NWCC Banner Task Force, 5 January 1988, NAA: A463 1987/2824.

39　Sue Heard to Edith Hall, 7 January 1988, NAA: A463 1987/2824.

40　Edith Hall to Di Lucas, 29 January 1988, NAA: A463 1987/2824.

41　Andrea Coelli, 'Historic Banner Returns', *Canberra Times*, 9 March 1988, 18.

42　Office of the Status of Women, news release, 8 March 1988, NAA A463 1987/3770.

43　Coelli, 'Historic Banner Returns', *Canberra Times*, 9 March 1988, 18.

44　Conservation of Australian Women's Suffrage Banner, NAA A463 1988/3222 part 1.

45　On 12 June 2002 custodianship of the banner was fully transferred to the Parliament House Gifts Collection to mark the 100th anniversary of women's suffrage in Australia. In December 2003 the Royal Australian Mint celebrated the centenary of women's suffrage with the release of a dollar coin based on a representation of the banner. Approximately ten million of the one-dollar 'suffrage coins' were minted.

46　Women's Suffrage Banner Historical Research Report NAA A463 1987/3770. My many attempts to locate and contact Dale Spender to confirm whether the kit was printed were not successful.

Select Bibliography

ABBREVIATIONS

LSE – London School of Economics and Political Science
ML – Mitchell Library, State Library of NSW
MMS – Muriel Matters Society, Adelaide
NAA – National Archives of Australia
NLA – National Library of Australia
SLV – State Library of Victoria
TWL – The Women's Library, London

PRIMARY SOURCES

A.J.R. *The Suffrage Annual and Women's Who's Who*. London: Stanley Paul, 1913.

Ackermann, Jessie. *Australia from a Woman's Point of View*. London: Cassell, 1913.

—. *What Women Have Done with the Vote*. New York: WM Feakins, 1913.

anon. 'Australian Women in Politics.' *British-Australasian*, 1911.

anon. 'Not Prophecy but History.' 1908? *Nineteenth Century Collections Online*, Gale Group.

anon. 'Our Comrade Dora B. Montefiore in Melbourne.' *Justice*, 21 January 1911.

anon. 'Womanhood Suffrage Justified: What Australia Says.' London: People's Suffrage Federation, 1910?

Artists' Suffrage League. 1911, NA1047, TWL, LSE.

Australian Women's Suffrage Banner. 1990. National Women's Consultative Council of Australia, ML, MS Q929.92 4.

Billington-Greig, Teresa. *The Militant Suffrage Movement: Emancipation in a Hurry*. London: Frank Palmer, 1911.

Bramwell Booth, Mrs. *Mothers of the Empire and Other Addresses*. London: Salvation Army Book Department, 1914.

Butler, Josephine. 'Letter to New Zealand Press Regarding Contagious Diseases Act.' 30 April 1895, collections held by the Fawcett Library relating to Australia and New Zealand, AJCP, SLV MS M2308.

Coates, Dora Meeson. 'Letter to Dr Mary Booth.' 1933, ML, MSS 2109 Box2 Item 4.

de Holstein, Alexandra and Montefiore, Dora. *Serf Life in Russia: The Childhood of a Russian Grandmother*. London: Heineman, 1906.

Deakin, Alfred. *The Federal Story*. Melbourne: Robertson, 1944.

Deakin, Alfred. *Federated Australia: Letters from the Morning Post 1900–1910*. Melbourne: Melbourne University Press, 1968.

Deutsch, Regine. *The International Woman Suffrage Alliance: Its History from 1904 to 1929*. Vida Goldstein Memorial Collection Commemorating Women's Achievements in National Development. London 1929.

Doughty, Lady Eugenia. *The Cheerful Way*. London: Adam and Charles Black, 1912.

Fawcett, Millicent Garrett. *What I Remember*. London: Fisher Unwin, 1924.

Fawcett, Millicent Garrett. *Women's Suffrage: A Short History of a Great Movement*. London: TC and EC Jack, 1912.

Festival of Empire: Souvenir of the Pageant of London. London: Bemrose and Sons, 1911.

Fisher, Andrew. *Andrew Fisher Papers*. 1883, NLA, MS 2919.

Fox, Frank. *The British Empire*. London: Adam and Charles Black, 1911.

Fox, Frank. *Peeps at Many Lands*. London: Adam and Charles Black, 1911.

Gardiner, A.G. *Pillars of Society*. London: James Nisbet, 1913.

Gay, Florence. *In Praise of Australia: An Anthology in Prose and Verse*. London: Constable, 1912.

Goldstein, Vida. *Papers*, State Library of Victoria, MS 7865.

—. *Vida Goldstein Collection*, The Women's Library, London School of Economics (formerly the Fawcett Library), 7VDG

—. 'Letters of Vida Goldstein.' Fawcett Library, Australian Joint Copying Project, State Library of Victoria MS 2309.

—. 'Report on Visit to America.' 1902, Fawcett Library, Australian Joint Copying Project, State Library of Victoria MS 2309.

—. 'Should Women Enter Parliament?' *Review of Reviews*, 20 August 1903.

—. 'The Australian Woman in Politics.' *Review of Reviews*, 20 January 1904.

—. 'The Political Woman in Australia.' *Nineteenth Century* 56, no. 329 (1904).

—. *Diary*, 1908, *Vida Goldstein Papers*, collections held by the Fawcett Library relating to Australia and New Zealand, AJCP, SLV MS 2309.

—. 'Record of Visit to England.' 1911, collections held by the Fawcett Library relating to Australia and New Zealand, AJCP, SLV MS 2309.

—. 'Woman Suffrage in Australia.' 1911, collections held by the Fawcett Library relating to Australia and New Zealand, AJCP, SLV MS 2309.

—. 'Senate Candidacy.' *Vida Goldstein Papers*, collections held by the Fawcett Library relating to Australia and New Zealand, AJCP, SLV MS 2309.

—. *To America and back : January–June 1902: a lecture by Vida Goldstein*, prepared for publication by Jill Roe (2002).

Hamilton, Cecily. *A Pageant of Great Women*. London: Marian Lawson, 1948.

Cicely Hamilton; with sketches by M. Lowndes, D. Meeson Coates, C. Hedley Charlton, *Beware! A Warning to Suffragists*. London: Artists Suffrage League, 1909.

Hansard. 'Commonwealth Franchise Bill.' Senate, 1902.

—. 'Commonwealth Franchise Bill.' Second Reading, April 1902.

—. 'Electoral Bill.' Senate, 1909.

—. 'Womanhood Suffrage (Resolution).' Senate, 17 November 1910.

—. 'Womanhood Suffrage (Resolution).' House of Representatives, 25 November 1910.

—. 'Electoral Bill' Senate, 1911.

Hasluck, Alexandra (ed.). *Audrey Tennyson's Vice-Regal Days: The Australian Letters of Audrey Lady Tennyson*. Canberra: National Library of Australia, 1978.

Henderson, Leslie. Vida Goldstein 1869–1949: Biographical notes by her niece, Leslie M. Henderson, 1966 January, State Library of Victoria, MS 7930.

Hill, Ethel and Shafer, Olga. *Great Suffragists and Why: Modern Makers of History*. London: H.J. Drane, 1909.

Hobbs, J.B. *Recovering the 'Ashes': An Account of the Cricket Tour of Australia 1911–12*. London: Pitman and Sons, 1912.

Holder, Lady Julia. 'Equal Suffrage in Australia.' In *Congressional Publications on Woman Suffrage*: National American Woman Suffrage Association, 1904.

Holmes, Marion. 'Concerning Muriel Matters.' *The Vote*, 19 February 1910.

International Woman Suffrage Alliance, *Report of the Fourth Conference of the International Woman Suffrage Alliance, Amsterdam, 1908*. Amsterdam: F. Van Rossen, 1908.

International Woman Suffrage Alliance, *Report of the Sixth Congress of International Woman Suffrage Alliance, Stockholm, June 12–17, 1911*. London: Women's Printing Society, 1911.

Judkins, William (ed.). *Review of Reviews*, January to December 1911.

Kenney, Annie. *Memories of a Militant*. London: Edward Arnold, 1924.

Langton, Rivers. 'The Coronation One Year After.' Imperial Federation League of Australia, 1912.

Lowndes, Mary. 'On Banners and Banner-Making.' *The Englishwoman*, 1909.

Mack, Louise. *The Romance of a Woman at Thirty*. London: Alston Rivers, 1911.

Mann, Tom. 'The Political and Industrial Situation in Australia.' *Nineteenth Century* 56, no. 331 (September 1904).

Martel, Nellie A. *The Women's Vote in Australia*. London: The Women's Press, 1907.

—. 'Women's Votes in New Zealand and Australia.' In *The Case for Women's Suffrage*, edited by Brougham Villiers. London: T.H. Unwin, 1907.

Martin, C.J. 'What Women are Doing in Australia', *Womanhood: the magazine of woman's progress and interests, political, legal, social, and intellectual, and of health and beauty culture*, vol. 10 no. 58, 1903.

Matters, Muriel. *Muriel Matters Archive*, Muriel Matters Society, South Australia.

—. *The Christian Commonwealth*, 21 December 1910.

—. 'Our Tour in Australia.' *The Vote*, 1 October 1910.

—. 'Commonwealth Resolution.' *The Vote*, 1911.

—. 'Violet Tillard Obituary.' 1930.

Matters, Mrs Leonard. *Australasians Who Count in London and Who Counts in Western Australia*. London: Jas. Truscott, 1913.

Meeson Coates, Dora. *George Coates: His Life and Work*. London: Temple Press, 1937.

Mitchell, Geoffrey (ed.). *The Hard Way Up: The Autobiography of Hannah Mitchell, Suffragette and Rebel*. London: Faber and Faber, 1968.

Mitchell, J. Malcolm. *Colonial Statesmen and Votes for Women: Lord Curzon Answered*. London: Women's Freedom League, 1912.

Montefiore, Dora. 'Why Women Need Woman Suffrage; and Why We Need It Now.' *Shafts*, December (1896). DM1

—. 'Women Uitlanders.' Union of Practical Suffragists within the Women's Liberal Federation, 1899.

—. 'A Bundle of Fallacies.' *The Social Democrat* 5, no. 2 (15 February 1901): 48–9.

—. 'Women Voters in Australia.' *New Age*, 24 December 1903.

—. 'Woman Suffrage Resolution.' *New Age*, 14 February 1904.

—. 'Women Voters in Australia.' *New Age*, 22 September 1904.

—. 'Taxation without Representation Is Tyranny.' *New Age*, 22 June 1905.

—. 'Pageants.' *Justice*, 16 April 1910.

—. 'The "Conciliation" Bill.' *Justice*, 23 July 1910.

—. 'A Labour Party in Power (I).' *Justice*, 15 April 1911.

—. 'A Labour Party in Power (II).' *Justice*, 22 April 1911.

—. 'A Labour Party in Power (III).' *Justice*, 29 April 1911.

—. 'Australian Workers Condemn the Coronation.' *Justice*, 6 May 1911.

—. *From a Victorian to a Modern*. London: E. Archer, 1927.

National American Woman Suffrage Association. 'Congressional Hearing on Woman Suffrage.' House of Representatives. Washington, DC, 1915.

Northcott, Clarence H. *Australian Social Development*. New York: Columbia University Press, 1918.

Office of the Status of Women. Women's Suffrage Banner—Historical Research Report. 1987, NAA, MS A463 1987/3770.

Office of the Status of Women. 'Proposal to Buy Back Women's Suffrage Banner.' Second National Women's Consultative Council—Bicentennial Project 1987, NAA, A463, 1987/2824

Office of the Status of Women. Conservation of Australian Women's Suffrage Banner, 1988, NAA, A463 1988/3222.

Palliser, Edith. 'The International Movement for Women's Suffrage.' In *The Case for Women's Suffrage*, edited by Brougham Villiers, London: T.F. Unwin, 1907.

Pankhurst, Christabel. 'Letter of Christabel Pankhurst to Dora Meeson Coates.' 1930, NLA, MS M9688.

—. *Unshackled: The Story of How We Won the Vote*. London: Hutchinson, 1959.

Pankhurst, Emmeline. *My Own Story*. London: Everleigh Nash, 1914.

Pankhurst, E. Sylvia. *The Life of Emmeline Pankhurst: The Suffragette Struggle for Women's Citizenship*. London: T. Werner Laurie Ltd, 1935.

—. *The Suffragette Movement: An Intimate Account*. London: Longmans, 1931.

—. *The Suffragette: The History of the Women's Militant Suffrage Movement 1905–1910*. London: Gay and Hancock, 1911.

Pember Reeves, Mrs (Maud). *Round About a Pound a Week*. London: Bell and Sons, 1913.

Pember Reeves, William. 'The Effect of Woman Suffrage in New Zealand and Australia.' *Congressional Publications on Woman Suffrage*, National American Woman Suffrage Association 1, no. 6 (1904).

—. *State Experiments in Australia and New Zealand*. London: Grant Richards, 1902.

Pethick-Lawrence, Emmeline. *My Part in a Changing World*. London: Victor Gollancz, 1938.

Pethick-Lawrence, Frederick. *Women's Fight for the Vote*. London: The Women's Press, 1910.

Pethick-Lawrence Memorial Committee. *Memories of Fred and Emmeline Pethick-Lawrence*. Middlesex: Pethick-Lawrence Memorial Committee, 1963.

Phillips, Mary. *The Militant Suffrage Campaign in Perspective*. London: self-published, nd.

Rischbieth Papers, National Library of Australia, MS2004.

Rischbieth, Bessie. *March of Australian Women: A Record of Fifty Years of Struggle for Equal Citizenship*. Perth: Paterson Brokenshaw, 1964.

Robins, Elizabeth. *Way Stations*. London: Hodder and Soughton, 1913.

Rowland, Percy. 'The Beginnings of an Australian National Character.' *Nineteenth Century* 52, no. 307 (1902).

Scott, Rose. *Rose Scott Papers*. ML, MS 3888.

Seddon, The Rt Hon. Richard. 'On Women's Suffrage.' (pamphlet). London, 1902.

Senate, US. 'Joint Resolution Proposing an Amendment to the Constitution of the United States Extending the Right of Suffrage to Women.' Select Committee on Woman Suffrage. Washington DC: Government Printing Office, 1902.

Smith, W. Sidney. *Outlines of the Women's Franchise Movement in New Zealand*. Dunedin: Whitcombe and Tomes, 1902.

Snowden, Ethel. *The Feminist Movement*. London: Collins, 1913.

—. *The Woman Socialist*. London: George Allan, 1907.

Spence, Catherine Helen. *Catherine Helen Spence: An Autobiography*. Adelaide: WK Thomas, 1910.

Spence, William Guthrie. *Australia's Awakening: Thirty Years in the Life of an Australian Agitator*. Melbourne: The Workers' Trustees, 1909.

Stanton, Elizabeth Cady, Susan B. Anthony, and Matilda Joslyn Gage. *History of Woman Suffrage*. Rochester, NY: Charles Mann, 1887.

Street, Jessie. *Truth or Repose*. Sydney: Australian Book Society, 1966.

Turner, Henry Gyles, *The First Decade of the Australian Commonwealth: A Chronicle of Contemporary Politics, 1901–1910*. Melbourne: Mason, Firth and McCutcheon, 1911.

Villiers, Brougham. 'Introduction.' In *The Case for Women's Suffrage*, edited by Brougham Villiers, 1–21. London: T.H. Unwin, 1907.

Walker, Henry de R. *Australasian Democracy*. London: T. Fisher Unwin, 1897.

Wells, H.G. *The New Machiavelli*. London: The Bodley Head, 1911.

Zimmern, Alice. *Women's Suffrage in Many Lands*. London: The Athenaeum Press, 1909.

SECONDARY SOURCES

Allen, Judith. *Rose Scott: Vision and Revision in Feminism*. Melbourne: Oxford University Publishing, 1994.

Anand, Anita. *Sophia: Princess, Suffragette, Revolutionary*. London: Bloomsbury, 2015.

Anderson, Margaret. *When Australia Was a Woman: Images of a Nation*. Perth: Western Australian Museum, 1998.

Atkinson, Diane. *The Purple, White and Green: Suffragettes in London 1906–14*. London: Museum of London, 1992.

—. *The Suffragettes in Pictures*. London: Museum of London, 1996.

Banks, Olive. *Becoming a Feminist: The Social Origins of First Wave Feminism*. London: Wheatsheaf Books, 1986.

Blainey, Ann. *I Am Melba: A Biography*. Melbourne: Black Inc., 2009.

Boldrick, Stacy. 'Iconoclasms Past and Present: Conflict and Art.' In *Art under Attack: Histories of British Iconoclasm*, edited by Lena and Boldrick Mohamed, Stacy. London: Tate Publishing, 2013.

Bomford, Janette M. *That Dangerous and Persuasive Woman: Vida Goldstein*. Carlton: Melbourne University Press, 1993.

Brett, Judith. *The Enigmatic Mr Deakin*. Melbourne: Text, 2017.

Burke, Janine. *Australian Women Artists*. Collingwood: Greenhouse Publications, 1980.

Caine, Barbara. 'Australian Feminism and the British Militant Suffragettes.' In *Department of the Senate Occasional Lecture Series*. Canberra: Parliament of Australia, 2003.

Cass, Deborah and Rubenstein, Kim, 'Representation/s of Women in the Australian Constitutional System', *Adelaide Law Review*, vol. 17, 1995, 3–48.

Cockroft, Irene. *New Dawn Women: Women in the Arts and Crafts and Suffrage Movement at the Dawn of the Twentieth Century*. Compton: Watts Gallery, 2005.

Cockroft, Irene and Croft, Susan. *Art, Theatre and Women's Suffrage*. Twickenham: Aurora Metro Press, 2010.

Collette, Christine. 'Socialism and scandal: the sexual politics of the early Labour Movement', *History Workshop Journal*, vol. 23, no. 1, 1 March 1987, 102–11.

Crawford, Elizabeth, *The Women's Suffrage Movement: A Reference Guide 1866–1928*, London: UCL Press, 1999.

Crawford, Elizabeth, ed. *Campaigning for the Vote: Kate Parry Frye's Suffrage Diary*. London: Francis Boutle, 2013.

Crisp, L.F. *Federation Fathers*. Melbourne: Melbourne University Publishing, 1990.

Daley, Caroline, and Melanie Nolan, eds. *Suffrage and Beyond: International Feminist Perspectives*. Annandale, NSW: Pluto Press, 1994.

Damousi, Joy. *Colonial Voices: A Cultural History of English in Australia*. Melbourne: Cambridge University Press, 2010.

Day, David. *Andrew Fisher: Prime Minister of Australia*. Sydney: Fourth Estate, 2008.

Docker, John. *The Nervous Nineties: Australian Cultural Life in the 1890s*. Melbourne: Oxford University Press, 1991.

Fry, Ruth. *Maud and Amber: A New Zealand Mother and Daughter and the Women's Cause, 1865–1981*. Canterbury: Canterbury University Press, 1992.

Gammage, Bill. 'Anzac' in John Carroll (ed.), *Intruders in the Bush: The Australian Quest for Identity*. Melbourne: Oxford University Press, 1982.

Glass, Margaret. *Charles Cameron Kingston: Federation Father*. Melbourne: Melbourne University Press, 1997.

Grimshaw, Patricia, Lake, Marilyn, McGrath, Anne and Quartly, Marian. *Creating a Nation*, Ringwood, Vic.: Penguin, 1994.

Goot, Murray. 'The Aboriginal Franchise and Its Consequences', *Australian Journal of Politics and History*, 52:4, 2006, 517–61.

Ham, Paul. *1914: The Year the World Ended*. North Sydney: Heinemann, 2013.

Headon, David. '"On the Side of Angels": E.W. O'Sullivan as Republican, Feminist and Federationist.' In *Makers of Miracles: The Cast of the Federation Story*, edited by David Williams and John Headon, Melbourne: Melbourne University Publishing, 2000.

Hirst, J.B. *The Strange Birth of Colonial Democracy*, Sydney: Allen and Unwin, 1988.

—. *Sense and Nonsense in Australian History*. Melbourne: Black Inc. 2009.

Hunt, Karen. 'Journeying through Suffrage: The Politics of Dora Montefiore.' In *The Suffrage Reader: Charting Direction In British Suffrage History*, edited by Clare Eustance, Ryan, Joan and Ugolini, Laura. Leicester: Leicester University Press, 2000.

Irving, Helen. *Gender and the Constitution: Equity and Agency in Comparative Constitutional Design*. Melbourne: Cambridge University Press, 2008.

—. *To Constitute a Nation: A Cultural History of Australia's Constitution*. Melbourne: Cambridge University Press, 1999.

—. *Citizenship, Alienage and the Modern Constitutional State: A Gendered History*. Cambridge: Cambridge University Press, 2016.

Keating, James. '"The Defection of the Women": The New Zealand Contagious Diseases Act Repeal Campaign and Transnational Feminist Dialogue in the Late Nineteenth Century.' *Women's History Review* 25, no. 2 (2016): 187–206.

—. '"An Utter Absence of National Feeling": Australian Women and the International Suffrage Movement 1900–1914.' *Australian Historical Studies* 47, no. 3 (2016): 462–81.

Laing, Kate. '"The White Australia Nettle": Women's Internationalism, Peace and the White Australia Policy in the Interwar Years.' *History Australia* 14, no. 2 (2017): 218–36.

Lake, Marilyn. '1914: Death of a Nation.' *History Australia* 12, no. 1 (2015): 7–24.

—. 'Feminist History as National History: Writing the Political History of Women.' *Australian Historical Studies* 27, no. 106 (1996): 154–69.

—. '"In the Interests of the Home": Rose Scott's Feminist Opposition to Federation.' In *Makers of Miracles: The Cast in the Federation Story*, edited by David Williams and John Headon, Melbourne: Melbourne University Publishing, 2000.

—. 'The Inviolable Woman: Feminist Conceptions of Citizenship in Australia, 1900–1945.' *Gender and History* 8, no. 2 (1996): 197–211.

—. 'Mission Impossible: How Men Gave Birth to the Australian Nation—Nationalism, Gender and Other Seminal Acts.' *Gender and History* 4, no. 3 (1992): 305–22.

—. 'Personality, Individuality, Nationality: Feminist Conceptions of Citizenship, 1902–1940.' *Australian Feminist Studies* 9, no. 19 (1994): 25–38.

—. 'State Socialism for Australian Mothers: Andrew Fisher's Radical Maternalism in International and Local Contexts.' *Labour History* 102, no. May (2012): 55–70.

—. 'Women and Whiteness.' *Australian Historical Studies* 32, no. 117 (2001): 228–342.

Langmore, Diane. *Prime Ministers' Wives: The Public and Private Lives of Ten Australian Women*. Melbourne: McPhee Gribble, 1992.

—. 'Prime Ministers' Wives: Women in the Background.' In *Makers of Miracles: The Cast of the Federation Story*, edited by David Williams and John Headon, Melbourne: Melbourne University Publishing, 2000.

Lees, Kirsten. *Votes for Women: The Australian Story*. St Leonards, NSW: Allen & Unwin, 1995.

Liddington, Jill. *The Life and Times of a Respectable Rebel: Selina Cooper 1864–1946*. London: Virago, 1984.

—. *Vanishing for the Vote: Suffrage, Citizenship and the Battle for the Census*. Manchester: Manchester University Press, 2014.

Linklater, Andro. *An Unhusbanded Life: Charlotte Despard, Suffragette, Socialist and Sinn Feiner*. London: Hutchinson, 1980.

Lumsden, Linda J. *Rampant Women: Suffragists and the Right of Assembly*. Knoxville: University of Tennessee Press, 1997.

MacIntyre, Stuart. *A Colonial Liberalism: The Lost World of Three Victorian Visionaries*. Melbourne: Oxford University Press, 1991.

Magarey, Susan. *Passions of the First Wave Feminists*, Sydney: UNSW Press, 2001.

McCalman, Janet. *Sex and Suffering: Women's Health and a Women's Hospital*, Carlton: Melbourne University Press, 1998.

McMullin, Ross. *Will Dyson: Australia's Radical Genius*. Melbourne: Scribe, 2006.

Mills, Carol. 'Expatriate Australian Black and White Artists: Ruby and Will Dyson and Their Circle in London.' In *Working papers in Australian Studies*. London: Menzies Centre for Australian Studies, 1988.

Mohamed, Lena. 'Suffragettes: The Political Value of Iconoclastic Acts.' In *Art under Attack: Histories of British Iconoclasm*, edited by Tabitha Barber and Stacy Boldrick, London: Tate Publishing, 2013.

Newmarch, Geoffrey. 'Ruby and Will: The Art of Ruby Lind and Will Dyson.' edited by Creswick Museum, 2008.

Nugent, Ann. 'Nellie Alma Martel and the Women's Social and Political Union, 1905–09.' *Hecate* 31, no. 1 (2005): 142–59.

—. 'Sister Suffragettes', *National Library of Australia News*, February 2003, 7.

Oldfield, Audrey. *Woman Suffrage in Australia: A Gift or a Struggle?* Cambridge: Cambridge University Press, 1992.

Piper, Alana Jayne. '"A Menace and an Evil": Fortune-Telling in Australia 1900–1918.' *History Australia* 11, no. 13 (2014): 53–73.

Priestley, Susan. *Henrietta August Dudgale: An Activist 1827–1918*. Melbourne: Melbourne Books, 2011.

Pugh, Martin. *The March of the Women: A Revisionist Analysis of the Campaign for Women's Suffrage, 1866–1914*. Oxford: Oxford University Publishing, 2002.

Purvis, June. *Christabel Pankhurst: A Biography*. London and New York: Routledge, 2018.

—. *Emmeline Pankhurst: A Biography*. London: Routledge, 2002.

—. 'Remembering Emily Wilding Davison (1872–1913)'. *Women's History Review*. 22 (3): 353–362.

Marian Quartly, 'The Australian Women's National League and Democracy, 1904–1921', *Women's History Review*, vol. 15, 2001, 35–50.

Rees, Anne. 'Lessons from Australia: Persia Campbell and the International Afterlives of Federation-Era Welfarism.' *Australian Historical Studies* 48, no. 3 (2017): 1–17.

Reynolds, Henry, *Unnecessary Wars*, Sydney: NewSouth, 2016.

Rowbotham, Sheila. *Dreamers of a New Day: Women Who Invented the Twentieth Century*. London: Verso, 2010.

Scalmer, Sean. 'Peace, Patriotism and the Australian Commonwealth: Historiographical Observations on Nations and Movements.' *History Australia* 14, no. 2 (2017): 285–90.

Scott, Myra. 'The Art of George James Coates (1869–1930) and Dora Meeson Coates (1869–1955).' MA thesis, University of Melbourne, 1992.

—. 'How Australia Lead the Way: Dora Meeson Coates and British Suffrage.' Canberra: Parliament of Australia, 2003.

Searle, Betty. *Silk and Calico: Class, Gender and the Vote.* Sydney: Hale & Iremonger, 1988.

Smart, Judith. 'Modernity and Mother-Heartedness: Spirituality and Religious Meaning in Australian Women's Suffrage and Citizenship Movements.' In *Women's Suffrage in the British Empire: Citizenship, Nation and Race*, edited by Ian Christopher et al. Oxon: Routledge, 2012.

Souter, Gavin. *Lion and Kangaroo: The Initiation of Australia.* Melbourne: Text, 1976.

Stretton, Pat and Christine Finnimore, 'Black Fellow Citizens: Aborigines and the Commonwealth Franchise', *Australian Historical Studies*, 25:101, 1993, 521–35

Tavan, Gwenda. *The Long Slow Death of White Australia.* Melbourne: Scribe, 2005.

Tickner, Lisa. *The Spectacle of Women: Imagery of the Suffrage Campaign 1907–14.* London: Chatto and Windus, 1987.

Tregenza, John. *Professor of Democracy: The Life of Charles Henry Pearson, 1830–1894, Oxford Don and Australian Radical.* Melbourne: Melbourne University Publishing, 1968.

Wainwright, Robert. *Miss Muriel Matters.* Sydney: Harper Collins, 2017.

Williams, Joan. 'Women Carrying Banners.' In *Carrying the Banner: Women, Leadership and Activism in Australia*, edited by Joan Williams. Perth: UWA Press, 1999.

Woollacott, Angela. 'Australian Women's Metropolitan Activism: From Suffrage to Imperial Vanguard to Commonwealth Feminism.' In *Women's Suffrage in the British Empire: Citizenship, Nation, Race*, edited by Ian Fletcher. Oxon: Routledge, 2012.

—. *To Try Her Fortune in London: Australian Women, Colonialism, and Modernity.* Oxford: Oxford University Press, 2001.

Wright, Clare. *The Forgotten Rebels of Eureka.* Melbourne: Text Publishing, 2013.

—. 'Golden Opportunities: The Early Origins of Women's Suffrage in Victoria', *Victorian Historical Journal*, Women's Suffrage Centenary Issue, vol. 79, no. 2, 2008, 210–24.

—. 'A Splendid Object Lesson': A Transnational Perspective on the Birth of the Australian Nation. *Journal of Women's History*, 26(4), 2014, 12–36.

Index